Remaking Respectability

Remaking

Victoria W. Wolcott

Respectability

African
American
Women in
Interwar
Detroit

The University of North Carolina Press
Chapel Hill and London

© 2001 The University of North Carolina Press
All rights reserved
Manufactured in the United States of America

Designed by Jackie Johnson
Set in Bembo
by Tseng Information Systems, Inc.

The paper in this book meets the guidelines for permanence and
durability of the Committee on Production Guidelines for Book
Longevity of the Council on Library Resources.

"Elegies for Paradise Valley," by Frederick Glaysher, editor. © 1978 by
Robert Hayden, from *Collected Poems of Robert Hayden*, by Robert Hayden,
edited by Frederick Glaysher. Used by permission of Liveright Publishing
Corporation.

Portions of this book have been reprinted in revised form with
permission from the following works: "Mediums, Messages, and Lucky
Numbers: African-American Female Spiritualists and Numbers Runners in
Inter-War Detroit," in *The Geography of Identity*, edited by Patricia Yeager,
273–306 (Ann Arbor: University of Michigan Press, 1996); "'Bible, Bath,
and Broom': Nannie Helen Burroughs's National Training School and
African-American Racial Uplift," *Journal of Women's History* 9 (Spring 1997):
89–110; and "The Culture of the Informal Economy: Numbers Runners in
Inter-War Black Detroit," *Radical History Review* 69 (Fall 1997): 46–75.

Publication of this work was aided by a generous grant from the Z. Smith
Reynolds Foundation.

Library of Congress Cataloging-in-Publication Data
Wolcott, Victoria W.
Remaking respectability : African American women in interwar
Detroit / by Victoria W. Wolcott.
p. cm. — (Gender and American culture)
Includes bibliographical references and index.
ISBN 0-8078-2637-5 (alk. paper) — ISBN 0-8078-4966-9 (pbk. : alk. paper)
1. African American women—Michigan—Detroit—Social conditions —
20th century. 2. African American women—Michigan—Detroit—
Economic conditions—20th century. 3. Social classes—Michigan—
Detroit—History—20th century. 4. African Americans—Michigan —
Detroit—Social conditions—20th century. 5. African Americans—
Michigan—Detroit—Economic conditions—20th century. 6. African
Americans—Migrations—History—20th century. 7. Rural-urban
migration—United States—History—20th century. 8. Detroit (Mich.)—
Race relations. 9. Detroit (Mich.)—Social conditions— 20th century.
I. Title. II. Gender & American culture
F574.D49 N488 2001
305.48'896073077434—dc21   2001018125

05 04 03 02 01   5 4 3 2 1

For Erik, Nora, and Maya

Contents

Illustrations

Acknowledgments

Many institutions and individuals supported me as I researched and wrote this book. In the early stages of work, I was fortunate to receive the Henry J. Kaiser Family Foundation Research Grant from the Archives of Labor and Urban Affairs, Wayne State University; a graduate student award from the Coordinating Committee on Women in the Historical Profession, Conference Group on Women's History; a research grant from the University of Michigan's Center for Afroamerican and African Studies Ford Foundation project, "From Margin to Center: Towards a New Black Scholarship"; and the Charlotte W. Newcombe Doctoral Dissertation Fellowship. My year as a resident graduate fellow at the University of Michigan's Institute for the Humanities was a crucial one, and I thank the faculty, graduate students, and staff of the institute for their valuable input and help. A postdoctoral fellowship at the University of Rochester's Frederick Douglass Institute for African and African-American Studies provided a collegial and supportive atmosphere in which to rework the manuscript. I am particularly grateful to Joseph Inikori and Karen Ferguson for their comments on my work during my tenure there.

A number of scholars read all or part of the manuscript and offered valuable advice and guidance. The distinguished members of my dissertation committee—Earl Lewis, Elsa Barkley Brown, Robin D. G. Kelley, and David Scobey—were valuable critics and model scholars. They offered me intellectual and emotional support when it was most needed. Stephanie Shaw made insightful and perceptive suggestions as an outside reader for the University of North Carolina Press and a commentator on a 1999 American Historical Association panel. Nell Irvin Painter's reading of the manuscript for the University of North Carolina Press proved invaluable. I am also grateful to an anonymous reader for his or her criticisms. My editor, Kate Douglas Torrey, helped shepherd me through the publishing process with a minimum of hassle. Paula Wald's editing of the manuscript was masterful. Friends and fellow historians Robin Bachin and Georgina Hickey carried me through the highs and lows of writing a book. Finally, my colleagues at St. Bonaventure University were more than supportive as I completed the manuscript while starting a demanding new teaching career.

The staffs at the Bentley Historical Library, Archives of Labor and Urban Affairs, and Burton Historical Collection helped me discover an untapped wealth of material on Detroit's black women. I am also indebted to Thomas Featherstone at the Archives of Labor and Urban Affairs, Karina McDaniel at the Tennessee State Library and Archives, and Paul Spaeth and Theresa Shaffer at St. Bonaventure University Library for assistance in obtaining illustrations for the book.

I owe thanks as well to all four of my parents—Nancy, Jeff, Ilene, and Peter—and to my siblings—Joel, Jennie, and Lauren. In the last three years, I gave birth to Nora and Maya, who kept me grounded as I struggled to develop and teach new courses and polish the manuscript. Balancing parenthood, teaching, and research would have been an impossible task without my husband, Erik Seeman. Erik read and commented on the entire manuscript throughout the process of researching, writing, and revising. He also cared for Nora, Maya, and our home as an equal partner, ever sensitive to my need to finish the manuscript in a timely manner. Our family has brought me immense joy, and this book is dedicated to them and to us.

Abbreviations

The following abbreviations are used throughout the book.
An additional list of abbreviations precedes the notes.

AME African Methodist Episcopal

CAS Children's Aid Society

CIO Congress of Industrial Organizations

CRC Civic Rights Committee

MUC Mayor's Unemployment Committee

NAACP National Association for the Advancement of Colored People

NACW National Association of Colored Women

NNC National Negro Congress

NYA National Youth Administration

TOBA Theater Owners' Booking Association

UAW United Auto Workers

UNIA Universal Negro Improvement Association

VHA Visiting Housekeepers' Association

VNA Visiting Nurses' Association

WPA Works Progress Administration

YMCA Young Men's Christian Association

YNPA Young Negroes' Progressive Association

YWCA Young Women's Christian Association

Remaking Respectability

Introduction

And Belle the classy dresser, where is she,
who changed her frocks three times a day?
  Where's Nora, with her laugh, her comic flair,
  stagestruck Nora waiting for her chance?
Where's fast Iola, who so loved to dance
she left her sickbed one last time to whirl
in silver at The Palace till she fell?
  Where's mad Miss Alice, who ate from garbage cans?
  Where's snuffdipping Lucy, who played us "chunes"
on her guitar? Where's Hattie? Where's Melissabelle?
  Let vanished rooms, let dead streets tell.
    Robert Hayden, "Elegies for Paradise Valley"

In his poem "Elegies for Paradise Valley," Detroit native Robert Hayden invokes the forgotten women who walked the streets of Paradise Valley, Detroit's interwar black neighborhood. These intrepid women traveled from southern states such as Georgia, Tennessee, and Alabama between 1915 and 1925 to build better lives for themselves and their families in Detroit. Many settled near Paradise Valley's heart—St. Antoine Street, which, recalls Hayden, teemed with "restaurants, barbershops, pool halls, cabarets, blind pigs, gamblin' joints camouflaged as 'Recreation Clubs.' Shootings, stabbings, blaring jazz, and a liveliness, a gaiety at once desperate and releasing, at once wicked—Satan's playground—and good hearted."[1] This book attempts to recapture the complexity of Hayden's childhood world, the good-heartedness, the gaiety, and the desperation.

In much the same way that "Recreation Clubs" could hide "gamblin' joints," a narrow focus on male industrial workers in Detroit's historiography has hidden the complexity of this city's African American community.[2] By focusing a narrative of migration and urban growth on African American women, who were excluded from industrial labor during the interwar period, this book views a Detroit that encompassed reformers, preachers, prostitutes, and domestic servants. This range of individual experiences complicated African American social reformers' attempts to construct a cohesive community identity during and after the Great Migration. African American women were at the center of these contestations over community formation as both symbols of racial reform and active agents of migration and urban resettlement. Understanding the variety of female experiences represented in Hayden's poem, therefore, is essential to understanding a broader story of African American life in the urban North.

This book employs two intertwined approaches to examine the lives of African American women. It is a women's history that uncovers some of the quotidian details of African American women's lives. Such detail prevents overgeneralizations about black women's ideologies, motivations, or class positions. A social history of black women also highlights their remarkable achievements in the face of racial discrimination practiced by white employers, landlords, police, and city officials. But *Remaking Respectability* is also a gender history that examines broad cultural, political, and economic shifts in Detroit's black community.[3] This gender analysis reveals a significant transformation in racial discourse from a focus on bourgeois respectability in the 1910s and 1920s to a more masculine ideology of self-determination during the Great Depression.

Both approaches are structured by the nature of the available sources. Institutional histories and manuscript collections reveal much about the major reform organizations, uncovering fascinating changes in African American leaders' priorities and rhetoric. The personal papers and recorded oral histories of some African American women allow us to reflect on their daily struggles for respect and survival in the face of staggering obstacles. These sources, however, leave major gaps in our understanding of black women's lives. Migrants, for example, formed numerous working-class clubs that left almost no records behind. Reform institutions' manuscript collections rarely include clients' criticisms of their work. Oral histories often contain romanticized and selective visions of the past. As I worked with all of these sources, I was cognizant of their limitations and possibilities. Thus, the daily lives of ordinary African American women and the institutional context in which they operated are only partially revealed in this work. Yet access to a surprising amount of material previously unmined by historians allowed me to record community conversations about the role of black women in an industrial city.

The key to capturing these conversations was my examination of the interactions between African American women of different classes. In her study of blueswomen, Angela Davis argues that there are "multiple African American feminist traditions."[4] Until recently, black clubwomen and reformers who left behind written records have received the most scholarly attention as the source of these traditions.[5] This book takes reformers' work seriously by examining their role in defining institutional responses to the Great Migration. However, understanding the interaction between middle-class black women and the working-class migrants they sought to aid and influence is key to capturing the full range of African American women's experiences. This perspective necessitated that I study not only the "successful" migrants described in other works but also the "unsuccessful" migrants who have been largely lost to history.[6] Prostitutes, gamblers, and performers shaped black Detroit as vitally as club leaders, church founders, and social workers did. Some women remained desperately poor despite years of struggle to obtain viable employment, whereas others achieved significant social mobility.

In order to document the lives of migrants who did not fit into the model of respectable womanhood, I needed to confront Detroit's cultural history. Blueswomen's lyrics, accounts of numbers running, and ethnographies of storefront churches provide a glimpse of the lives of migrants who fell outside the norm. Indeed, it was in the realm of culture that reformers defined bourgeois respectability and their class status. "Middle-class blacks and members of the elite," argue Shane White and Graham White, "were keen to distance themselves from the dress and demeanor of ordinary African Americans, and, at the same time, to curb what they viewed as the sartorial and kinetic excesses of these they saw as their social inferiors."[7] Curbing these excesses was central to creating a respectable community identity. Yet cultural expressions of independence and creativity also challenged white stereotypes of the black working class and provided an expressive outlet for urban migrants.[8] Reformers' responses to migrant culture structured the institutions, politics, and local economy of interwar Detroit.

Detroit's culture may have been slighted by historians, but the city has long attracted scholars of labor and black politics.[9] In Detroit, organized labor won its most significant battle with the birth of the United Auto Workers (UAW). This victory was possible only through interracial activism among Detroit's industrial working class. For years, labor organizing was stymied by the Detroit chapters of the Urban League and the National Association for the Advancement of Colored People (NAACP), which maintained an alliance with the city's white elite well into the 1930s. By the early 1940s, black political organizations that embraced a more strident, working-class perspective undermined this alliance. Although this story has been told before, the roots of this political transformation have been only partially described. An analysis of Detroit's rich cultural life can illuminate the motivations and desires of members of the black working class, who demanded greater civil rights in the workplace and in their communities. These women and men challenged established institutions, such as the Detroit Urban League, to abandon old allegiances and develop new strategies of racial reform.

As a result of this shift in perspective, the neighborhood rather than the shop floor is this book's central terrain. In their neighborhoods, blacks debated racial reform strategies, appropriate behavior, and community development. Neighborhoods were also the purview of African American women, whom many viewed as the caretakers of homes, streets, and local institutions. African American women were instrumental in creating, and at times transgressing, community norms. Therefore, shifts in racial reform took on gendered meanings. During the late 1910s and early 1920s, reformers used the language of female respectability to "uplift" incoming southern migrants. By the 1930s, however, reformers rarely invoked female respectability, focusing instead on male self-defense, civil rights, and industrial unionism. These changes in the language of racial reform are revealed when African American women's lives are fully incorporated into the analysis of migration and resettlement. Placing women at the center of these developments, moving the focus away from the industrial workplace, and tracing the changing role of female reformers all enhance our understanding of intraracial dynamics in the urban North.

During the Great Migration, these dynamics were particularly complex. As southern African Americans moved to the urban North in unprecedented numbers, black leaders embraced the opportunity to shape new urban communities by reforming migrants' dress, demeanor, and deportment. To carry out this project, they drew on a language of bourgeois respectability developed by black female reformers in the decades prior to the Great Migration. Because this discourse was so central to the migration experience, I chose to focus on how African American women used and transformed respectability throughout the interwar period. Respectability encompassed a set of ideas and normative values that had tremendous power among African Americans and was particularly open to competing definitions, inflections, and meanings. Individual black women understood respectability in very different ways depending on their social, political, and cultural context. This malleable discourse, then, reveals how individuals situated themselves in an ever-changing community.[10]

Although African Americans developed unique ideas about respectability in the nineteenth and twentieth centuries, much of the historical work on respectability has focused on how Anglo-American society used this discourse. These examinations provide a useful background to the distinctive history of African American respectability. In general, two overlapping discourses of respectability have predominated in Anglo-American society. The first encompassed the values of hard work, thrift, piety, and sexual restraint — values that were, theoretically, accessible to all classes and races and therefore routes of social mobility. This definition was often used to differentiate the "rough" working class from the "respectable" working class in the eighteenth and nineteenth centuries in the United States and Great Britain.[11] The second discourse emerged with the rise of the bourgeoisie in the nineteenth century and denoted class status and privilege through dress, deportment, and organizational affiliation. These very broad definitions overlapped in different social contexts and periods, diverging and converging. At times, the "respectable" working class used respectability to point out the hypocrisy of upper-middle-class women and men who were not temperate, religious, or sexually restrained. At other times, cross-class coalitions were constructed around shared notions of respectability.

When individuals deployed respectability, the discourse frequently took on gendered characteristics. Ellen Ross has noted that in England, because "respectability" was a term used to describe class divisions outside the workplace, it became the project of white working-class wives, who largely controlled the appearance of home and neighborhood.[12] Ross suggests that "women . . . *embodied* respectability or the lack of it, in their dress, public conduct, language, housekeeping, childrearing methods, spending habits, and, of course, sexual behavior."[13] This female embodiment of respectability was also central to a middle-class self-definition. Numerous historians have noted the increase in the number of etiquette manuals and other prescriptive works aimed at women and the greater public display of white respectable women on urban streets and in private parlors in the nineteenth century.[14] Sexual restraint and traditional sex roles were important components of both valences of respectability and were areas in which women were more harshly judged than men. Respectability, then, was a gendered language usually deployed and defended by women.

Because public displays were crucial to the enactment of respectability, the city was often the theater in which the drama of respectability was most elaborately performed. Women and men living in close quarters could effectively police the behavior and demeanor of their neighbors. Or as Brian Harrison puts it, "Public visibility enabled the respectable to make converts; they made the most of their numbers by advertising themselves and their lifestyle."[15] Such publicity also excluded those who did not live up to the established standards, thus constructing more intricate hierarchies and class divisions. In urban neighborhoods, potent symbols such as clothing, mode of transportation, or the state of a front yard or stoop signaled the level of respectability to others. A whole neighborhood that displayed these symbols could, in a sense, "communicate" the residents' respectability to the rest of the city. This power of respectability appealed to African American reformers, who wanted to communicate messages to both African American urban newcomers and the white community.

Although bourgeois respectability's roots can be found, in part, in Anglo-American culture, the particular forms that respectability took in the African American community were unique. Sexual restraint among women, for example, was a direct rebuttal of white stereotypes of African American female sexuality as innately licentious. Similarly, the cleanliness and orderliness of African American homes had symbolic value for black women who labored cleaning white homes and could compare their own favorably. Recently, African American women's historians have effectively captured this distinct history. In her groundbreaking work, *Righteous Discontent*, Evelyn Brooks Higginbotham defines a "politics of respectability" through which middle-class and elite black women sought to "earn their people a measure of esteem from white America" by striving "to win the black lower class's psychological allegiance to temperance, industriousness, thrift, refined manners, and Victorian sexual morals." This bourgeois respectability received a degree of support from the black working class that gave rise to numerous institutions of racial reform. However, asserts Higginbotham, it also led to class tensions as black elites "disavowed and opposed the culture of the 'folk'—the expressive culture of many poor, uneducated, and 'unassimilated' black men and women."[16] Other historians of black women have built on Higginbotham's formulation in their studies of middle-class and elite black clubwomen and professionals. Clubwomen at the turn of the century, argues Anne Meis Knupfer, used respectability as both a "collective strategy" to enhance the reputation of all African American women and a means to define class distinctions in the black community.[17] Thus, bourgeois respectability shaped black female activists' desire to act as unblemished representatives of the race and to reform the behavior of their working-class sisters.

In the late nineteenth and early twentieth centuries, African American female reformers embedded bourgeois respectability in racial uplift ideology. This ideology refuted racist stereotypes of African Americans as biologically inferior by stressing the respectability of an African American elite and the evolutionary progress of the African American masses only a generation after slavery. Female activists such as Fannie Barrier Williams, Anna Julia

Cooper, and Nannie Helen Burroughs wrote copiously in African American periodicals and lectured nationwide, arguing that issues of particular relevance to African American women—the expansion of the female labor market, the need for training programs in domestic service, sexual exploitation of women, temperance, and education—should be central to racial reform. Through their writing and activism, these women propagated an ideology of racial uplift that focused on the unique role women would play in racial advancement. This female uplift ideology constituted a central strategy of racial reform by the early years of the twentieth century.

The development and implementation of racial uplift ideology led to significant divergence over the meaning of respectability in the African American community.[18] This divergence reflected class tensions that became more acute during the Great Migration. Working-class women stressed family survival and individual self-respect more than the public propriety encouraged by uplift ideologues. Some working-class women engaged in paid labor that was deemed inappropriate by community elites and established small evangelical churches that encouraged ecstatic religious practices criticized by reformers. Female uplift ideologues, more concerned about a public appearance of respectability, attempted to police these behaviors, which they believed would undermine the effort to uplift the race.[19] Reformers simultaneously defined their own class status by constructing working-class and poor African Americans as less "respectable." These conflicts were heightened when African Americans migrated to cities in the South and the North and debated community norms and standards. Although reformers hoped to instill bourgeois respectability in migrants, African American women and men with divergent values sometimes resisted their efforts.

There is evidence, however, that aspects of the uplift ideology expressed by middle-class elites resonated strongly with the preexisting values of poorer African American women. Respectability, therefore, reflected more than simply bourgeois Victorian ideology; it was a foundation of African American women's survival strategies and self-definition irrespective of class. This broader concept of respectability has been used by historians who have explored ideologies and lifestyles common to black women. Some studies have carefully examined how chastity, domesticity, and racial pride shaped the childhood and early education of black women from different class backgrounds.[20] Stephanie Shaw, for example, argues that black families viewed respectability as an essential tool to achieve social mobility.[21] Although middle-class and elite families were better positioned to give their daughters the education that would allow them to achieve professional status, the desire to protect and uplift young black women was shared across classes. As Sharon Harley has noted, "Even among the poorest blacks, whose own standards of respectability were largely determined by the church and by the community in which they lived, their domestic ideology was not always diametrically opposed to middle-class norms of behavior." [22]

The shared norms of behavior in the black community reflect a greater degree of "circularity" between dominant and subordinate classes than was present in white society. Segregation and racial discrimination heightened reciprocal cultural influence among African Americans.[23] Thus, at times working-class and middle-class women's notions of respectability converged. Both focused on domesticity as the central terrain of uplift, on the need to defend African American women against sexual harassment and rape, and on racial pride. These convergences continued beyond the Progressive Era, when racial uplift ideology began to lose its dominance. Indeed, black women throughout the twentieth century have used respectability to enhance their reputation, ensure social mobility, and create a positive image for their communities.[24] To be "respectable" was an identity that any African American could embrace, whatever his or her economic standing.

Neighbors and social reformers at times disputed an individual's claim to respectability. One can view this contested nature of respectability clearly when examining the interwar period. When southern African Americans migrated to Detroit, they encountered institutions that relied on an ideology of bourgeois respectability. In the early years of the Great Migration, the city was dominated by a relatively small number of reform institutions and organizations. These institutions, most significantly the Detroit Urban League, were partly backed and funded by white elites and supported integrationist goals. Generally speaking, reformers in this period foregrounded the presentation of a respectable community, and particularly respectable women, as a primary goal of reform. To fulfill this goal, they sought to transform migrants into respectable, self-sufficient citizens. Reformers designed this work to aid fellow African Americans by providing charity, shelter, and recreation. In addition, creating a new community of well-adjusted migrants might demonstrate to white elites that these new residents were capable workers and trustworthy neighbors. African American leaders hoped this would lead white employers and city officials to reexamine racist hiring practices, spatial segregation, and discriminatory welfare policies.

By the 1930s, many black Detroiters had become disillusioned by bourgeois respectability's lack of success as a reform strategy and remade this discourse in dramatic ways. Throughout the late 1910s and 1920s, individual migrants transgressed community norms by participating in the informal economy, commercial leisure, and nationalist groups. These transgressions alarmed reformers and the black elite, who sought to shape migrant behavior. By the 1930s, reformers considered such transgressions less problematic for a variety of reasons. Middle-class African Americans moved out of the overcrowded East Side and therefore no longer focused as intently on their working-class neighbors' behavior. The crisis of the Great Depression made male employment and economic survival top priorities. Finally, it became clear that focusing on respectability had not made major inroads in racial discrimination. New political organizations that proliferated in the city during the Great Depression were quick to point out these facts to an older generation of reformers. Many of them, like the Nation of Islam, had a nationalist orientation that countered the integrationist platform of existing institutions. In addition, labor unions and New Deal agencies provided new models of interracial cooperation that challenged the traditional relationship between white industrialists and black leaders.

In the midst of these struggles and debates, female respectability lost its salience as a reform strategy. Although individual African American women continued to work at the forefront of reform and bourgeois respectability remained an important aspect of black culture, black women were no longer central symbols of racial progress. When black Detroiters invoked respectability in the 1930s, they most often referred to the respect African American men demanded in order to protect and defend their homes and neighborhoods. Male self-defense was an aspect of respectability that placed self-determination and community survival above public presentations of bourgeois life. By World War II, racial leaders did not cite domesticity, chastity, and self-restraint as the primary goals of respectable citizens. Instead, they focused on civil rights, unionization, and self-determination.

The first half of this book traces the establishment of female respectability as a dominant but contested discourse in Detroit. Chapter 1 analyzes how class-based convergences and divergences around the meaning of respectability shaped southern African Americans' daily lives and their approaches to racial reform before the Great Migration. It then describes racial uplift ideology's influence on Detroit's social, economic, and political climate just prior to the Great Migration. Chapter 2 traces the response of Detroit's racial reform institutions to the Great Migration by using female respectability to both refute white stereotypes of African Americans' innate inferiority and "uplift" incoming African American migrants. These efforts were stymied by Detroit's extremely restricted job market for black women. Chapter 3 describes how some African American working-class women transgressed bourgeois notions of respectability through their participation in the informal economy, storefront churches, commercial leisure activities, and Garveyism. These activities, however, did not necessarily transgress working-class notions of respectability that foregrounded economic survival and racial pride.

The final three chapters trace the gradual decline of bourgeois respectability as a prominent reform strategy. Chapter 4 argues that the increased spatial dispersion of African Americans lessened elites' need to discipline and sanitize the East Side neighborhood where the majority of poor and working-class African Americans lived. Despite this, the language of bourgeois respectability continued to be employed by the growing number of women's clubs and established churches throughout the 1920s. Chapter 5 explores the effects of the Great Depression on Detroit's black community. As traditional institutions found themselves unable to handle skyrocketing unemployment, new nationalist organizations proposed alternative organizing strategies. In addition, black leaders no longer focused on the informal economy's negative effects and the behavior of individual female migrants. The final chapter traces the emergence of new interracial organizations that challenged the dominance of the Detroit Urban League, women's clubs, and mainline churches. Working-class activism in the Communist Party and industrial unions undermined the traditional relationship between Detroit's black elite and white industrialists. New Deal agencies also allowed African American women to bypass racial reform institutions that had aided them since the Great Migration. These new agencies and organizations, as well as the nationalist groups discussed in Chapter 5, used a more masculine language of self-defense and self-determination rather than female respectability when discussing their priorities and strategies.

The dominant narrative of black Detroit has focused on male industrial employment and struggles for civil rights, relegating black women to a secondary role in the development of an African American community. Yet it was female migrants and their middle-class allies who created and supported the homes, businesses, and institutions that made up black Detroit. Black women challenged the virulent racism that relegated their families to the worst housing and lowest-paying jobs and made them vulnerable to harassment from police, employers, and white neighbors. Their ability to not only combat racism through social activism but also create a community in which to worship, work, and live was remarkable. Only by fully integrating black women into the migration narrative can we begin to view interwar Detroit as the lively, contested, and ever-changing city captured in Hayden's poetry.

1   Female Uplift Ideology, the Politics of Class,
    and Resettlement in Detroit

*I was really proud to hear from you and know that you are getting on so well.
Indeed I'm uplifted to hear what you are doing. I'm forced to write these para-
graphs. . . . Now you are doing so well and I'm sure looking likewise you
are going to have many temptations along your pilgrim journey. Let me urge,
intreat and beseech that you continue to pray asking God for his comfort that
his Guiding arms will be around you his eye will direct you to the better paths
of life. Now you will have no time to pause, for satan you will find very busy
and is like God somewhat. . . . With all our prayers and carefulness we are
made to have the path of righteousness.*

"Aunt Sarah" to Mary Etta Glenn, 29 January 1922

When Mary Etta Glenn migrated from Bibb County, Georgia, to Detroit in 1917, she left behind her mother, grandmother, and aunt, but she carried the ideas and values she
was raised to uphold. After settling in the North, Glenn continued to receive advice from her family on how to behave as
she grew to womanhood. "Hold up your head and be a sweet
girl," advised her grandmother in a letter. "I am glad to know
you are having a good time," wrote her mother, adding the
caution, "Don't take so much air riding in your friends' new
car." Aunt Sarah entreated Glenn to follow a "path of righteousness" now that she was older and vulnerable to the "many
temptations" of urban life. Yet this plea was tempered with a
sense of pride in Glenn's accomplishments.[1] Glenn's mother
and grandmother similarly stressed their pride in her, while
encouraging her to be cautious in her new surroundings.

The Motor City had already welcomed thousands from
Georgia, the most common point of origin for Detroit migrants, when fifteen-year-old Mary Etta Glenn arrived to
join extended family members.[2] Indeed, May 1917, the month
Glenn arrived in Detroit, was the beginning of the most active
summer of north-bound migration to Detroit, and Glenn

was one of an estimated thousand migrants to arrive in that month alone.[3] By 1922, the year Glenn's Aunt Sarah wrote her from Georgia, Detroit's African American population had increased sixfold. By 1925, another 40,000 African American migrants joined Detroit's burgeoning black community.[4] Although many of these migrants were African American men attracted by the promise of employment in Detroit's booming automobile industry, the majority of migrants cited noneconomic reasons for their movement north.[5] These noneconomic motives included the availability of public education for migrant children, an opportunity Glenn and others quickly took advantage of.

After she arrived in Detroit, Glenn attended public school, completing a commercial course at the Detroit High School of Commerce in 1922.[6] A year later, she obtained a white-collar job with the Detroit Post Office. The pride her family felt at this accomplishment, an accomplishment directly related to her migration, is clearly expressed in the letters quoted above. Yet this pride is tempered with a sense of concern from her female relatives. Would Glenn be "tempted" by the city's commercial recreation and secular lifestyle? How would she handle the virulent racism of Detroit's white employers and homeowners? Perhaps it was this concern that led Glenn's mother to encourage her to visit a friend living in Detroit. "I am sending you one of my friends addresses and I want you to go to see her," wrote Glenn's mother; "she said she had been expecting you to see her so be sure and see her."[7] Glenn's mother hoped her friend could guide her daughter through young adulthood and help her uphold the values of respectability Glenn had first learned in the South.

The letters from Glenn's female relatives reflect the continuing impact of southern norms of respectability on northern female migrants. Racial uplift ideology, which espoused bourgeois respectability and flourished in the South, shaped the social and institutional context Glenn entered when she arrived in Detroit. Glenn was an active member of Detroit's Second Baptist Church, for example, whose pastor hired social workers and developed programs to instruct new migrants in cleanliness, domestic skills, and deportment. She also helped organize a neighborhood improvement organization that publicized the need to keep homes and yards clean and orderly, a preoccupation of many African American reformers during the early twentieth century.[8] In order to appreciate Glenn's migration experience, one must understand the continuities between her childhood in Georgia and her adulthood in Detroit.

Glenn's family in Georgia encountered local and national conceptions of respectability in the decades prior to the Great Migration. Bourgeois respectability was most fully articulated in middle-class reformers' rhetoric of uplift ideology in the late nineteenth and early twentieth centuries. This national discourse emerged in dialogue with southern working-class women, who were targeted by reformers as most in need of "uplift." The interaction of elite and working-class women both strengthened uplift ideology and helped define class differences in the African American community. The emergence of a public discourse of respectability also shaped the African American community's institutional response to the Great Migration. During the late 1910s and 1920s, the Detroit Urban League, established churches, women's clubs, and other organizations used the language of female respectability and uplift prevalent in the years prior to migration. Middle-class notions of Victorian womanhood, a key component of the discourse of respectability, whose salience had declined in the white community by the late 1910s, continued to be espoused by African American reformers in Detroit through the 1920s. For Glenn and thousands of other migrants like her, the language of respectability was a central part of the migration experience.

Female Uplift Ideology

In 1903, Charles Chesnutt wrote: "The rights of the Negroes are at a lower ebb than at any time during the thirty-five years of their freedom, and the race prejudice more intense and uncompromising."[9] It was during this dark period of disenfranchisement, segregation, and violence that a number of ideological strands coalesced around racial uplift ideology. This ideology viewed the empowerment of African Americans as an evolutionary struggle, celebrated individual hard work in the tradition of Protestantism, and stressed a bourgeois moral code of appropriate behavioral norms.[10] Racial uplift at times operated as a "public transcript"—an open discourse that would appeal to moderate whites in the South, which has led some scholars to focus on its accommodationist tendencies.[11] However, uplift ideology also operated within African American traditions of reform and evangelical progress. A close examination of uplift leaders reveals a diverse and complex range of ideas behind their reform efforts. These educators and activists can also be credited with building the institutional base that would serve African Americans throughout the twentieth century.[12] Ida B. Wells's courageous efforts to curb lynching, for example, were clearly not the actions of an individual avoiding confrontation with southern political leaders. Thus, rather than representing accommodation to racist politics, uplift ideology sometimes masked resistance to the South's dominant power structure. It was essentially neither accommodationist nor resistant but part of a shifting strategy by community leaders who were both reacting to the oppressive political climate and creating new routes to empowerment through institution building and reform work.[13]

Uplift ideology emerged during the "woman's era," a period in which African American female school founders, lecturers, writers, and artists gained widespread notoriety for their activism. Writing at the height of this period in her landmark 1892 book, *A Voice from the South,* educator and scholar Anna Julia Cooper argued: "Now the fundamental agency under God in the regeneration, the re-training of the race, as well as the ground work and starting point of its progress upward, must be the *black woman*."[14] At the turn of the century, African American periodicals contained numerous articles linking the needs and aspirations of black women to the advancement of the race.[15] As a result, womanhood and domesticity became powerful tropes in the language of racial uplift during the Progressive period. This language linking female respectability to racial empowerment shaped the institutional and ideological response to the Great Migration in Detroit well into the 1920s.

In racial uplift ideology, clear divisions between classes and distinct social roles for men and women provided evidence of racial advancement. Advocates of racial uplift viewed the gender and class integration of the African American community as an impediment to racial progress and a sign of social disorganization. Crowded urban neighborhoods became targets of reformers disturbed by the mixing of classes, races, and genders on city streets. Prominent female reformer Fannie Barrier Williams, for example, wrote in a 1906 article on Chicago: "The huddling together of the good and the bad, compelling the decent element of the colored people to witness the brazen display of vice of all kinds in front of their homes and in the faces of their children, are trying conditions under which to remain socially clean and respectable."[16] Similarly, Detroit's African American reformers viewed the endemic crowding of the East Side as a barrier to creating a "socially clean and respectable" community. Establishing such a community, they hoped, would simultaneously counter negative white racist stereotypes and "uplift" newly arrived migrants. This project of sanitizing public space through class and gender segregation and hiding or removing evidence of vice dominated the reform agenda of migration-era black Detroit.

Northern racial uplift ideologues often presented a distorted image of southern migrants. They frequently described them as backward and primitive. A 1926 study of Detroit's African American migrants, for example, characterized the typical migrant as a "rural, uneducated farmhand."[17] More than half of the migrants, however, had lived in cities before making their final journey to Detroit.[18] Despite this fact, African Americans who lived in Detroit before the Great Migration shared reformers' perceptions. "People came out of the plantation and tenant farms and their whole life, their culture was different," argued one black Detroiter; "there is much difference in the culture of people who were tenant farmers down South than people who were raised up here."[19] In order to construct a positive community identity, reformers believed these perceived cultural differences had to be erased. The symbolic transformation of southern rural disorder into northern urban order through teaching migrants "respectable" behavior and self-presentation was a reform strategy that shaped major African American institutions in the early twentieth century. Yet by presenting a distorted view of the migrants' past, this discourse ignored the extensive experience many middle-class and working-class migrants had with southern reform organizations and urban life. Likewise, reformers exaggerated the advantages and opportunities available in the urban North to migrants who accepted bourgeois norms of respectability.

The motivations for embracing racial uplift ideology differed along class lines. For the growing bourgeoisie, female uplift ideology helped to define middle-class and "respectable" working-class African Americans against a lower class whose members they believed did not follow rules of cleanliness, religiosity, and sexual purity.[20] Uplift ideology also spurred them to initiate a variety of reform programs to materially aid African American migrants in a period when the state and white private charities ignored the black needy. Underlying these programs was the effort to negate pervasive and pernicious white stereotypes of blacks. Many working-class African Americans understood the class-coded nature of racial uplift and used it to achieve social mobility, reinforcing norms of bourgeois respectability while using them for their own ends. Working-class women were particularly hopeful that the new reform organizations would help them break into white-collar and industrial employment and leave domestic service behind. Therefore, African American Progressive Era reform organizations had a broad base of support throughout the black community. For Mary Etta Glenn and thousands of other African American female migrants in Detroit, the common experiences of southern life would inspire institution building, political activism, and reform work on a large scale. These same women, however, would continue to debate categories of respectability that shaped class and gender relations in the urban North in fundamental ways.

In order to legitimate their own class status, racial uplift leaders contrasted their behavior and demeanor with those of poor and working-class African Americans. This reveals a central paradox in the logic of uplift ideology: on the one hand, African American elites were attempting to help the poor and working classes achieve middle-class standards of respectability; on the other hand, doing so would weaken the unique positions of leadership these men and women held. This paradox was resolved by an assertion of class hierarchy as a necessary aspect of racial evolution that would provide evidence to skeptical whites of African Americans' progress. One white woman suggested at the turn of the century that "the best sign for the negroes of our land is that they are fast separating into classes, — a fact to which their white fellow-citizens but too often fail to attach the importance it deserves."[21] Kelly Miller, the dean of Howard University, believed industrial training and higher education were compatible strategies for racial uplift that would help reproduce class relations. "After making provision for the few people of any race who are capable to direct," argued Miller, "there will be left sufficient to toil. The value of the triangle depends upon its altitude as well as upon its base."[22]

This geometric metaphor, the triangle of class hierarchy, was very much present in the discourse of female uplift ideology. For many female African American elites, it was a source of a painful contradiction. They viewed themselves as middle class and respectable, following Victorian rules of decorum; however, some whites viewed them as inherently licentious and unclean because of their race. Numerous articles and speeches touched on this subject, revealing the class consciousness of elite women. In 1904, Sylvanie Francaz Williams published one such article, "The Social Status of the Negro Woman," in *Voice of the Negro*. Williams was responding to a statement published in 1904 in the *Independent* by a white women who argued: "I cannot imagine such a creature as a virtuous black woman." This article became the focal point of numerous discussions about social purity and racial uplift in the African American community because it stated plainly what so many felt to be true: when a southern white man or woman saw an African American woman, he or she saw only a depraved and degraded individual. Williams wrote in response: "We could not, nor would not feel aggrieved, if in citing the immorality of the Negro, the accusation was limited to the pauperized and brutalized members of the race. But it is that broad condemnation without exception; that uncharitableness of thought and deed that casts a shadow of distrust over the women of an entire race, that offends. . . . Of all God's creatures, the educated Negro woman is the most to be pitied."[23] Having achieved middle-class status through education and having adopted the norms of respectability prescribed by female uplift ideology, Williams was still unable to become a "virtuous woman" in the eyes of southern whites. Her racial status superseded all other aspects of her identity in the South; she was not at the pinnacle of a triangle but within a shapeless, classless mass.

African American female reformers who sought to transform this racist vision of the black community used the gendered rhetoric of Progressive Era reform to their advantage. In 1897, Fannie Barrier Williams wrote in the *AME Church Review*: "Never before has the world been so interested in woman and woman's work, and never before in our history have the people of this country been so much interested in colored women as it is to-day."[24] African American women broadened and extended the Victorian "cult of true womanhood" to include goals of racial empowerment.[25] The practical limitations that shaped all African American women's lives—the necessity to engage in wage work, to dispute accusations of immorality, and to protect themselves and their families from the daily psychological and physical violence of segregation—set them apart from their white counterparts and forged a different, if related, version of Victorian bourgeois ideology. Anne Firor Scott has suggested that "even more vehemently than white women, black women emphasized the home as the vital center of reform, and taught gentility as a counter to racial stereotypes, particularly those that labeled all black women as immoral."[26] The virulent attacks on African American female morality and the difficulty of directly challenging the southern power structure led to this emphasis on domesticity and female gentility. Nevertheless, female uplift ideology also emphasized teaching young African Americans about the historic struggles of their predecessors and instilled racial pride in a society that continually denigrated people of African descent.

A major weapon in this fight for respectability during the Progressive Era was the language of social purity. Social purity linked the evils of prostitution to a more general decline in morals in the late nineteenth century and promoted religious education and the protection of home and family.[27] African American clubwomen used social purity discourse to offset the stereotypes of immoral black women at the turn of the century. In *An Appeal for Social Purity in Negro Homes*, a sermon delivered at Fisk University in 1898, Eugene Harris stated: "There are no young women in this country who are more liable to insult, and for whom the foul-hearted tempter more often spreads his snares than the women of my own race. Unseen danger is lurking around them upon every side; and as they walk unattended the streets of our cities, hidden pitfalls are put before them. The purity of no class of women is put to a severer test. The chastity of no other women is more often assailed."[28] Preserving and protecting the "chastity" of young women became major priorities for uplift ideologues. These reformers encouraged young African American women to practice modesty, thrift, and sexual chastity to not only improve and protect themselves but also uplift the entire race.

The greatest threats to chastity, argued many black clubwomen, were white employers who sexually exploited African American domestic workers. In the Jim Crow South, few barriers deterred white men from sexually harassing or raping African American women who worked in their homes. Although sexual harassment and rape occurred in the African American community, reformers seeking to highlight the inherent purity of black women focused on the actions of white men who exploited negative stereotypes of black women as inherently promiscuous to justify their abuse. Because white employers barred African American women from entering other forms of paid labor, domestic service was also symbolic of racial oppression. Domestic service, therefore, was a central topic in the discourse of female uplift ideology. Reformers believed domestic training programs could instill norms of respectability and improve the economic well-being of their working-class sisters. If household labor was professionalized and rationalized, argued reformers, African American women would be viewed as workers rather than sexual objects.

Thus, in the late nineteenth and early twentieth centuries, the most common programs directed at black women involved household or domestic service training. These programs consisted of classes taught at schools, churches, voluntary associations, or branches of the Young Women's Christian Association (YWCA) by a graduate of a southern industrial school, a "home missionary," or a professional in the new field of household economics and domestic science. A model house or apartment usually served as a classroom for proper methods of cooking, cleaning, and serving. Many schools also had a model laundry that brought in extra funds while simultaneously training future laundresses in "modern" methods of cleanliness. The ubiquity of these programs and the wide-scale support of them by female uplift ideologues make them a useful example of the direct application of female uplift ideology. Because few African Americans viewed household labor, paid or unpaid, as inherently modern or enlightened, reformers had to work particularly hard to "uplift" the occupation.[29] Thus, they stressed two primary themes when advocating domestic training programs: training for domesticity and motherhood to improve African American homes and training for service work with better wages and working conditions.

Female uplift ideologues continually emphasized black women's talents as homemakers in their writing. "The time is certainly coming when it will be discreditable, yes, a disgrace, to any woman who has had no training in household economics," declared Fannie Barrier Williams in a 1904 article; "the accomplished woman of the future must be the woman whose accomplishments will include the kitchen and pantry as well as the drawing-room and the piano. If women are to keep pace with men in expanding the fields of usefulness and honor, they must learn to give a new value to the fundamental things that are now considered degrading and unimportant."[30] Working at an occupation that was "fundamental" fulfilled several central tenets of racial uplift: the Protestant work ethic, the modesty of a true woman, and the primary importance of the home. "What a miserable creature the woman to whom house-keeping and home-making are drudgery!," declared Williams in the same article; "think of the high uses and obligations that gather around the term home."[31] Inherent in Williams's discussion was a critique of African American women who avoided the duties of a housewife; reformers made this critique of both lower-class women who were deemed lazy and upper-class women whose love of "finery" and leisure led to a degraded home. The untrained poor and cosseted ladies could both be reformed through the teaching of domestic work. Thus, African American reformers redefined domestic labor as a noble pursuit that was essential to racial uplift and not "drudgery." Only by elevating household labor could blacks view domesticity as a central component of racial uplift. As a result, reformers argued that not only the labor itself but also the women who performed it would be elevated in standing.

In African American etiquette manuals published at the turn of the century, thrift and household cleanliness were deemed integral to the definition of a "lady."[32] An illustration in Elias M. Woods's 1899 manual, *The Negro in Etiquette*, shows two contrasting images of African American women. The woman answering the door is wearing a head scarf and apron, her hand is resting on her hip, and she is leaning forward. She is portrayed as a failed housewife whose home is not ready to receive visitors and whose personal appearance is equally unladylike. In stark contrast, the visiting woman, who is identified as a "lady," is wearing fashionable clothing and standing upright. Separating them is the dirt of an unruly home. Through this image, Woods suggests that by removing dirt and reforming her physical appearance, the woman answering the door could be transformed into the lady visitor.

Educators taught African American women and girls that the home had to appear spotless and that women should take responsibility for their self-presentation—in particular, their dress. Similarly, reformers in the social purity movement viewed dress as a clear indicator of respectability, separating the licentious from the sexually pure. This theme resonated throughout household-training manuals and etiquette books. In a 1909 article, B. E.

"Come in, if You Can Get in for the Dirt."

Illustration from Elias M. Woods, The Negro in Etiquette: A Novelty *(1899).*

Bradford cautioned against the elite woman dressed in "gaudily decorated silks" and "coarse, vulgar ornaments" in place of "the plain woman dressed in simple, becoming gowns, her eyes beaming with love and tenderness."[33] "Respectable" dress, then, was neither too plain and homely nor too gaudy and vulgar. Speeches, articles, and etiquette manuals instructed African American women to spend their money carefully on demure and practical clothing that would reflect social status and moral standing. This self-presentation, as much as the presentation of a clean and orderly home, could aid racial uplift through a communal public display of respectability. African American women, then, potentially embodied norms of bourgeois respectability as they traversed public spaces dressed in appropriate, demure attire. Respectable self-presentation took on a heightened importance in urban areas such as Detroit where city dwellers judged women's dress and demeanor.

Exalting household labor, thrift, and modesty of dress and equating these characteristics with respectability were integral to middle-class women's efforts at racial uplift. The focus on the home as the front line of racial uplift also reflected the continued denigration of African American women in public spaces. A woman might be forced to mingle with "unrespectable" men and women in a Jim Crow streetcar, but in her home, she could fully embody the ideals of respectability and be recognized as a model "mother" to the race. Sylvanie Francaz Williams noted that "to judge her, she must be seen in her home, where her detractors never can enter."[34] Improving the home could also reflect well on the neighborhood, presenting a clean and orderly picture to the white community. In a 1909 article, Fannie Barrier Williams argued that it was the role of a "few energetic and sympathetic club women" to reform African American communities and create "attractive home surroundings so that no longer shall uncleanliness or shiftlessness advertise the color of certain neighborhoods."[35] The discourse surrounding household training, then, was directly linked to the reform of entire communities. This crucial link was made by female reformers in Detroit as they transplanted southern strategies of racial uplift to the North.

Although educators designed domestic training programs to improve African American homes, with an emphasis on thrift and cleanliness, Williams, Nannie Helen Burroughs, and other proponents of domestic training recognized that young African American women would use the skills they learned primarily in white homes as domestic servants. They therefore sought to redefine domestic service as a "professional" occupation that was not to be shirked.[36] When women were trained to be better servants, argued reformers, both their wages and their social status would increase. Given the fact that between 60 and 90 percent of southern domestic servants were African American, this solution was pragmatic and highlighted the importance of domesticity in racial uplift.[37] Thus, young African American women were taught domesticity and domestic science to make them better wives and workers. African American domestic science programs were aimed at "home uplift" as a route to "racial uplift" and at the professionalization of domestic service as a way to mitigate the stigmatization of African American workers. This linking of domesticity and domestic service continued after the Great Migration. Domestic service training in Detroit became the centerpiece of nearly every reform effort aimed at female migrants in churches, settlement houses, the Urban League, and, by the 1930s, government-sponsored programs.

Reformers believed housewives and household workers alike benefited from rigorous domestic training programs. Indeed, the dual nature of domestic training resolved a central conflict in female uplift ideology: although many blacks viewed African American women as the caretakers of the race, they were in a subordinate economic position in American society. Household labor was associated with dirt and disorder; however, homemaking in the Progressive Era was associated with purity and reform. By focusing on the positive attributes of household labor—cleanliness, religiosity, and efficiency—reformers hoped the negative attributes would eventually be ameliorated. The discourse of domestic training, then, had many of the same inflections as the discourse of social purity and female racial uplift more generally. Uplift ideologues politicized domesticity by emphasizing bourgeois respectability during the nadir of race relations.

Training women to be better servants and wives was also a pragmatic solution. Like the training that African American men received in agriculture, domestic training had the support of moderate southern whites and northern philanthropists. It was a solution, however, that reinforced the structure of the labor market and gender relations in the community. The persistence of domestic service training in northern cities such as Detroit well into the Great Depression reflected both the durability of female uplift ideology and the stagnation of the labor market for African American women. Nevertheless, the motivations of the African American working women who entered such training programs differed in complex ways from those of the middle-class women who set them up. Despite these differences, a common concern of all African American women was domestic servants' vulnerability to sexual harassment and rape.

Collective Visions of Sexuality and Domesticity

Sexual exploitation was a quotidian reality for southern African American women. In an anonymous article published in the *Independent* in 1904, a presumably southern African American woman dared to speak out about these daily injustices: "It is commonly said that no girl or woman receives a certain kind of insult unless she invites it. That does not apply to a colored girl and woman in the South. The color of her face alone is sufficient invitation to the southern white man. . . . Few colored girls reach the age of sixteen without receiving advances from them—maybe from a young 'upstart,' and often from a man old enough to be their father, a white haired veteran of sin."[38] The woman who wrote this article did not have to labor outside her home after marriage. Her husband was a doctor, and they owned property from which they obtained some income. If she had found it necessary to bring in wages to support her family, her exposure to sexual harassment and rape would have increased dramatically. In southern cities, as many as 70 percent of all adult African American women were employed at the turn of the century, and married African American women were five times as likely to be employed in wage labor as married white women.[39] The vast majority of these women worked in domestic service and were therefore vulnerable to sexual exploitation in private homes.

In 1912, an anonymous article published in the *Independent* by "a Negro nurse" exposed the sexual harassment of domestic workers in the South.[40] Reflecting on a thirty-year career as a southern domestic servant, this woman described in detail the poor wages, long hours, and loss of freedom experienced by household workers. She wrote of her first dismissal from a job:

> I lost my place because I refused to let the madam's husband kiss me. He must have been accustomed to undue familiarity with his servants, or else he took it as a matter of course, because without any lovemaking at all, soon after I was installed as cook, he walked up to me, threw his arms around me, and was in the act of kissing me, when I demanded to know what he meant, and shoved him away. I was young then, and newly married, and didn't know then what has been a burden to my mind and heart ever since: that a colored woman's virtue in this part of the country has no protection. . . . Many and many a time since I have heard similar stories repeated again and again by my friends. I believe nearly all white men take, and expect to take, undue liberties with their colored female servants.[41]

Sexual harassment in private homes led African American women to leave household labor and seek better employment options for themselves and their female family members. Fannie Barrier Williams reported in a 1904 article: "It is a significant and shameful fact that I am constantly in receipt of letters from the still unprotected colored women of the South, begging me to find employment for their daughters according to their ability . . . to save them from going into the homes of the South as servants, as there is nothing to save them from dishonor and degradation."[42] Living under the constant threat of rape and harassment and unable to defend themselves openly or to ask their brothers and fathers to defend them—an act that could result in lynching—African American women developed what historian Darlene Clark Hine has called "the culture of dissemblance." This culture "created the appearance of openness and disclosure but actually shielded the truth of their inner lives and selves from their oppressors."[43]

It was in self-help clubs, private homes, mothers' meetings, settlement houses, and churches that working-class African American women found safety, solace, and space to develop strategies of resistance. These strategies incorporated notions of respectability, a self-image that was the polar opposite of white men's perception of black women as they passed them on the street. Often this self-image coincided with the descriptions of respectability in female uplift ideology. For example, the physical spaces where working-class African American women found refuge were often same-sex venues that discouraged heterosociability and were thus lauded by female uplift ideologues. It was the convergence over a defense of their sexual selves, however, that was the most powerful cross-class aspect of respectability. Working-class mothers and middle-class reformers continually sought to protect their daughters from the indignities and dangers of sexual assault and harassment.

Erma Calderon's mother, for example, kept a constant eye on her behavior while she was growing up in Savannah, Georgia, in the early twentieth century. "Never take candy from a man," she warned; "never get in a car or a truck or any kind of vehicle or buggy or hack with a man. If a man said anything to you, keep on going."[44] Annie Mae Dickson, an African American woman who grew up in the South, remembered other restrictions placed on African American girls: "In those days, you know, a lot of our people didn't let the girls get out much. I got many a whipping for slipping off and easing on in to town to the ballgames on Sunday afternoons when we had nowhere else to go."[45] Mahalia Jackson's aunt, known as "Aunt Duke," made sure that Jackson, who grew up in New Orleans in the early twentieth century, did not engage in the temptations of the "sporting life" of the city. "She believed in the church and hard work and no frills—and little as I was, I had to learn to toe the line."[46] For these women, as well as for the Detroit migrant Mary Etta Glenn, female relatives provided essential lessons for self-protection that were echoed by female-headed institutions promoting racial uplift ideology.

Although the messages of self-protection were similar, the motivations that lay behind these messages differed at times. Whereas writing a public transcript that denied the inherent immorality of African American womanhood was a project taken on primarily by female uplift ideologues, working-class African American women articulated sexual purity primarily as a defense against the sexual abuse of their daughters, sisters, nieces, and themselves. Thus, a "strong will to survive" and self-respect were the legacies of many working-class mothers. These legacies often coincided with the rhetoric of Victorian morality expressed in female uplift ideology. African American reformers, like individual black women, were motivated by a desire to protect vulnerable women. Therefore, African American women adapted sexual propriety as both a public discourse and a private strategy of protection and "dissemblance."

This common ground helped black women form powerful alliances in the Progressive Era institutions they founded. Working-class women had a long history of organizing and sustaining benevolent societies and mutual aid organizations in their communities. This legacy of activism, combined with the need to counteract images of immorality, led to the support of institutions and programs set up by female uplift ideologues. By 1914, the National Association of Colored Women's Clubs (NACW), for example, had a membership of 50,000. Settlement houses such as Atlanta's Neighborhood Union, domestic training classes, extension services of the women's schools, and other programs all attracted the support of working-class women. Despite the elitism of reformers like Margaret Murray Washington, who saw mothers' meetings as a way for the "superior class of Negro women" to teach domesticity to the masses, these groups gained the widespread support and interest of ordinary African American women who *already* valued domesticity and sexual restraint.[47] Describing her missionary work at St. Helena Island, South Carolina, for example, Rossa Cooley, a northern white woman, remembered her frustration over trying to find a topic that female islanders would consider appealing: "When I had a course in hygiene and home emergency nursing the next year, we found we had struck the nail on the head, and ever since that has been the 'course of study' and they never weary of it. . . . It lay near to their traditional functions as home-makers and tenders of sick."[48] The "traditional functions" noted by Cooley reflected a cross-class understanding of domesticity and good housekeeping. Although working-class women did not foreground a notion of "uplift" that emphasized class divisions and class markers of respectability, they understood and responded to a common language that transcended class and elevated their role in the home.

Values of domesticity centered around the image of clean, efficient, and comfortable homes. Although cleanliness was a recurrent theme in the discourse of racial uplift, it also struck a strong chord among working-class women, who had long labored to uphold standards of cleanliness.[49] Erma Calderon, whose mother was a domestic servant, remembered her childhood: "My mother was spotless. And we had to be the same way. We washed our socks and our hair ribbon every day. They were washed, and the ribbon was ironed. The socks were put up to dry. . . . The dresses that we wore were hung up."[50] Calderon also had to keep her mother's stove as "clean as her table." "Where the ashes went—your bread box couldn't be any cleaner," she remembered; "that box was taken outside and washed, rinsed out, dried, and inside it was clean. The oven—spotless."[51] Mahalia Jackson had similar memories of her mother: "We lived in a little old 'shotgun' shack. It rained about as much inside our house as it did outside, and we were always putting out pots and pans to catch the water and sweeping it out with brooms, but those floors were always scrubbed clean."[52] The pride that women and their families took in keeping their houses clean despite the hardships of poverty was a testament to an enduring legacy of self-respect and community building. Although these women may have been influenced by the standards of cleanliness emphasized in the programs run by female uplift ideologues, these norms were already pervasive in southern African American culture.

It could be extremely difficult to keep a clean home in the rural South, where African American families often lived in small cabins with poor facilities. Sara Brooks, who grew up in rural Alabama, remembered her family's insistence on being clean even though they had no running water or bathtub: "We'd wash in the wash pan when we get ready to go to bed. You really took that good bath on Saturday night in the tin tub, but all the rest of the time we'd wash up in the pan. We'd wash our face and hands and underarms and privates and wash our feet."[53] Olivia Young, a resident of the Coffins Point Plantation on St. Helena Island, described her participation in "cleanup" week: "I have raked up all the yards, gather up all the old rubbish carried them to the trash pile and burn them. Have painted the walls and ceiling inside the house, remove and dusted all the rugs and put them back in their places, have cleaned the flowers yard and set out more flowers, have washed and cleaned up all my heaviest bedclothes and laid them aside, clean out the poultry coop and put in clean straw, washed and iron curtains and hang them up again and have dusted all the rooms and furniture."[54] These rural women worked long days in order to meet the expectations of not only middle-class reformers but also the working-class community at large.[55]

Normative standards of cleanliness captured the attention of national African American leaders who were interested in uplifting southern African Americans. W. E. B. Du Bois's 1914 study, *Morals and Manners among Negro Americans*, reported the views of community leaders in southern states on African American standards of cleanliness. In general, the comments were very positive: "Habits of cleanliness are far above the average; The percentage of those who observe a fair degree of personal and home cleanliness is encouragingly large; In housekeeping and cleanliness there is a wonderful change. . . . Clean-up days have been instituted among the colored people and there are few yards that are not overgrown with beautiful flowers and fern. . . . Their homes are beautiful thruout."[56] African Americans continually expressed pride in clean homes, neighborhoods, and bodies during the Progressive Era. Domestic servants would often comment that their own standards of cleanliness surpassed those of the white families they worked for. For servants, who were associated with "dirt" because of their occupation and their race, high standards of cleanliness refuted dominant stereotypes of African American women. Keeping a clean house also indicated that a woman did not place her wage labor over her household duties. Thus, in myriad ways, cleanliness could represent resistance to poverty and oppression; it was a symbol of self-respect, whose importance was understood by elite reformers and working-class women alike.

Housewifery and domesticity were pragmatic arts for African American women, and they often took advantage of opportunities to improve these arts at mothers' meetings or in domestic training courses. Like their teachers, the students of domestic training preferred to use these skills in their own homes rather than as wage workers in the homes of whites. Through the discourse of household training, then, respectability was firmly linked with the physical cleanliness of homes and bodies. In the eyes of reformers, keeping a "clean" home was an important first step toward respectability for working-class women. For all African American women, the presentation of clean homes and bodies could refute white stereotypes of black disorder and dirt and thus aid in the uplift of the race. In Detroit, this link between cleanliness and respectability was reinforced through domestic training programs, instructions to incoming migrants, and settlement houses. Female migrants who arrived in Detroit had encountered these lessons before from their mothers, aunts, and grandmothers, as well as from southern reform institutions.

Divergent Visions of Household Labor and Religion

Although many working-class women and their middle-class counterparts shared an ideology of domesticity, their views of domestic service often differed. African American educators wished to raise domestic work out of the category of "drudgery" and professionalize it as a means of improving wages and working conditions. This approach paralleled the programs of other progressive reformers who sought to rationalize labor to improve workers' lives. Most working-class African American women, however, wished to get out of domestic labor altogether, if possible. Meanwhile, the many women who remained domestic servants used a variety of alternative strategies of resistance and reform to shape the occupation to their own needs. These strategies were, for the most part, out of the purview of those initiated and promoted by middle-class clubwomen, missionaries, and schoolteachers.

Domestic science was the centerpiece of the National Training School for Women and Girls' curriculum.[57] The school's founder, Nannie Helen Burroughs, set up a model house and a commercial laundry on the Washington, D.C., campus and promoted domestic science courses in school brochures. Despite this, one woman interested in the school wrote Burroughs: "I sincerely hope you have 'fields' for girls of average intelligence besides domestic service!"[58] When students arrived at the school, they often avoided taking courses in domestic service training. Between 1918 and 1931, for example, 51 percent of the students majored in sewing, 29 percent in business, and only 15 percent in domestic science.[59] Unfortunately for these students, white employers largely shut African American women out of white-collar work such as stenography, typing, and other clerical employment. Although some jobs opened during World War I, mostly in government agencies, increased racism in the years after the war further narrowed the employment opportunities for African American women.[60] Sewing offered autonomy and independence for African American women who could open small shops for themselves or work as seamstresses out of their homes. Any of these occupations were higher in status than domestic service because they helped women escape from sexual harassment in private homes and generally provided better wages. It is not surprising, then, that the majority of students chose to train in these trades rather than domestic science. Students' preferences for commercial and business training demonstrated their desire to escape low-paying and demeaning service work, their optimism in the face of a severely circumscribed job market, and perhaps their skepticism toward reformers' efforts to "professionalize" domestic service.

Students drew from their experiences in their homes and communities to make their curriculum choices. Many had watched their female relatives labor in domestic service and agricultural work and sought training in occupations that provided more autonomy, economic security, and social mobility. Mildred Holly Farren, for example, reported to her teacher: "I want to be a stenographer when I finish school because it seems very businesslike."[61] Students' families also hoped their daughters, nieces, and granddaughters could achieve social mobility by avoiding household labor. Although Burroughs skillfully crafted a discourse on domestic service that sought to incorporate racial uplift with wage labor and housewifery, working-class women who attended the school continually challenged the identification of domestic service with African American womanhood. In other training schools, such as Hampton and Tuskegee, female students entered domestic service training because of the need to work for tuition. Working in school laundries, dining rooms, kitchens, and dormitories was mandatory for all students, and for those on scholarship, such work took up most of their days. James Anderson found that students at Hampton "protested against the menial level of training, hard labor, low wages, and poor working conditions."[62] African American students and their families sacrificed a great deal to further their education, and remaining in low-paying, demeaning service work after such sacrifices was unthinkable to many.

Yet the reality was that most African American women turned to domestic service as a reliable means to bring home wages. Melnea Cass, whose mother was a domestic servant and father was a janitor, grew up in Virginia in the early twentieth century. She attended a private Catholic school in Rock Castle where she was taught domestic work. "We learned how to keep the house and all that, because mostly colored girls at that time were hired out as domestics," remembered Cass. "We had cooking classes. And all sorts of things that made you learn how to do things in a house, if you were going out to work in a house. It was very good, because most of us did go out and work in the houses; we couldn't go on to college, you know."[63] Despite her generally positive memories of domestic training, Cass later resented being restricted to employment in domestic service:

I couldn't get a job when I came out of school, I told you, in any of the stores or any place else. The only resort for most black people was domestic work. . . . You always could make a living. But it wasn't always what you wanted to do. But you had to do it. I didn't want to do it, because I felt I could have done something else. I could have gone in as a trainee in some of these offices, receptionist, and all these things that I see people doing now, I could have easily done it in my young days. But they wouldn't hire me, because I was a colored woman. . . . That's how they [African American women] educated their families and did everything else, doing domestic work.[64]

Cass's inability to find wage labor outside of domestic service was the reality for almost all African American women, even those who had received a fairly good education.

Annie Mae Dickson had similar memories of limited choices for employment: "I had wanted to be a secretary for a long time because once I saw the secretary to the high school principal and that seemed to be the most important job I saw a black woman have. But if you lived where I did you did domestic work or farming, even if you finished high school. . . . For a black girl there wasn't anything like working at the stores . . . and I don't remember any registered nurses that was colored working in the hospital then. The only nursing that you did was taking care of people's children. It was easy to find a job baby-sitting, or somebody to cook for and houseclean. So that's what I did."[65] Women such as Cass and Dickson, however, were not passive employees. They actively shaped the nature of domestic service to fit their own needs and the needs of their families.

Married African American women, for example, preferred to work as laundresses rather than live-in domestic servants in private homes. This work allowed them to remain at home to care for their children and gave them more independence and protection from sexual harassment than labor in private homes.[66] After Charleszetta Waddles gave birth to her first child in St. Louis, for example, she said she "started helping Mama do the nurse's uniforms by doing them at home and that allowed me to be home with my baby and baby sister."[67] Southern African American women also set a precedent in domestic service by insisting on "living out" rather than staying in employers' homes, as northern white domestic servants traditionally did.[68] Another strategy of resistance included taking time off to attend religious revivals, public holidays, and other communal events. Domestic servants' high turnover rates reflected their understanding of their labor's value in the southern economy. Moving from job to job in order to find one that was more tolerable was possible because of the high demand for household workers. The practice of "pan-toting," taking home food from an employer's house, helped to stretch the meager wages of domestic servants.[69] Finally, in a few cases, domestic servants formed organizations and implemented work stoppages to demand improvements in wages, hours, and work conditions.[70]

All of these quotidian forms of resistance differed from middle-class women's reform strategies. Domestic servants sought to improve their immediate situations in whatever way they could rather than joining in a project to "rationalize" labor in private homes that was dependent on a personal relationship between employer and employee.[71] Not surprisingly, then, for working-class women, the ultimate reform of domestic service was to escape it altogether. African American women, like their immigrant counterparts in the North, did what they could to avoid domestic service. Jacqueline Jones notes that in regions that provided alternative employment opportunities for African American women, for example, in seafood-processing plants or tobacco factories, domestic servants were in short supply.[72] In cities, African American women peddled fresh produce, opened beauty shops or lunch counters, and engaged in other innovative entrepreneurial strategies to avoid domestic service and expand their job opportunities. These strategies were not antithetical to working-class women's notions of respectability. Rather, by leaving domestic service or helping their children do so, women were directly addressing the threat of sexual harassment and rape, countering the traditional images of the "black mammy," and asserting independence and self-respect, which were integral to their notions of racial pride. "There is no sacrifice I would not make, no hardship I would not undergo," wrote one southern African American woman, "rather than allow my daughters to go in service where they would be thrown constantly in contact with southern white men, for they consider the colored girl their special prey."[73] By refuting the notion that black women and service were inextricably linked, however, many southern African American women were at odds with the Tuskegee-Hampton ideology that circumscribed their educational opportunities. Thus, views of domestic service reflected a growing class-based schism in the ideology of respectability. Although they converged over the importance of domesticity and the family, African American women diverged over training a new generation for servitude.

The workplace was not the only arena in which notions of respectability diverged by class. The church, a center of local activism and community life, was another terrain of conflict in the premigration South. Before reformers established settlement houses, YWCAs, community centers, and schools, the local church served as both a spiritual meeting place and a source of empowerment. As female racial uplift ideologues increasingly stressed bourgeois respectability, however, particular forms of religious worship came under attack. Reformers viewed "excessive" emotionalism, shouting, speaking in tongues, spirit possession, and other forms of ecstatic worship as negative legacies of slavery, remnants of an African past. By the 1870s and 1880s, established Methodist and Baptist churches began actively to discourage ecstatic worship, emphasizing instead the decorum and worship styles of white denominations. At the same time, the social gospel movement encouraged churches to expand their activities to secular concerns of community reform, leaving behind the "otherworldly" aspects of ritual and religious teaching and promoting a well-educated ministry.[74] As a result, religion increasingly became an arena of conflict and dissension over definitions of female respectability and class position. The most prominent targets of attack were women in the Sanctified churches established in the late nineteenth century.[75] These self-described "saints" directly confronted stereotypes of African American womanhood while discarding many bourgeois conceptions of respectability. The churches they founded in the South, and in cities such as Detroit during the Great Migration, reflected a powerful commitment to religious values, racial pride, and self-respect.

In 1867, a massive camp meeting was held in Vineland, New Jersey, attended by whites and African Americans from a variety of denominations who sought to "make common supplication for the descent of the Spirit upon ourselves, the church, the nation, and the world."[76] This revival, which grew out of a general dissatisfaction with a perceived decline in morality and religiosity at the eve of the Civil War, led to the founding of the National Holiness Association. Theologically, the Holiness sects differed from the Methodists, the denomination from which most Holiness evangelicals sprang, by preaching the doctrine of entire sanctification. Reaching a state of "sainthood" or "holiness" required a second blessing or conversion experience. This second blessing was obtained through ritual worship styles that emphasized emotionalism, shouting, singing, spirit possession, and glossolalia (speaking in tongues). Traveling south in the years after the Civil War, white missionaries found these rituals abhorrent and recommended their elimination from black religious culture.[77] Mainstream African American denominations, such as the African Methodist Episcopal (AME) and Baptist churches, sought to prove their own respectability in the religious community during this period. Therefore, they discouraged ecstatic worship in their own congregations and condemned its practice in other denominations.[78]

By the 1880s and 1890s, those who had experienced the second blessing broke off from Methodist and Baptist denominations and formed separate churches. The largest African American Holiness church, the Church of God in Christ, was incorporated in Memphis in 1897. By the 1910s, the Church of God in Christ would declare that the only true evidence of the second blessing was the gift of glossolalia. This distinction became the foundation of the Pentecostal church.[79] By the eve of World War I, a variety of sects, including the Holiness, Pentecostal, and Primitive Baptist churches, had a common belief in sanctification and stressed emotionalism in their religious worship. The creation of these new denominations, which refused to subscribe to the restrained worship practices of mainstream churches, led to schisms in the African American community that centered around the issue of respectability.

Although critics of the Sanctified church focused on its ecstatic worship, the church's teachings also emphasized chastity, cleanliness, abstinence from liquor and tobacco, and the abandonment of "worldly amusements." These strict proscriptions may not have been followed to the letter by all adherents to the faith, but most congregants at least strove to achieve the second blessing and sainthood by following the teachings of their church. Thus, a powerful irony emerged in the discourse of racial uplift ideology. On the one hand, ecstatic worship drew criticisms of moral laxity; on the other, members of the Sanctified church seemed to be following the tenets of social purity and domesticity with great fervor. This apparent contradiction can be explained by definitions of respectability emanating from the working class: members of Sanctified churches did not accept the class-based standards of "respectable" worship styles, but they maintained strict standards of every-day behavior. Nevertheless, in the eyes of racial uplift ideologues, female saints who had no self-restraint in their religious practices could never be considered "ladies." Yet the saints had already reached the peak of respect-able self-identity in their spiritual and social lives. For them, this spiritual identity was more important than presenting a public face of self-restraint.

One of the attractions of the Sanctified church for African American women was the possibility of gaining greater status than was available in more established denominations. "Sects' rejection of the status in the secu-lar world," argues Edward Ayers, "opened them to the possibilities of female leadership."[80] All members of the church could achieve the status of saints, and many Sanctified churches also allowed women to preach directly to con-gregations rather than relegating them to the "Women's Departments" of Methodist and Baptist denominations. This led reformers to criticize "overly religious" women who paid more attention to their spirituality than to their families. For example, in a social purity tract, Reverend R. A. Adams la-mented: "Many a girl has gone to ruin while her mother was at church shout-ing or making a speech at the missionary society where oftentimes they weep over the heathen in the jungle and lose their children at home."[81] Evange-list and domestic worker Amanda Smith countered such charges by arguing that devout women did not neglect their domestic duties: "Many times over my wash-tub and ironing table, and while making my bed and sweeping my house and washing my dishes I have had some of the richest blessings. . . . How many mothers' hearts I have cheered when I told them that the blessing of sanctification did not mean isolation from all the natural and legitimate duties of life, as some seem to think. Not at all. . . . For we have to learn how not only to bear, but also to forbear with infirmities of ourselves and others as well."[82] Smith often found forbearance in prayer meetings with other women. "We would tell each other our joys or sorrows, our victories and defeats," remembered Smith, "and if Satan had buffeted us, how we bore up or if we yielded under the pressure . . . and then we would advise each other and pray for each other."[83]

Forbearance and solace were sources of power and personal identity that African American women found in the Sanctified church. Besides complying with strict behavioral proscriptions and guidelines for modest dress, saints abided by their own codes of respectability while continuing to express their spirituality. Yet the dancing, shouting, and speaking in tongues that characterized ecstatic worship also provided a source of identity and power because it diverged from the self-restraint that African American women had to exercise as domestic servants in white homes or in public spaces, where they were under threat of sexual harassment and rape. It allowed them to get beyond the "culture of dissemblance" that defined much of their public existence. In addition, female saints saw their worship style as evidence of their sainthood and their eventual redemption in heaven. Despite some ministers' pronouncements that "noise cannot save us," these women were not willing to give up their worship styles for surface attributes of middle-class respectability and refinement.[84] Thus, the religious identity of many working-class African American women was rooted more in notions of self-respect than in bourgeois public displays of respectability. When these deeply religious women opened new churches in small Detroit storefronts, they soon felt the wrath of African American religious and secular leaders who accused them of undermining a respectable public identity defined by a self-restrained worship style and male leadership.

Another point of conflict in religious worship styles centered around music. Mahalia Jackson remembered the Sanctified churches in her native New Orleans: "Those people had no choir and no organ. They used the drum, the cymbal, the tambourine, and the steel triangle. Everybody in there sang and they clapped and stomped their feet and sang with their whole bodies. They had a beat, a powerful beat, a rhythm we held on to from slavery days, and their music was so strong and expressive it used to bring tears to my eyes. I believe the blues and jazz and even the rock and roll stuff got their beat from the Sanctified Church."[85] Jackson was not the only one who associated the powerful music of the Sanctified church with "slavery days." Often critics of Sanctified music dismissed it as "uncivilized" or "backward." In reality, Sanctified musicians combined emerging secular styles of music with more traditional rhythms to develop what would eventually be known as gospel music.[86] As the secular and sacred worlds grew further apart in the early twentieth century, the Sanctified churches continued to combine the two worlds in their music. "They brought into the church not only the sounds of ragtime, blues, and jazz," states historian Lawrence Levine, "but also the instruments. They accompanied the singing which played a central role in their services with drums, tambourines, triangles, guitars, double basses, saxophones, trumpets, trombones, and whatever else seemed musically appropriate."[87] By experimenting with music in their churches, African

American women participated in the development of blues and jazz without going to the saloons or jook joints that many saw as potentially dangerous or at odds with their religious beliefs.

The musical style of the Sanctified churches was perhaps the best example of how popular religion in the South transgressed the dichotomies that structured racial uplift ideology. The churches incorporated ecstatic styles of worship and music that reformers considered overly exuberant by contemporary standards. Yet the female saints who were the backbone of the churches saw themselves as equal to or above other women in society because they had attained a second blessing and thus sainthood. In an increasingly materialistic and urban society, the Sanctified church also stressed simplicity in dress and lifestyle. Most important, the Sanctified church was a profoundly democratic institution where women's voices were as loud as men's, where the possibility of interracial harmony existed during the nadir of race relations, and where class divisions had less meaning than whether one had achieved the blessings of the Lord. Perhaps the ability of the church and its female leaders to transgress these boundaries led to the vociferousness of the attacks on the congregants. As urban migration progressed and even more sects sprang up in city storefronts founded and led by African American women, these criticisms only increased in fervor.

Mobility, Leisure Workers, and Urban Space

Attending Sanctified camp meetings and revivals was one reason for southern African American women to travel throughout the South. A more common motivation was the search for wage labor and better schools for their children. Like progressive reformers in the North, southern racial uplift ideologues grew increasingly concerned about urbanization's toll on the "purity" of women. Mobility was the opposite of the domesticity advocated by reformers, which implied settling down and making a commitment to community building. But mobility was essential for African American women's survival. Despite this fact, reformers argued that leaving their rural and small-town communities for southern and northern cities made African American women vulnerable to urban vices. In contrast, female migrants who saw the city as a means to improve living conditions and standards for themselves and their families believed the potential benefits of mobility outweighed its dangers.

African American women who sought to escape domestic service and agricultural work developed new niches in urban labor markets. Segregated communities offered economic opportunities for owners of shops, lunch counters, and other small businesses and founders of storefront churches. By the late nineteenth century, an informal economy also began to flourish in African American communities based primarily on gambling and prostitution. Finally, black women found jobs ranging from singing to waiting tables in honky-tonks and jook joints as jazz and blues gained popularity. I have labeled women who worked in these occupations "leisure workers." They provided services to African American men and women who sought leisure after a hard day's work, while at the same time earning wages for their families. African American women found the entrepreneurial skills they learned in these occupations particularly useful when they migrated to northern cities, where their employment opportunities were equally circumscribed in the traditional labor market. For those who worked in honky-tonks, as prostitutes, or in dance halls, however, the opportunity to be recognized as "ladies" by the respectable middle class was lost.[88]

As urbanization and consumer culture accelerated into the twentieth century, more entrepreneurial opportunities for women emerged, and debates about "respectable" occupations increased. In the city of Detroit, known for its powerful underworld, the link between a respectable identity and a respectable occupation became particularly strained. One occupation that combined the dangers of mobility with the dangers of illicit activities was working the vaudeville circuit singing the blues, playing music, or dancing.[89] In 1909, the Theater Owners' Booking Association (TOBA) organized a southern and midwestern circuit of vaudeville acts and tent shows. The TOBA hired dancers, comedians, blues singers, magicians, musicians, and singers of popular vaudeville songs.[90] The women who joined these traveling shows could earn up to $50 a week, at least five times the salary of a domestic worker. Historian Daphne Duval Harrison argues that some women migrated to urban centers and worked as domestics with the hope of eventually starting a career onstage.[91] Female performers such as Bessie Smith, Ethel Waters, Fannie Wise, Ma Rainey, and Ida Cox did gain fame and a degree of wealth through the TOBA. Countless other female dancers, musicians, comedians, and backup singers were paid much lower wages and had to endure the difficult conditions of travel and work on the TOBA circuit. Furthermore, by appearing onstage in "gaudy" outfits and performing sexually suggestive songs, female performers often incurred the wrath of clergymen and other guardians of bourgeois respectability. Nevertheless, for many women, the risk of moral censure and uncertain working conditions was outweighed by the economic opportunities and geographic mobility that a life on the circuit offered. Because they could send their wages back to family members to support the educational efforts of sisters, brothers, or children and because they were able to escape domestic service, performers did not necessarily transgress their own codes of respectability.

Esther Mae Scott was one young African American woman who decided to face the risks and potential rewards of traveling with a vaudeville show. Scott was born in 1893 in Warren County, Mississippi, where her parents were tenant farmers on the Polk Plantation. When she was fourteen, Scott left home and joined the Rabbitfoot and Woolcott Traveling Minstrel Show. She demonstrated the hair pomade that the show sold and played the guitar. In return, Scott received $1 per day and the use of her costume. "I thought I was the happiest and the biggest person in the world," remembered Scott. When she tired of the minstrel show, Scott worked as a domestic, taking time off to travel briefly with Leadbelly, Bessie Smith, and Louis Armstrong. Scott recalled escaping her work as a domestic for a memorable trip with Leadbelly to see Bessie Smith for the first time: "I'm trying to tell you, we didn't have no weeks. The world go round, and the weeks go round from can to can't, when you could see until you couldn't see. . . . Nobody give you no time off. . . . Baby, I left there running, going, me and Leadbelly. I said, 'If you don't get me out the way, they'll change their mind and call me back. Let's go.' And we didn't waste no time, and on to Clarksdale. We got in his car and off we went."[92] The sense of freedom Scott felt when she was on the road with Leadbelly contrasted sharply with her life as a live-in domestic. This freedom of travel and of expression was reflected in the blues songs sung by African American women during the early twentieth century.

The emergence of the blues singer defined a new generation of young urban women who would take the second step of migration from southern to northern cities. "I remember when I used to listen to Bessie Smith sing 'I Hate to See That Evening Sun Go Down,'" recalled Mahalia Jackson. "I'd fix my mouth and try to make my tones come out just like hers. And I'd whisper to myself that someday the sun was going to shine down on me way up North in Chicago or Kansas City or one of those faraway placed that . . . the other Negroes that roamed away from New Orleans always talked about."[93] Soon Jackson boarded a train to Chicago and began a journey duplicated by hundreds of thousands of southern African American women. This journey transformed not only their lives but also the nation as a whole.

In the years before and after World War I, many southern African American women, like Mahalia Jackson and Mary Etta Glenn, chose to leave the South for Detroit. "In the never-ending procession, they came, lured by stories of easy money, girls who asked nothing of life save an opportunity to earn money to help tired and over-burdened parents; girls who wished only to be self-supporting and so relieve the strain at home . . . ;

girls who were seeking adventure; girls who longed for the bright lights and a good time, and to whom a job was only a necessary means to this end."[94] Progressive reformers viewed this "never-ending procession" of young female migrants to urban centers as a major concern.[95] African American female reformers feared that the South-to-North migration would exacerbate problems of female vice because of crowding, the availability of unwholesome commercial amusement, and the economic degradation of women workers. These reformers attempted to counteract the perceived negative effects of urbanization by founding organizations and institutions that promoted female virtue. Settlement houses, "respectable" rooming houses, YWCA branches, and numerous other institutions proliferated as the Great Migration brought increasingly larger numbers of African American women to northern cities.[96]

During the period of migration and resettlement, respectability became the watchword of middle-class reformers who wished to construct a collective public identity in the North based on bourgeois values of thrift, sexual restraint, cleanliness, and hard work. Reformers believed this public identity would have two primary effects. First, white city officials and employers would view African Americans as respectable urban citizens and employees, improving their working conditions, employment opportunities, and level of city services. Second, in the community, teaching respectability to incoming migrants would aid in their assimilation to the urban North and "protect" them from the city's dangers. Reformers attempted to encode this public identity in visible displays of respectability; thus, they repeatedly stressed dress, demeanor, and neighborhood cleanliness. They hoped that these symbols of respectability, often embodied in the behavior and attire of African American women, would simultaneously "uplift" African American women and men and create a positive image of the African American community.

The segregation of Detroit's African Americans limited the effectiveness of this approach to racial uplift and community building. Near the commercial center of the city, the small and crowded African American community was bounded by the Detroit River to the south, Mt. Elliot Street to the east, Harper Street to the north, and Brush Street to the west. Located in Detroit's East Side, this neighborhood was identified by whites as the primary vice district, with numerous speakeasies, houses of prostitution, and gambling dens. The existence of illicit spaces in the East Side also encouraged the growth of black reform organizations that hoped to "purify" the neighborhood for the betterment of its inhabitants. Thus, bourgeois respectability operated during the Great Migration to reform both the physical space of the African American neighborhood and the behavior of individual African American women and men.

The self-consciousness of community leaders who wished to display a "proper" public face to white Detroit and protect incoming migrants was reflected in their efforts to control large public crowds of African American migrants. When the Negro National League opened the 1921 baseball season in Detroit, for example, an African American newspaper, the *Detroit Contender*, stressed the link between individual behavior and community identity. "The league should be considered your personal league," it argued; "if it succeeds you should feel you have succeeded; if it fails, you should consider it a personal failure. Your heart should vibrate sympathetically with the heart of the league. If the league succeeds, the race succeeds; if the league fails, the race fails."[97] The uplift of the race was considered the personal responsibility of individual migrants, who were to present reliable, respectable, and constrained public selves. Because Mack Park, where the Detroit Stars played, was a long streetcar ride away from the East Side and many white fans also attended the games, community leaders instructed African American "rooters" to dress well and present a reserved demeanor.[98] When the white press noted the presence of gamblers and the "gallons of perfumery and tons of powder" on fashionably dressed women, it was evident that the policing of the Negro National League was a battle Detroit's African American leaders were going to lose.[99] In fact, some African American fans consciously displayed their social mobility by wearing expensive clothing and cosmetics, which transgressed boundaries of bourgeois respectability. These alternative images undermined the project of constructing a community identity and contradicted the stereotypical image of the naive, vulnerable migrant painted by African American reformers.

Overcrowded living conditions in black Detroit made public displays of bourgeois respectability particularly hard to promote and enforce in the early twentieth century. Racial segregation led to class integration, with elites and working-class blacks living in close proximity; therefore, orderly class relations were difficult to achieve.[100] The overcrowding of Detroit's housing and the scarcity of "respectable" recreation also led to gender mixing, which suggested the possibility of illicit encounters between the sexes and thus could reflect negatively on the community. The crowding of the African American community meant that there were few homosocial spaces available where African American women could congregate apart from men.[101] Clubwomen worked to create spaces—in churches, the Detroit Urban League's settlement house, and the YWCA—to offer female migrants classes and clubs that taught domestic skills, health, hygiene, and social mores. Reformers also attempted to shut down "disorderly" houses, shame prostitutes working on the streets, and close down the numerous "unsightly" storefront churches that occupied the abandoned stores of fleeing white merchants. These efforts were only partially successful in a period when heterosociability and the informal economy thrived.

Detroit before the Great Migration

Detroit's African American residents had almost uniformly fond memories of the years before the Great Migration. The black community, they suggested, was thoroughly integrated, and discrimination was barely evident. James E. Cummings remembered: "There was no such thing as resistance to blacks until that surge of blacks coming up during World War I. That's when attitudes began to change and resistance set in."[102] The "old settlers" of premigration Detroit contrasted this romantic past with the overcrowded, segregated, and underserved postmigration African American community. These Detroiters distinguished themselves from the uncouth, rural migrants whom they viewed as the cause of deteriorating race relations in Detroit. One longtime resident of Detroit complained that the "underprivileged Negro from the rural South has been responsible for changing the Negroes' position in Detroit." He argued that "a proper discrimination between individuals is no longer shown on the part of the whites. Negroes are taken as members of a race and not on individual merits."[103] Given this perception, many of the city's original residents hoped to force migrants to conform to bourgeois standards of respectability promoted by African American elites. This old settler versus newcomer dichotomy, however, masked a more complex set of class relations and migration patterns.

In 1870, Detroit's African American community comprised less than 3 percent of the overall population of the city. Although the actual number of African Americans doubled by 1900, to 4,111, the percentage of African Americans actually declined to 1.4 percent due to an influx of European immigrants.[104] Many late-nineteenth-century African American migrants were ex-slaves who had escaped to Ontario, Canada, and later returned to the United States.[105] Others migrated to Detroit from the rural hinterland of Michigan. Yet a substantial number of migrants between 1880 and 1900 were southern-born. These vanguard migrants tended to be relatively well-off and well-educated in contrast to the image of the poor, rural migrant that emerged during the Great Migration.[106] However, the prosperous black middle class did not make up the majority of black residents in late-nineteenth-century Detroit. The urban poor did not arrive with southern migrants after 1917 but rather had always been part of Detroit's segregated East Side. Most African Americans lived in single-family dwellings that housed boarders or several families. Few were homeowners, and rents were consistently higher than those charged to whites.

Perhaps most significant, African American women and men were almost completely shut out of the emerging manufacturing industries of Detroit. David Katzman notes that in 1910 only twenty-five African Americans were employed in the burgeoning auto plants.[107] Men as well as women worked in service jobs such as waiting tables, private domestic service, and laundering. The exclusion of African American women from the emerging sector of female white-collar work was almost total. The 1910 census identifies no African American female telephone operators, only one saleswoman, three clerks, and ten clerical workers. The latter most likely worked for African American businesses in the East Side.[108] Before World War I, then, the labor market for all African Americans was extremely circumscribed. Although members of the small African American community may have been able to mingle with whites somewhat more freely in public spaces, these interactions were defined by the occupational roles of service workers such as waiters, barbers, laundresses, and domestic servants. Patterns of racial discrimination in the workplace, housing, and the public sector were not products of the Great Migration, as many old settlers believed, but patterns set in nineteenth-century Detroit.

A minority of the old settlers were from relatively prosperous families. Elite nineteenth-century southern migrants included women such as Frances E. L. Preston, a native of Richmond, Virginia. Preston became a lecturer and organizer for the National Women's Temperance Union, traveled throughout the country as an orator, and served as president of the Michigan Federation of Colored Women's Clubs for four years.[109] Another middle-class female migrant, Emma Azalia Smith Hackley, was born in Tennessee in 1867 and migrated to Detroit with her family in the 1870s, where she later became a public school teacher and prominent musician. Hackley was a leader in the cultural programs of racial uplift, conducting folk festivals to celebrate the "negro spiritual" throughout the country. In 1916, she published *The Colored Girl Beautiful*, compiled from lectures she gave at boarding schools and her experiences teaching young African American women in Detroit. This etiquette manual combined familiar prescriptions of Victorian womanhood with calls for racial pride and uplift. "Each colored girl may be an Esther," wrote Hackley, "especially in all matters of cleanliness, manners, and self sacrifice, to advance and change the prevalent opinion of the Negro."[110] Individual self-help would lead to racial uplift, in Hackley's formulation. This notion of evolutionary progress shaped the response of members of prominent families among Detroit's old settlers to a new generation of twentieth-century migrants.[111] The influx of southern migrants, who did not always share old settlers' norms of bourgeois respectability, signaled the advent of a massive reform effort.

Holding a tenuous position in the economic structure of Detroit left working-class African American women vulnerable to poverty. These women received charity from black neighborhood churches and women's clubs; however, they also interacted with white social welfare agencies more frequently than they would after the Great Migration. Mrs. Lucien Moore, a white nurse who worked with the Visiting Nurses' Association (VNA) of Detroit, remembered accompanying a nurse on a visit to an African American family in 1903:

> Ascending the stairway leading from the alley, we found an attic room, lighted by one small window; it was furnished with a single bed, two chairs and a table, and accommodated a family of three. In the dirty bed was a young colored woman and her babe, born some twenty-four hours before, the mother very ill, and the child greatly in need of care. The room was very cold, for there was no stove; there were no clothes for the child, except the soiled ones it had on, no clothing for the mother, no sheets for the bed—nothing but dirt and utter misery. It may show great heroism to go as a missionary to Africa, but . . . to go as a visiting nurse to an African attic on Hastings street, and do the work I saw your nurse do . . . [was] acting the gospel of kindness and cleanliness.[112]

The "gospel of kindness and cleanliness" was emblematic of Progressive Era female reform efforts.[113] For white Progressive Era organizations, charity depended on proof of a family's or individual's worthiness, most clearly evidenced by cleanliness. A year prior to Moore's report, another nurse had visited the family only to find "not a clean article in the house." The mother was told that she would receive no aid from the VNA unless she made more of an effort to keep her attic apartment clean, ill as she was. Upon her return, the nurse found "a clean bed, only straw to be sure, but in a freshly washed tick, and several clean sheets, and other necessary articles, this, though the father had been out of work, and the mother had supported the family all winter by washing."[114] The mother in this case clearly knew how to clean her small home as she was a laundress by trade. But she was sick, with little money, and living in cramped quarters; the visiting nurses saw only the dirt and not the desperation of a woman struggling to survive. Unfortunately for her, only with cleanliness would kindness follow.

The VNA was founded in 1894 and served both the large European immigrant community and the small African American community. It was not until 1918, after the establishment of the Detroit Urban League, that an African American nurse was hired to care for black patients.[115] This pattern of excluding African American professionals from social agencies or hiring them only to serve among other African Americans was characteristic of the practices of agencies in Detroit and other cities. Racist definitions of the "worthy poor" also meant that some state agencies were reluctant to give aid to any African American women. From October 1912 to October 1913, for example, the Associated Charities of Detroit reported that only 45 African American women received mothers' pensions, as opposed to 327 Hungarian and 542 "white" women.[116] Furthermore, white charity organizations generally did not offer programs promoted by black female reformers, such as instruction in African American history, training programs to improve employment, and day care for young children.

Despite this pattern of discrimination, before World War I, African Americans were more fully integrated into Detroit's network of public and private charity organizations than they were after the war. For example, in the late nineteenth century, the Young Women's Home Association housed white immigrant and African American women and placed them in domestic service jobs. Its employment registers from 1877 to 1882 included Irish, Canadian, Polish, French, German, English, and "colored" women and specified religion (Catholic or Protestant) to fit the preferences of employers.[117] The Children's Aid Society (CAS) and Department of Public Welfare, run by white reformers, also worked with the African American community. Despite these programs, the primary focus of Detroit's public and private reform efforts during the Progressive period was on the "Americanization" of European immigrants, primarily those from Germany and East Europe.[118] With the advent of the Great Migration, white social agencies focused on the African American community mainly to gauge potential racial violence and criminal activity. By the end of World War I, most white charity groups left reform work up to African American organizations, creating a two-tiered system of public and private welfare: one for blacks and one for whites. Thus, the process of segregation in reform was occurring just as the African American women's club movement expanded its charity efforts. In this process, the policing of respectable norms of behavior shifted from the purview of white reformers to that of black reformers, who emphasized female respectability, racial pride, and economic self-sufficiency.

By the turn of the century, middle-class black women stepped up their reform efforts by establishing clubs and charity organizations to cater to "less fortunate" African American men and women. This work was part of the larger national racial uplift movement and used the language of evolutionary change through education and behavioral prescriptions. Historian Sara Evans has suggested that voluntary associations became "free spaces" located "between the state and domestic life" that allowed women to express communal self-interest and gain useful political experience.[119] Detroit's early women's clubs were emblematic of this overall trend, with elite clubs often beginning as cultural and literary forums and by 1900 turning to explicitly reform-minded political concerns. One early club enthusiast remembered:

> At that time [1898], Detroit was in the small city class with less than 10,000 colored inhabitants. Our women were not in industry and professions as these of latter days, with their clubs and many activities, but they moved in a very limited sphere, so that no matter how bright a scholar they might have been before graduating from High School or college before marrying and settling down, as was the custom, except those who elected to become teachers, they were apt to become dull by the cobwebs collecting in their brain and not able to keep pace with the march of time, being so engrossed in the care and comfort of their families, as there were few good lectures and meetings of educational nature.[120]

Middle-class women sought to remedy the lack of educational and political opportunities for black women by founding numerous clubs at the turn of the century. Responding to the challenge of racial uplift, this matrix of women's organizations formed a female public sphere in the African American community. Because African Americans were excluded from organized political reform and state-run institutions until mid-century, this public sphere remained vital throughout the interwar period. In contrast, white women's clubs lost their salience in this same period because of the greater inclusion of women in Progressive Era politics. As a result, bourgeois female respectability, an ideology that was pervasive in the black women's clubs, remained a powerful strand in the discourse of racial reform until the 1930s.

The Detroit Study Club was a typical early African American women's club. It was founded in 1898 by the wife of a leading African American newspaper editor, Robert Pelham. Originally the club members studied the works of Robert Browning, fulfilling a need for social and intellectual engagement. In 1900, the club became the first African American group to join the Detroit Federation of Women's Clubs and, like many women's clubs, began to turn its attention to the study of progressive reform and other contemporary issues. Writing a history of the club in the mid-1950s, Frances Welker remembered: "The founders of the Detroit study club felt the need of an organization which would bring to the attention of the women of this community who hold places of leadership, the need of continual study and the need of being kept informed in progressive thinking in all educational fields in order to render a better job in whatever work they find themselves engaged."[121] By limiting its membership to thirty-five, the club ensured that only a small number of female community leaders had access to the discussions of the group. Through the study of "progressive thinking," these women would train themselves to become community leaders and materially aid those who were less fortunate.

Women such as Lillian Johnson, one of the founding members, considered the Study Club a central part of their lives, a space free from wage work or family duties. "I remember how eagerly I would look forward to the meetings, one afternoon a week," recalled Johnson; "I would hurry thru [sic] my household duties that day, partially prepare my husband's supper . . . bundle up my infant daughter, carry her around the corner to my mother's home, then rush off to the meeting."[122] Temporarily leaving the duties of a wife and mother behind, Johnson actively engaged in the study and reform work of the club, writing numerous papers for recitation and discussing both national political issues and local concerns involving employment, charity, and segregation. By 1911, the yearbook noted that the club had studied the origins and growth of the settlement house movement, the "oppressed masses of Europe," Detroit's Juvenile Court, and "laws relating to women and children in Michigan."[123] By 1916, members established a Department of Philanthropy and Reform, and the club continued to meet and discuss a variety of social and cultural topics throughout the first half of the twentieth century. The Detroit Study Club also sent delegates to the NACW conventions and the Detroit Federation of Women's Clubs meetings.

Several characteristics of the Detroit Study Club were emblematic of Detroit's African American women's clubs. After the turn of the century, the club increasingly focused on urban reform work, while continuing its study of literature, music, and art. The club also carried out social rituals such as teas, card parties, and dances that embodied bourgeois female respectability. In order to be a member of such a club, a woman had to be well versed in these social rituals and in a position of leadership in the community. The programs carried out by the Study Club through the 1930s resulted in clear class demarcations; in their reform and charity work, clubwomen sought to "uplift" working-class African Americans, while in their social rituals, they sought to distinguish themselves from the working and lower classes. The leadership of the Detroit Study Club was made up of premigration elite women whose husbands were politicians, businessmen, and ministers. Therefore, in their class distinctions, club members reinforced the dichotomy of old settler versus newcomer.

Other early Detroit women's clubs included the In As Much Circle of King's Daughters, a charity club organized in 1895; the Labor of Love Circle of King's Daughters, organized in 1908; the Ladies' Benevolent Society, a Baptist women's club founded in 1867, which offered health and death benefits; the Lydian Association, organized in 1899 as part of a national society, which provided benefits to its members as well as performing charity work; and the Willing Workers' Club, founded in 1887, a prominent club that raised money for needy children.[124] By the early twentieth century, Detroit women established settlement houses, an old-age home, and an orphanage to aid the "worthy" poor. Many of these institutions targeted young black women who had recently arrived in the city. For example, reformers founded the Christian Industrial Home in 1904 to provide accommodation for African American "working girls." Originally this work was done at the Second Baptist Church, but a separate building was rented in 1914 and named the Frances Harper Inn. This home, of which few records remain, seemed to have served many of the functions of the Phillis Wheatley Homes in other cities, which sought to protect young female migrants.[125] One Detroiter recalled why it was established: "In the early part of the life of the home a girl came to our city and missed her train, went to the white Y.W.C.A. and asked to stay there. They refused. She begged them to let her sleep in a chair in the hall for the night as she knew nobody, but they refused her even that privilege. She had to go in the park and sit on a bench. She sat in this park for two days and nights until some one came by that knew of this home and took her there. The girl stayed in the home until she married."[126] According to this narrative, the segregated YWCA would not help the young migrant girl, so Detroit's women's clubs stepped in to assist her. They created a "home" that sheltered her until she could make her own home, protecting her from the sexual and social dangers of the city.

In 1897, Detroit clubwomen established the Phillis Wheatley Home for elderly women.[127] All of the women's clubs worked to provide the money necessary to care for the approximately forty residents of the home, and the community continually pointed to its existence with pride. In order to care for the very young, Detroit's elite women organized McCoy's Orphanage. Mary McCoy, sometimes referred to as the "mother of clubs," was the wife of African American inventor Elijah McCoy, a prominent Detroit businessman. She played a central role in founding the Phillis Wheatley Home and was also a member of the Lydian Association, the Willing Workers, and the In As Much Circle. From 1909 to 1911, the McCoy Orphanage provided "the care and training of orphaned and other children in need of home and moral rearing." Many of the children who boarded in the home were not orphans but rather had mothers who worked as domestic servants. One such household worker kept her five children at the home. "The mother who has left the father on account of cruelty and neglect, works during the day and boards at the Home, and helps pay for her children by assisting in the care of the others." This woman performed a double load of paid domestic work in order to support herself and her children. "Two other children have been placed there recently . . . and the mothers of the remaining two are employed in domestic service and cannot have their children with them."[128] The need for child care for working mothers was readily apparent to Detroit's clubwomen, and these early institutions prefigured decades of private charity work by African American women.

Besides founding institutions to meet the particular needs of Detroit's black community, Detroit clubwomen were very much part of the national movement for racial uplift. Like the southern reformers migrants had encountered in their early lives, Detroit's clubwomen stressed motherhood, cleanliness, and home life as central to uplift. In 1906, they discussed these priorities with clubwomen around the country when Detroit hosted the fifth biennial convention of the NACW.[129] It is notable that the NACW chose Detroit as the site to celebrate its tenth anniversary. Prominent Atlanta clubwoman Addie Hunton praised Detroit as a beautiful city "with no note of discrimination." "While we of the South have sometimes felt that these conventions, because of their influence and great power to challenge the aspersions so often placed upon colored women, were best held in the section where the storm and stress are greatest," argued Hunton, "still we must concede that the vision and touch—yes, the intellectual and spiritual awakening—of the meeting just held in Detroit could scarcely be equaled."[130] During the convention, Detroit clubwomen had an opportunity to show off their accomplishments, hosting receptions at the Phillis Wheatley Home, holding events at the Second Baptist and Bethel AME Churches, and giving tours of the city.

After ten years of organizing, reform-minded African American women throughout the country assessed their failures and successes in Detroit. "We all realize how discouraging it is to work in our various local societies," reported one delegate. "It seems as if we are going round and round . . . as if the very members from whom we justifiably expect the most, fail us at the very time we need them. . . . Then there comes a meeting . . . and our eyes are opened to the fact that hundreds, nay thousands, of women are working just as hard as we are."[131] At the height of both the Progressive Era and a period of deepening racial violence, the Detroit meeting provided strength for the delegates, who carried their message back to their local communities. The meeting also provided a sense of comradeship, a confidence that a new class of educated and enlightened race women had finally succeeded in rising to the forefront of racial uplift in part through their respectable trappings. "The women were modest in demeanor, so quiet in dress," remembered a delegate, "so sane in their deliberations that I was proud to be identified with them." [132]

Conclusion

Detroit's clubwomen were part of a national community of African American female uplift ideologues who defined norms of bourgeois respectability through their reform work. The premigration women's clubs and the middle-class female reformers who founded them presaged Detroit's institutional responses to the Great Migration. Their focus on respectability—cleanliness, restrained religiosity, and sexual morality—pervaded the language of Detroit's black reformers. Like clubwomen, African American leaders who responded to the massive influx of migrants firmly believed urban life posed a threat to young African American women. These leaders placed old settlers and new migrants in a dichotomy of good urban citizen versus uncouth rural southerner. Reformers defined this dichotomy by promoting behavioral norms and public displays of respectability that focused on African American women's roles as homemakers and caretakers of the community.

This gendered emphasis on respectability continued to be a dominant theme in reform discourse well into the 1920s. Meanwhile, the migrants themselves proved to be a much more diverse group of women and men than represented by reformers. Middle-class social workers arrived along with working-class sharecroppers, and the majority of the migrants had some experience living in urban areas. The structure of the labor market, the local economy, and the physical layout of the city affected the development of the new, largely migrant, African American community in profound ways. Female migrants like Mary Etta Glenn displayed extraordinary ingenuity while challenging pervasive white racism to create a future for themselves and their children. For Glenn and her companions, however, survival and social mobility at times entailed practices that social elites found problematic. Taking the first steps toward migration and creating homes in the city embodied an ethos of respectability not always reflected in the reform discourse of middle-class women's clubs.

2 Reform and Public Displays of Respectability in Great Migration Detroit

The club woman in Detroit, more than any other distinct type, is turning her attention to substantial and constructive things. The social service work which she is doing is assuming more of a scientific character; she is taking an intelligent interest in political affairs, and her religion, recreation and general activities are of the vital sort. The leisure which she has at her command, and her rather high average of intelligence; her zeal for the right and her will to act, together with her willingness to learn — all operate to make her a force to reckon with.

Citizens' Research Council, The Negro in Detroit

Clubwomen were indeed a "force to reckon with" in migration-era Detroit. When thousands of young African American women and men streamed into the city during the 1910s and early 1920s, it was Detroit's middle-class clubwomen who took the lead in developing programs to assimilate and aid the migrants. These women built a vibrant club movement in the late nineteenth century, and their ranks were invigorated with new members as the migration accelerated. In the city's leading churches, African American women developed innovative programs to materially aid and educate new migrants. When the YWCA expressed interest in opening a segregated branch in Detroit, black clubwomen eagerly participated in developing programs targeted at the female migrants pouring into the city. These female reformers embraced racial uplift ideology as the basis of their work and were instrumental in shaping Detroit's major black institutions.

The city's most prominent institution by the early 1920s was the Detroit Urban League. The Urban League provided a wide variety of services to incoming migrants and legitimized other racial uplift efforts that conformed to its reform strategies. In particular, it lauded women's clubs and the established

Baptist and AME churches for their efforts to uplift and materially aid migrants. Although the Detroit Urban League's leaders and the prominent churches' ministers were male, African American women made up the rank and file of these organizations. These public women led the effort to sanitize Detroit's streets, making them safe for female migrants and thus providing sanctuary for African American families.[1]

Black reformers had to deal with a severely restricted job market for African American women in the industrial city of Detroit. Because female migrants had few employment options when they arrived in the city outside of domestic service, reformers quickly became concerned about their potential poverty. More alarmingly, without steady work in "respectable" occupations, young women might turn to suspect sources of income such as prostitution. Therefore, opening up employment for black women was intricately linked to the larger project of racial uplift. Protecting young migrants such as Mary Etta Glenn from exploitation and despair would aid not only individuals but also the community as a whole. Black women working in sacred and secular institutions responded to this challenge by building homes to shelter female migrants, lobbying white employers to hire black women, and developing recreational programs. Building on decades of reform work both in the South and in Detroit, these institutions promoted bourgeois respectability and sought to protect young women from the dangers of the migration process.

Despite the centrality of activist women in the Great Migration, most migration narratives cast the southern male agricultural worker who became a northern industrial laborer as the central protagonist.[2] Female migrants were generally secondary to this story, portrayed as supportive wives and mothers or family members left behind.[3] Ironically, although most historians have largely left women out of their narratives, contemporaries viewed female migrants as "seeds" of a new northern community, carrying morality, education, and religiosity to the homes that formed the center of African American urban neighborhoods. Reformers deeply imbued the institutions they established to aid migrants with feminine images of respectability formulated in previous decades. As caretakers of the home, members of churches, and the foundation of a new community, African American female migrants embodied the hopes of urban African American communities. Because of female migrants' central role in resettlement and community building, reformers policed their behavior in order to construct a public identity that emphasized bourgeois respectability, sexual restraint, and thrift.

Reformers Respond to the Great Migration

By 1916, migrants crowded Detroit's Michigan Central Railroad station. By the summer of 1917, an estimated 1,000 migrants per month were arriving, primarily from West Georgia, Alabama, and Tennessee. By 1920, 35,000 migrants had settled in Detroit, increasing Detroit's African American population by 611 percent. As dramatic as this initial wave of migration was, it would be matched between 1920 and 1925 when an additional 41,000 black southerners made the journey to Detroit.[4] Because Detroit, unlike Chicago, was not a central stop on the North–South railroad lines, migrants often traveled first to Cincinnati on the Louisville and Nashville Railroad and then changed trains to arrive in Detroit via the Michigan Central Railroad.[5] The transportation of migrants who were hired by labor agents was typically paid only to cities such as Pittsburgh, St. Louis, or Cincinnati, and therefore migrants had to pay their own fares to Detroit.[6] Some migrants feared that because Detroit was not a railroad center, "it would not be as easy to get away" from as cities such as Chicago.[7] As a result, Detroit became known as a "repository city" where most migrants came to stay after experiencing disappointments in other urban centers. Of the 250 families surveyed in 1920 by Forrester B. Washington, the Detroit Urban League's first director, 63 percent or 158 heads of household had come from southern cities. As well as being urban, most migrants were relatively young, between twenty and forty years old, and men outnumbered women in this industrial city.[8]

The significance of Detroit's migration pattern is evident when one compares it to the broader images of migration spread by the national media, which often portrayed migrants as rural dupes lured to the North by labor agents. Yet the vast majority of Detroit's migrants had lived in cities, at least for a short period, and almost all had paid their own way to Detroit, deliberately seeking a better future with no plans to return to the South permanently. African American women were even more likely to have lived in urban areas than their male counterparts because of the probability that they worked in domestic service at some point before migrating, a job that was typically located in cities.[9] Despite these facts, well known to Urban League officials, reformers insisted on portraying the migrants as rural, backward, uneducated, and vulnerable. Migrants came from "some of the culturally most backward sections of the South" or the "backwoods of the south," wrote journalists.[10] These representations were contrasted with the equally unfounded image of Detroit's old settlers as "sophisticated" urbanites who had long lived in a racially integrated and prosperous city.

Reformers explicitly linked geographic origins with an individual's personal identity. A southern migrant was an object of reform and uplift, whereas a native-born Detroiter was a teacher of urban lessons. One reformer who set this agenda was George Edmund Haynes, a founding member of the National Urban League, who wrote *Negro New-comers in Detroit, Michigan* for the Home Missions Council in 1918.[11] Contemporary observers of the migration widely quoted this book, which provided an enduring blueprint for reform.[12] The work of the Associations for the Protection of Colored Women, a pioneering organization developed to protect black female migrants arriving in northern cities in the late nineteenth and early twentieth centuries, influenced Haynes's response to the Great Migration. While writing his Ph.D. dissertation at Columbia University, Haynes worked closely with the organization's female founders.[13] Haynes began his survey of Detroit by characterizing the old settlers as "self-respecting and respected for their intelligence and moral character." He noted that these older residents resented the influx of migrants due to a real or perceived increase in segregation resulting in a "class feeling." The incoming female migrants, meanwhile, were "so untrained that they are unemployable even in laundering, cleaning and other domestic service in private homes."[14] Urban reformers needed to introduce these untrained female migrants and their male counterparts to the disciplined, scientifically managed industries of the North, according to Haynes.

As significant as employment, however, were the twin problems of housing and recreation, which remained the centerpiece of assimilation efforts for years to come on a national as well as a local level.[15] Migrants were lured to cities not only by jobs but also by promises of the "high life," or what one author referred to as the "silk shirt era."[16] With higher wages and more leisure time came the ability to purchase luxuries such as clothes, liquor, and even a Ford automobile. Such consumer excesses went against the tenet of thrift central to uplift ideology. Meanwhile, African American migrants were segregated into the cramped East Side district in dilapidated housing, and white landlords charged them exorbitant rents. Although the housing crisis was a direct result of a racist housing market and outright exploitation by white landowners, discussions of housing in the African American community were often couched in terms of the dangers of crowding: class crowding, gender crowding, and the perceived immorality that resulted. Crowding could lead migrants to illicit urban spaces because rooms in "disorderly" houses were readily available, and saloons, dance halls, and cabarets provided escape from cramped quarters.[17] The fall from grace that resulted from even a short stay in a disreputable boardinghouse was a continual concern for Detroit's reformers. As a result, housing and recreation became inextricably linked in the discourse of migration reform.

In Haynes's discussion, housing involved "not only the question of physical shelter" but also the problems of providing a "sanitary and moral environment." Crowding caused by housing too many boarders threatened the sanctity of African American homes. The presence of lodgers represented to Haynes "a pressure against wholesome family life which is serious in the extreme." In addition, for migrants who were encountering "a more liberal atmosphere than they have known before," amusements such as pool, gambling, commercial dances, and vaudeville theater also posed a constant threat to morality and thrift. The crowded home and the crowded city neighborhood were twin evils that could be combated through recreational alternatives sponsored by the churches and the Detroit Urban League.[18] The image of the crowded home threatened by the encroaching city was a particularly powerful one for urban reformers, who viewed the home as central to racial uplift. In order to teach the tenets of bourgeois respectability in such an environment, reformers had to develop new and more direct methods. In Detroit, the Urban League was at the forefront of these efforts.

The Detroit Urban League and Female Respectability

In 1917, the *New York Evening Post* ran an editorial praising the Detroit Urban League as an exemplary model for the assimilation of migrants. "The human material coming from the South is plastic," the editorial stated. "It can be made industrious, law-respecting, and progressive, or can be abandoned to the saloonkeeper, gambler and drug-vender."[19] This national attention resulted from the stellar presentation of Forrester B. Washington, Detroit's first Urban League director, at the National Urban League's Conference on Migration held in New York City.[20] After only eight months in Detroit, Washington had set up a comprehensive plan to assimilate incoming migrants, which he relayed to his fellow district officers, a plan that was emulated in cities across the country. Summing up the purpose of the Detroit Urban League in 1916, Washington said: "You cannot do much for a man spiritually until you have given him a healthy and wholesome physical environment. In other words, 'You cannot grow lilies in ash-barrels.'"[21] In Washington's eyes, Detroit's segregated East Side community was the ash barrel, and the migrants were potential lilies who only had to be nurtured by an enlightened elite to reach their full potential.

When Washington arrived in Detroit in 1916, he undertook a cursory survey of the community's housing, health conditions, employment, and "morality." Although approximately 100 African Americans were arriving every week, noted Washington, nothing was being done "in the way of adjusting strange negroes to their new environment or assimilating them healthfully." [22] The survey produced a laundry list of problems that needed to be solved: there were "no wholesome amusements" furnished by social centers; the death rate of African Americans was twice as high as that of white Detroiters; there were no foster homes available for African American children; and "industrially the negro was found in the least skilled, the lowest paid and the most unhealthful occupations." [23] Of primary importance to Washington was the need to open up better employment opportunities for African American men and women. In order for this to be done effectively, Washington believed, white employers had to be impressed with the character of their potential African American employees, both in the workplace and on the streets. The Urban League used the language of racial uplift to pioneer an assimilationist program that was built on notions of bourgeois respectability. Cleanliness, thrift, domesticity, and sexual chastity would have to be maintained if employers were to be convinced that African Americans were responsible workers and if white Detroiters were to view the African American community in a positive light. These values would also aid the migrants' adjustment to urban life and guide them away from crime and vice.

Washington argued that the first week was the most critical time for migrants. "In a few days idling in search of a job," argued Washington, "the immigrants may come into contact with conditions and people whose influence is demoralizing and may destroy his chance of ever becoming a useful citizen." [24] These people, "the saloonkeeper, the poolroom proprietor, the owner of the gambling club and of the disorderly house," often gave the newly arrived migrant the "warmest welcome." [25] Concerned that migrants would be waylaid by such attractions, Washington had cards printed up directing migrants to the league and enlisted the popular African American theater, the Vaudette, to run lantern slides announcing the availability of aid.[26] The Urban League set up a makeshift employment bureau that placed male migrants in industrial jobs and female migrants in "day work" (domestic service jobs available for one day only). Washington worked closely with Detroit's white philanthropic elite, white industrialists, and existing African American charity organizations in this early stage of the Urban League's existence. He persuaded the police department, for example, to appoint a special officer to "mingle with crowds on the streets where the newcomers congregate and urge them not to make a nuisance of themselves by blockading the sidewalks, boisterous behavior and the like." [27]

During the height of the Great Migration, much of the league's work revolved around behavioral suasion, epitomized by the "special officer" who met the trains and chastised migrants for their "boisterous behavior." The train station was the first of a number of public spaces where reformers expected migrants to display personal characteristics of respectability. In addition, migrants were to be on their best behavior at Mack Park, where the Detroit Stars played; on streetcars; at their workplaces; and in the streets. The Urban League urged migrants to avoid other public spaces altogether, such as the disreputable saloons and dance halls springing up in the East Side community. To counteract the influence of this commercial recreation, league officials developed recreation programs designed to transform migrants into thrifty, hardworking northern citizens. These programs offered migrants alternative spaces to spend their leisure time.

The most popular of these efforts was the public community dance. The dance cost ten cents, significantly less than commercial dance halls' entrance price, and the Urban League distributed cards to migrants inviting them to partake in this "respectable" amusement. "The rougher the type the heartier the welcome," bragged Washington.[28] The first dance held in 1916 attracted a fairly small crowd of thirty or so; by early 1917, however, over 300 African Americans were flocking to the dances.[29] Using the proceeds from the community dance, the Urban League also organized the first African American basketball teams for men and women, a recreation that proved popular for many years to come. Hoping to recruit young female migrants, whom they viewed as particularly vulnerable to urban vice, the Urban League also founded a Campfire Girls group in the early years of the migration.[30]

A group of twenty-five young African American men attending colleges in Detroit who called themselves the Young Negroes' Progressive Association (YNPA) helped Washington with his endeavors. Arguing that the "majority of the organizations catering to the young men of this age, have for the object selfish pleasure," the YNPA worked to promote "wholesome" recreation and raise the status of Detroit's African Americans generally.[31] These men distributed Urban League cards publicizing community dances, the employment office, and other league services. They took over much of the athletic endeavors of the Urban League, expanded the basketball teams, and in 1917 organized a baseball league.[32] The YNPA viewed the training of efficient industrial workers as crucial to the success of migrants. They lectured male factory workers during their lunch hour on the need for punctuality, reliability, and industrial efficiency and distributed "Why He Failed" cards to employees.[33] The industrial worker failed, argued the Urban League, because he "watched the clock. . . . He asked too many questions; He did not put his heart in his work; He didn't learn that the best part of his salary was not in his pay envelope—SUCCESS."[34] The YNPA's approach reflected the racial uplift ideology developed in previous decades. Although it was a men's group, its protective and prescriptive work with migrants used the rhetoric and tactics of female uplift ideologues. Through moral suasion, it hoped to persuade migrants to abide by the tenets of bourgeois respectability. Migrants' behavior could then uplift the race, present a positive community image, and offset the racism of Detroit's white employers and city officials.

The Great Migration provided African American elites such as the young men of the YNPA an opportunity to construct a public community identity in northern cities. The "misbehavior" of individual migrants who were singled out by whites as representative of the group weakened this community image. In Washington's eyes, this "loud, noisy, type of Negroes unused to city ways" had to be transformed or the larger project of opening up employment opportunities for African Americans would be at risk.[35] Therefore, early league programs targeted behavior, appearance, and public displays of respectability. The Detroit Urban League, for example, was determined to stop the female migrant from "wander[ing] down to the business district . . . in calico 'Mother Hubbards.'"[36] To address the problem of African American migrants' "disorderly" attire, Washington established the Dress Well Club in 1917. At the founding meeting of the club, Washington gave a speech asking the question, "Why is . . . segregation increasing?" He answered: "Chiefly on account of the loud, noisy, almost nude women in 'Mother Hubbards' standing around in the public thoroughfares."[37]

To members of the Dress Well Club, African American women carried an unequal burden in the public display of respectability. Reformers viewed women as the caretakers of neighborhoods and homes, responsible for the appearance of community, family, and private property. In the increasingly overcrowded city of Detroit, this visible presentation of a respectable public identity was of paramount importance as whites and blacks interacted in workplaces, public transportation, and city streets. Whites judged individual African Americans' appearance, behavior, and demeanor in these public spaces. Migrants' houses, churches, and stores were also on public display in the city. Washington and his colleagues hoped that focusing on changing the behavior and appearance of female migrants would both shape the opinions of a white public and improve the living standards of the entire community as husbands and children followed the female migrants' example.

Like the YNPA, the Dress Well Club was formed by "earnest race men resolved to create a better impression of the Negro by attention to dress, personal appearance and public behavior."[38] Members were recruited from the Loyal Christian Brotherhood of the Second Baptist Church, the YNPA, and the Detroit Urban League. They distributed cards and pamphlets on the importance of dressing well to migrants arriving at train stations as well as newcomers already settled in Detroit. In a speech to the Dress Well Club in 1917, Washington suggested that "members should ask any person who is making himself a nuisance by vulgar clothing or loud mouth, to digest this card and hand it to others."[39] By receiving the card listing "dos and don'ts" of dress, Detroiters became "honorary members" of the club and were expected to pass the advice on to others. The "helpful hints" listed on the Dress Well Club brochure included proscriptions targeted specifically at African American women: "Don't . . . go about the streets in bungalow aprons and boudoir caps," and "don't do your children's hair up into alleys, canals and knots." In the public theater of the streets, the occupation of domestic servant, which the boudoir cap marked, should be hidden behind modest and unassuming attire.[40]

Exhorting African Americans to be "individual apostles of the doctrines of better dress, better personal appearance and better public behavior" was central to the strategy of forming a visible community identity that appealed to whites.[41] "Carelessness in regards to dress," warned the Dress Well Club, "will lead to discrimination and segregation."[42] Even in this early period of the migration, however, the reformers saw another possible danger of public appearance and behavior. Rather than dressing too much like rural southerners, migrants might start wearing "flashy clothes" or too much finery, outward signs of profligacy and immorality. Warnings against audacious dress had long been a theme of female respectability and the women's club movement. The Detroit Urban League applied this reform strategy to all newcomers, men as well as women. Thus, Washington and the men of the YNPA and Dress Well Club used a feminine reform discourse to counteract the negative effects of migration. Indeed, many Urban League affiliates embraced this strategy.[43] Urban League officials, however, were not the first reformers to address working-class African Americans' behavior. For decades, African American middle-class women had preached that reforming individual comportment and appearance would mitigate the worst ills of racism. The Urban League simply applied this ideology to incoming southern migrants.

In 1918, the Detroit Urban League produced another pamphlet that directly addressed the need to promote bourgeois female respectability. This pamphlet reinforced many of the proscriptions of the Dress Well Club through two juxtaposed photographs. The first depicts a woman sitting on trash-covered steps outside her home. The woman wears a housecoat, nightcap, and slippers and sits with her legs spread apart. Directly opposite is a second photo of the same woman. In this image, the steps are clean and the

General Disorderly Appearance   Neatly Clothed and Orderly Appearance

Illustrations from a brochure of the Detroit Urban League, 1918. Courtesy of Michigan Historical Collections, Bentley Historical Library, University of Michigan.

woman is demurely dressed, her hair well groomed, and her legs pressed together.[44] These two images reflected a dichotomy central to the discourse of urban migration and resettlement: on one side were disorder, dirt, licentiousness, and carelessness of appearance; on the other, self-restraint, cleanliness, and respectability. Throughout the interwar period, Detroit's elites viewed African American female migrants as embodiments of the rural South's disorder and backwardness. By policing the behavior and appearance of female migrants, these elites sought to instill "northern" and "urban" characteristics in the community as a whole.

Echoing the concerns expressed by the Dress Well Club, the Urban League brochure targeted practices that were identified as distinctly southern: the wearing of work clothes in public spaces, not wearing shoes in public, sitting in front of one's house, and using patent medicines. In his study of Chicago, James Grossman suggests that these southern-identified traits reflected a different cultural standard "because in the South whites expected blacks to be dirty and poorly attired."[45] Although whites may have expected such low standards of southern African Americans, many migrants had quite a different set of standards for themselves and their neighbors. Many "southern" habits such as wearing work clothes in public spaces, a practice that occurred among domestic workers in the South, seem to have quickly dissipated in cities such as Detroit and Chicago. Migrants followed other suggestions offered by the Urban League: most, particularly women, did join churches soon after arriving in the city, and the growth of black-owned banks reflected the efforts of migrants to save their wages. These migrants, however, were forging a new identity for themselves in the urban North that combined aspects of southern culture with norms of respectability shared across class lines.

When the Detroit Urban League appeared on the scene, white social service agencies gladly turned African American casework over to the league. White charity organizations worked with the league through the Associated Charities, an umbrella group of social service agencies that disbursed funds.[46] Many of the league's cases involved girls suspected of "immorality." Asked to investigate one such fifteen-year-old, the league discovered that "she lived in the so-called 'Bear Trap' on Eliot St., and that of all the miserable families living there, hers was the worst. . . . She associated with grown men and indicated her haunts etc."[47] Here was the worst-case scenario of Haynes, Washington, and Detroit's clubwomen: a young woman living in an overcrowded boardinghouse exposed to adult men and the dangers of the city.[48] A 1916 investigation of all cases that came before the Juvenile and Police Courts' Probation Department brought more such incidents to light. "Colored cases were reported as constituting the greatest number of failures simply because the probation officers found no institutions or organizations to co-operate with them," reported Washington. "This difficulty is particularly disheartening in dealing with colored girls, especially those arrested for the first time for sex offenses. Because of the lack of public and private institutions where they can be sent or reliable homes where they can be placed under supervision of a strong minded woman, they must be returned to the streets from which they came. Inevitably they become victims of their unfortunate environment and eventually hardened criminals."[49] As a result of these reports, black reformers stepped up their efforts to protect girls from the physical environment and immoral atmosphere that could lure them into prostitution or at the very least make them vulnerable to arrest for suspected immorality. Indeed, the vulnerable young female migrant was a central image in Urban League reports and literature throughout the 1920s.

Like Haynes, Washington stressed that overcrowding was the root of migrants' social problems and that it particularly endangered the morality of young women. Because domesticity was central to reform efforts during this period, overcrowded apartments were barriers to an effective implementation of reform work based on bourgeois respectability. How could African American women uplift the race by keeping clean and efficient homes when those homes held boarders and extended families and lacked basic amenities? In 1916, almost all African American migrants lived in the crowded environs of the original East Side community, a neighborhood they shared with the remaining Jewish population, which moved out in large numbers in the next decade. Most African American families were paying $18 to $20 a month for three or four rooms with no bath or inside toilet. Despite this, survey workers who carried out research for the 1926 report noted the cleanliness of the cramped apartments. "In various places the deterioration of the houses was so great that rats could not be kept out," reported the survey, "yet the interior was clean."[50] Clearly, African American migrants kept up the standards of cleanliness that had been so important to working-class perceptions of respectability in the South. Yet the mixing that overcrowded dwellings engendered could not be solved by cleanliness alone.

Washington reported that the average rent per room in Detroit was $4.60 per week, higher than the rent for a comparable room in New York City and nearly impossible for one working family to afford. White landlords exploited the desperate need for housing by raising their East Side rents exorbitantly. During the era of migration, some African American women paid up to $50 a month for a house in which they could run gambling, prostitution, and other illegal activities that earned them a considerable profit despite the high rent. Reformers blamed these "disorderly resorts," also known as "buffet flats," for putting additional pressure on the housing market.[51] To combat this problem, the Urban League encouraged the police department to raid buffet flats and then took over the leases and transformed them into "respectable" boardinghouses. Only by gaining a familiarity with the "urban geography of vice" could Urban League officials locate buffet flats and carry out their plans.[52] Thus, Washington and his associates mapped vice in order to eradicate it. This strategy reinforced the importance of domesticity in the creation of a respectable community. By replacing "disreputable" houses, reputable homes could begin to exert a positive influence on incoming migrants.

Despite the best efforts of the Urban League, many migrants arriving in the city had difficulty finding a "respectable" place to board. Out of necessity, male migrants took rooms in "disorderly" houses or even slept on pool tables.[53] Female migrants had even fewer options. Urban League officials viewed the end result of overcrowding as "adult delinquency" due to the "good and bad, especially of the poorer classes, being thrown together, the corruption of the former by the latter."[54] Reformers expressed concerns over the negative effects of crowding well into the 1920s. In his 1924 speech on housing to the Ohio State Conference on Social Work, for example, John C. Dancy, Washington's successor, stated: "Conditions of this sort bring about a breaking down of the family life and later on means poor health, juvenile delinquency, and a lower moral tone."[55] To offset these conditions and separate the "good" from the "bad," the league provided a physical space in the city where young men and women, in sex-segregated groups, could meet. Reformers felt that young women in particular needed a place to hold club meetings, attend classes, and generally engage in uplift "free from undesirable and vicious attentions."[56] After Washington's departure from Detroit in 1918 to direct Atlanta's School of Social Work, the new director of the Urban League, John Dancy, established such a space.[57] In 1919, the Columbia Community Center opened its doors.

Dancy would be a charismatic leader of Detroit's African American community for the next four decades. His views on migrant assimilation, like his predecessor's, focused on recreation, housing, and employment through an ideology of racial uplift and public displays of respectability. Dancy often met the trains at the Michigan Central station himself, directing the incoming migrants to the Urban League employment office and the community center. Like Washington, he worried about migrants looking "presentable" upon arrival and about their ability to adjust to a "northern, urban atmosphere."[58] He continually blamed the perceived deterioration of race relations on migrants' appearance and background. "The great majority of Negroes in Detroit were brand new," remembered Dancy; "they had grown up in the rural South, without access to any education worthy of the name, without training in personal cleanliness, without familiarity with most of the features of civilization which the average white person took for granted."[59] The familiar themes of evolutionary change and uplift ideology are present in this image: migrants were "brand new" naïfs who would become "civilized" through the labor of the Urban League.

The community center flourished in its early years. During 1920, the average daily visits numbered eighty-five as migrants made use of its employment office, reading rooms, and educational programs.[60] Dancy also established a small music school, implemented dancing classes, and continued the league-sponsored dances and parties initiated by Washington.[61] The most immediately successful program was the league's baby clinic, established in response to the influenza epidemic of 1919. African American mothers brought their babies to the clinic five mornings a week to be cared for by two trained nurses and a doctor. In 1920, nearly 400 babies were brought to the clinic in a two-month period.[62] Dancy recalled that "the mothers who

The popular Detroit Urban League baby clinic. Courtesy of Michigan Historical Collections, Bentley Historical Library, University of Michigan.

brought their children were those who had come from the rural deep South and had little or no familiarity with health service and medical science."[63] The health professionals were particularly shocked by southern mothers' use of folk medicine. The enthusiastic participation of migrant mothers in this program, however, belies Dancy's interpretation of a cultural clash. Indeed, access to improved health care was one of African American women's many motivations for migration. Migrant mothers took advantage of free medical care with enthusiasm, while not completely letting go of southern traditions of folk medicine. As migrants would continue to do throughout the interwar period, these mothers combined a variety of cultural practices from the North and the South to improve their lives and the lives of their families.

Other center activities that targeted female migrants included a domestic training school and a temporary boardinghouse for female migrants. Reformers were particularly concerned about female migrants who were stranded in an unfamiliar city, as the following case testifies: "Monday night at 10:30 a woman with her three year old child failed to meet up with her husband when the train came in. She was forced to sleep on the wooden benches in the station in the morning, when the Travelers' Aid worker brought her to the offices of the League. The baby by that time had become ill with a cold and lack of food, while the mother was worn out and despondent. . . . Had a room been fitted out for this specific purpose, she could have been cared for immediately upon her arrival at the station."[64] Soon the Columbia Community Center housed such women temporarily, offering free health care for their babies, a dwindling list of "respectable" rooms, and employment in domestic service. Although men also used the facilities, almost all of the activities and physical spaces were sex-segregated: the reading room, for example, was used exclusively by men. Thus, the center provided a physical space in the overcrowded neighborhood where "respectable" women could meet without mixing with disreputable neighbors or men of either race.

Sex-segregated leisure activities that offered alternatives to the city's commercial amusements completed the Columbia Community Center's mission. Dancy continued Washington's athletic programs, arranging basketball and baseball leagues for both young men and women and adding track teams as well. Games between teams of different races provided a unique opportunity to display the positive characteristics of African American migrants in public. For example, Dancy described in his autobiography a game between the accomplished Center Girls Five, the Urban League's girls' basketball team, and the white Grosse Pointe Neighborhood Club basketball team. Before the game, the girls were schooled about the fine points of hygiene by league nurses. "The word had gone around that Negroes had a different odor from whites," recalled Dancy, "and these girls did not want to leave any such odors in the ritzy Grosse Point gymnasium." The girls, therefore, took baths *before* the game started and wore freshly laundered uniforms. "Far more important than winning the basketball game was making a good impression," said Dancy.[65] Although this example may appear extreme, it epitomized the work of the Urban League. Young African American women's cleanliness and proper demeanor symbolized the upward evolution of the whole community throughout the 1920s. These women would serve as models, argued Dancy and other reformers, for other recent migrants and symbolize the African American community's respectability to white employers and city officials.

After the center offered migrants physical space to hold meetings, they quickly formed their own clubs and organizations. In 1920, an estimated twenty-one different clubs made use of the center.[66] During the economic slump of 1921, which left many autoworkers temporarily unemployed, the center was filled with young men playing checkers, reading, and playing music on the Victrola and piano. In just one month, January 1921, an estimated 4,000 people visited the center, many of them unemployed men.[67] At other times, during the baby clinics, for example, the center was filled with women. Thus, throughout the late 1910s and 1920s, the Detroit Urban League successfully established itself as the locus of black reform activity in

Detroit. Recognized by public and private charity organizations, employers, and religious leaders throughout the community, the Urban League exercised control over the daily lives of migrants by parceling out scarce housing, jobs for men and women, and behavioral mandates. The prominence of the Urban League was due in part to its alliance with white elites who sanctioned its existence, but it also provided valuable services to the African American community when housing was scarce and discrimination rampant. The Urban League employed a discourse of respectability that focused on domesticity, thrift, and outward appearance to assimilate migrants to a new urban industrial culture. Its efforts were intrinsically linked with those of Detroit's other major reform institution, the Second Baptist Church.

Respectable Religion and the Assimilation of Migrants

As in southern cities, black churches in Detroit were a mainstay of community organizing and reform and a center of African American women's activism. By the early 1920s, the oldest black Baptist church in the state, the Second Baptist Church, had the largest and most active congregation among the migrants. Besides expanding the membership of the Second Baptist Church, the Great Migration swelled the number of all African American churches in Detroit, which increased 400 percent from 1915 to 1920, from nine to thirty-eight.[68] Washington estimated that 52 percent of Detroit's African Americans during this period were Baptists, with Methodists making up the next largest group at 25 percent.[69] Most of these Baptists attended the Second Baptist Church, which was located in the heart of the East Side neighborhood.[70] Even with rapid church expansion, there were never enough seats for all parishioners in Detroit's churches; indeed, hundreds had to be turned away from the Second Baptist Church each Sunday. Many black Detroiters stood outside the church to listen to the charismatic Reverend Robert Bradby when they could not find seats in the pews. By the mid-1920s, as many as 4,000 were reported to attend the Second Baptist Church for Sunday services.[71]

Under the leadership of Bradby, the Second Baptist Church played a key role in the assimilation of migrants—second only to the Detroit Urban League. Because so many migrants were Baptists, the church dramatically increased its membership by 1925 and expanded its physical space to an adjoining annex.[72] The church's establishment of the Christian Industrial Club in 1904, founded by prominent church member Etta Taylor, presaged its work with migrants. In 1906, a group of churchwomen also formed the Earnest Workers' Club, which raised money for the church and aided in charity cases.[73] These early-twentieth-century religious women's clubs expanded their work significantly as church membership grew. The old settlers who founded them, such as Lillian Johnson, a founding member of the Earnest Workers and the Detroit Study Club, remained in leadership positions throughout the interwar period. Thus, although migrants were welcomed into the church, the old settlers maintained their dominance in the female auxiliaries and clubs that carried out the bulk of the church's charity work. As a result, the old settlers' vision of the newcomers as uncouth, rural, and naive dominated much of the agenda of assimilation and reform during the Great Migration.

In 1917, Reverend Bradby set up a system of committees to meet trains arriving at Michigan Central and offer housing and employment assistance to the new migrants.[74] Soon thereafter, Bradby hired an assistant pastor to help organize charity and educational programs for the burgeoning membership. Bradby clearly recognized the key role his church could play during the migration. As in most congregations, women predominated in the church; therefore, in 1919, Bradby called a mass meeting of all women affiliated with the church to organize the church's first Big Sister auxiliary. The 100 women who showed up at the meeting divided into fifteen smaller groups and began to discuss fund-raising for the founding of a home for young women. The original 100 Big Sisters recruited 300 more, and in four years, they raised $5,000 and purchased a building to stand "as a beacon-light for the protection of our girls." The home was on the corner of St. Aubin and Antietam Streets in the heart of the African American East Side community. The Big Sisters adopted the motto "Lift As We Climb," an adaptation of the NACW's motto, "Lifting As We Climb," which suggests their allegiance to the tenets of racial uplift ideology. The women of the church engaged in charity work throughout the 1920s and 1930s, focusing on young women in the community who, they felt, needed to be guided through the dangers of a new city.[75] By caring for the new migrants, Detroit's churchwomen were playing a traditional role in the church hierarchy. "In the black church tradition," argues historian Milton C. Sernett, "much of the burden for assisting the poor and needy and of building up new missions fell to women."[76]

The church's female congregants founded numerous other women's clubs in the late 1910s and early 1920s to draw new members: the Silver Leaf Club in 1915, the Ladies' Aid Society in 1918, the Naomi Circle in 1920, and the Nurses' Guild in 1921.[77] In 1922, church members organized the American Beauty Club to help migrants "become better acquainted" with each other through fund-raising for the church.[78] All of these clubs remained active for many decades to come, forming a backbone of community organizing that, like the Urban League, was based on the tenets of female uplift. By the mid-1920s, the church expanded its work to provide day care for the children of employed women and classes in a variety of fields including domestic service. The Second Baptist Church and other large churches also offered "respectable" leisure activities, such as picnics and excursions. Indeed, 500 heads of families surveyed in 1920 cited church socials as the "chief form of recreation" after movies.[79] The church's activities paralleled those of the Urban League and the segregated YWCA, and these institutions formed a network dedicated to assimilating migrants and protecting them from the dangers of urban life.

Reverend Bradby worked with the white community through the city-wide Metropolitan Detroit Council of Churches, organized in 1919 to "speak with one voice" on all "matters of public interest."[80] This large-scale effort was an institutionalization of the social gospel movement, which attempted to address secular concerns of poverty and social reform. By joining the council, Bradby helped shape white perceptions of the African American community and developed reform programs that he felt would aid recent migrants. The council's social service department was particularly active, working to pass censorship laws regulating the content of movies, supervising the growing number of dance halls and burlesque theaters, and calling for the "suppression of vice of all kinds."[81] This department also hired probation officers to reform the "home life" of juvenile offenders and coordinated the many interchurch athletic activities.[82] Because Detroit's "red-light" district was located primarily in the African American East Side neighborhood, the reform work of the council was inextricably linked with the work of the Second Baptist Church and the Urban League.[83] The Urban League, for example, assisted the council in locating centers of commercial recreation deemed problematic by reformers. By 1922, the Department of Race Relations and International Good-Will invited African American ministers to become more involved in activities such as censoring inflammatory newspaper articles that "might breed racial disorders," meeting with the police department to discuss police brutality, and holding conferences with the Board of Commerce and Real Estate Board to address the growing housing crisis in the African American community. The council, however, coupled this relatively progressive interracial work with calls to forestall the "tremendous moral danger of the congestion of our colored sections."[84] The social mixing of classes, genders, and races in illicit spaces united the reform efforts of Detroit's religious leaders and marked a consensus on the need to promote public respectability citywide.

The women and men of the Second Baptist Church organized yet another set of programs targeting newcomers' needs. Modeled after a settlement house, the Baptist Christian Center was designed to be "purely a social application of Christian teaching" open to African Americans of all denominations in 1920.[85] By 1922, attendance at the popular center exceeded 5,000 per year. During the early 1920s, a Red Cross nurse taught the center's most popular class on the "care of homes, babies, and personal hygiene."[86] The instruction in medical care was essential during a period when tuberculosis, influenza, and other diseases took a serious toll in the African American community. This class and others like it also paralleled the home mission work popular throughout the South. The four employed staff members at the center carried out home visits, undertaking a total of 250 in one three-month period in 1921, primarily targeting mothers by offering instruction in housewifery and information about available services. During that same period, forty "personal talks with mothers and girls" were also held at the center.[87] Because the thrust of this settlement work was moral reform and educational training, including classes in domestic service, women were the main targets of the center's work and made up the majority of the staff.

The Christian Center, like the Urban League, was chiefly concerned with helping migrants adjust to their new surroundings. The discourse used by the center's workers continually emphasized the vulnerability and passivity of female migrants and the dangers they and their families faced in the over-crowded East Side. In the words of the women who ran the Christian Center, migrants came to Detroit with "little training or experience . . . accustomed to living, working and sleeping in the open air," "utterly bewildered by the social surroundings, living conditions and the climate," "coming largely from rural regions of a primitive type of civilization."[88] These newcomers had to be guided and taught by social workers, religious leaders, and activists in order to be protected from urban vice and transformed into responsible citizens, productive workers, and respectable women. Who better to carry out this transformation than African American women, who could set an example and serve as the unpaid stalwarts of the church, settlement houses, and clubs? The overwhelming thrust of reform work focusing on domesticity was indicative of the cultural continuity of migration. These programs had been pioneered in the South and shaped in part by working-class women's needs and activism. In order to get funding from the white-dominated Community Union and to construct a respectable community identity, reformers presented migrants as ingenues who could be taught and cajoled into becoming the urban citizens envisioned by religious and political leaders.

The fine line that Bradby was able to walk between providing sermons and services that appealed to southern migrants and maintaining the respect of secular leaders was the reason for much of the church's phenomenal success during the Great Migration. Some migrants, however, found the large congregation unwelcoming. Unless they had been among the early members, no one knew their names and there was little opportunity to gain a position of authority in such a large church. Therefore, migrants founded their own storefront churches and even their own religious sects. Significantly, many of these church founders were women, who were explicitly excluded from the Baptist and AME leadership. Bradby, Dancy, and other community leaders saw this plethora of new urban churches as blemishes on a community they were attempting to cleanse. In their vision, religious life would be centralized at the Second Baptist Church and other large traditional churches. Small Sanctified storefront churches led by women presented a threat to this model. As in the South, religion became a terrain of conflict over female respectability and public identity in the North.

The YWCA and Female Migrants

Although the Urban League and Second Baptist Church developed many programs aimed at African American women, the segregated YWCA was explicitly founded to respond to black women's migration to Detroit. In 1919, the Colored Work Committee of the YWCA published a study of female African American urban dwellers during World War I. Their findings paralleled those of the Associations for the Protection of Colored Women before the war. The committee reported a "deplorable lack of facilities for amusement for the more than a million colored girls in this country." "Colored girls looking for rooms in a strange city," noted the YWCA workers, "were usually compelled to take quarters in the squalid sections."[89] Once again it was the lack of "respectable" leisure and domestic life that most distressed these female reformers. Responding to the need to protect young female migrants, the workers in Detroit's segregated YWCA sought to provide physical shelter and respectable recreation.

When Nellie Quander, a war worker for the YWCA, reported her findings on the plight of Detroit's African American women in 1918, her descriptions of the city and its dangers mirrored the words of Forrester B. Washington. Housing was perhaps the most serious problem, suggested Quander: "It was particularly difficult for girls and women drawing small wages to secure decent rooms." Only one "respectable hotel" accepted African Americans; however, few young women could afford to stay there. Dining rooms open to African Americans also "catered to the poor and undiscriminating."[90] These descriptions reflected reformers' concern for young female migrants who could not separate themselves from the "disreputable" and the "undiscriminating" in the crowded streets of Detroit. African American women were vulnerable to urban vice under such conditions, and the YWCA promptly set out to protect and aid them.

In November 1918, the YWCA opened the Industrial Women's Service Center to cater to the needs of African American female war workers. When Olive Williams, a "special industrial worker" for the YWCA, visited the center several months later, she found that "some five hundred girls are using the center and regular meetings are held in three of the factories."[91] The center organized numerous women's clubs, eleven by the end of 1918, and perhaps most important, it provided a physical space in the city where young migrants could congregate. "The women and girls are enthusiastic over their new home," reported Williams, "a beautiful building with plenty of club rooms, large recreation hall and, best of all, a spacious, airy cafeteria."[92] Building a well-regulated, sex-segregated space in which female migrants could live, eat, and relax was a direct response to the YWCA workers' perception that the social mixing and lack of domesticity in the city posed the greatest dangers to women.

Although the Industrial Women's Service Center remained open into the early 1920s "for those activities which seem best fitted to further physical, mental and moral well-being," eventually the segregated St. Aubin YWCA supplanted its work.[93] YWCA officials noted three reasons for the eventual failure of the center: the building was located too far from the factories where women were employed; after young women married, "home interests" prevented them from using the center; and, finally, in the post–World War I era, "colored women were thrown out of industrial employment."[94] Rather than challenging the sex and racial segregation of industrial employment, YWCA workers turned toward organizing clubs for the service workers they had made contact with.[95] Thus, the St. Aubin YWCA, opened in 1920, contained all of the contradictions of racial uplift work during the Great Migration. It provided a safe physical space for African American women; however, it never directly addressed the problem of a racialized labor market and other discriminatory practices experienced by female migrants.

The St. Aubin YWCA became a central gathering place for young African American female migrants throughout the 1920s. Like Urban League officials, YWCA workers met incoming trains and helped migrants find appropriate lodging, dissuading them from staying in disreputable boardinghouses. Some young women stayed at the YWCA for a few weeks while they looked for work, often through the employment office located at the St. Aubin branch.[96] YWCA workers found that after women married, "home activities take the place of recreational interest . . . and this tends to draw them away from club or group connections."[97] This admission was significant because reformers often targeted female migrants' domestic life as an area needing improvement. Lacking time and money, many young married women, however, found it difficult to engage in recreation of any kind, respectable or disreputable. Unable to keep older women in the YWCA's programs, the St. Aubin branch workers decided to focus on younger women and girls, organizing them into clubs and offering recreational and educational programs.

One such program was a camp for girls located across the Belle River in Ontario, Canada. YWCA instructors believed this rural location provided a haven from the dangers of city life for vulnerable young migrants. "Here the camper finds everything a real girl dreams about," reported the *Southern Workman*, "the magic campfire, the romance and mystery of the woods, and valuable instruction in the guise of play."[98] This "valuable instruction" included lessons in canoeing, tennis, and cooking meals for the camp using local produce. The cooking lessons were the most pragmatic because they provided young women with domestic training. More important, their parents could be assured that they were safe and well cared for, away from the dangers posed by the city. Girls were taught to swim at the camp's bathing beaches without having to face the segregation of the city's public beaches, and they engaged in recreation normally reserved for the middle class. These advantages made the Belle River camp popular among African American Detroiters, attracting as many as 600 campers during the summers.

By 1923, 260 African American women belonged to twenty different YWCA clubs. Unlike the clubs organized at the Industrial Women's Service Center in the late 1910s, these clubs were organized primarily around recreational activities. Two clubs were distinctly service-oriented—the Entre Nous Club and the Mothers' Club—and the rest provided young migrants with sex-segregated leisure activities designed to keep them off urban streets. With names like Lilies of the Valley, Bright Starts, Wide Awakes, and Merrymakers, the YWCA clubs emphasized femininity and domesticity, offering arts and crafts activities and dramatic and musical performances. During the early 1920s, the St. Aubin YWCA also introduced educational and occupational classes for women. The most popular, with an enrollment of fifty-five women in 1921, was a millinery class, since sewing and selling hats could be a relatively profitable occupation for African American women. Not surprisingly, young African American migrants flocked to classes that taught skills other than domestic work, such as sewing, tailoring, and typing.[99] The YWCA's foray into education heralded the availability of a large

YWCA camp on the Belle River. From John Marshall Ragland, "The Negro in Detroit," Southern Workman 52 (November 1923): 536.

number of classes for African American women by the late 1920s. Generally, most women preferred courses that provided them with the skills needed to work outside of domestic service, either as self-employed small entrepreneurs or in black-owned businesses as clerks and clerical workers.

The clubs and classes were supplemented by talks and demonstrations on "personal hygiene, proper dress," and "better homes," which, like the Dress Well Club and Urban League pamphlets, targeted the behavior and appearance of migrants.[100] Indeed, one of the stated goals of the YWCA was to cooperate with other agencies "to maintain high character standards among all girls."[101] Reformers coordinated the efforts of African American agencies to prepare young women for life in urban Detroit and to produce a generation of black women who would set an example for the entire community. They influenced young female migrants such as Cora M. Brown, a native of Alabama who came to Detroit with her family at the age of seven. Mamie Cole Franklin, the YWCA's Girl Reserves secretary, charged with organizing young black women, urged the talented Brown to attend Fisk University. At Fisk, Brown studied with E. Franklin Frazier and earned a degree in sociology. After returning to Detroit, she worked for the police department's Women's Division, obtained a law degree from Wayne State University, and in 1953 became the first black woman elected to the Michigan senate.[102]

Brown exemplified the high standards set by the YWCA workers, educated middle-class African American women who promoted racial uplift ideology in migration-era Detroit. As well as encouragement and moral suasion, these workers provided desperately needed resources to black women facing a deeply racist and segregated city that denied them affordable housing and a living wage. The female migrants who lived at the YWCA, ninety-one women in 1920, eagerly accepted this shelter and support.[103] Although they did not always become the "model migrants" envisioned by the YWCA founders, African American women enthusiastically embraced job training outside of domestic service and recreational programs in the "safe spaces" reformers provided.

The Limits of Respectable Labor

Female migrants arriving in Detroit during the Great Migration faced an extraordinarily limited job market. Although some found jobs in munitions factories during the war, by 1921, African American women were all but absent from any paid occupations in the formal economy outside of domestic service. These women faced both unsympathetic white employers and white female workers who refused to work alongside them. In addition, a secondary level of discrimination based on skin color among African Americans determined who would be employed in the handful of factory and white-collar jobs that were available. Therefore, most working-class women had to make choices between domestic service, "legitimate" entrepreneurial endeavors such as beauty shops, and the informal economy.

Negotiating the local job market in order to provide for their families was a central experience in black women's daily lives. Female migrants often cited the desire for employment opportunities as a primary motivation for migration to the urban North. In 1921, for example, Mary Etta Glenn received a letter from her friend, Lucile, a young African American woman who had remained in Macon, Georgia, while friends and relatives migrated north. "Mary Etta," lamented Lucile, "I got the railroad blues. . . . I am so lonesome here Mary Etta. I want you to rite [sic] and tell me about a job at once so I can leave here. . . . I can do most anything like clean up and Laundry by the day. . . . What are you doing and what do you get a week?"[104] Lucile, like many southern women, sought inside knowledge about the labor market in Detroit—what kind of jobs were available and how much they paid. Leaders of Detroit's African American community were concerned about migrants like Lucile, who arrived in the city with expectations of improved employment opportunities. Would there be enough jobs for the many incoming female migrants, what kind of jobs would be made available, and how well would female migrants serve in these positions?

For a brief period during World War I, industry opened its doors to African American female workers, but shortly thereafter, employers offered few jobs outside of domestic service. In 1919, Forrester B. Washington reported in *Life and Labor*:

> They pulled a bedraggled mass of cloth and mud out of a creek of the Toledo River recently. "Why, it's a colored girl," the policeman said. . . . Her landlady, when interviewed, said that on account of the end of the war they were discharging colored girls from the "decent" jobs which they had secured during the labor scarcity. The suicide, who was a graduate of a southern college, had declared, she added, that she would kill herself before she would go back to work in a kitchen. "There's no chance for us colored girls, even if we have an education," the unfortunate girl had told her friends. "In the South they try to make us immoral, and in the North they won't let us keep a decent job."[105]

Although this story is most likely apocryphal, it accurately reflects the black community's despair at the war's end. Social mobility for female migrants seemed imminent during the brief war years. This hope was dashed when white employers promptly fired African American women in industrial and white-collar jobs when the soldiers returned. Going back to the kitchen was the only choice for the majority of Detroit's black female workers. In addition, discrimination based on skin color limited job choices for some women. Employers offered the few jobs in factories and stores that were available to light-skinned "cultured" African American women. This color distinction created a secondary level of job-market discrimination sometimes sanctioned by community leaders who wished to employ "respectable" women in highly visible occupations. Eager to place as many women as possible in industrial and clerical jobs, community leaders were forced to acquiesce to white stereotypes of employable black women. Therefore, definitions of respectability and occupational ability became closely linked in the labor market.

Urban reformers seeking to protect and uplift young female migrants were eager to improve the job market for black women in the early 1920s. Washington, for example, devoted a chapter of his 1920 study *The Negro in Detroit* to African American women in industry. His intensive study of the employment situation of Detroit's African American women reveals both the stratified nature of the job market and the Detroit Urban League's tendency to downplay the racism of white employers. Discussing the status of African American women's employment prior to 1915, Washington primarily bemoaned the lack of distinction between different groups of women. "In 1910 the mass of the colored women, whether they were members of the oldest Negro families of Detroit or whether they were recent arrivals in the city; whether they were graduates of high-schools and higher institutions of learning or whether they had no formal education whatever—if they had to work, were forced to seek employment in the field of personal service." Washington went on to admit that some of the "more cultured types" did have skilled personal-service jobs in private homes, such as hairdressing. "The larger portion of the cultured and practically all of the uncultured however," Washington argued, "were employed in the more dull tasks of personal service."[106] The mixing of the "uncultured" and "cultured," distinguished only by their labor in either skilled service work such as cooking and hairdressing or unskilled service work such as cleaning, was a grave concern of Washington's. Separating out the "cultured" through a differentiated labor market would aid racial progress because *all* African American women could no longer be identified with servitude. According to the logic of the Urban League, any progress in stratifying the labor force was evidence of the community's progress as a whole.

By 1920, African American women had found work in a handful of industries, including the metal trades, meatpacking, and cigar factories.[107] Many of these so-called industrial jobs, however, were thinly disguised service jobs. Women working in automobile plants were usually employed as janitors, for example. Industrial jobs were also held tenuously. Washington noted that most African American industrial workers hired in the metal trades during World War I were fired immediately after the war's end. White women workers were also let go after the war, leading Washington to note that "the colored woman suffers as much from sex limitation as from color limitation."[108] The understood result of the removal of all women workers from industrial labor was that white women now comprised an available reserve industrial labor force, and only in times of severe labor shortage would African American women be employed in any substantial numbers. Complaints of white women workers who refused to work alongside African American women or even share locker rooms or showers with them in industrial plants further strengthened the "double bind" of racial and gender discrimination. In 1917, for example, the Detroit Urban League reported that "one firm discharged about thirty girls . . . first because the white girls objected and secondly because the manager claimed the colored girls were too rough and rowdy."[109]

The policy of firing black women workers when white female workers complained of their presence continued throughout the 1920s. In 1925, for example, the Detroit Urban League reported: "Some office managers would be willing to take on colored girls in capacities such as mentioned but for fear of disturbances by the girls already employed[;] usually these girls threaten to quit if placed side by side with a colored woman worker."[110] White workers' objections to African American female workers represented an active policing of the strict racial and gender barriers of the job market. Indeed, white women felt that the status of their own paid labor would decline if they worked with African American women. Job market segmentation was deeply rooted in cultural representations of African American women as "beneath" white women in culture, education, morality, and thus occupation. In order to maintain their own relatively "high" position in the labor market, then, white female workers engaged in "hate strikes" throughout the first half of the twentieth century, segmenting the already narrow labor market by race. Employers and managers acquiesced to white women's demands, reflecting their acceptance of negative stereotypes of African American female workers.

Despite the paucity of jobs, by the early 1920s, Washington and his cohorts prematurely claimed success in improving the "industrial status" of the recent southern female migrant. "Her change in environment," stated Washington, "has caused an immediate improvement in her industrial status." The improvement was a matter of not only wages but also the "character . . . and the conditions surrounding her work."[111] Community leaders viewed the entry of a few women into industry and the relatively higher wages of the North as evidence of racial progress. These advances would improve not only working conditions, reformers implied, but also the moral conditions of the workers and their workplace—in short, their respectability. Efforts to improve the social conditions of industrial workplaces, however, were limited by the reluctance of employers to include African American women in their recreational and welfare programs. Factory owners and managers did not open women's clubs, athletic teams, and social outings to African Americans.[112] Therefore, like domestic workers, African American women in industry and retail employment had to seek recreation outside of their workplaces, leaving them, in the eyes of elites, vulnerable to the dangers of urban commercial entertainment.[113]

Although the cost of living in Detroit was substantially higher than the cost of living in the South, some young African American women workers had more money and time to spend on entertainment. A woman working as an elevator operator in a department store, for example, could make $16 per week in 1920 and work a relatively short week of forty-eight hours. Women working and boarding in hotels and restaurants and earning $22 dollars a week had the advantage of avoiding high rents and food prices while working regular hours, as compared to live-in domestic workers, who were expected to be available to their employers twenty-four hours a day.[114]

These jobs were appropriate primarily for unmarried women without family duties, a group that represented a minority of African American female workers. The wages of all black female workers reflected the racial discrimination inherent in Detroit's job market. African American women working in scarce industrial jobs, for example, earned an average of $14.71 per week, whereas the average wage for white women was $18.90.[115] Nevertheless, for a few hundred African American female workers employed in factories and department stores, migration led to higher wages, increased leisure time, and improved job status.

Whether African American female migrants experienced improvement in their working lives is a question that cannot be answered by merely comparing wages. For example, in his 1920 study, Washington noted that the "more favored class" of migrants in the South had been schoolteachers, earning about $27 dollars per month. After migrating north, "women that formerly earned not over $27.00 per month teaching school in the South are earning $60.00 per month operating elevators in the various department stores of Detroit."[116] Thus, for Washington, these women both experienced and represented racial progress, despite the improbability that the women themselves would have found the experience of operating an elevator more fulfilling than teaching. What is most striking about Washington's statement is that women of the "more favored class" were chosen for this particular niche in the tight job market. The fact that light-skinned, well-educated African American women obtained jobs in white department stores was a result of white employers' preferences and African American reformers' desire to place the most "respectable" women in public view. Black reformers constantly sought to present the black community in the most "attractive" way possible in order to improve race relations and economic conditions for African American migrants. Because white employers defined "attractive" as educated, well-mannered, and fair-skinned, reformers placed black women who fit this profile into the most public positions.

At least a few African American women broke free from the constraints of Detroit's job market by "passing" as white women in the workplace. The sales department of an automobile factory hired one such woman in a clerical position. When her employer discovered her racial identity, the factory filed a complaint with the Detroit Urban League, which was viewed by white employers as responsible for African American workers' behavior. In this case, the Urban League declined to respond. It is possible that community leaders helped some women find employment by "passing." In 1917, Jesse O. Thomas, principal of Voorhees Normal and Industrial School in South Carolina, wrote to Washington asking him to help find employment for two female schoolteachers. In his letter, he noted that "one of these young women could readily pass for white, without any difficulty whatever."[117] This light-skinned woman may have been placed in a department store with other former schoolteachers. Or perhaps she was able to gain more lucrative employment by "passing" in the workplace.

When Washington noted that "the factory and store employer gets the cream of colored womanhood for these occupations," his use of the word "cream" had more significance than he may have intended.[118] It was well known that the most coveted jobs, in department stores, factories (other than laundries), and theaters, were assigned based on skin color. Although department stores had the reputation for being particularly "fastidious" on this account, factories, where the workers were more or less hidden from view, also preferred to hire light-complected women. In factories, there were also hierarchies of color, with "mulatto girls" working the machines and "dark complexioned girls" working as janitors. During World War I, there was such a high demand for light-skinned women that a "pulling and hauling of the girls from one industry and then another" led to high turnover.[119] When employers had to hire dark-complected women because of a labor shortage, they sometimes changed their views on the significance of skin color. For example, when a garment factory and two cigar factories began to hire darker women, "they discovered that some of the darker women had quicker reactions and were more regular in attendance than many of the lighter complexioned women, and that on the whole, with equal training there was no crucial differences [sic] in the ability of the light and dark Negro women."[120] In fact, southern migrants, who were often the ones labeled "uncultured," were much more likely to have worked in tobacco factories than northern-born Detroiters. Despite this, during and after World War I, skin color and job status became intricately linked for African American women.

Washington and other community leaders acknowledged that these practices could be detrimental to racial uplift; however, they often went along with the wishes of employers for pragmatic reasons. Some improvement in the labor market for African American women was better than no improvement at all. At times, their negative views of southern migrants shaped their attitudes toward employment. Washington, for example, felt that it was important that northern-born "cultured" women take factory jobs because "it is in the field of the factory employment where each worker is contributing to the productive wealth of society that real respect for the Negro will be developed."[121] Mulatto women were not superior because of skin color, insisted Washington, but because "they were as a rule girls who have had better opportunities than the pure blacks who were mostly southern girls from the rural districts."[122] The assumption that "pure blacks" would not be exemplary workers was built into the discourse of migration. Rural, untrained, and naive female migrants could become successful workers only by gaining more education, training, and exposure to moral uplift programs. Such characterizations reified the color discrimination of employers by identifying light-complected women with "cultured" northern cities and dark-complected women with the rural, "uncultured" South. Thus, the discourse of migration and reform unintentionally helped to justify color discrimination in the job market.

When John Dancy placed light-complected women workers in coveted industrial and clerical jobs, he did so as part of a conscious scheme to improve the image of African American female workers in Detroit. "I have thought of this plan as a means of working colored girls into places where they have previously never been employed and where the white girls will raise objections to them," argued Dancy. "It is to go to these girls placing before them this picture: after spending the day in the open, breathing nature's fresh air and bathing our faces in sunshine, night comes on and suddenly a star appears, and later on another star and still another one until finally the Heavens are brilliant, illumined by many stars. That could be likened to the girls, in their positions, in that first we place one girl and then another and still another until finally the whole place becomes a picture of beauty."[123] Dancy's vision may have been poetic, but it was not immediately prophetic — the color line in white-collar employment would not be broken until after World War II.

Dancy took a very active role in placing his "stars" in Detroit's night sky. When Dancy encouraged Hudsons, a large department store, to hire African American women as elevator operators, he met resistance from the management. Attempting to assuage their fears, he gathered together "some of the prettiest girls you ever saw. Many had gone to good schools in the South; some were college graduates." The manager wanted to reject one woman who was, in Dancy's words, "very dark . . . not as good looking as the others." Dancy encouraged him to hire this woman because her intelligence and graciousness "proved more important than surface beauty."[124] To Dancy, a dark complexion was not the ultimate test of refinement; a good education and manners could overcome the deficit of skin color. Because the Detroit Urban League exercised control over which women were hired at department stores, they could consciously shape the black community's public image into a model of bourgeois respectability. "These elevator girls were far more than just elevator girls," argued Dancy; "they were ambassadors of the Negro race."[125]

These industrial "ambassadors" were sent by the Urban League to a newly established factory that was an experiment in African American women's employment. The league's involvement with this factory demonstrates that Dancy's ultimate goal was to help a larger number of African American women break into the industrial labor market. In 1916, the Detroit Urban League began negotiations with a wealthy industrialist, Julian Krolik, to open a garment factory that would exclusively employ African American women. Krolik's wife was a member of the board of Detroit's Urban League and no doubt helped persuade her husband to undertake the experiment.[126] Since no female white workers would be employed in the factory, hate strikes would not occur, and African American women would gain valuable industrial experience. The industrialist also proposed building a gymnasium, club room, and restaurant for the workers—social services from which African American women were excluded in other factories. When the Urban League advertised the new positions in the newspaper and through ministers who made "appeals for girls from their pulpits," the response was immediate: 165 women applied for half as many positions.[127] In 1917, the A. Krolik Company opened a pants factory that employed seventy-five African American women in all capacities except management, including clerical work in the company office.[128] Krolik and his associates built the promised facilities and planned to extend other social services to workers, such as lectures at a branch library and monthly dances.[129] The women workers at Krolik were selected from the large number of applicants for their good looks, education, and "cultured" manners.[130] As in other factories, most of the operatives were light-skinned.

When it appeared in 1917 that the "Krolik experiment" was a success, the Buhl Malleable Iron Company approached Washington about hiring some African American women as core makers in its plant. Washington selected four "clean-cut refined colored girls" to accompany him to Buhl, "ostensibly to show them just what core-making means." "As a matter of fact," explained Washington, "the trip was made in order that the Board of Managers might have an opportunity of observing a number of the type of colored girls they could expect to obtain through the Urban League. They were so pleased at the appearance of the young women that they have informed me that they have definitely decided to employ colored women in this process."[131] Once again, the "appearance" of the workers rather than their experience or skill was paramount. The Urban League used employers' growing interest in "attractive" African American female workers to make inroads into industrial employment. For example, when Boyd Fisher, of Detroit's Board of Commerce, contacted Washington about hiring African American women as telephone operators, he said he was "very much impressed by a photograph of the community dance and the type of girls shown there." Washington promptly invited both Fisher and the general manager of the Michigan Telephone Company to the following week's dance to "look over some of the young ladies first hand."[132]

Hiring "attractive" young women to serve the white public often had unintended consequences for both employers and employees. One hotel that hired only "good-looking mulatto girls" as chambermaids and elevator operators discharged the women three months later. Apparently, continuous "indecent and unwelcome attentions of the male guests" led to extremely high turnover. The hotel management responded to this situation by hiring "a less attractive type . . . of dark colored girls" in their place, fully expecting the problem to stop—but it did not.[133] Clearly, sexual harassment was not a problem that African American women had left behind in the South after the Great Migration. Washington argued that white men harassed African American women in factories and other workplaces both because they viewed the black woman as "a person of lesser morals and consequently easier approached" and because there was less danger that the man would be chastised or prosecuted if caught.[134] Emphasizing African American women's respectability was a time-honored method of fighting sexual harassment in the workplace.

African American women, however, did not rely solely on reformers to defend their honor. At times, victims of sexual harassment stood up to their white employers. One young woman who worked in an auto factory and was harassed by a foreman complained to a social service agency, which investigated the case and confronted the superintendent of the department. Washington reported that "the superintendent misunderstood the investigator's mission and voiced his approval of the foreman's judgment, stating that he was from the South himself and had always possessed a colored mistress 'down home.'"[135] Another woman who worked as an usher in a theater was raped by the manager and later gave birth to his child. Despite the odds, she pressed charges, which he countered, "using every method in his power financial and otherwise."[136] As is evident from these cases, African American women had few weapons with which to fight sexual harassment and rape in the workplace. This was particularly true for the group of workers most vulnerable to sexual harassment, domestic workers, who represented the majority of Detroit's black female workforce. Consequently, household labor remained the least desirable occupational choice for Detroit's African American women.

Much to their chagrin, African American women found that domestic service was the only reliable means of wage work that employment offices offered them after they migrated to Detroit. Domestic service in Detroit was different from domestic service in other large cities such as Philadelphia, New York, or Chicago. Detroit had a large working-class population due to the rapid growth of the auto industry. As a result, only a small elite in the city could afford either a live-in domestic, work that many African American women declined, or a maid who would work several days a week on a regular basis.[137] For African American women, therefore, almost all domestic service meant "day work." Women would arrive at employment offices at the Detroit Urban League, YWCA, or Second Baptist Church and be sent to work at a private home for eight or ten hours. The rate for this work was usually $2 per day, although some workers were paid even less.[138] Day work also meant that household workers had more arduous cleaning duties. Ernestine Wright, a day worker in the 1920s and 1930s, remembered: "They didn't want you but once a month. That's why the dust was so heavy under the beds, and that's why the floors were so dirty you didn't know the color of them."[139] Sexual harassment in private homes also remained a constant problem. "They was afraid if you sent a young person that their husband would flirt with them, which they did," recalled Wright.[140]

Although day work was irregular, difficult, and underpaid, it had the advantage of being flexible—a factor that women with families found helpful. African American women could leave their children with a neighbor or occasionally at a day nursery associated with a church and work several days a week. Some women alternated child care duties with day work by taking care of a neighbor's children while she worked in exchange for the same service. If their husbands or other family members were temporarily laid off (on a "starvation vacation" as some workers referred to it), women might do more day work to bring in extra income or have their daughters do day work as well.[141] This need for temporary labor was marked in a city where male employment was dominated by factory work that did not provide a steady income. In many ways, the day worker was the female equivalent of the unskilled male laborer who got jobs on a day-by-day basis.

Like their male counterparts, African American women had to rely on employment agencies to assign day jobs. Located at the YWCA, churches, and the Detroit Urban League, these agencies ensured that reformers and social workers interacted daily with working-class African American women. As in the South, domestic service became a focal point of reform efforts in northern cities. Reformers sought to improve wages and working conditions for day workers and elevate the status of the African American women who dominated the occupation. The impetus for the training of day workers in the northern context, however, was also rooted in a larger migration discourse. White employers viewed African American women as rural, naive, and unprepared for the urban North. African American reformers worked to refute these stereotypes by training and certifying domestic workers. They hoped these efforts would help professionalize domestic service, and they welcomed the opportunity to interact directly with recently arrived migrants.

One of the primary difficulties African American female domestic servants faced was white employers' preference for white servants, particularly in the better-paid positions such as cooks and housekeepers. Elizabeth Ross-Haynes, a noted African American social scientist, expressed concern about the plight of African American domestics in Detroit in 1922, noting that "from eighty to ninety percent of the calls for domestic workers are for white girls." [142] Between 1910 and 1920, the use of African American domestic servants increased by 300 percent as white servants began to fill industrial and white-collar jobs. [143] This shift in the racial makeup of household laborers, part of a national trend, was not welcomed by white housewives, who complained incessantly about the quality of the new southern-born servants. One social worker noted in 1926 that she had difficulty placing African American women as domestics because "a great many white people will not take them." [144] A study of classified advertisements for domestic servants in 1926 found that in a two-week period, 61 percent specified a preference for a white servant. [145] Despite the preference for white servants, by 1930, African American women and domestic service were inextricably linked in Detroit.

Advertisements also provide evidence of African American women's resistance to adverse labor conditions. High turnover and a shift to day work transformed domestic service in 1920s Detroit. African American female migrants who were entering domestic service in large numbers applied their southern strategies of resistance to a northern context. [146] Newspaper advertisements seeking domestic labor reflect the high turnover common in the occupation, and black workers consistently requested day work. This choice reflected their rejection of live-in work. [147] Although many white employers preferred to hire white servants, African American women found it relatively easy to obtain day work in Detroit. White working-class housewives who could not afford the higher wages of a live-in white housekeeper could afford an occasional African American day worker. During the economic recession of 1920 and 1921, when large numbers of male African American autoworkers were laid off, the Detroit Urban League placed thousands of African American women in day work. Dancy argued at this time: "All of us can't be professional men; some of us have got to be domestics. We must stress these jobs as domestics." [148] Dancy's statement reflects his understanding of the crucial role that African American women's wages played in the economy of black households.

The employment office of the Detroit Urban League, whose primary role was the placement of day workers, was the league's busiest and most lively department. Dancy remembered one "problem" with the office space: "At first we had seats—chairs, so that people could sit down, particularly women who came in looking for day work. They would come in sometimes when we opened the office at 8 A.M., and would sit around until say, 11 waiting for calls to come in. We found out they were making a social rendezvous of the place. They would continue to occupy space long after it would be too late to get a call for day work; some seemed to come there primarily for the chance to sit around and talk. . . . We finally decided it was hindering our real work of finding jobs for people, and so we took out the chairs."[149] Dancy and the employment office secretaries felt African American women were "misusing" the space made available to them. The alternative to sitting in an office, however, was to stand on street corners and wait to be hired by housewives who drove by, a practice, known as the "slave market," that occurred in other northern cities.[150] No doubt Detroit's Urban League employment office became a de facto meeting place for African American female workers who, because they worked in private homes, ordinarily had little contact with one another except on the streetcars that took them to their jobs. It is likely that these women shared information about which jobs were preferable, how to complete tasks quickly and efficiently, and where to get reliable child care, as well as simply talking and relaxing. Making the space less hospitable undercut the organizing capacities of domestic servants and discouraged their use of the Urban League facilities for leisure and relaxation. This disjuncture between Urban League officials' notion of how their offices should be used and the wishes of domestic servants illustrates the different priorities of community leaders and the female workers they sought to reform. Clearly, though, the Urban League provided a valuable service to African American women workers by making it possible for them to pick up day work from the relative comfort of an employment office rather than an inhospitable street corner.

In the 1920s, the most common complaints of reformers and employers about domestic servants were that they were untrained, unable to operate "modern" appliances, and generally unreliable. As in the South, community leaders responded to these complaints by setting up training programs to certify domestic servants in their craft. The teachers at the Baptist Christian Center, which offered domestic training classes in the mid-1920s, viewed female migrants as "utterly bewildered by the social surroundings, living conditions and the climate. The women and older girls were willing enough to work as domestics, but the electrical appliances, the mechanical devices frightened them. It was necessary to gather these people, instruct them in the work that would be expected of them and help them to fit into their new surroundings."[151] Despite this description of recent migrants, the most popular classes at the Baptist Christian Center were not domestic service courses but educational and commercial classes that offered a means to escape service work altogether.

The Detroit Urban League agreed with the Second Baptist Church's estimation of Detroit's female migrants' skills as domestic servants. In 1920, Washington argued: "The largest proportion of colored women in Detroit who seek domestic employment come from the rural sections of the South. They are not good house-maids, at first, because they have never been inside a modern city home in the South much less in the North. They have come to Detroit from the little cabins on the plantations. Gas stoves and set tubs—not to speak of electric washing machines, vacuum cleaners and other modern house-hold appliances are entirely new to them." Washington went on to point out that "after a few weeks of systematic supervision in use of modern household appliances," African American women could become successful domestic workers.[152] Although the electrical appliances used in Detroit may have been unfamiliar to some recent migrants, it did not take long for household laborers to learn how to use them. Dancy, who promoted domestic service training throughout his career, also admitted that African American domestics "learned fast" even though they "had no experience with the appurtenances of a modern household."[153] When the Urban League stressed the technological challenges of a "modern household," it reinforced Detroit's image as a foreign urban territory to "untrained" female migrants. If these migrants could learn to work in "modern" households, they would be transformed into the urban citizens and reliable workers that employers desired and in turn aid in the uplift of the race.

In 1920, Dancy oversaw the expansion of the Detroit Urban League's Domestic Service Training School, initially a small program at the Columbia Community Center.[154] This school had originated as the Day Workers' Training School, which trained and certified newly arrived migrants from 1916 to 1920. During this period, 600 women took the course and were in turn guaranteed employment and good references. Nevertheless, when African American women realized that day work was fairly easy to get without any training or certification, the program lost its popularity. Therefore, the Detroit Urban League found it necessary to expand the purpose of the school to include home economics.[155] In general, training in domestic service with no larger purpose in mind was never particularly popular among African American women. For recent migrants who were eager to earn the promised higher wages in Detroit, taking classes at the day workers' school in exchange for assured employment was a worthwhile endeavor. When they realized that certification was unnecessary, however, the school's mission had to be expanded to include skills that would lead to better service jobs and could be applied to African American women's own homes.

With the assistance of the Visiting Housekeepers' Association (VHA), the school set up a "model flat" as a practicing laboratory. Classes included sewing, cooking, home economy, laundering, home nursing, diet, and hygiene. After ten lessons, students were sent out to do day work on a trial basis. After two days of work, they had to report to their instructor with recommendations from their employers. If the employers were satisfied, the women were awarded diplomas and became certified domestic workers.[156] Workers were also given advice about maintaining their own homes, deportment, and dress and other tips on maintaining a respectable self-presentation. Before graduating, workers took a pledge to be punctual, work hard, have a "pleasant manner," and "maintain good health habits."[157] Thus, training and placing African American day workers allowed the Detroit Urban League to promulgate a bourgeois ideology of respectability that had a dual nature. On the one hand, it attempted to instill a work ethic of efficiency and dependability; on the other hand, it stressed personal hygiene, household cleanliness, dress, and deportment. Thus, as in the South, African American women in Detroit were being taught to be both good household laborers and good housewives. These women, however, made use of the services selectively. They took classes that ensured employment or that offered to teach skills for jobs outside of domestic service. When they had learned the skills necessary to gain employment as day workers, usually in a short amount of time, they used the Second Baptist Church or the Urban League primarily as an employment office and day care facility.

For many African American women, the ultimate badge of respectability was to escape domestic service altogether and enter the white-collar labor force. Only a handful of African American women in Detroit reached this goal. By 1926, there were approximately 150 African American women employed as teachers, social workers, skilled clerks, or stenographers in Detroit.[158] This relatively small number of workers formed the elite of the occupational structure of Detroit's African American women. Their positions were beyond reproach: they were "clean" jobs dissociated from dirt and disorder, and they were relatively new occupations for African American women. Many African Americans viewed these workers as the vanguard in opening up white-collar work, and jobs in social work and teaching were directly linked with racial uplift and reform movements.[159] During the interwar period, however, the number of skilled white-collar jobs for black women would not increase significantly. Although this ensured the social superiority of the small number of black women in white-collar work, the stagnation of the job market reflected a failure in African American leaders' reform strategy. The hard work and attractive appearance of African American white-collar workers never translated into the hiring of large numbers of African American women in offices, schools, or reform agencies.

Clerical work, for example, was a rapidly growing field for white women by the early 1920s; however, for Detroit's African American women, the only jobs available in white office buildings were those that involved cleaning.[160] Social workers trying to place African American women in offices reported that "employers . . . give the excuse that their white office staff will not stand for the introduction of Negro labor." Thus, hate strikes were not limited to the factory floor.[161] Black-owned banks and insurance companies provided the only readily available clerical jobs, but these were extremely coveted and competitive. Middle-class migrants with some higher education would most likely have become schoolteachers in the South, working in the seg-regated school system. Teaching opportunities in northern cities were more scarce. By 1927, Detroit's public school system employed approximately fifty African American teachers.[162] Most worked in predominantly black schools; however, a few taught white students exclusively.[163] Despite the slow influx of African American women into Detroit's school system, no African Ameri-can administrators or counselors were assigned to even predominantly black schools during the 1920s.[164] Thus, the handful of African American school-teachers and clerical workers were members of a female elite in the paid labor force.

Middle-class African American women were well qualified for social work. It required education, experience, and a dedication to racial uplift that many African American women had displayed in voluntary associations. Applications to Detroit's United Community Services from 1926 to 1928, a clearinghouse of social service agencies, reveal the educational and social background of many of Detroit's African American social workers. A woman born in 1893 in Pensacola, Florida, filed a typical application. She attended Knoxville College from 1912 to 1916 and after obtaining a bachelor's degree worked as a schoolteacher in Florida until 1918, earning $50 per month. After migrating to Detroit, she worked first as a housekeeper for J. L. Hudson Company from 1923 to 1924 for $56 a month and later for Simon J. Mur-phy Company in a similar capacity. Moving from a job as a schoolteacher to one as a service worker was a typical pattern among migrant women, as the above example of schoolteachers who became elevator operators illustrates. Married with three children, this migrant attended a Methodist church and was a "solid" member of the community who hoped to improve her employment situation by entering social work. Initially, the interviewer from United Community Services wrote "not very promising" on her application, but this comment was later crossed out and "Mr. Dancy recommends" was written alongside it. Clearly, this migrant's social standing in the community, her respectability, was verified by Dancy, whose aid may have helped her obtain a job as a social worker and escape the relative drudgery of household labor.[165]

Female migrants often asked the Detroit Urban League's director to place them in social work. In 1917, Sarah Jane Bannister, a migrant from Virginia, wrote to Washington: "I have adopted Detroit as my home and am deeply touched with the conditions that I find here. . . . I am interested in Social Service work and am well fitted for it as to education and temperament and as a minister's daughter, having served my people as a teacher, and lastly as a trained nurse."[166] Offering her services to research housing conditions, Bannister hoped to simultaneously find paid employment and aid in the uplift of her new community. Indeed, the two motivations were directly linked since an educated black female social worker was the embodiment of racial uplift. This link was further strengthened because appearance as well as education and training often played a part in the hiring of white-collar workers. These educated women represented and policed the respectability of the entire community. The executive secretary of the St. Paul Urban League, for example, wrote to Dancy seeking employment for an African American woman as a chemist. "Permit me to say that she is a fine looking brown-skin girl," he wrote, "with a very pleasant face and pleasing manner. . . . She is attractive, dresses neatly but not gaudily."[167] Skin complexion, modest dress, and physical attractiveness all served to reflect a particular level of refinement to African American leaders who sought to place such women in highly visible positions.

Most of the applicants for social work were born in the South, had at least some college training, and were married. Many had been schoolteachers prior to their arrival in Detroit and clearly hoped to obtain white-collar jobs that would give them both social standing and a decent income. These women were often dedicated volunteers, teaching in the Baptist Christian Center or working with juvenile delinquents in the Recorders' Court. In 1929, a survey of Detroit's social workers revealed that African American women who did obtain jobs were highly trained and experienced. Bessie

Carney, the supervisor of the Columbia Community Center, had earned a degree from Talladega High School and attended the University of Chicago. She also had worked at Hampton Institute and in Harlem as a settlement worker. Other Urban League social workers included Geneva Mercomps, who had received a bachelor's degree from Bethel College in Kansas, and Odessa McCullough, who had attended Wilberforce University and worked at several settlement houses and the CAS in Detroit.[168] The African American workers at the YWCA and VHA also had college education and considerable experience in social work.[169] Although many of these women migrated north along with their working-class counterparts, they differentiated themselves from these "other" migrants through their occupational status and devotion to racial uplift. These women illustrate the diversity among female migrants, belying the old settlers' characterization of migrants as an undifferentiated mass of rural, naive workers. Educated in black colleges throughout the country and with work experience in numerous settlement houses and YWCA branches, they were well versed in the tenets of racial uplift and employed the "scientific" knowledge of early-twentieth-century social science.

Many well-educated migrants found the search for white-collar jobs exceedingly difficult. This difficulty is aptly illustrated by Mary Etta Glenn's struggle to find clerical work. After Glenn graduated from Detroit's High School of Commerce in 1921, she began to apply for clerical jobs in the city.[170] For decades, Glenn kept the stinging replies she received from prospective employers, perhaps the most poignant evidence of how deeply racial discrimination in the job market shaped her early life and the lives of so many other African American women in Detroit. One letter in the summer of 1922 simply read: "I am very sorry to say that it has never been the custom of the Company to employ colored girls. Due to that fact we feel that we could not place you."[171] Glenn finally found a clerical job in 1923 at the only public agency that hired African American women—the post office. Throughout her long career there, she labored to help other women workers. For example, beginning in 1925, the year of her own marriage, Glenn began a campaign to oppose the firing of married female post office employees.[172]

The significance of Glenn's early struggles to find employment lay in the nature of both her search and the rejections she received. Discrimination in the job market was not a passive economic measure but an active process. White employers had policies against hiring African American women, and white female workers often refused to work alongside African American women; together, these groups actively and forcefully rejected black women's continuing efforts to get white-collar jobs. This process of exclu-

sion and racism further fueled middle-class African American women's determination to improve the image of black women. With the exception of
a handful of women who found jobs as teachers, social workers, and post
office employees, African American female migrants who had education
and training often settled for jobs as elevator operators or cleaning women
in department stores and factories. They did so out of economic necessity
and in the hope that such work would begin to break down racial barriers.
Another way to expand white-collar work for African American women was
to help black-owned businesses grow and prosper. Because some of those
businesses were part of a growing commercial leisure industry that elites
considered disreputable, developing black entrepreneurship was somewhat
controversial.

Most businesses founded by Detroit's African Americans in the interwar
period were small and service-oriented, requiring little capital. Lunch counters, many serving southern-style food, barber shops, beauty parlors, grocery stores, and drug stores predominated.[173] Between 1920 and 1930, the
number of African American retail stores in Detroit increased 20 percent,
with the largest increase occurring among restaurants and lunch rooms.[174]
Many of these small enterprises were staffed and run by African American
women who gained valuable experience as small entrepreneurs in the early
1920s. Shut out of white-owned and -operated retail shops, African American women found employment in stores and restaurants on the East Side.
Some African American women opened their own establishments, creating
employment where formerly there was none. Music teachers, often well-
educated African American women, also advertised their services widely
in the local press and church circulars. All of these entrepreneurial activities met with a spectrum of success, from women who worked out of their
homes to women who opened their own shops. These small establishments
offered escape from the drudgery of domestic service and the racism of white
employers.

For African American women, beauty shops and dressmaking stores were
promising entrepreneurial endeavors.[175] Female migrants could choose from
an array of beauty and fashion services by the early 1920s. For example,
in 1921, the African American newspaper the *Detroit Contender* advertised
"Madame Washington's School of Dressmaking and Coatmaking" as well
as "Madam Nora Johnson's Chiropodist and School of Beauty Culture and
Hairdressing, Manicuring, Shampooing, Facial, Scalp Treatment, Dyeing
Hair, Clipping, Singeing, Bleaching, Arching Eyebrows, Marcelling and
Fancy Hair Dressing and Manufacturing."[176] By 1926, African Americans
operated twenty-eight beauty parlors, two millinery shops, and twenty-

eight dressmaking shops, and the number of such shops would increase in the ensuing years.[177] Because African American reformers emphasized self-presentation during the Great Migration, beauty culture took on political meanings. "Racial pride," argues Kathy Peiss, "often took the guise of a beautiful woman on display."[178] Well-dressed and groomed female migrants potentially reflected the entire community's respectability in the workplace and on city streets. Young female migrants embraced beauty culture both as a means of employment and as a form of self-expression.

Often reformers linked the success of reputable individual entrepreneurs to the uplift of the community. These businesses employed African American women who desperately needed jobs, and their success became public signs of community pride. For example, in 1920, the *Detroit Contender* published an article on Eleonora A. DeVere, whom it described as "one of our women of Detroit who is forging ahead in the world of business." De-Vere had worked as an employee in another beauty shop before setting out on her own in 1919. Her success was due in part to her role as a representative of Madame C. J. Walker's beauty products, which were advertised in the African American press nationwide. DeVere was part of a network of female entrepreneurs who captured a growing urban market of African American women. Noting that she employed other women in her shop, the *Contender* concluded that "Detroit cannot have of our race too many women of the type and stamina of Eleonora A. DeVere."[179] In 1927, an ad for the "DeVere School of Beauty Culture" appeared in the *Detroit Independent*, indicating that DeVere's business had become profitable enough to reach the next level of entrepreneurial success—training other African American women to work as beauty culturalists and be self-supporting.[180] In the African American community, working-class and middle-class people embraced the label "businesswoman" as a positive sign of racial uplift and community pride. As commercial leisure exploded in popularity and the informal economy grew, however, a businesswoman might become involved in illicit activities not sanctioned by community leaders.

For Detroit's African American women, earning an income was an ongoing struggle. Mary Etta Glenn and her fellow migrants constantly sought to push the boundaries of a segregated job market by applying for white-collar or industrial jobs. For the most part, however, white employers refused to consider hiring black women for any but the most menial positions, and white employees resisted working alongside female migrants. African American reformers responded to this situation by placing educated and attractive black women in the most visible positions to prove to white employers that African American women were capable and trustworthy employees. Recognizing that most women would be relegated to domestic service, reformers also developed training and certification programs designed to introduce recent migrants to urban life and reassure white employers that these workers were qualified to perform domestic tasks. Above all, reformers were eager to steer female migrants away from disreputable wage work—employment in commercial entertainment or prostitution. When female entrepreneurs escaped domestic service by opening legitimate new businesses, they were lauded by community leaders and fellow migrants alike. However, migrants who found wage work outside of what reformers deemed reputable challenged the principles of bourgeois respectability.

Conclusion

Many historians have suggested that World War I marked the end of the Victorian Era, a time when middle-class American women traded in their ideology of true womanhood for a more emancipated image of companionate wives and young flappers.[181] Two factors slowed this ideological transformation in the club activities and reform work of middle-class African American women: white assumptions of African American women's inherent immorality and the dangers of sexual harassment and rape that continued to shape black women's lives. The Great Migration exacerbated these factors because it appeared that young African American women were even more vulnerable to sexual violence in the urban North and because young women's involvement in leisure activities that reformers deemed disreputable threatened to tarnish the African American community's image. Therefore, in black Detroit, the work of protecting women and promoting sexual purity and chastity remained central to reform in the 1920s.

Because the Great Migration enlarged Detroit's segregated black community so dramatically, elites were alarmed by the overcrowding and concomitant social mixing. Different classes and genders commingled in northern urban streets and overpriced apartments, making the dream of well-regulated domesticity and differentiated moral and class boundaries unattainable. Thus, African American churches, clubs, and other institutions promoted programs that separated the sexes and attempted to instill values of domesticity, cleanliness, and thrift in women and dependability and community responsibility in men. Fueling these programs was a concern for the development of respectable leisure in a period when commercial amusements were growing at a rapid rate. African American reformers built these strategies for racial uplift around bourgeois respectability and taught these tenets to incoming southern migrants. Many migrants, however, had a very different list of priorities when they arrived in Detroit. Some saw illicit occupations and leisure activities as opportunities for economic prosperity and a more varied social life. These varied visions of urban life ensured that the image of Detroit's black community would be fractured from the outset of the migration process.

3 The Informal Economy, Leisure Workers, and Economic Nationalism in the 1920s

The fact is that Black Bottom was like that during Prohibition, the sort of neighborhood that could be as lyrical as church chimes and at the same time keep you up at night with an assortment of commotion that was by no means restricted to the belfry.

Coleman Young, Hard Stuff: The Autobiography of Coleman Young

"I basically had two role models in those days," wrote Coleman Young of 1920s Detroit—"the hustlers, with their flashy clothes and money clips, and the Ford mules, as they were called, straggling home from work all dirty and sweaty and beat."[1] Detroit was very much a city with a dual nature during the 1920s: a thriving industrial city and a "wide open" town of gamblers and prostitutes. Because gambling, drinking illegal liquor, and hiring prostitutes were common pastimes for male workers, these two images were closely linked. By spending their relatively high wages, the "Ford mules" fostered a thriving informal economy during the height of Prohibition. Factory workers also spent their wages and leisure time on new forms of commercial entertainment: cabarets, dance halls, movie theaters, and poolrooms. African American women, shut out of industrial and white-collar labor, found desperately needed employment in these commercial and illegal forms of leisure. The wages of male industrial workers were thus spent on the services provided by African American women leisure workers.

The male hustler and "Ford mule" had their female counterparts in the flapper who dressed flamboyantly and transgressed her elders' norms and the hardworking domestic who labored tirelessly to support extended family. These dichotomous images, however, were not accurate pictures of African American women, who both transgressed and combined these identities as they labored to support themselves in a hostile economic climate. Just as male industrial workers emerged in Detroit's nightlife as urban "sheiks," many young African American women enjoyed the varied leisure activities that Detroit's East Side offered. Because these women did not have the steady income available to their male counterparts, their participation in the informal economy and commercial leisure was often as workers rather than customers. Community leaders responded to this expansion of female leisure work by mapping and policing illicit and respectable occupations for women.

For African Americans, the dual image of Detroit was geographically embedded in their East Side community. As in many cities, the vice district and the central African American neighborhood were coterminous as city officials segregated crime and vice along the same geographic lines as they segregated racial groups through zoning laws and selective policing. Therefore, African American community leaders had to work doubly hard to present a community image of bourgeois respectability. Many middle-class African Americans viewed visible signs of disorder and vice as an affront to the race as a whole. Nevertheless, for some working-class African American women, an informal economy that included illicit activities such as prostitution provided a means to escape domestic service and support themselves and their families. For these leisure workers, individual self-worth and economic survival took precedence over presenting a public face of decorum and self-restraint.

African American women's participation in the informal economy undermined a community identity that placed women in the roles of mother, homemaker, reformer, and "respectable" worker.[2] The emergence of an African American female sector of the informal economy was shaped by the extremely limited job market after World War I. But choosing to work in the informal economy came with costs—women who became prostitutes, for example, could have their children taken away, be arrested, or contract a venereal disease. Some female migrants were unwilling to take such risks, preferring to rely on neighborhood employment bureaus for day work. These choices, however, were not always as stark as Urban League officials made them out to be. Although community norms demarcated a hierarchy of reputable occupations for women, the formal and informal economic sectors were not distinct. As historian Luise White notes in her study of prostitution in Kenya, "The illicit often supported the respectable."[3] This dynamic was equally true in Detroit. The informal economy both circulated African American male industrial wages throughout the community and, by attracting white customers, established new sources of income for African Americans.

Indeed, the informal economy, generally defined as economic activity outside of or hidden from state regulation, is often an imagined category, a legalistic distinction not always made in everyday life.[4] This was perhaps most apparent during the interwar period in urban America, when Prohibition led to the spectacular rise of organized crime and most Americans broke the law on a regular basis by taking an occasional drink.[5] Although the informal economy is usually gendered in the popular imagination as a male world of danger, bravado, violence, and exploitation, illegal activities that involved monetary exchange also employed women. In some cases, women were entrepreneurs in the informal economy, creating employment opportunities where none had previously existed.[6] Spiritualist mediums involved in the numbers business provide one such example of female entrepreneurship. Although many African American women did not make strict distinctions between work in the informal and formal economies, African American reformers during the 1920s were very concerned with these distinctions because the presence of "vice" in the East Side would reflect on the community as a whole. Therefore, community leaders differentiated reputable and disreputable employment and recreation by identifying characteristics that were evidence of participation in the informal economy: "finery," extra income, and too many boarders were all enumerated by the Urban League social workers and gossiped about by church members and neighborhood watchdogs as evidence of informal economic participation.

In contrast to the stark warnings of community leaders about the dangers of illicit leisure work, individual decisions about employment and urban survival strategies most often revolved around working-class notions of respectability that focused on self-worth, family survival, and racial pride. For many African American women, these norms, rather than a bourgeois definition of respectability, dictated their actions. Perhaps most emblematic of this trend was the wide-scale involvement of African American women in Marcus Garvey's Universal Negro Improvement Association (UNIA), which offered them entrepreneurial skills and a source of racial pride as they were settling into their new homes in Detroit. Similarly, storefront churches founded by African American women that offered ecstatic worship to their mostly female parishioners were sources of both extra income and spirituality. Both of these institutions became targets of the Detroit Urban League, mainline churches, and women's clubs because they undermined the project of creating a respectable community identity. Elites perceived marching in a UNIA parade or opening a storefront church as a public act that marked the community as a whole as disreputable. Increasingly, these elite criticisms fell on deaf ears as African American migrants quickly learned to navigate and make use of the myriad economic and social opportunities available in an urban setting.

Leisure and Vice in the 1920s

Many seemingly legitimate businesses in the African American community thinly disguised the world of the informal economy. With the onset of Prohibition and increasingly strict state regulation of prostitution and gambling in the 1920s, small stores and restaurants often hid gambling, drinking, and prostitution. In his autobiography, Coleman Young describes how seemingly legitimate small businesses often served as fronts for illicit activities: "In our neighborhood, Prohibition was a period of enthusiastic debauchery in which nothing on the street was what it seemed to be. . . . The local hat shop was a front for the biggest numbers operation on the east side. Dave Winslow made whiskey in the rear of his sweet shop. If you were stupid enough to walk into Lonnie's shoe shine parlor and ask for a shine while the poker and black jack games were going on—which was most of the day and night— you were liable to get your ass beaten."[7] Thus, visible, outward-facing storefronts that seemed to indicate a level of economic prosperity hid a different economy—one that was within the purview of African Americans. In this way, an image of community respectability was shakily maintained while an underground informal economy thrived. Detroit's crowded urban setting facilitated this multiple use of space as migrants created a distinct culture and economy.

The uneasy truce between the need to "protect" a respectable community identity and the promotion of illicit commercial activity reflected the creation of a broader understanding between Detroit's city officials and the growing organized crime syndicates that controlled the traffic in illegal liquor. The line between formal and informal economies and reputable and disreputable behavior was blurred in a city profiting from the illegal liquor trade and numbers gambling. This blurring revealed contradictions in the project to foster a community identity, a project dependent on clear demarcations between vice and virtue determined in part by economic activity. New migrants who participated in the informal economy did not adopt the Urban League image of a respectable hardworking citizen or retain an imagined rural southern identity but instead fostered new sets of identities in conjunction with the dynamic surroundings of Detroit. This creation of new urban identities began the process of remaking respectability as it dismantled the simplistic dichotomies of the migration era. Commercial leisure, definitions of vice, and the growth of the informal economy were all central to this process.

Commercial recreation was a major area of concern for the Detroit Urban League, women's clubs, and churches that wished to "assimilate" southern migrants to a northern industrial city. Integral to the control of recreation was the policing of urban space. The most illicit, most dangerous spaces of leisure were those that encouraged unsupervised mixing of different races, genders, and classes. Lewis Erenberg suggests that reformers' concern over illicit leisure spaces in the 1920s was the culmination of three decades of declining Victorian values regarding appropriate leisure activities.[8] Similarly, in the African American community, reformers had been concerned about "appropriate" leisure activities since the late nineteenth century, which had led to the denunciation of popular music, jook joints, inappropriate dancing, public drinking, and indecorous dress in the South by the 1880s and 1890s. These worries centered on women, who were perceived as uniquely vulnerable to the lures and dangers of commercial leisure in cities. Indeed, fear of the dangers of illicit leisure shaped the initial response to the migration of African Americans. Reformers presented an image of young female migrants who were lured into dance halls and disorderly houses and became prostitutes—and thus embodiments of the white stereotype of African American women. The downfall of these potential "mothers of the race," suggested uplift ideologues, would lead to the downfall of the race as a whole.

As commercial leisure in cities grew throughout the 1920s, African American reformers continually focused on its dangers, particularly for women. During this period, reformers hoped that by offering supervised recreation such as the Detroit Urban League's community dances, they could teach moral lessons about temperance, sexual behavior, dress, and deportment. With the proliferation of commercial recreation by the mid- to late 1920s, this optimistic outlook on the possibilities of controlled recreation seemed somewhat naive. Several studies of recreation among African Americans in cities presented the dangers of illicit leisure in stark detail and documented the phenomenal growth of commercial dance halls, theaters, cabarets, and poolrooms.[9]

In 1928, Forrester B. Washington published the results of one such study, based in part on his work on the Detroit surveys of 1920 and 1926. Washington argued that African American migrants' primary motivation for leaving the South was the "quest for happiness," which would be satisfied by an increase in leisure time and activities. Migrants who sought better employment opportunities, he argued, did so to improve their access to commercial leisure.[10] A survey of 1,000 Detroit migrants found that fishing, hunting, and "sitting down" were the primary leisure activities in the South.[11] Therefore, argued Washington, migrants left the South to take advantage of the opportunities of commercial entertainment. Once a migrant arrived in the city, however, "in nine cases out of ten the kind of leisure time activities available to him have been more harmful than otherwise."[12] In part, this was due to the segregation of the "wholesome" recreation offered at local branches of the Young Men's Christian Association (YMCA) and YWCA, schools, and parks and the commercial entertainment offered at theaters and amusement parks. In Detroit, for example, African Americans could not go to the Boblo Island or Tashmoo amusement parks and could only visit Put-in-Bay and Sugar Island, popular excursion destinations, on particular days. Middle-class African Americans, such as the Dancy family, vacationed in segregated resorts such as Idlewild, Michigan.[13]

Working-class African Americans had even fewer choices, according to Washington. Migrants had to be content with the "degraded forms of leisure time activities" found in saloons, gambling houses, and houses of prostitution. Washington concluded his study by blaming the lack of "wholesome" recreation facilities on the African American migrant's "reputation for crime": "He idles about the streets because he has no other place to go, and wanders into pool rooms and more vicious places in large numbers."[14] The image of the African American criminal in the white mind was the root of the recreational problem for Washington; therefore, providing better recreational options for African Americans could be urged "on the basis of self-protection." As recreational facilities improved, the image of African Americans in cities would improve as well.[15]

The image of the African American community, its public identity, was the central concern of other reformers who studied recreation in African American communities. The public nature of the new commercial entertainment led to unsupervised mixing, allowing races to observe each other (and even dance and drink with each other) in an illicit setting. This illicit world also promoted sexual experimentation, in particular, the development of vibrant gay and lesbian subcultures. Gay men and lesbians of both races frequented speakeasies and buffet flats in the black community, where they felt welcomed and even celebrated. The blueswomen of the 1920s frequently sang about bisexuality, and in Harlem, the "panzy craze" of the 1920s pioneered popular black drag shows that were imitated in other cities. When Ruby Smith traveled to Detroit with her aunt, the famous blues singer Bessie Smith, she remembered one buffet flat that offered a gay sex show to paying customers. "People used to come there just to watch him make love to another man," remembered Smith. "He was that great."[16] Such activity alarmed the moral guardians of Detroit's black community, for whom heterosexuality was an integral part of bourgeois respectability. "Sexuality," argues George Chauncey, "became one of the critical measures by which the black middle class differentiated itself from the working class and constituted itself as a class."[17] Immoral single women, gay men, and anyone who frequented the underworld of 1920s Detroit had to be policed carefully by black reformers, who asserted normative models of sexuality. Indeed, because these activities were largely ignored by white city officials unconcerned with the welfare of recent migrants, it was up to the black middle class to discourage this "deviant" behavior.

Deviancy was fostered, argued Henry McGuinn in his 1928 study of commercial recreation in African American communities, by unsupervised mixing.[18] Dance halls and poolrooms in African American communities, he noted, were less closely supervised by city officials than similar white establishments.[19] Policewomen in Detroit did occasionally go undercover to supervise African American dance halls by "rescuing" young women who appeared to be in trouble (women who were very young or very intoxicated) and identifying prostitutes.[20] Interestingly, the 1926 study *The Negro in Detroit* noted that "according to the policewomen whose duty it is to supervise public dancing the conduct of the patrons . . . is very good. In their opinion, the people seem very eager to *preserve* the order and decorum, and to meet the approval of the policewomen."[21] This report could suggest that the result of supervised dancing was relative decorum. However, many establishments and informal dances held in the city had no such supervision.

Public dances that attracted domestic servants and industrial laborers particularly concerned McGuinn. "In places of this kind," he argued, "drunkenness, bootlegging, prostitutes in search of men, and men in search of easy prey, are frequently seen." "Lewd" women caused McGuinn alarm, such as prostitutes who danced with "foreigners," women fighting over a man who took their fight out on the street, and women who wore costumes that "easily rivaled those of the bathing beauties." McGuinn saw similar behavior in unsupervised cabarets, which he labeled "sluiceways through which vice pours into the community."[22] Of most concern to McGuinn and others was the interracial nature of that vice and its location outside the purview of either African American community leaders or white public officials.

Comparing commercial entertainment in white and African American communities, McGuinn concluded that the primary difference "is the degree to which different classes mix in the colored places of amusement. There are white dens that are the hangouts for pickpockets, prostitutes and their ilk;

but the respectable working classes do not go there frequently. In the colored community, however, lack of wholesome recreation often leads the servant girl and workingman into these dens of vice and crime."[23] Keeping the respectable and the licentious apart meant keeping social classes separate. It was through supervision, argued McGuinn and many others, that this could be done most effectively. If the police department refused to provide thorough supervision, then clubwomen, church workers, and Urban League social workers would. This push for supervision reflected the genuine concern of middle-class reformers for incoming migrants who were not familiar with the dangers of commercial leisure. The "immoral landscape" they supervised, Detroit's East Side, was also the neighborhood of the "respectable" working class.[24] The final goal of reformers was the creation of a "moral" landscape where divisions between reputable and disreputable people and places were clear.

Often overlooked by reformers was the potential for commercial recreation to provide employment opportunities for African American women. Because such jobs were on the borderline of bourgeois respectability and were visible to white city dwellers, Urban League officials and social workers were concerned that they might reinforce negative white stereotypes of black women. Although being a ticket-taker or a hostess at an African American theater, such as the Koppin Theater on Detroit's East Side, was a job that many African American women would prefer to domestic service, the Urban League employment bureau did not list such openings. Performing at the Koppin Theater was even more problematic than working there. Blues historian Daphne Duval Harrison estimates that African American female performers could earn up to $50 a week at a theater like the Koppin—a powerful incentive to enter the world of entertainment.[25] Despite this, community leaders throughout the country expressed concern about young women working in blues shows. Harrison notes that the 1922 Chicago Commission on Race Relations objected to one café because "it offered jazz, vulgar dances, and mixed couples, all considered immoral enticements for the young black women who performed there."[26] As in the general discourse about female migration, African Americans concerned about female performers depicted them as vulnerable and naive rather than portraying them as women who made an active choice for economic betterment.

Detroit's community leaders sounded warnings about the dangers of blues throughout the 1920s. An editorial in a 1921 edition of the *Detroit Contender* called for an end to blues singing. "Such rot only poisons the soul and dwarfs the intellect," the editorial read. "We need the song of hope, which will start the wheels of fortune rolling."[27] Such warnings cut across class lines in the black community. Detroit-born poet Robert Hayden recalled the reaction to Bessie Smith: "Religious people . . . thought her songs immoral, and my staunch Baptist foster father, for instance, didn't want Bessie's low-down songs played on our 'victrola.'"[28] Although the audiences for blues performances were largely working-class migrants, devoutly religious migrants shared the concerns of community elites. Washington was particularly appalled by newspaper advertisements of "race records" that were "distinctly immoral in their title and context . . . accompanied by obscene pictures."[29] Such advertisements, he believed, reinforced the negative stereotype of African American women as licentious. They depicted singers like Ma Rainey backed up by a chorus line of "brown skin beauties" — light-skinned dancers who were a popular part of vaudeville entertainment. Rainey frequently performed at the Koppin, a theater attended by all classes of African Americans, and her shows drew large crowds. Smaller clubs and cafés, however, offered more risqué shows and attracted a mixed crowd of gamblers, numbers runners, prostitutes, whites who were "slumming," and "ordinary" working men and women.[30] These establishments most concerned reformers and most clearly negated the dichotomous images of the newly arrived rural southern migrant and the established, trustworthy old settler. The blues queen and her chorus line of dancers were clearly not respectable, yet these women were quintessentially urban and earned a decent living. Their emergence into the public imagination marked a new challenge for community leaders and a new model for incoming female migrants to emulate.

Despite attempts by African American and white social reformers to "clean up" the city by closing down illicit dance halls and saloons, Detroit in the 1920s was known as a "wide open town." Judge Brennan of the Recorders' Court said of this period: "There was an abundance of almost everything, vice included."[31] This description of the Motor City was offered with pride by many city dwellers and with shame by city reformers in both the white and black communities. A number of factors led to Detroit's reputation for vice and the rapid growth of an "illicit" informal economy that became intricately linked with the African American community: the proximity of Detroit to Canada, the closing of Chicago's "red-light" district in 1912, and the large number of male industrial workers who earned relatively high wages and were the primary consumers of leisure. No Detroit neighborhood was as closely associated with vice as the African American East Side. In the urban geography of Detroit, the East Side *was* the "immoral landscape" — a repository of gamblers, prostitutes, rum runners, and gangsters. Speaking of African American gangsters, one black journalist stated: "They got out their guns and went to work, and the race in general has been made to share in their shame."[32]

In the first decade of the twentieth century, as many as 10 percent of African American adults worked in the city's saloons, in gambling parlors, or as prostitutes.[33] In the community, lines between immorality and respectability were drawn based on dress, occupation, church membership, and family status. The thousands of women who worked in illicit entrepreneurial activities, however, also made judgments about respectability and self-worth. By choosing not to engage in domestic service, these women hoped to leave behind the low-wage, low-status occupations that left them vulnerable to sexual harassment. Although leisure workers faced community censure and sometimes arrest, they also brought in much-needed wages to their families, at times sending money back to family members in the South. Many of these women attended church or engaged in other community activities that were deemed "respectable" by elites. Thus, individual identities shaped by the racist job market and prevailing social morays were much more complex than the images of recent migrants put forth by the Urban League for public consumption.

Reformers were first alerted to vice activity among Detroit's African Americans in the late nineteenth century. In 1885, black gamblers began to visit two Detroit racetracks.[34] After betting at races became illegal in the United States, entrepreneurs in Windsor, Ontario (just across the river from Detroit), built new racetracks to attract American customers. Thus, according to Washington, "the proximity of the Windsor (Canada) races, attracted the touts, the gamblers, book-makers and all the undesirable followers of the race track from all over the country."[35] George Edmund Haynes also made this observation: "Disreputable characters of other kinds than those who follow the race-track were drawn from other large cities. The beginning of a Negro ghetto in the region of St. Antoine . . . was made."[36] John Dancy remembered a famous race in 1920 when "St. Antoine was a deserted village; all of the men were at the track."[37] For many African American leaders, the initial influx of this African American "underworld" paved the way for a flourishing informal economy and stigmatized the community in the eyes of whites.[38]

Another undesirable migration occurred as a result of the 1911 vice campaign in Chicago.[39] Washington noted that "when the reform wave struck Chicago and cut out at least a large part of the colored Red Light district, a great many proprietors of disorderly resorts and their hangers-on came to Detroit because it had the reputation of being a wide open town."[40] Whether or not successful madams from Chicago opened businesses in Detroit is difficult to ascertain; however, it is true that houses of prostitution were abundant in Detroit throughout the 1920s whereas their numbers were declining in other cities. More important, Detroit's city officials did not have the political will to carry out the type of progressive reforms that led to the vice campaign in Chicago. This lack of supervision reinforced Detroit's image as a city susceptible to crime and vice.

Detroit's proximity to Canada was perhaps the primary reason for its reputation as a "wide open town" during Prohibition. After the manufacture and sale of alcoholic beverages were declared illegal in April 1918, "blind pigs"—illegal saloons that sold liquor—proliferated.[41] Before Prohibition was declared, approximately 1,200 saloons operated in Detroit. After Prohibition, the illegal sale of liquor became the second largest industry in the city after the production of automobiles.[42] By 1923, the Detroit police department estimated that 3,000 blind pigs were operating in Detroit, and the Detroit News put the number at 10,000. By the late 1920s, the number of blind pigs had grown to between 15,000 and 20,000.[43] The language and lifestyle of illegal liquor running pervaded Detroit's culture. During this period, the Detroit-Windsor tunnel was referred to by locals as the "Detroit funnel."[44]

The proliferation of new establishments that operated outside the law was a boon to Detroit's African Americans, who had trouble finding employment elsewhere or preferred the flexible hours and higher pay that the informal economy offered compared to factory labor or domestic service. In 1923, a Detroit News article estimated that 5,000 people were employed in bringing liquor into Detroit from Canada, and many more worked in the blind pigs and other liquor operations throughout the city.[45] Because blind pigs operated outside the law, they were not subject to health codes or other city regulations and could be operated almost anywhere—in storefronts, private homes, apartments, and former saloons. Historian Mary Murphy has suggested that Prohibition both created "new social spaces for drinking" that "accelerated the advent of heterosocial night life" and allowed women to engage in commercial enterprises by selling liquor in speakeasies.[46] Drinking and serving liquor also changed gendered definitions of acceptable public behavior—as public drinking became increasingly heterosocial during Prohibition, it also became more reputable. Thus, as Murphy notes, "women [were] able to expand the boundaries of recreational behavior and still retain respectability."[47] In Detroit, the blurring of the line between respectable and unrespectable behavior accelerated with the advent of Prohibition. Illegal drinking establishments were ubiquitous in the city, particularly in the African American community, and in them men and women mixed freely.

Female blues performers sang about the central place of blind pigs in African American urban culture and the role of female entrepreneurs in establishing them. In 1929, for example, blues performer Mary Johnson recorded "Barrel House Flat Blues." A "barrel house" was another name for a blind pig, often used for speakeasies that also had stills to brew illegal liquor.

> I got a barrel house flat in Detroit
> and one in St. Louis too
> I got a barrel house flat in Detroit
> and one in St. Louis too
>
> But my barrel house flat in Detroit
> really gets me blue.[48]

Numerous other blues singers wrote and recorded songs about drinking establishments and the effects of alcohol.[49] These performers often began their careers in small jook joints and blind pigs, where drinking was a central activity. Some performers, such as Bessie Smith, became known for their heavy drinking, but others, such as Ethel Waters, consciously avoided alcohol. The blueswomen's songs about running speakeasies and drinking alcohol linked the image of the glamorous female urban resident with illicit behavior. These songs also provide evidence, difficult to obtain in traditional manuscript sources, that African American women did play a role as employers, employees, and consumers in a burgeoning new commercial enterprise.

Detroit's speakeasies took many forms. Besides blind pigs, there were "neighborhood pigs, apartment pigs, back-room pigs, and front-room pigs."[50] These establishments ranged from small rooms in apartments to large saloons. Because a blind pig was so easy to open and so profitable, competition was fierce. In 1927, one blind pig owner lamented the growth of neighborhood pigs that took business away from the downtown establishments. "The little birds have opened up places wherever they can find a roof to cover them in the residential district," he complained. "They're sort of becoming a gang of apartment drinkers."[51] The "little birds" this proprietor was referring to were women of both races who were active not only in the establishment of blind pigs but also in the production of illegal liquor. During Prohibition, approximately 1,000 illicit breweries were discovered by Detroit police officers, and it is likely that many more were in operation. The distillation of raw alcohol in home stills was also a popular and profitable industry that supplied "white lightening" to pigs in Detroit and throughout the Midwest.[52] Popular images of Prohibition—such as the gangster, bartender, and workingman with a beer—were primarily male. Nevertheless, Prohibition fostered the growth of an informal economy that employed women, children, and sometimes whole families and brought millions of dollars weekly into Detroit's local economy. The perception of a prosperous African American community in Detroit during the 1920s, despite a restricted job market for women and periodic layoffs for men, is mainly due to the growth of the informal economy and the large amount of cash circulating throughout the city. Although it is difficult to know how many African American women were employed or were entrepreneurs in the illegal liquor industry, the development of the industry had two significant effects: it fostered the growth of a larger informal economy, and it broke down some of the proscriptions against illegal activity among the African American working class.

The response to the proliferation of blind pigs was selective. City officials and the police department made distinctions between more "respectable" former saloons and cabarets and those that catered to prostitutes or adolescents or invited social mixing of races and genders.[53] Not surprisingly, the latter types were often located in the East Side and run by African Americans who had neither the political clout nor the capital to encourage law enforcement to pass over their establishments.[54] Therefore, it was generally more dangerous for an African American man or woman to open a blind pig, and proprietors became adept at closing down and moving their establishments at a moment's notice. City officials had the aid of the Urban League in locating black speakeasies. Emmett Scott noted in 1920: "The league itself kept a close watch on the negro underworld of Detroit and immediately apprised the police when dives were developed especially to prey on the immigrant."[55] In fact, by "protecting" migrants, the Urban League was also cutting off a lucrative area of employment, especially for African American women. Because "respectable" employment was central to the community identity reformers were attempting to create, they did not acknowledge this negative consequence.

Urban League officials carefully mapped commercial recreation in Detroit's African American community. They kept tabs on which poolrooms and dance halls were fronts for gambling operations or prostitution and which ones were legitimate places of business. When Washington arrived in Detroit to take over the directorship of the Urban League, he found "twenty-three saloons, seven pool-rooms, twelve gambling clubs, and houses of prostitution and buffet-flats galore where most of the colored people now live."[56] By the mid-1920s, the amount of "commercialized vice" had grown dramatically because of the influx of money through the informal economy and the growing number of working-class consumers. Working with city officials and civic groups, the Urban League acted as a mediator between the African American community and concerned white reformers and law enforcers. League officials investigated suspected disorderly houses and reported their findings to the police and welfare agencies, often deciding African American women's fate based on their perception of whether or not they were "reputable." In no area did city officials depend on the knowledge and expertise of the Urban League more than in the policing of prostitution.

Policing Prostitution

For middle-class reformers, African American prostitutes were the ultimate victims of migration. They represented for clubwomen, argues Wanda Hendricks, "the corruptibility of young, poor black women and lent support to the demoralizing stereotype of black females."[57] Thus, "rescuing" such women from their fate would aid both individual migrants and the fight against negative stereotypes of African American women. For some whites, African American prostitutes represented both the criminal and physical contamination of the African American community. Black prostitutes exposed white Johns (and their families) to venereal disease and were physical manifestations of a racialized criminal population. In the white community, containing African Americans was synonymous with containing vice and disease. Historian Kevin Mumford has argued that prostitution was driven deeper into black communities during the 1920s as a result of the vice crusades of the Progressive Era.[58] In this period, reformers of both races joined forces to restrict the movement of prostitutes, punish them, and treat their physical ailments as part of a larger project of "purifying" the city.[59]

However reformers may have seen them, in reality, African American prostitutes were neither "Jezebels" nor victims but workers who provided a variety of services to the African American and white communities, including but not limited to sex in exchange for money. In a city where housing was scarce and young migrants sought lively entertainment, houses of prostitution offered shelter and recreation. In the 1926 *Negro in Detroit* study, the authors noted that "to many male newcomers the house of prostitution furnishes a social center to which he has ready access and where he receives a cordial welcome."[60] The house of prostitution as "social center" was exemplified by Detroit's many buffet flats. A buffet flat was usually a small private house that offered a variety of services to customers, including gambling, "erotic shows," prostitution, illegal liquor, and musical entertainment. These houses were run by women who provided shelter and recreation for a price. Customers would even use a favorite buffet flat as a bank, leaving their money with the madam.[61]

Buffet flats originated as places where transient Pullman porters could stay overnight to enjoy illicit pleasures, have a bed to sleep in, and keep their money safe. Another group of transient workers also made use of buffet flats—TOBA performers who traveled from city to city throughout the 1920s. Many of these performers were women—blues-singing headliners such as Bessie Smith, Victoria Spivey, and Sippie Wallace and numerous female dancers, comedians, and musicians. After performing at Detroit's Koppin Theater, for example, Bessie Smith and her companions would regularly visit a nearby buffet flat run by a female friend. The madam would send several cars to the Koppin to pick up Bessie and her dancers and drive them to her establishment. This buffet flat offered a variety of sex shows in different rooms, but the primary show was a musical "after hours" performance. In 1925, Bessie Smith recorded "Soft Pedal Blues," which she wrote to immortalize her favorite Detroit buffet flat.

> There's a lady in our neighborhood
> Who runs a buffet flat
> And when she gives a party
> She knows just where she's at
>
> Early in the morn'
> So put that soft pedal on
> I'm drunk and full of fun
> Go and spread the news
> 'Cause I got them soft pedaling blues.[62]

Bessie's song describes a heterosocial world of sexual, musical, and social experimentation. The buffet flat she sang about was a "social center" not only for male workers or traveling Pullman porters but also for a group of female performers who, having worked all night, spent their wages at the establishment of a fellow leisure worker—the madam. Thus, madams and female employees pooled their resources to run highly lucrative establishments that blended images of home and workplace.[63]

Buffet flats and houses of prostitution prospered in Detroit at the same time that they were declining in other cities. Most likely, this was due to the lack of a well-organized antiprostitution drive in Detroit.[64] The biography of one woman who ran a Detroit buffet flat illustrates the circuitous route many madams took before founding their own houses. When Doris was seventeen and living in the South, she became pregnant after having an affair with a local musician. Her father, a Baptist minister, threw her out of the house, and she migrated to Detroit to stay with a married sister. When her sister also refused to take her in, Doris got a job as a waitress and lived in a boardinghouse after her baby was born. After she lost her job, she sent her child to Ohio to stay with another sister and moved in with a friend who was in "the racket." Soon afterward, Doris and her friend opened a buffet flat that sold whiskey and offered sexual services. In a few years, she had "a good-sized savings account" and, with her friend, owned the well-furnished house.[65] Doris's story was shaped by the norms of morality held by her father and other family members who were unwilling to assist her when she was pregnant. After years of trying to "make good" in Detroit by working as a waitress, Doris turned to a lucrative occupation for African American women and became a successful entrepreneur. In the context of a severely limited job market and the disciplining she received from her own community, her choice to become an entrepreneur with a community of other women gave her more financial, and perhaps moral, support than attempting to live a "respectable" life in a boardinghouse. For Doris, the road to bourgeois respectability led to poverty, not social mobility.

The buffet flat was the ultimate threat to community order because of the social mixing it fostered. Not only did different classes and genders frequent buffet flats, but the activities in them were also diverse. Bessie Smith's niece Ruby Smith remembered: "They called them buffet flats because buffet means everything, everything that was in the life."[66] For many African American women, buffet flats provided a lucrative employment opportunity outside of domestic service. One buffet flat prostitute from Chicago stated, for example: "When I see the word *maid*—why, girl, let me tell you, it just runs through me! I think I'd sooner starve."[67] In contrast, for reformers, buffet flats exemplified the disorder of unsupervised and uncontrolled urban life. Urban League officials argued that migrants and itinerant workers arriving in an overcrowded city who stayed in buffet flats were in immediate danger. George Haynes warned that a buffet flat was especially dangerous "because it is usually in a private house in a neighborhood of homes, is run with all signs of respectability and caters especially to the youthful and unwary." Haynes recognized the elevated status of the buffet flat in the informal economy, defining it as a "high-class combination of a gambling parlor, a 'blind tiger' and an apartment of prostitution."[68] Locating buffet flats became a specialty of the Detroit Urban League, which sent investigators to inspect "suspicious" houses. Armed with the knowledge necessary to identify a buffet flat, the Urban League workers acted as mediators between the white and African American communities.[69]

In 1916, for example, the CAS contacted the Urban League to determine whether a mother was a "proper guardian" for her child. Upon investigation, the league found that despite working only occasionally, "this woman was always expensively clothed and claimed to live alone in a luxurious apartment." Their suspicions were immediately aroused. Reformers and social workers viewed overly luxurious clothes as a sign of moral depravity—too much finery was worse than wearing "southern" clothing such as a head scarf because of its association with illicit leisure work. The league concluded that this woman maintained a buffet flat and sold liquor illegally and recommended that the CAS remove the child from the mother's care.[70]

A case documented by the registration bureau, which tracked "trouble cases" (in which families contacted several social service agencies for aid), reveals both the dangers and the possibilities of running a buffet flat. An African American woman, Mary, migrated to Detroit in 1916 accompanied by her twelve-year-old daughter and began keeping a boardinghouse. When this house was raided as a "sporting house," the CAS was asked to investigate. With aid from the Detroit Urban League, the CAS identified Mary's establishment as a "disorderly house" and recommended the removal of the daughter. With the help of a brother, Mary sent her daughter to Tennessee to live with her grandmother. A few months later, Mary's house was identified as a buffet flat and closed by the police department.[71] This case reveals both the role of the Urban League in locating and closing buffet flats and the ways in which female migrants such as Mary learned to maintain illegal businesses while aiding their families. Mary opened her buffet flat within months of arriving in Detroit rather than sliding down an imagined "slippery slope" of immorality. When her daughter was in danger of being removed, Mary quickly sent her to live with relatives, to whom she likely sent money for support. Thus, Mary's story challenges the prevailing stereotypes of the naive southern migrant and the prostitute as the helpless victim of urban vice.

African American women who kept boarders and had no other obvious means of income ignited middle-class community leaders' suspicions. In 1925, John Dancy received a letter from Ruth Franklin of the Detroit Public Schools about a seven-year-old boy. "We believe that this family would bear investigation," wrote Franklin. "From the history we obtained from the child we judge home conditions to be very poor. . . . Robert states his mother is away from home during the day, but does not know where she works. There are several men roomers and the environment seems rather questionable."[72] The nature of Robert's mother's job would determine her fate. Domestic service was the most acceptable and "safe" employment in the eyes of city officials such as Franklin. The lack of direct knowledge of "respectable" employment combined with any sign of luxury or excess income aroused suspicion that a woman was a leisure worker. In a city where women could earn a good income through the informal economy, social mobility was not necessarily indicative of respectability.

Another female migrant, Belle, who was the subject of several different agencies' investigations, was given employment as a day worker by the YWCA in the hopes of diverting her from prostitution. This tactic was common in the 1910s and early 1920s — if young women could be shown alternatives to a "disorderly" lifestyle, perhaps they and their families could be rescued.[73] Unfortunately for black reformers, low-paying domestic work was not always an attractive alternative to leisure work. In addition, the boundary between reputable and disreputable employment was not always clear. Some African American women combined these categories by working as domestic servants in "disorderly houses." When the CAS threatened to take one young mother's two children from her because she worked as a cook in a "questionable home," the woman fled the city with her children. In his 1933 study, "Prostitution in Detroit," sociologist Glen S. Taylor argued that "many instances were found of colored girls who got started in the racket through associations while working as maids in sporting houses."[74] Other women interchanged prostitution with other forms of wage labor depending on the availability and quality of the work.

By combining day work with prostitution, African American women could earn a dependable income. Allie, for example, worked as a prostitute irregularly, earning a few dollars to supplement more regular day work.[75] Indeed, day work and casual prostitution had some similarities: both were irregular forms of employment that offered flexibility. Women could pick day work or exchange sex for money when they needed to bring in extra income. The difference between the occupations was that wages for a full day's housework were equal to wages for one trick — between $1 and $3. Significantly, women like Allie did not fit into the models of respectable and disreputable workers presented by reformers and civic leaders. Allie and other women like her used available forms of employment to survive in the city without making stark distinctions between having a "respectable" identity as a domestic worker or having "fallen" as a prostitute.

The sexual harassment experienced in domestic service and sexual favors in prostitution were sometimes compared by prostitutes — the difference being that prostitution was better paid and actively chosen. Myrtle, an African American prostitute who grew up in a middle-class neighborhood in a home where discipline was "strict and old-fashioned," lost her virginity when she was raped by her employer while working as a domestic servant. After this experience, Myrtle had a variety of other jobs, routinely returning to day work. Frustrated, she and several other young women decided to join a house of prostitution. Fourteen years later, Myrtle was working both on her own and occasionally for a madam, hoping to earn enough money to open her own "sporting house."[76] Millie, another African American prostitute, left day work altogether to become a prostitute because she found it difficult to live on the meager wages of a domestic servant. "I figured I could make just as much hustling," she said to an investigator, "as I ever could on the 'legit' and it wouldn't be as hard work."[77] Millie recognized prostitution's "illegitimacy," but for her, its advantages far outweighed the risk of public censure.

In 1926, a study by the American Social Hygiene Association declared Detroit "the American Mecca of prostitutes" and the "blackest hole of crime and vice in the United States." Detroit's vice squad was formed in response to this study, and the number of arrests of black prostitutes increased dramatically. One finding, which was already well known but still distressing to African American community leaders, was that the "vice district" mapped by investigators "overlaps a large section of the colored residential area."[78] Dancy noted that soon after the establishment of the vice squad, "great numbers of women [were] arrested for prostitution."[79] The black community recognized that a larger number of African American prostitutes would be arrested than white prostitutes. In the early 1930s, for example, three-quarters of the prostitutes in prison at any given time were African American.[80] City officials claimed that the lack of jobs was the primary reason for the overrepresentation of African American prostitutes among those who were arrested. For example, Eleanore Hutzel, head of the Women's Division of the police department, pointed to the lack of employment and uneven sex ratio as the social roots of African American prostitution.[81] Racial discrimination practiced by Detroit police officers, however, also explained the large number of black prostitutes arrested. One study observed that "it is a noticeable policy of the Detroit police to arrest colored girls almost exclusively on week-ends, the days when business is most brisk." This policy of racial discrimination was reportedly "keenly felt" by prostitutes, who lived in a city where police brutality was endemic. The popularity of buffet flats and houses of prostitution reflected the police's policy of arresting street-walkers rather than raiding private houses.[82] The increased likelihood that a prostitute soliciting on the street would be arrested reflected an abhorrence of "visible" vice and resulted in the classification of streetwalkers as a "lower" type of prostitute.

Soliciting on the streets was a dangerous endeavor for African American women. On the streets, they were vulnerable to police harassment, and when arrested, they could be imprisoned in what was known as the "power house." The health department's Social Hygiene Clinic was primarily interested in the treatment of venereal disease—literally "cleaning up" prostitutes in order to keep the Johns (and their families) healthy. The Board of Health had the legal right to examine anyone suspected of having a venereal disease. Women who exhibited evidence of venereal disease included "females without visible means of support and found on the street late at night or about restaurants or places of amusement" and "girls found in questionable hotels or rooming houses unchaperoned."[83] Thus, being in public alone or with other young women was enough evidence for a police officer or official from the Board of Health to bring a woman in for questioning and a forced physical exam. Women who refused to be examined or continually escaped from the Social Hygiene Clinic were confined in the "power house" while receiving treatment. This facility consisted of a single room with twenty cots, some shared by two women, and iron bars from floor to ceiling in front of a frosted window. A matron, locked in a secure cage, surveyed the imprisoned women twenty-four hours a day. They were not allowed any physical freedom or recreation. "The most common and popular amusements," noted Taylor, "are loafing, chatting, swearing, talking shop, screaming and engaging in frequent but ineffectual riots." Considering this alternative, it is not surprising that many prostitutes registered with the Social Hygiene Clinic in order to receive lighter sentences when arrested and reassure customers that they were, in fact, "clean."[84]

As the city attempted to crack down on streetwalking, physical violence by white policemen against suspected African American prostitutes increased. One celebrated case concerned Gertrude Russian, a young African American woman who migrated to Detroit from Arkansas in 1924. A year later, Russian was arrested by three police officers for soliciting on the street. After throwing her in the patrol car, two of the officers left to investigate a nearby incident. The third officer, left alone with Russian, struck her with his blackjack. Russian retaliated by pulling out her knife and slashing the officer's torso; the officer then shot Russian in the leg. When the two other policemen returned, the wounded officer yelled, "She cut me!," and Russian replied, "He shot me!" The two officers jumped into the car and drove away swiftly. Bystanders heard two more shots as the car sped away, and Russian died at the hands of the Detroit police.[85] Russian's initial arrest for solicitation was likely based on her mere presence on the street at night. Her defiance of police harassment and her self-defense unfortunately cost her her life. This brutal incident illustrates the prevalence of police brutality in interwar Detroit and the risks associated with leisure work.

In the spectrum from reputable to disreputable occupations, prostitution lay at one extreme. By venturing into the informal economy, prostitutes faced losing their children, frequent arrest, and police brutality. Despite these negative consequences, some female migrants actively chose to engage in prostitution. Although reformers described a prostitute's life as one of vice and immorality that undermined community respectability, the reality was more complex. Buffet flats, a unique social institution developed by female entrepreneurs, were social centers that provided rooms and lodging as well as sex, gambling, and illegal liquor. Some women labored as prostitutes and domestic workers simultaneously, and others did service work in houses of prostitution. Madams earned respect from fellow leisure workers, male and female, and employed other women who were excluded from occupations in the formal job market. Wages of prostitutes also made their way into family economies and community institutions such as churches. These women had achieved some level of social mobility and did not necessarily view themselves as failures. In the minds of African American elites, however, the presence and visibility of prostitutes stymied efforts at racial uplift and the creation of a respectable community identity.

Storefront Churches and Numbers Running

Buffet flats and blind pigs were not the only establishments that undermined the bourgeois respectability of Detroit's East Side. African American reformers also targeted small storefront churches as social evils. Debates over respectable religious practices proliferated in postmigration Detroit as working-class African American women proselytized and expanded their southern Sanctified denominations in the urban North. As in the South, Sanctified churches in Detroit promoted ecstatic worship styles and incorporated secular music into their services. In contrast, the ministers in mainline denominations sought to foster churches that were models of decorum and self-restraint. This older conflict was amplified when female migrants founded new churches that were linked with Detroit's burgeoning informal economy. These new denominations, most notably the Spiritualists, infuriated mainline ministers, old settlers, and social reformers throughout the 1920s. Thus, religion in interwar Detroit was intertwined with the complexities of the labor market and changing definitions of respectability.

"Before I joined this church I used to play as big as fifty cents almost every day in policy and never hit," reported an African American resident of Detroit. "I went to visit the church, got a private reading. She told me to fast. I did three days and one day I played fifty cents and won. I then thought I ought to've played more so I put in fifty cents the next day and won. Nobody can tell me she's a fake. That woman knows what she's talking about."[86] "That woman" was an African American Spiritualist medium, part of a thriving informal economy of gamblers, bootleggers, and, ironically, church leaders that shaped urban life in interwar Detroit. The Spiritualist church led by this medium provided its parishioners with religious teaching and a space for ecstatic worship; less conventionally, it also offered tips on what numbers to play in the immensely popular game of policy. This coupling of sacred and secular space and practice was scorned by African American community leaders, who attempted to curtail the immorality and female disorder they associated with Spiritualism. For the Spiritualist mediums, however, participation in the informal economy and a religious sect led to cultural authority and economic independence. During the Great Migration and for the ensuing two decades, community leaders and female participants in the informal economy clashed over whether urban space would become a site of respectable public behavior.

Storefront churches became a primary target of reformers during the interwar period. Migrants, who often felt alienated in Detroit's larger congregations, founded small churches in empty storefronts. Women were the mainstay of these small churches, just as they were the mainstay of the African American church generally; yet unlike women in more established denominations, women in storefront churches took on leadership roles as ministers, elders, saints, and founders.[87] Women could exercise power and cultivate a sense of self-esteem through their religious worship in storefront churches. They also developed entrepreneurial and organizational skills as they established their churches and built up congregations. Community leaders, however, viewed storefront churches as outward-facing symbols of southern primitivism. Their negative image was further reinforced when Spiritualist mediums began to work in the informal economy by providing numbers that African American men and women gambled in hopes of "hitting big."

Although storefront churches had diverse theological stances, urban reformers tended to group them together as an unfortunate by-product of the Great Migration.[88] A 1926 study of Detroit's African American community reported:

> There are scattered in various sections of Detroit a group of churches whose services cannot be better described than as religious hysteria. . . . They are characterized by the clapping of hands, shouting, yelling, moaning, rolling, and the exhibition of general emotional instability. Many of the members work themselves to the point where they roll up and down

the aisles, shake their bodies, jump, fall into trances. . . . The individuals who form the membership of these hysterical churches are extremely ignorant, which fact is exemplified in the noisy and irreligious manner in which they carry on their services. There seems to be a general impression among them that shouting, dancing hither and thither, groaning, howling, crying protracted prayers, frantic embracing, the waving of handkerchiefs, groveling on the floor, the throwing up of arms, and similar "hysterical" outbursts are the sole means of expressing devotion to God. . . . Often those who shout, cry and groan the most and pray the longest prayers are the most immoral and hypocritical people in the community, who are constantly getting into trouble for stealing and for committing other crimes which are supposed to be contrary to their religion.

This same report described storefront churches' congregations as "made up entirely of the unskilled laboring classes" and "the masses of Negro migrants."[89] Thus, reformers viewed storefront churches, with their ecstatic style of worship, as emerging directly from southern migration and cultural practices that went against a community identity of respectability, self-restraint, and sexual control.[90] Community elites saw those who belonged to the storefront churches as being unable to adapt to northern urban styles of worship and chastised migrants for their immorality, licentiousness, and undisciplined religious behavior.

In this report, African American church leaders and members of the Detroit Urban League lumped all storefront churches together as a cohesive and equally reprehensible group. There were, in fact, at least two significant types of churches that tended to be housed in storefronts: Sanctified churches and Spiritualist churches.[91] The Sanctified church is a general label given to Holiness and Pentecostal churches in which "saints" distinguish themselves from other Christians. Historian Cheryl Townsend Gilkes has suggested that the Sanctified church provided African American women "an alternative model of power and leadership" in Protestantism.[92] Women in Sanctified churches had access to leadership roles as elders, pastors, bishops, and teachers of the gospel. Their role in Sanctified churches was also an extension of the role of women in the neighborhood. For example, Lucy Smith, the founder of the Church of All Nations in Chicago, explained how she became a successful church leader: "I started with giving advice to folks in my neighborhood. This made me realize how much a good talking does to many people. Very soon they started coming more and more, and so for the last seven years I've been preachin' to larger numbers."[93] This female religious authority was possible in the alternative space of the storefront, where neighbors congregated in a more democratic and less hierarchical setting than established AME and Baptist churches.[94]

The rituals of shouting, spirit possession, speaking in tongues, and dancing had their roots in small southern churches, and many of the women and men who founded churches and made up congregations were reacting against what they viewed as "citified ritual."[95] A study of storefront religions reported: "A man in Detroit, deacon in a store-front church, told one of the workers that he could not pray in a big church. Further inquiry . . . revealed that the deacon really meant that he could not pray in the big Detroit church as he was accustomed to praying in the rural church of the South. His long, loud prayer would not be in place in the semi-sophisticated Detroit church. He therefore organized a church of his own."[96] The implication here is that the deacon's storefront church was unsophisticated and his worship style inappropriate in a modern, urban church. Because of its clear southern origins, the Sanctified church fit well into the southern/northern dichotomy so prevalent in discussions of African American migration. Elites, therefore, identified the worship styles of Sanctified migrants as "primitive" and "irrational" because of their southern roots.

The conflation of "southern" and "primitive" with immorality, however, did not fit within the teachings of the Sanctified church, which emphasized adherence to a moral and "clean" life in order to reach a state of sainthood. Bishop Ida Robinson's Mt. Sinai Holy Church in Philadelphia, known for its large number of female preachers and elders, prohibited "fornication, adultery, lying, stealing, backbiting, straightening the hair, impure conversation, swearing, participation in athletic games, attendance at football, baseball games etc., drinking intoxicants, smoking, polishing the nails, wearing short dresses, attending motion pictures, chewing gum, gambling in any form."[97] Sanctified church teachings hardly appear to warrant the charge of "demoralizing practices," nor were these teachings a "dangerous element in the community." Rather, the female members and founders of these churches were carrying out a commitment to religious beliefs, religious education, morality, and community strength. Why, then, did their style of worship cause such concern? Perhaps because the act of ecstatic worship was in itself a reclaiming of the body as a site of what cultural critic Michael Dyson calls "the intersection of the sacred and the secular, the spiritual and the sensual."[98] An integral part of the teachings of bourgeois respectability was the exercise of physical self-restraint, an ideal that ecstatic worship openly rejected. By blurring the lines between restrained religious practices and music and dancing, which could also be found in a blind pig, storefront churches continued to complicate definitions of bourgeois respectability.

The constant references to the "demoralizing" influence of the churches also linked the "hysteric" actions of church members to other actions that would demoralize women, such as prostitution, "immoral" dancing, and public entertainment. "These highly emotional services seem to produce an unbalanced state which robs the individual of inhibitions which would make him a reasoning being and capable of self-control in sudden uprushes of passion," wrote Washington in 1920. "He, or she, would steal, indulge in crimes of violence and not infrequently in sexual crime."[99] The loss of self-control in the churches, then, could lead to the unraveling of control elsewhere in the community, and the ubiquitous physical presence of the storefront churches was evidence of this potential. Furthermore, reformers feared that, like other "disorderly" spaces, storefront churches would lead to dangerous and unregulated race-mixing. Sanctified and Spiritualist churches often welcomed white parishioners, some also from the South, to join their services. Thus, the parallel between a relatively integrated church congregation and a blind pig where white and black customers were welcomed became a powerful image of the dangers of race-mixing. In both spaces, white Detroiters would see African Americans in an emotional state, leading to the potential disintegration of a respectable public identity. Likewise, African American congregants would be exposed to the "worst element" of the white community, leaving them vulnerable to negative influences.

Elites viewed dancing and playing secular music (which observers often noted included tambourines, banjos, and guitars) as additional evidence of the immorality of religious practices in storefront churches. A contemporary social scientist reported: "When the praying is over, and everyone is 'in tune with the Infinite,' a song is started. . . . The musicians . . . pick it up, always in good jazz rhythm, usually to the tune of one of the classical blues songs." Dancers start to perform in response to the music: "The worshiper who first began to speak in tongues is seized with an urge to dance. She dances with great vigor, a dance which she executes with a degree of gracefulness that indicates she has put in a great deal of time practicing it. Others join in the dancing until a large number are participating, and the building is creaking from rhythmic vibrations."[100] This blending of spiritual and secular music common in storefront churches led to the development of gospel music, which combines secular blues and jazz styles with spirituals and traditional music. "While many churches within the black community sought respectability by turning their backs on the past, banning the shout, discouraging enthusiastic religion . . . ," argues historian Lawrence Levine, "the Holiness churches constituted a revitalization movement with their emphasis upon healing, gifts of prophecy, speaking in tongues, spirit possession, and religious dance."[101] The Sanctified storefront church was a medium for these forms of cultural expression that became immensely popular in African American interwar communities throughout the country.

African American elites attacked this blending of sacred and secular practices as dangerous in part because of the contradictions it revealed in the community's identity. Storefront churches were social spaces that encapsulated both the urban practices of commercialized leisure, dance, and music and the rural-based religious "primitivism" that more established denominations were striving to leave behind.[102] Reformers linked the dangers of the dance hall with the dangers of ecstatic worship; both were locations where individuals could express emotion and spirituality through physical enactments. Moreover, the integration of sacred and secular culture in the storefront churches was made possible by the urban setting itself. In the city, musicians, religious women and men, and entrepreneurs mingled, exchanging religious ideas, dance styles, and musical innovations. Their location in storefronts reflected the crowding in the East Side neighborhood, where larger buildings could not be found or built. Storefront churches, then, were quintessentially urban, products of the social integration that community leaders were trying to impede.

Sanctified churches also symbolized the continued strength of working-class notions of respectability. Church saints wore demure long white dresses, and community members viewed them as moral leaders and positive role models. This alternative respectable identity had caused serious rifts in the South between mainline denominations and the Sanctified church, and with massive urban migration, these rifts grew larger. Female saints were embodiments of sexual restraint, yet their worship styles and religious organizations directly undermined the bourgeois respectability promoted by established denominations. Thus, many elites and reformers saw the visible presence of Sanctified storefronts as a threat to racial uplift and an eyesore in the physical landscape.

A target perhaps worthier of attack by social reformers was the Spiritualist church, a storefront church whose popularity grew quickly in Detroit in the 1920s and 1930s. As in Sanctified churches, women predominated in the leadership and membership of Spiritualist churches; a study of three such churches in Detroit noted that 88 percent of the members were women.[103] African American Spiritualism is a highly syncretic religion combining elements of Catholicism, voodoo and hoodoo, black Protestantism, and Islam as well as the messianic and nationalistic movements of the 1920s and 1930s. Whereas the Sanctified church emerged from the Holiness revivals of the 1860s and 1870s, Spiritualist churches emerged in the 1920s in urban areas primarily in the North.[104] Detroit was a central hub for the growth of Spiritualism. In 1924, black Spiritualist leaders in Detroit founded the National Colored Spiritualist Association, which had split from its white counterpart, the National Spiritualist Association of Churches. By 1940, between 200 and 300 Spiritualist congregations existed in Detroit.[105] Spiritualist churches were in no way southern imports but urban institutions founded by women and men who sought both to make sense of the uncertainty inherent in urban life and to actively engage in the informal economy. Like Sanctified congregations, Spiritualist congregations were located in storefronts in neighborhoods dotted with gambling dens and houses of prostitution; however, congregants in Spiritualist churches did not set themselves apart from this world in their clothing or through moral proscriptions, as did congregants in the Sanctified church.

The largest Spiritualist church in Detroit during the interwar period was the Father Hurley sect, a church that provides a useful example of the syncretism of the churches and the inventiveness of their founders. After having received religious training at the Tuskegee Institute in Alabama, George Hurley arrived in Detroit in 1919 and joined a storefront Holiness church, Triumph the Church and Kingdom of God in Christ, originally founded in Georgia in 1906. After he rose through the ranks to become the Presiding Prince of Michigan, he began attending the meetings of a white Spiritualist organization, the International Spiritual Church. He then became a Spiritualist preacher, leaving the Holiness church to teach that God was a spirit and that "Heaven and Hell are states of mind, existing in the here and now."[106] Soon after joining the Spiritualist movement, Hurley reported that he had seen a vision of a "brown-skinned damsel" who turned into an eagle. Interpreting this as a sign that he should found his own church, in 1923, Hurley opened the Universal Hagar's Spiritual Church, and a year later, he established the School of Mediumship and Psychology.[107] In his church, Hurley combined aspects of Spiritualism, communication with the spirit world and the deceased, rituals of black Protestantism, magico-religious rituals such as the use of charms and incense, astrology, and an altar similar to altars used in Catholic services. Hurley was also an active member of Marcus Garvey's UNIA and incorporated black nationalism into his teachings. Hurley's personal history—his study of traditional religion in the South, his conversion to the Sanctified church in Detroit, and his eventual decision to found his own Spiritualist church—provides an alternative mapping of respectable religion. Hurley's traditional "respectable" religious roots were southern, whereas the urban North provided access to a variety of secular and sacred teachings that Hurley drew on to fashion his own church, which reformers viewed as "unrespectable." Notably, it was Hurley's northern migration that led to his participation in an alternative religious group that undermined the established denominations' hegemony.

Universal Hagar's Spiritual Church quickly gained a following among Detroit's African American women. Hurley, who conducted his services in the evening so members of other churches could attend, became particularly well known for two popular sermons: "The Purity of the Blessed Water," which he delivered while standing in a large tank of water up to his neck, and "Domestic Peace," in which he offered a "free reading to every woman who wished to know where her husband spent his spare time." [108] These sensationalist services rivaled other neighborhood entertainment and attracted large crowds. A Spiritualist church was a relatively innocuous space for an African American woman to visit, despite the protestations of community leaders. It was not as suspect as a poolroom or blind pig but could offer music, entertainment, and rituals that were thought to bring luck. In addition, women could maintain membership in established churches while still enjoying Hurley's evening sermons, further blurring the division between respectable and suspect religious practices.

By the late 1920s, Hurley faced competition from new Spiritualist churches in the city, most founded and run by African American women. Many of these church founders and the mediums who assisted them had learned their trade in Hurley's school. One female church founder, Dr. Johnson, remembered: "When I first came to Detroit from Red Bank, Georgia, I never dreamed that I would be doing this kind of work. You see my husband was a Baptist preacher in Red Bank and after his death, I sold out and came to Detroit. That was in 1919, just after the war. I met a lady at Providence Baptist Church and she asked me to go into this type of work. While I was in Georgia people were always coming to me for advice. I was a midwife and traveled in all parts late at night. . . . Well, before I opened this church I studied Spiritualism under Rev. Hurley. He tried to keep me with him by telling me I wasn't ready to head out for myself, but I tried it. Many people from his church came over here with me." [109] Johnson, like Hurley, left her traditional denomination behind when she migrated from the South, embracing Spiritualism after her arrival in Detroit. Her southern identity as a midwife and confidante translated into her authority as a preacher in Detroit. In Johnson's case, her identity as a Spiritualist leader was based on both her southern experiences and her willingness to strike out on her own in the North. Johnson employed business skills and entrepreneurial know-how to build a congregation and keep her church running efficiently. Such skills and the potential payoff of running a storefront church provided an alternative employment option for some African American women. In contrast to domestic service, which many African American women found demeaning, serving as a spiritual leader, even one vilified by some elites, provided income and self-respect.

By 1926, all but one of the Spiritualist churches in the United States were located in urban centers, and all of them incorporated secular services and eclectic teachings.[110] Indeed, one contemporary scholar called the Sanctified church the "most urbanized of the religious institutions."[111] Like the dance hall and the disorderly house, the Spiritualist church combined aspects of northern/urban and southern/rural culture. Although the church's ecstatic worship style and combining of secular and sacred music were pioneered by southern Sanctified churches, it was in the urban North that migrants such as Johnson came across messianic movements like Garveyism, a thriving gambling racket, and the many religious practices embraced by Spiritualism. Thus, the cultural practices introduced by Spiritualist leaders were products of the urban milieu.

The Spiritualist church's most urban, secular practice was the numbers business, which, along with bootlegging, formed the economic base of the informal economy. Numbers, policy, and mutuels were all forms of gambling that became immensely popular during the interwar period in African American urban communities. In numbers, a game that can be traced back at least to the eighteenth century in America, the winning number was determined by the last three digits of the daily stock market average or by using combinations of numbers based on racetrack results (mutuels), generally giving the bettor a 1 in 1,000 chance to win. Policy was a game in which numbers between 1 and 78 were randomly drawn twice a day. Detroiters believed that Casper Holstein, an immigrant from the Virgin Islands, first introduced policy in Harlem in the early 1920s.[112] Like many other cities, Detroit had banned gambling and lotteries in the late nineteenth century; however, policy, dice, and other types of gambling remained underground forms of entertainment in such institutions as the Waiter's and Bellman's Club, an African American gambling club dating from the early twentieth century.[113] In the early 1920s, the numbers business expanded as the Great Migration brought many more customers to urban centers.[114] In response, middle-class reformers sought to warn migrants of the dangers of the numbers game. These reformers were particularly concerned about the practice of numbers gambling on street corners, in speakeasies, in cigar stores, and in storefront churches. The allure of this informal economy, many in the Detroit Urban League and mainline churches felt, would undermine efforts to teach thrift and hard work to newly arrived southerners.

Middle-class concerns, however, did not slow the growth of the numbers game in the Prohibition Era. In 1925, Bill Mosley, who was to become the most important numbers baron in Detroit, opened his first large establishment, the Michigan. By 1935, there were thirty-five such houses in the city, many located in closed bank buildings. During the early years of the Great Depression, many considered the numbers banks more viable than legitimate financial establishments, so it was fitting that they took over the physical space of these formal economic institutions. It is particularly significant that Detroit's African American numbers bankers, unlike those in New York or Chicago, were able to retain control of their businesses against the encroachment of white mobsters. They formed the Associated Numbers Bankers in 1928 in response to an attempt by a group of Cleveland mobsters to break into the business. This association regulated the payment of winnings, divided the city into districts, organized payoffs to law enforcement officers, and hired its own lawyer.[115] The domination of black numbers bankers over this sector of the informal economy also ensured that the profits gained from whites who played the numbers would circulate in the African American community. Such organization in the informal economy also lessened competition among African American entrepreneurs, who otherwise might have engaged in turf wars, and decreased potential violence among rival bankers.

Each bank employed between 300 and 500 writers or runners who solicited bets on street corners, in barbershops, in poolrooms, and even door-to-door. Charleszetta Waddles was a typical numbers runner. She migrated to Detroit from St. Louis in the early 1930s and remembered walking "from house to house" picking up numbers to earn extra cash.[116] Like many runners, working for the numbers bank was only one source of income for Waddles. She also worked as a domestic servant and sold barbecue ribs in front of her home during the summer. Many barbers, beauticians, newspaper vendors, and lunch counter workers were expected to sell numbers as part of their work duties, thus blending formal and informal economic practices in African American businesses. One Detroit dentist who felt ambivalent about his role in the numbers game reported: "What can I do when one of my patients asks me to buy a number? If I don't play with him he'll go somewhere else for his dental work."[117] Given the difficulty of keeping a small business solvent, few business owners or professionals could afford to displease customers who expected to play numbers at their establishments.

A runner would usually receive 25 percent of his or her overall take, as well as a percentage of a winner's earnings. The runner gave his or her bets to a pickup person, who brought them to the house or bank. At the bank, cashiers, clerks, and checkers collected and counted the money and determined the results when the numbers were chosen. Like other illicit spaces in the community, the numbers banks were places of energy, bustle, and excitement in contrast to the demure reading rooms of the Urban League or the well-regulated club meetings of the YWCA. Numbers running was big business in Detroit, and many felt that the African American community could not have survived without it. A longtime Detroit resident remembered: "One of the largest businesses among Blacks is the numbers business. . . . Everyone played either the numbers . . . or policy or both. . . . It offered its players daily chances to pick up on a few quick bucks without any questions asked. It was very popular . . . because it was inexpensive and convenient; and perhaps because as it grew, it employed many blacks as runners and clerks who could not find more socially acceptable employment elsewhere."[118] Another resident recalled: "One of the areas that is not talked about, and why our dollars turned over in the community, was the black numbers business. Our local people here developed it, and we controlled it. Of course, it was considered illegal, but that money was put to good use in the black community, with the dollar turning over in the community five or six times. The pickup man, the lady that wrote the number, pickup man, the other pickup man, to the owner. The owner had all blacks working for his area."[119] The numbers business by the late 1920s, then, formed the basis of a local informal economy that was quickly becoming an accepted part of African American culture in Detroit. Many African Americans saw the numbers business as a positive force in the community rather than a detriment to the race.

Although many customers were women hoping to make ends meet by placing an average bet of ten cents per day, African American men were the primary direct employees of the business.[120] As in so many aspects of the informal economy, however, African American women found a way to participate in this subeconomy as more than just numbers players. The primary way in which women could gain income from numbers running was to work as independent Spiritualists or mediums in Spiritualist churches. Mediums were thought to have the power to foresee numbers or feel a person's "vibrations," which might indicate what number he or she should play. From their vantage point in the storefront churches, mediums were able to take part in a lucrative entrepreneurial business. Thus, the same mixing and crowding that had engendered storefront churches also encouraged a complex circulation of money in the community, a containment of the wages earned and spent by African American men and women. In addition to circulating male industrial wages, African American numbers runners profited from whites who played the numbers in Detroit, bringing new sources of revenue into the community.

Church members received numbers from mediums in several ways. Sometimes a medium would call out a hymn number that represented the number parishioners should play that day. This practice spread to other churches, whose members played hymn numbers because they felt they were lucky and therefore more likely to hit. More common in Spiritualist churches was a direct method usually conducted by the female medium. During the service, members who wished to receive numbers were asked to stand and march in single file past the medium, who stood near the altar. The medium would dip her hands in holy water, sprinkle each person, and whisper a number in his or her ear. Generally, the person would then give a quarter to a waiting assistant. One variation on this method was to create a fictitious funeral scene by placing the medium in a coffin. Parishioners would file past the coffin and receive their numbers from the "deceased," who was presumably able to communicate directly with the spirit world. Another common way to receive numbers was through the "test message." Before the service, assistants sold numbered cards to congregants for a quarter. At the appropriate moment during the service, the medium would call out a number and the person holding that card either stood or raised his or her hand. The medium would then relay the message she had received from the Holy Spirit. Occasionally, the message would include an actual number, but usually it was coded as a "key word" message. The words that were most clearly stressed by the medium were then looked up in a dreambook, an "encyclopedia of symbols," that translated the words into numbers.[121] A test message recorded verbatim from St. Ruth's Spiritualist Church in Detroit in 1935 read: "When I come in touch with you, all right, a beautiful *cloud* is over you. The spirit brings *cotton* to you. Watch yourself very carefully and you will succeed, said the spirit. A *bridge* is standing before you and you will be successful in crossing this condition."[122] The parishioner would look up "cloud," "cotton," and "bridge" in a dreambook and play the numbers they represented. Mediums might also encourage members to approach them after the service to receive a "special" message, for which they would expect to receive an additional donation.

Besides giving lucky numbers during church services, mediums worked as independent entrepreneurs, holding consultations to give numbers and advice on customers' personal lives.[123] Mediums also sold lucky products— incense, holy oil, candles, amulets, and charms—during Spiritualist services and private consultations. These products were thought to aid numbers players in choosing numbers that would hit, and contemporary newspapers were full of advertisements for them.[124] Thus, African American women were integral to what became known as the "confidence racket," a sub-economy that grew up around the numbers business by promising customers a better chance to win.

Mediums actively engaged in the informal economy, seeking potential customers through proselytizing. In the 1930s, an African American migrant who had arrived in Detroit in 1916 with her husband and three children reported that her family would have been destitute "if it weren't for that Spiritualist woman." She described her initial encounter with the Spiritualist:

> One day I was riding on the trolley and a spiritualist woman sat across from me. She kept watching me, and when I got off she got off behind me. She told me that I was a woman of great trouble. She said if I would come to her house she would tell me how to improve the condition that is around me. I went home and went to see her that night. . . . She called me and just gave me a box of incense and a candle and told me to burn the incense and look to the west each night before I go to bed. She told me to put the candle in the altar down stairs in the church and light it. It was supposed to bring me success. It seemed that my luck changed when I joined this church.[125]

Meeting on a streetcar, a "moving theater" of urban relations, and conducting their business in a storefront church, these two women engaged in a kind of commerce and religious practice that had their roots in both the North and the South but were quintessentially urban in flavor.[126]

Like prostitution, running disorderly houses, and other "illicit" occupations, mediumship was a form of service work that depended on the circulation of wages in the community and was part of the broader leisure industry. The consternation of community elites over the activities of Spiritualist churches also paralleled their attempts to discipline other forms of leisure work. Although reformers viewed Spiritualism as emblematic of a rural, primitive, southern past, the work of mediums in fact derived from a distinctly urban milieu. Mediums were trained in urban Spiritualist schools and combined their religious knowledge with business acumen to create a customer base among those who sought ecstatic worship without the condemnation of gambling or commercialized vice. When congregations became disillusioned with a medium who was not able to give them winning numbers consistently, the medium would often move to another location and the process would start again. Thus, the relative anonymity possible in the city was also conducive to the smooth running of a Spiritualist church.

The Spiritualist church could only engage actively in the informal economy if it did not condemn behavior that was considered reprehensible by the "saints," most notably gambling. Father Hurley stated in the 1930s: "I play numbers because it helps the poor fellow. Gambling is a God-sent blessing to the poor."[127] Many Detroiters felt that the Spiritualists' acceptance of gambling and other forms of "vice" was a welcome respite from the moralizing of other churches. Detroiters became attached to Spiritualist leaders who were able to help them financially and counsel them through personal crises and, in return, bought Spiritualist paraphernalia and encouraged others to attend services. Spiritualist churches, unlike Sanctified ones, encouraged ecstatic performance without the enforcement of strict codes of morality. African American women made use of this liminal space to gain authority and power in the community, as well as bringing in cash to the family economy.

The particular nexus of practices and beliefs that was the Spiritualist church could only have occurred in an urban center where lines of geographical identity and norms of respectability constantly shifted and crossed. Indeed, the syncretism of Spiritualist theology is an apt metaphor for the diverse cultural and political practices that the public discourse of bourgeois respectability failed to capture. Reformers who worked to separate illicit and licit behavior through racial uplift work did not take into account working-class African American women's own norms of respectability and self-worth. With few employment options available to African American women in the formal sector of the economy, their ability to garner income from the informal economy was a creative response to widespread job discrimination. This entrepreneurial spirit was expressed in another widely popular movement—Marcus Garvey's UNIA. Like Spiritualists, Garvey made use of diverse cultural symbols and rituals to communicate an ideology that empowered working-class African Americans. Economic nationalism was a central component of this emerging ideology and one that particularly attracted African American women seeking paid labor for themselves and their children.

Garveyism and Economic Nationalism

Reformers believed that African American women's participation in the UNIA's Detroit chapter, like their participation in storefront churches and numbers gambling, undermined a respectable community identity. However, elite attempts to discourage participation in the UNIA failed in the face of popular support for the charismatic movement. Garvey first launched his UNIA in the United States in the late 1910s. By 1922, the Detroit chapter was the second largest local chapter in the world, with over 5,000 members.[128] Garvey and his associates preached a powerful self-help ideology and urged black Americans to connect with their African roots. He countered feminine uplift ideology with nationalist rhetoric that placed black manhood at the center of racial reform. This trend was emblematic of the 1920s New Negro movement, which encompassed the artistic endeavors of the Harlem Renaissance and a newfound militancy in black politics. "The proponents of New Negro ideology," argues historian Deborah Gray White, "made race progress dependent on virile masculinity."[129] The UNIA introduced working-class African American migrants in cities like Detroit to this new militancy, arguing that black men should be more confrontational and less accommodationist. This emphasis on masculinity did not deter African American women from becoming active participants in the movement. It did, however, undermine the potency of racial uplift ideology and female respectability in 1920s Detroit by providing an alternative vision of masculine self-determination.

As in other major cities, Garveyites in Detroit held mass meetings, organized excursions and other leisure activities, and participated in large-scale parades along city streets dressed in the regalia of the UNIA. Female members wore the military uniforms of the Universal African Motor Corps and the white garments of the Black Cross nurses as they marched alongside men in military attire.[130] These women shifted the definition of respectable clothing from community leaders' focus on demure, restrained fashions to the uniform of the UNIA. In doing so, they advertised their allegiance to an organization that offered a viable alternative to female uplift ideology. The number of black Detroiters who made this choice is remarkable. UNIA marches and meetings attracted as many as 15,000 during the early 1920s.[131] In 1922, Garvey recalled his popularity in Detroit during a lecture tour: "I spoke two nights at a hall . . . wherein were jammed two thousand people to hear me each night, and there were turned away twice as many on both occasions."[132] Even after the movement's popularity waned at the end of the decade, many Detroiters stood by the UNIA. In 1927, after Garvey's imprisonment on fraud charges, organizers staged a silent parade and mass meeting on Detroit streets that attracted thousands of participants who walked behind a large portrait of Garvey mounted in an automobile.[133]

These public displays of racial nationalism and the widespread support for Garvey incensed community leaders who promoted racial integration and fostered racial uplift. Garvey's rejection of integrated leadership and light-skinned leaders was a direct attack on organizations such as the Urban League and women's clubs.[134] Detroit's black reformers had to work with white community leaders to obtain private funds for their organizations. Garvey denounced such alliances, arguing that African Americans should be entirely self-reliant. Garvey also attacked elitism based on skin color in the black community. For example, he claimed that Robert W. Bagnall, the pastor of St. Matthew's Episcopal Church, did not allow dark-skinned African Americans to join his Detroit congregation. He supposedly verified his allegation when "one Sunday night" he "attempted to occupy one of the empty seats, not so very near the front, and the effort nearly spoiled the whole service, as Brother Bob, who was then ascending the pulpit, nearly lost his 'balance' to see such a face so near the 'holy of holies'"[135] Exposing the hypocrisy of Detroit's religious leaders did not endear Garvey to elites, who saw themselves as the African American community's legitimate authority figures.

Community leaders responded to these attacks by pointing out that Garvey and his associates undermined images of respectability. Bagnall declared that Garvey was "a lover of pomp and tawdry finery and garish display."[136] Many elites argued that such "garish displays" would subvert the project of racial uplift, antagonize whites, and perpetuate segregation. In his autobiography, John Dancy recalled the image of Garvey with distaste: "They would have parades, and he would deck himself out in regalia and strut down the street."[137] The sharp contrast between the demure clothing recommended by the Dress Well Club and the uniforms of parade participants symbolized the disjuncture between middle-class championing of bourgeois norms of respectability and working-class support of black nationalism. The arrival of the UNIA signaled the first major challenge to Detroit's dominant reform organizations. Particularly appealing to African American women, however, was the UNIA's support of entrepreneurial projects in the African American community.

Economic nationalism was central to the ideology of the UNIA. "The UNIA is determined to lift the American Negro . . . to a higher plane of economic independence," declared Garvey in a 1919 editorial written in Detroit's Biltmore Hotel, "and to this effort every man and woman of color should lend support."[138] In Detroit, the income of the local UNIA division came from members' dues and donations, as well as restaurants, laundries, shoeshine parlors, drugstores, theaters, and gas stations run by Detroit Garveyites.[139] John Charles Zampty, the leader of Detroit's UNIA throughout much of the twentieth century, remembered that "we did all that was possible to raise our economic standards."[140] Indeed, the message of economic self-sufficiency was central to the Detroit chapter's popularity. Small businesses run by the UNIA that employed black women and men served as advertisements for the movement. Because of their limited employment opportunities, African American women found the possibility of economic self-sufficiency particularly appealing and flocked to UNIA rallies and meetings.

Detroit resident Ruth Smith remembered that in 1920 her mother "carried all of the girls into the UNIA." Smith, a longtime community activist, recalled that she "grew up in the organization. . . . Instead of going to church on Sunday, we would get up early and go to the Detroit division of the UNIA. . . . The UNIA people would gather and the hall would be crowded every Sunday and we had a time. In the halls they would be selling papers and pop. . . . The man I married was a member of the UNIA—my life, my ideas revolve around the organization."[141] The powerful speeches of the UNIA's female leaders such as Amy Jacques Garvey and Maymie L. T. De Mena also galvanized Garvey's female following. These leaders and the Detroit women who flocked to UNIA meetings and events contradicted Garvey's focus on masculinity. Deborah Gray White suggests that the women of the UNIA "persistently fought against the masculine impulse of the New Negro era."[142] Some women even found a voice in the UNIA to criticize Detroit's African American leaders. In a letter published in the UNIA newspaper, the *Negro World*, a Detroit woman expressed her anger at community leaders: "The so-called big Negroes will sell you out for a cigar that is bigger than his mouth to see the smoke as it goes up."[143]

The work of the UNIA celebrated and supported the racial pride and entrepreneurship that were central to a bottom-up notion of respectability among Detroit's African American women. Community elites, however, viewed Garveyism as a threat to the project of constructing a cohesive identity. Thus, conflicts over Garveyism illustrate a larger schism in the African American community about identity, appropriate occupations for women, and public displays of respectability. By parading down city streets in uniforms, denouncing racial integration, and criticizing traditional black leaders in public forums, the UNIA's mass membership weakened the dominance of John Dancy, Reverend Robert Bradby, and other African American reformers.

Conclusion

In the 1920s, Detroit's African American community leaders used a variety of spatial and geographic metaphors to construct a respectable public identity. As southern migrants arrived in Detroit, they were seen as an undifferentiated group of rural, naive, and disorderly workers who had to be taught how to live in an urban community. In the city itself, reformers discouraged these migrants from engaging in activities or frequenting establishments where people of different classes, races, and genders could mix freely. An elite focus on public displays of respectability as a reform strategy, however, had unintended consequences for race relations in Detroit. Reformers reinforced the respectable/licentious dichotomy by emphasizing bourgeois norms of respectability, making this vocabulary accessible to the white community. Whites continued to segregate African Americans in the East Side and identify them with the physical space they inhabited. The efforts to sanitize this space and the women who symbolized its possibilities and dangers were doomed to failure as long as racial segregation and workplace discrimination persisted. Thus, the assertion of a model female urban identity reinforced and reproduced images of women migrants as deviant, other, and eternally southern.

African American women, meanwhile, created their own social spaces and economic opportunities in Detroit that did not conform to a top-down notion of respectability. Spiritualism and numbers running, for example, were cultural practices that could not be easily encapsulated in a public identity of female respectability, thrift, and self-restraint. Nevertheless, women who worked as mediums, elders, and preachers in the Spiritualist church did not represent the polar opposite of bourgeois respectability. Rather, their codes of behavior incorporated aspects of African American culture that they felt *were* compatible with a respectable life: communal expressions of religious ecstasy and participation in the informal economy to support their families. Finally, ecstatic forms of worship flourished in Detroit not merely because of the southern rural roots of these practices but also because the city brought together women who had the ability and acumen to create new sacred spaces within the streetscape of the informal economy.

Ironically, the informal economy's growth negated the stereotype of the migrant as rural, backward, and unsophisticated. When a Packard pulled up to Mack Park and young African American men and women dressed in furs, wide-brimmed hats, silk suits, and short dresses stepped out to join the interracial crowd, African American leaders found they had to deal with a new problem different from the woman who left her house wearing a mother hubbard and head scarf. These migrants were neither dependable workers nor part of an educated cultured elite; they were working people who used all of the resources the city offered—licit and illicit. By the late 1920s, this diversification of social identities was also reflected in the movement of middle-class, and some working-class, African Americans out of the East Side. This movement, as well as the emergence of new clubs and social institutions, began to undermine bourgeois respectability's dominance as Detroit's primary reform strategy.

4 Neighborhood Expansion and the Decline of Bourgeois Respectability in the 1920s

The Negro problem in Detroit is of minor importance only as long as those residents realize that they are to be restricted to a type of area of their own. As long as they stay in this area it becomes typically Negro. The congestion and carefreeness of the population is evidenced by the ramshackle character of their buildings, by the multiplicity of their store types, by the picturesque gaudiness of their decorations and street attire, the teeming colorfulness of their street life, the lounging and lolling groups of all ages, sexes, and colors who bring to Detroit a landscape type far different from that which existed in the same region, on the same streets, and veritably in the same buildings only a few short years ago.

    Jerome Gale Thomas, "The City of Detroit"

In 1928, white social scientist Jerome Gale Thomas conflated the physical space that African Americans inhabited with their personal characteristics. This conflation of the "ramshackle character of their buildings" with the "picturesque gaudiness" of their persons concerned African American leaders throughout the 1920s. Increasingly, however, those leaders did not inhabit the same physical space as the working-class migrants whose behavior they attempted to modify in the years following the Great Migration. As a new spatial order more accurately reflected an emerging class order in the African American community, reformers no longer had the same motivation to "clean up" the congested East Side neighborhood. Yet middle-class African Americans' movement into new neighborhoods challenged racial segregation and white supremacy in interwar Detroit. The white community responded swiftly to black mobility by instigating a series of violent housing riots designed to terrorize black Detroiters.

    The most notorious of these incidents resulted in a criminal trial that placed African Americans squarely in the public eye. On 8 September 1925, a young woman from one of Detroit's old-settler families and her well-educated husband, a practicing doctor, attempted to move into a predominantly white neighborhood on Detroit's West Side. They were met by a mob of whites throwing stones and shouting racial insults. In self-defense, Ossian Sweet, his brothers, and his friends shot into the crowd, killing one man and wounding another. The police arrested all African Americans present, including Gladys Sweet, for first-degree murder. The resulting trial brought the Sweets notoriety in the national African American community. Black newspapers presented Sweet and his brothers as heroes who had the courage to defend their home and family during a time of deepening racial animosity. The Sweets' elite and cultured status, their unblemished respectability, became the central focus during the ensuing trial for murder. Although employing the discourse of bourgeois respectability had not substantially helped African American women find employment in white-collar and industrial work, the NAACP successfully linked respectability with citizenship and the rights of manhood during the Ossian Sweet trial. The Sweet case illustrates how a masculine self-defense of a female domestic sphere became a central component of a remade discourse of respectability. This masculine emphasis had wider appeal in the late 1920s than a discourse of bourgeois respectability that focused on female self-restraint.

Central to the Sweet case was the development and codification of racial segregation in Detroit. As middle-class, and some working-class, African Americans migrated from their East Side neighborhood to find new and better housing in the city, they encountered powerful white resistance. As a result, African Americans celebrated the movement out of the East Side as evidence of racial progress and the lessening of spatial segregation and racial discrimination. The new neighborhoods created by black migrants tended to be more class-specific than the older East Side neighborhood. In a contradictory discourse, John Dancy and other African American leaders praised the middle-class West Side neighborhood where many of Detroit's African American professionals lived as visible proof that blacks could be entrusted with keeping a community clean, well groomed, and crime-free. Meanwhile, working-class developments outside the city limits offered a more problematic picture. Some elites regarded the "shacks" and gardens established by working-class migrants on undeveloped land as a return to a rural southern lifestyle and feared that the lack of middle-class role models in these communities would stymie reform efforts.

The African American community's increasing class stratification was reified on Detroit's maps with the increase of suburbanization. This stratification was also reflected in the growing differentiation of women's clubs, reform organizations, churches, and charity groups. By the late 1920s, a vibrant female public sphere in Detroit encapsulated a variety of activities and viewpoints that tended to be divided along class lines. New urban identities—such as that of the businesswoman—emerged, and women established corresponding organizations and clubs that expanded the ranks of the middle class. Thus, by the eve of the Great Depression, Detroit's African American community had become spatially and socially stratified along lines of occupation, wealth, status, and geographic location. Although female uplift ideology continued to be a potent discourse, embodied in the case of Gladys Sweet and in middle-class women's clubs, migrants were remaking respectability by emphasizing the need for masculine self-defense. As class differentiation became more spatially pronounced—and materially real—the need to define public identity on the East Side lessened. In a similar way, with more class differentiation, there was less need to imbue a classless lower group with respectable middle-class norms. Thus, by the end of the 1920s, the proliferation of social identities in the city lessened the effectiveness and appeal of older reform efforts and class markers. Underlying these trends was the infiltration of "scientific" norms of charity and reform into the African American community, setting the stage for the intervention of the federal government during the 1930s.

New Neighborhoods and Social Stratification

Although we associate suburbanization and middle-class flight with the postwar world, by the late 1920s, middle-class African Americans were already moving out of the crowded East Side. This movement helped facilitate the decline of an ideology of respectability as the cornerstone of racial uplift and reform. Much of the effort to contain and reform vice in the African American community in the 1910s and 1920s was expressed in a language of crowding. The mixing of classes, genders, and races in unsupervised spaces of leisure was invoked by religious leaders and reformers as debasing the image of the entire community. As African Americans moved into new neighborhoods, the problem of crowding became less prominent in reform discourse. The dispersal of the African American community created a physical mapping of class identity in the city. This mapping was never stable as elite African Americans resented wealthy entrepreneurs in the informal economy who purchased homes in middle-class neighborhoods. More important, whites ferociously resisted attempts to desegregate their neighborhoods, limiting the ability of African Americans to create new communities.[1]

Detroit experienced phenomenal growth in the early decades of the twentieth century, both in population and in size. One result of this growth was the rapid expansion of suburban communities on the outskirts of the city. The development of streetcar transportation and the increasing availability of automobiles made the city's periphery both more accessible and more attractive.[2] The central business district was no longer considered the most desirable residential area, as whites began to develop suburban neighborhoods.[3] For black Detroiters, the dividing line throughout the interwar period was Woodward Avenue. Although the northern and eastern boundaries of the East Side neighborhood would expand, Woodward was a racial line that few would cross. The creation of a West Side African American neighborhood that crossed over Woodward Avenue, then, became a major point of pride among racial reformers. This community traced its roots to the late 1910s, when middle-class southern migrants began to buy homes in the area and established it as an enclave in which the majority of homes were owned and lodgers were a relative rarity.[4] "This was an attractive neighborhood," recalled John Dancy, "and the Negroes who moved there took great pride in their achievement and determined to keep their homes on a high level."[5]

In order to maintain the "high level" of the new middle-class African American enclave, a group of African American women formed the Entre Nous Club. Wielding the slogan "The West Side Is the Best Side," the self-appointed female caretakers of the neighborhood organized cleanup campaigns and offered awards to homemakers whose property met their standards of cleanliness. Contemporaries noted that the new African American residents had improved the housing and the adjoining property deserted by fleeing white residents.[6] Block clubs were formed to keep an eye on neighbors and maintain high property values. Club members reported "slovenly" neighbors to the Urban League, which reprimanded the irresponsible homeowners.[7] This need to police behavior and appearance in a relatively affluent neighborhood reflects the Entre Nous Club members' belief that wealth did not always translate into responsible homeowning. Given the income generated by numbers running or blind pig proprietorship, it is likely that a few of the new homes bought on the West Side were owned by members of the "sporting" class. Despite clubwomen's concerns, the West Side became known as a model neighborhood. "It was a place that gave me a sense of right and wrong," remembered Berry Gordy, "a sense of safety in the family, a sense of love and kinship in a community where being good was actually a good thing to be."[8] To ensure that the West Side remained a community where "good" and "bad" were clearly delineated, Urban League workers and female club members continued to organize contests and cleanup campaigns throughout the interwar period.[9]

For southern migrants, the movement across Woodward Avenue entailed a second, class migration that linked social and spatial mobility. Describing the residents of the West Side in 1920, Forrester B. Washington said: "The majority of them are migrants who have been in Detroit over two years, who have worked in the factories of this city, earned good wages, saved a portion of them and who have emerged from the East side District class into the 'home owning group' of the West side."[10] The social mobility that was symbolized by the movement across Woodward Avenue was recalled by Frederick N. Cureton, who migrated with his family from South Carolina in 1921. His family's "escape" from the East Side to buy a home on the West Side was a prominent memory for Cureton. "They had two or three families, or more, living in that house," recalled Cureton, describing his East Side residence. "I had an aunt downstairs. I had an uncle; I had cousins started coming in from the South. The first thing I know we ain't got a house without twelve people in the house. And then when they got money enough to get them a house, they broke away."[11] One by one, the extended family members "broke away" from the overcrowded East Side to buy their own homes on the West Side or the new working-class suburbs. But Cureton noted: "Everybody over here was not able to put a down payment on a house, so they were not able to escape. They had mishaps, and families, and they just stayed there."[12] Those who stayed and those who "escaped" were increasingly differentiated by the spatial distance between their neighborhoods as well as their occupations, clubs, and church memberships. This "escape" to the West Side, however, was often partial. Many West Siders continued to have relatives on the East Side, and businessmen and professionals who worked in the African American West Side community had clients and customers on the East Side.

By the mid-1920s, the West Side district had approximately 7,200 African American residents, and it had become the favored neighborhood for middle-class and elite African American Detroiters.[13] Working-class African Americans who could not afford to buy homes on the West Side, however, had few opportunities to move out of the overcrowded East Side into other urban neighborhoods due to white resistance. By the early 1920s, white city residents had developed a variety of strategies to prevent racial integration, ranging from legal action to violence. Although the U.S. Supreme Court declared zoning ordinances that restricted residents by race unconstitutional in 1917, the Michigan Supreme Court's 1923 *Parmallee v. Morris* decision upheld a private restrictive covenant that prohibited the use or occupancy of a residence by an African American in the Russel Woods subdivision northwest of the city. This decision established a precedent that stood until 1948. Neighborhood improvement associations and realtors had the legal right to draft contracts that excluded persons of a particular race or religion. In the case of the Russel Woods subdivision, African Americans and blind pigs were both excluded—a linkage of race with criminal activity that was of primary concern to African American elites.[14] Restrictive covenants enforced by neighborhood improvement associations proved fairly effective in keeping African Americans out of newly developed neighborhoods by placing restrictions directly on deeds when whites first bought the land. In more established areas where homeowners had to enter into joint agreements, such as the West Side, African Americans were more likely to be able to infiltrate a previously white neighborhood. The development of suburbs in the Detroit metropolitan area, therefore, was synonymous with the development of racial segregation.

White resistance to African American mobility led to an increasing number of housing riots by the mid-1920s. In response, Urban League director John Dancy and other community leaders began to search for vacant property on the city's outskirts that could be developed for African American families. Henry Stevens, the chairman of the Detroit Urban League's board of directors, owned one such parcel of land north of Eight Mile Road. He agreed to subdivide the land and make it available for African Americans to purchase.[15] Unfortunately, few African American residents were able to obtain bank loans to build homes, and fewer still had adequate savings to build homes outright. Therefore, many families simply built whatever structures they could on their lots. With no running water, paved roads, or electricity, life on Eight Mile Road was initially quite primitive, leading to concerns by social workers that some migrants were "reverting" to their southern roots. In 1926, one social worker stated: "Living in subdivisions aggravates the health problem and people who adopt it slip into the old southern rural ways of doing things."[16] An African American real estate dealer argued that migrants who moved to subdivisions tended to "remain in a static condition, raising vegetables."[17] More accurately, southern migrants were using gardening and building skills they had developed in the South to create a northern community that was not part of an inner-city neighborhood. For those who viewed urban assimilation as part of the project of racial uplift, however, working-class families growing their own vegetables and living without "modern" conveniences signaled a regression to a southern "primitive" past.

In addition to the concern that the Eight Mile Road suburb kept migrants in a state of "southernness," elites worried about the lack of a middle-class influence in the new subdivision. "The presence of large isolated groups of Negroes in an area is apt to cause a lack of care of property," argued an African American social worker who visited the subdivision. "If they lived in better communities, suggestion and public opinion would force them to keep up their standards of property and conduct."[18] "Public opinion" referred to both middle-class African Americans who disciplined the behavior of their working-class neighbors and the white audience who observed the neighborhoods and made judgments about the community's worth. Left to their own devices, a relatively homogeneous group of African Americans who worked as industrial laborers, domestic servants, or entrepreneurs in the community would be "free" to create their own identity, which would then be communicated to whites. The fear that this identity would be a disorderly one without "standards of property and conduct" reflected a strong middle-class belief in the need for social control. Working-class suburbs were, suggested reformers, in dire need of an Entre Nous Club.

Eager to escape the overpriced and overcrowded housing of the East Side, African Americans flocked to the new development. Eight Mile Road quickly became a predominantly working-class subdivision, with male workers taking the streetcar to industrial jobs at the River Rouge Ford plant or other automobile factories. Their wives and daughters worked as domestic workers, grew vegetable gardens, raised small livestock, and ran businesses. A case record from the mothers' pension department of the city describes a typical female resident of Eight Mile Road. This woman was born in Georgia and worked in a laundry in Macon at the age of twelve. In 1915, she migrated to Cleveland with her parents, where she was able to find laundry work. After her marriage, she and her husband moved to Detroit, supporting her five children by doing laundry in her mother's home. In 1924, she moved to Eight Mile Road, where, because of the distance from the city, it was difficult to take in washing. Instead, she arranged to do day work in the city for two days a week, dropping her children off at her mother's home. Welfare workers reported that her home in the Eight Mile Road development was "a shack . . . set upon posts and has four small rooms."[19] This woman was typical of early female residents in the new black subdivisions—she was part of a larger family group that had to sacrifice convenient access to wage labor to live outside the city. In order to escape the overcrowded and exploitative conditions of the East Side, she was willing to move and take a first step toward owning her own home. Despite the concern of community leaders in Detroit that the Eight Mile Road suburb would "stagnate," steady wages from automobile workers (supplemented by wages brought in by women such as the one above) and continual community activism soon transformed the pioneer conditions of the subdivision.

The growth of the community—the activism of the residents in demanding city services, the buying of land and building of homes—was a powerful story that one Detroit resident, Burniece Avery, immortalized in a novel, *Walk Quietly through the Night and Cry Softly*. Many middle-class African Americans thought the subdivision's residents would be unable to obtain city services without the aid of a professional class. Avery and her neighbors, however, proved these African American elites wrong. In her autobiographical novel, the Parker family migrates from the South and, after a brief stay in Detroit, settles on Eight Mile Road. One female member of the family becomes a traveling evangelist, and others become involved in Marcus Garvey's UNIA. Notably absent from Avery's narrative are the Detroit Urban League, visiting social workers, male ministers, and women's clubs. Her characters derive their social activism and community strength from alternative working-class institutions.[20]

Despite the absence of middle-class role models, a 1927 article in *Opportunity* noted that the Eight Mile Road community had "improved in general appearance because of the cooperation in a 'Better Lawns' Committee among the families residing there."[21] Working-class women living in a newly established neighborhood used similar strategies to improve their communities to those of their middle-class counterparts on the West Side. Indeed, the community identity presented in the Eight Mile Road development in many ways conformed to the community identity presented by West Side residents in terms of public displays of cleanliness and orderliness. The militancy shown by Eight Mile Road residents in demanding their rights from a reluctant metropolitan government, however, differed from the more passive strategy of the Urban League and was remarkably successful.

Alice E. M. Cain Newman, one of the early Eight Mile Road residents, remembered the neighborhood with pride: "The community, as far as I can remember, was all black, and all had built their own homes. They were frame houses. It was very nice. It was safe, it was clean, and the businesses were black-owned."[22] Newman's father owned one of those businesses, a small restaurant on Eight Mile Road that sold hot dogs, chili, and her grandmother's sweet potato pies. A nearby restaurant that specialized in barbecue was owned and run by an African American woman. These recollections of the community starkly contrast with contemporary descriptions by social workers and reveal another potentially important dynamic in the development of African American satellite communities. In all-black suburbs, African American women could exercise their entrepreneurial skills. Land and housing were cheaper, and the relative isolation of residents created a guaranteed customer base. Newman herself earned a quarter a week dancing in a local stage show.[23] Indeed, the Eight Mile Road community transgressed the southern label that Urban League workers and other elites continued to place on migrants. The neighborhood could not be characterized as a southern rural-style settlement because most of the male workers labored in the automobile industry, riding the interurban rail lines to River Rouge and other factory destinations daily. Many of the early Eight Mile Road residents also employed uplift strategies that emphasized cleanliness, neighborhood development, and economic strength. In the Eight Mile Road community, the housekeeping skills of women were extended to the larger neighborhood, much as they were on the West Side.

The second largest working-class satellite community was Inkster, which became a popular destination for African American East Siders in the mid-1920s. The availability of land for purchase in Inkster was announced in Detroit's black churches, and John Dancy played a large role in publicizing the new suburb.[24] Like the Eight Mile Road subdivision, Inkster initially had no sewer, water, or electricity for incoming residents. What Inkster did have, however, was its own "benevolent despot" in Henry Ford, who saw the development of Inkster as an opportunity to create a model town for African American workers. Although the commute from Inkster to River Rouge was further than the commute from the East Side, it was a more direct trip via public transportation on the interurban line. During the depression, Ford spearheaded a massive reform effort in Inkster that provided food, better housing, and other aid to unemployed workers. This relationship was an extreme example of Ford's paternalism toward the African American community. However, as Howard O'Dell Lindsey has argued, Inkster's African American residents made use of their access to Ford in the 1930s and 1940s to gain much-needed city services. Indeed, in both the Eight Mile Road development and Inkster, the creation of satellite communities facilitated the political empowerment of African American residents who demanded basic services from a reluctant white suburban populace. As in Detroit, it was African American women like Burniece Avery who often spearheaded these community movements.

African Americans who moved to isolated enclaves in Detroit such as the Highland Park area had the most difficulty creating safe spaces for themselves and their children. Joseph Coles, for example, worked at a Highland Park factory and lived in the neighborhood. "There weren't too many Negroes. We had a little colony," remembered Coles. "This was the twenties. . . . There

was a lot of racism back in those days. You couldn't eat in restaurants. . . .
And I couldn't go to the theater down here on Monroe. Most of the theaters
downtown, you couldn't sit in the front rows."[25] Coles and others like him
had to negotiate racism daily after they moved out of the East Side to be
closer to their workplaces. Increasingly, racial violence ensued when African
Americans attempted to move out of segregated neighborhoods in search
of decent housing. The most dramatic of these cases involved a middle-class
family whose struggle marked a defining moment for the city of Detroit and
African Americans throughout the country.

Ossian Sweet and the Political Uses of Respectability

In 1926, African Americans throughout the country turned their eyes to
Detroit when a landmark case came to trial. In June 1925, Ossian Sweet
purchased a house in the northeast section of Detroit, a largely white immigrant neighborhood. Because the previous owners had been an interracial couple, Sweet's fears of a violent reaction from the neighborhood
were allayed. However, the residents had thought their former light-skinned
African American neighbor, Edward Smith, was white. When they heard
the house had been sold to an African American family, they organized the
Waterworks Improvement Association, named for the nearby Waterworks
Park. Like other neighborhood associations organized in Detroit during this
period, this group was formed exclusively for the purpose of maintaining
a "whites only" neighborhood. Cognizant of the growing resistance in the
neighborhood and hopeful that the tumult over a number of racial incidents
in the city that summer would die down, the Sweets decided to delay their
move until September.

On 8 September 1925, Sweet and his family moved into their house after
requesting police protection from the local precinct. Along with his wife
Gladys, Ossian was joined by his brothers Otis, a dentist, and Henry, a college
student, and three friends. They brought along a large supply of food, nine
guns, and ammunition. Although crowds formed near the house sporadi-
cally the first day, the night passed relatively peacefully. The crowd, however,
became increasingly belligerent the next day, so the Sweets asked four more
friends to help protect their property. When Otis Sweet and a friend arrived from work in a taxi that evening, they were stoned by the white crowd
and raced into the house as white residents screamed racial epithets at them.
The mob then began to hurl stones at the house, shattering an upstairs window. The Sweets and their friends took up firing positions inside, and shots
rang out both from the house and from the guns of police stationed nearby.

A member of the mob, Leo Breiner, was shot in the back and killed, and another man, Erik Halberg, was shot in the leg. Police immediately entered the house and arrested all eleven residents for murder.

The housing riot sparked by the Sweet family's move into northeast Detroit was one of many during the 1920s. As in the Sweet case, most of these riots involved relatively affluent African Americans who wished to escape the overcrowded East Side. For example, in June 1925, Dr. Alex L. Turner bought a house in an all-white northwest Detroit neighborhood. When the Turners attempted to move into their new home, a mob of 5,000 jeering and stone-throwing whites greeted them. They escaped only under police protection. The leader of the Tireman Avenue Improvement Association, who had orchestrated the ousting of the Turners, helped establish the Waterworks Improvement Association, whose members formed the bulk of the 9 September mob.

A few weeks after the Turner affair, an African American undertaker, Vollington A. Bristol, moved into a home he had built in a white neighborhood. After several nights of violent demonstrations, he was forced from the house. When it appeared that Bristol might hold out against the mob, a white woman reportedly stood on a box and shouted: "If you call yourselves men and are afraid to move these niggers out, we women will move them out, you cowards!"²⁶ Although large-scale race riots such as those in the Red Summer of 1919 tended to be incited by white working-class men, many small-scale housing riots during the interwar period were led by white women—residents of the neighborhoods that African American families were attempting to desegregate. In the Sweet case, the prosecution called many white women as witnesses, which reflected either their overrepresentation in the mob that attacked the Sweets' house or the prosecution's belief that they were more credible than male witnesses. Regardless, it is clear that white women played a major role in maintaining lines of residential segregation in Detroit. In the workplace, white women's hate strikes stymied African American women's occupational mobility; in the neighborhoods, their riotous behavior stymied African American women's spatial mobility.

In addition to the housing riots, in the two years before the Sweet case, fifty-five African Americans were killed by Detroit police with impunity. Besides the unrelenting police brutality and mob violence, during 1924 and 1925, the Ku Klux Klan openly ran a mayoral candidate, Charles S. Bowles, in a series of election campaigns. In 1924, Bowles nearly won the mayoral election as a write-in candidate. His opponent, John W. Smith, who was supported by the African American and European immigrant communities, was declared the winner only after the city disqualified 15,000 ballots. The Saturday prior to this election, the largest meeting of Klansmen and Klanswomen in Detroit's history took place in a field in nearby Dearborn.[27] The timing of the series of housing riots that led up to the attack on the Sweet family, then, was hardly accidental but indicative of an increase in racial tension and violence in the rapidly growing city.

As well as being emblematic of white racism, the Sweet case encapsulated several powerful themes in the discourse of racial uplift ideology. The home as a center of community, social mobility, family, and safety had been a powerfully resonant theme in much writing on racial uplift and social reform since the nineteenth century. In addition, the home and neighborhood were locations of female respectability, where women could display their skills as housekeepers and mothers and use them throughout the community in organizations such as the Entre Nous Club. Agreement on the importance of "home" in the community, even in the relatively divisive 1920s, was widespread among African American women of all classes, and it continued to be a linchpin of reform efforts. Indeed, reformers targeted the home and neighborhood as the sites of the formation of a respectable community identity. Therefore, as in the nineteenth century, the home was a location of class convergence over female respectability during the interwar period. When the Sweets' home, the symbolic location of the community's strength, was attacked, it struck a powerful chord among all African Americans.

A concomitant part of domestic ideology was the importance of a man's right to defend his home and the women in it. Although this aspect of domesticity was not highlighted during the Progressive Era, after World War I, discussions of male citizenship and masculinity as "rights" became more prominent. For example, in a letter to Reverend Robert Bradby, a field secretary of the NAACP wrote: "Whenever the price of our rights is made to be riot or death in any other form, we would prefer to pay the price rather than to give up the rights of man."[28] When whites treated African American soldiers, and later veterans, with scorn on American soil, they attacked not only the race but also the masculinity and citizenship of the soldiers. Indeed, Garveyism, with its uniforms and parades, displayed masculine pride and military discipline that engendered respect that was not given to African Americans by the white community during the 1920s.[29] Masculinity was defined, in part, by the ability of men to "protect" women in the domestic sphere and the rights of men to the perquisites of citizenship.[30] The Sweet case provided potent evidence that African American men could and would defend their homes and demand their rights as patriarchs and citizens. One early NAACP press release stated: "If in Detroit the Negro is not upheld in the right to defend his home against eviction at the hands of a riotous mob, then no decent Negro home anywhere in the United States will be secure." [31] African Americans were committed to fighting for the security of their homes and the corresponding rights of male citizenship. This ideology of self-determination and self-defense had widespread appeal in the late 1920s, uniting elite reformers with the migrant community.

The Sweet family itself represented a unity of social forces in the African American community. Gladys Sweet was from an old-settler family, the Mitchells. She had attended Detroit's Teacher College and was described as well dressed and attractive by the press.[32] She married Ossian Sweet, a doctor, in 1922, uniting her older elite family with a new middle-class one. Ossian Sweet was born in Florida and educated at Wilberforce and Howard Universities. In 1921, he set up business in Detroit as part of a migration of black businessmen and professionals. Gladys and Ossian traveled to Europe in 1924, and Ossian studied in Paris and Vienna, a fact brought up a number of times by the defense during the trial. The Sweets belonged to St. Matthew's Episcopal Church, a relatively elite congregation, and Ossian was a member of the Nacirema Club, an organization of educated African American men in Detroit.[33] Thus, the Sweets and their extended family were the epitome of the respectable African American middle class.

Although the Sweets were an established middle-class family, their worldview, revealed in trial documents, reflected a growing militancy in the African American community in the 1920s. Ossian Sweet was a follower of Marcus Garvey, a figure his minister at St. Matthew's, Robert Bagnall, derided. In one particularly interesting document, Gladys Sweet listed for the defense lawyers the publications she and her husband read regularly and the national events they followed closely. The Sweets read a variety of African American newspapers and journals, including the *Crisis* (the official publication of the NAACP), the *Messenger* (a socialist publication edited by A. Philip Randolph and Chandler Owen), the *Chicago Defender*, the *Pittsburgh Courier*, and the *Detroit Independent*.[34] Although these periodicals differed somewhat in content, they were all "race papers" owned and edited by African Americans and read largely by the black community.[35]

The Sweets' militancy was in part a reaction to the racial violence that erupted immediately following World War I. Gladys's uncle was murdered in the Chicago race riot of 1919, and she remained shaken by the event. When Ossian attended Howard University, he experienced the devastation of the 1919 Washington, D.C., riot firsthand. During the trial, he related seeing an African American man dragged from a streetcar and beaten. After their arrival in Detroit, the Sweets followed the city's housing riots closely, blaming both white residents and white police officers for not protecting the African American families involved. "After Dr. Turner's affair it was quite common to hear from time to time that mobs had gathered at the homes of colored people," recalled Gladys, "and either commanded them to move or began throwing missiles with the hope of damaging their property and of intimidating the negroes."[36] For the working-class African Americans who supported them, it was the Sweets' willingness to defend themselves openly against a white mob rather than their "respectability" that made them appealing heroes in a city rife with racism.

Why, however, were the Sweets' lawyers so interested in their perceptions of race relations before the riot and shootings? This was part of an innovative strategy employed in their defense. If the lawyers could show that Ossian Sweet's "state of mind" leading up to the riot was influenced by the knowledge of previous racial violence, they could explain his actions. "When I opened the door I saw the mob and I realized I was facing the same mob that had hounded my people throughout our entire history," stated Ossian during the trial. "I was filled with a fear that only one could experience who knows the history and strivings of my race."[37] During the trial, the courtroom became a classroom for jurors and spectators, who were instructed in the "history and strivings" of African Americans. By establishing the Sweets' irrefutable respectability, the lawyers hoped that no jury could deny their rights to citizenship and self-defense. This remarkable defense was devised by the national leaders of the NAACP and executed by a team of lawyers headed by the famous white defense lawyer, Clarence Darrow. Their use of a discourse of respectability was reported by observers to be no less than brilliant.

The NAACP's decision to grant the Sweet case financial and legal support was a key component of a three-pronged national attack on segregation. In 1917, the NAACP successfully argued in *Buchanan v. Warley* that the state could not pass legislation limiting individuals' right to own or use property because of their race. Just as the Sweet case began in Detroit in 1925, the NAACP was arguing *Corrigan v. Buckley* in the U.S. Supreme Court to overturn a residential covenant restricting African Americans in Washington, D.C. Having addressed housing segregation sanctioned by the state and housing segregation sanctioned by private agreement, it hoped to win a third battle against segregation by mob violence by defending the eleven accused in Detroit. Thus, almost thirty years before *Brown v. Board of Education*, the NAACP was directly challenging both legal and extralegal attempts to draw a color line in American towns and cities.[38] Skillfully deploying the language of middle-class respectability and male citizenship, the NAACP used the Sweet case to fight against northern urban segregation.

African Americans in many communities outside of Detroit also rallied to support the Sweet defendants, whose case had captured national attention. Events were held in major cities to raise the money necessary for the defense. After a mass fund-raising meeting in New York City, Walter White, assistant secretary of the NAACP, telegrammed Reverend Bradby, president of the local chapter: "It is felt here in New York that in making the fight you are making for Dr. Sweet you are fighting the battle of every one of the eleven million Negroes in the U.S."[39] Fund-raising efforts in Detroit gained much support throughout the community. "The people here are very much stirred," wrote White from Detroit immediately after the riot.[40] Indeed, the trial brought together disparate groups in the community in a common cause. In September 1925, the *Detroit Independent* reported: "Every organization in the city, including the NAACP, the Knights of Ethiopia, UNIA, churches, fraternities, and entire Detroit has turned their money and attention on this case of the martyrs of our city."[41] This alliance across class and ideological lines to support the defense of the Sweets presaged the alliances built during the 1930s, another period of tremendous crisis in Detroit's African American community. The alliance was further facilitated by the absence of the most condescending aspects of a middle-class discourse of respectability in the speeches in defense of the Sweets. UNIA followers and middle-class professionals understood the significance of spatial segregation for the future of the community and were fighting a common enemy. "The price of Dr. Sweet's defense," argued the *Detroit Independent*, "is the price of the defense of every colored man's rights in Detroit."[42] Defending "colored man's rights" rather than African American women's virtue became a new and powerful clarion call for racial uplift.

Judge Frank Murphy, who later became mayor of Detroit, governor of Michigan, and a U.S. Supreme Court justice, presided over the trial. Hundreds packed the courtroom each day, and after Darrow complained that African Americans were being denied seating, Murphy set aside half of the spectators' section for them. It was soon clear, however, that the African American audience would not be a passive one. When one prospective female juror declared, "I'm very prejudiced," early on in the trial, she received a vocal response from blacks in the courtroom. White had to assure Murphy that this incident would not recur, and he selected six "level headed people" to mingle in the large crowd and "keep down trouble."[43] This disciplining of the African American spectators in the courtroom was reminiscent of the mingling of police officers and social workers with crowds of incoming migrants in Detroit's railroad stations. Although Dancy and other community leaders supported Sweet's right to defend his home, they did not endorse outspoken black protests in the theater of the courtroom.

The prosecutor, Robert M. Toms, based his case on a conspiracy theory because he could not prove whose gun fired the bullet that killed Breiner or even whether the shot had come from the house.[44] Much of the prosecution's case consisted of the testimony of seventy-five witnesses who swore they saw no crowds near the Sweets' house on the night of 9 September. Apparently, the irony of having seventy-five witnesses testify to the absence of a crowd was lost on the prosecution. After discrediting the prosecution's witnesses, Darrow based his defense on sociological findings concerning race relations in America. John Dancy, the influential director of the Detroit Urban League, testified about housing conditions in Detroit, and Walter White testified about the history of the lynching and racial violence that had pervaded American society since emancipation. However, the most effective witness was Ossian Sweet himself. During his testimony, Sweet described his childhood in a small town in Florida where the fear of lynching was ever-present, his witnessing of the race riots in Washington, D.C., while studying medicine at Howard University, and his reaction to the series of racial incidents in Detroit that had preceded the events that landed him in jail. Using this strategy, Darrow demonstrated the defendant's state of mind on the night of the shootings and taught white jurors the basic history of racism in twentieth-century America.

"There are persons in the North and South who say a black man is inferior to the white and should be controlled by the whites," Darrow said in his eloquent closing argument, which moved many spectators to tears. "There are also those who recognize his rights and say he should enjoy them. To me this case is a cross-section of human history; it involves the future, and the hope of some of us that the future shall be better than the past."[45] The all-white jury deliberated for forty-six hours, arguing so loudly at times that those waiting in the halls could hear them. Finally, they announced that they were unable to reach a verdict. A large crowd of African Americans had remained in the courthouse to await the verdict, despite the fact that it was Thanksgiving eve.[46] Expectations had been raised in the African American community that an acquittal was imminent because of Darrow's skillful defense and Ossian's poignant testimony; therefore, a hung jury was a severe disappointment. However, White concluded that "the case has largely changed public sentiment in Detroit," as evidenced by the sympathetic portrayal of defendants by white newspapers at the close of the trial.[47]

The defendants were released on bail after the verdict, and on 20 April

1926, a second trial began. The state had decided to try the defendants separately and began with the prosecution of Henry Sweet, Ossian's younger brother, the only defendant who admitted firing his gun. This trial proceeded in a similar fashion to that of the first, with Darrow skillfully uncovering the lies of the prosecution witnesses and providing the sociological background to support his argument of self-defense. He also pursued another line of argument that proved to be particularly effective. He compared the "white mob" of rioters with the well-educated and genteel Sweet family, particularly the "refined" Gladys Sweet. Addressing the jury, Darrow remarked: "You have seen some of the colored people in this case. They have been so far above the white people that live at the corner of Garland and Charlevoix that they can't be compared, intellectually, morally and physically, and you know it. . . . There isn't one of you men but what know just from the witnesses you have seen in this case that there are colored people who are intellectually the equal of all of you. . . . Colored people living right here in the City of Detroit are intellectually the equals and some the superior to most of us." [48] In his remarks, Darrow skillfully used the jury's prejudice against eastern European immigrants to combat their racial prejudice.

Darrow used this tactic especially effectively when describing female witnesses. He referred to a young African American woman who had taken the stand as "modest, intelligent, beautiful." "The beauty in her face," he continued, "can't come from powder and paint or any artificial means but has to come from within, kindly, human feeling. . . . You seldom have seen anybody of her beauty and her appearance." Darrow went on to compare this idyllic figure of femininity to a white female witness, "the school teacher who for ten years has taught high school on what she called Gœthe Street [he pronounced this "Gopher" Street, presumably mimicking the incorrect pronunciation of the witness]. . . . Any sort of comparison?" [49] Darrow used this comparison of feminine virtues to convince the jury that only racial prejudice would lead them to convict the Sweets.

Darrow's assistant in the trial, Arthur Garfield Hays, recalled the effective contrast between the white and African American witnesses: "The defense witnesses, most of them colored, were people of a distinctly higher type than the whites who testified for the prosecution. Surely Sweet was moving to a neighborhood of his inferiors. Lies, evasion, prejudice and stupidity characterized their expression. Physically they were low-browed, mean and unintelligent looking, ugly. On the other hand, the colored witnesses were largely professional men and women, of clear features, good looks and unusual intelligence. At no point did the Nordics show to advantage." [50] Placing well-educated, attractive witnesses on the stand was reminiscent of Dancy's method of placing well-educated, "refined" women in jobs (such as that of elevator operator) where they were exposed to the white public in order to open up employment for African American women. In the theater of the courtroom, this tactic was much more effective. "They have good manners. They are clean," Darrow argued describing African Americans generally. "They are all of them clean enough to wait on us, but not clean enough to associate with."[51] The defense team's comparison of disreputable immigrants and respectable African American citizens resonated among the white jurors, who finally acquitted the Sweets. In his closing arguments, Darrow said: "If they had one colored family up there, some of the neighbors might learn how to pronounce Gœthe. It would be too bad to spread a little culture in that vicinity."[52] After deliberating for four hours on 19 May 1926, the jury found Henry Sweet not guilty, and the charges were eventually dropped for the remaining ten defendants. James W. Johnson sent a telegram to Walter White describing the moment: "When verdict of not guilty was rendered waiting women sobbed audibly and tears ran down the cheeks of men."[53]

After the Sweet family members were acquitted, the frequency of small-scale housing riots in Detroit decreased, and some African Americans found it easier to move into previously segregated white neighborhoods.[54] The case also led the city government to set up an interracial committee to study race relations.[55] This committee was chaired by the prominent theologian Reinhold Niebuhr and included African American representatives such as Bishop William T. Vernon of the AME church and numerous prominent lawyers and businessmen from the community. Finally, the 1924 campaign of Klan candidate Charles Bowles marked the high point of the Ku Klux Klan's waning influence in Detroit.[56] In many ways, the Sweet case brought the blatant discrimination against African Americans to the attention of liberal whites in the community and helped pave the way for more successful interracial work in the decades to come.

The Sweet case illustrates the power of social class in people's perceptions of rights. Darrow elided the Sweets' middle-class education, dress, and deportment with their race. Perhaps in the jurors' minds, the white Hungarians and Poles (depicted as uneducated, dirty, disrespectful) began to carry a more negative racial identity than the middle-class African American defendants and witnesses (depicted as well educated, clean, respectable). The NAACP and the legal defense team used male citizenship, which "respectable" blacks were entitled to, as a weapon against racial discrimination. Because in this case the men were protecting women and the sanctity of the home, the masculine nature of the language was heightened. The Sweet case, then, lies at the cusp of two racial reform discourses: a racial uplift ideology that emphasized female respectability and racial integration and an ideology of racial self-determination that emphasized masculine rights to citizenship and self-defense. The wide-scale support and interest that the trial engendered in the African American community reflected the power of these overlapping discourses. One could choose, for example, to identify with either the Sweets' gentility or their defiant act of self-defense. In the closing years of the 1920s, however, it was the masculine discourse that would prevail. Meanwhile, all reform efforts, club work, interracial organizations, and social movements were backed by a legion of African American women who had honed their organizing skills during a period when they were the central symbols and agents of racial reform.

The Growth of an African American Female Public Sphere

The increasing visibility and support of the NAACP among Detroit's African Americans during the Sweet trial reflected an ongoing diversification of racial reform organizations in the city. Before the trial, the NAACP had kept a relatively low profile in Detroit. By the trial's end, Detroiters saw the NAACP as a major player in local politics and community activism. This growth of African American social activism undermined efforts to present a community identity based on bourgeois respectability. During the early years of the Great Migration, the Detroit Urban League, the Second Baptist Church, the YWCA, and a handful of middle-class women's clubs dominated Detroit's African American reform organizations. By the mid- to late 1920s, African American men and women founded numerous new organizations and clubs that defined changing sets of social practices and urban identities. Categories such as "old settler" and "southern migrant," which reflected the structured hierarchies of bourgeois respectability, became increasingly fractured in this period.

These organizations fit well into a revisionist conception of the public sphere, which philosopher Nancy Fraser defines as "a theater in modern societies in which political participation is enacted through the medium of talk."[57] In these formal and informal institutions, relations between "civil society" (private citizens) and the state are mediated. During the 1920s, a period of tremendous growth in urban bureaucracies and businesses, professional and private identities that were constituted and articulated in the public sphere proliferated.[58] The creation and transformation of social identities in the public sphere did not always occur in opposition to a dominant power structure. Subordinate groups also unintentionally reproduced dominant ideologies and stereotypes. Perhaps the best example of this process was the use of Victorian ideology by black women's clubs to refute negative stereotypes of African American women. In this case, an oppositional discourse that asserted black women's respectability simultaneously reproduced wider gender stereotypes. Likewise, black women's club work in interwar Detroit both transformed and reproduced hegemonic ideas and practices.

It is necessary to examine both the public and private practices of clubwomen to determine how they shaped their communities. Sara Evans has noted that in voluntary associations "people draw directly and powerfully on private identities."[59] These private identities can create conflict in a group, leading to the exclusion of particular individuals. The creation of public opinion and the positing of a group identity, in contrast, represent a voluntary association's more unified public project. When the Entre Nous Club sponsored public events such as cleanup campaigns, for example, it attempted to shape public opinion by linking cleanliness with the black community. Although such projects are often explicitly oppositional to dominant ideologies, an examination of the "work" that such associations do should not be limited to such public and self-conscious projects. Many of these groups also restricted their memberships and meeting places to conform to particular definitions of inclusion, reproducing as well as transforming power relations.

Detroit's black women's clubs were oppositional in their relationship to the dominant white power structure; however, they also reproduced relations of power in the community and promoted racial reform strategies specific to their own agendas. The Entre Nous Club, for example, worked to gain city services for the West Side neighborhood but also disciplined residents who did not conform to community norms. In the 1920s, one effect of the proliferation of clubs and organizations was the emergence of new sets of social identities that were codified through the rituals of club life. Again, in part, these were oppositional—such as the African American businesswoman, an identity that went against every stereotype of white society— yet they also mediated and shaped class and gender relations in the community. The wide network of African American clubs and organizations also facilitated more direct challenges to white power structures that emerged in the 1930s and 1940s. As the Sweet case presaged, however, this new civil rights militancy led to the decline of women in visible leadership positions and the rise of a masculine discourse of citizenship and rights.

By the mid-1920s, older, more established black women's clubs stepped up their discussions of politics and culture while continuing their reform work of earlier decades.[60] The Detroit Study Club exemplified this change in focus. Club leader Lillian E. Johnson, in a paper delivered at a Study Club meeting, implored her fellow club members to take advantage of the recently obtained franchise. "Vote! Women, Vote!," entreated Johnson. "Running this government of ours is a joint job for both men and women. Now that we women have our full civic and political rights, it is just as much our duty to see that the right people are elected to office."[61] In another speech delivered to the club in 1925, Johnson analyzed an institution that was central to the development of a public sphere—the newspaper. "It serves as a medium of publicity for groups, and organizations, as well as individuals," argued Johnson. "Our own publications are needed to keep our race consciousness aroused, to stimulate cooperation in various efforts and enterprises and to cement us into a strong union to better combat the evils and injustices resulting from American prejudices."[62] Johnson, like many other middle-class African Americans, wanted Detroit's black newspapers to steer clear of "sensationalistic" journalism and work to inform the African American public of racial uplift efforts. As a "medium of publicity," newspapers shaped public opinion and public perceptions of group identity and were therefore central to the process of creating a community identity. Controlling this medium became a prominent concern for Johnson and other middle-class African Americans after the Great Migration.

Throughout the 1920s, the yearbooks of the Detroit Study Club were a testament to the increased involvement of black women in political and civic affairs as well as their continued commitment to charity work and reform. In the 1926–27 yearbook, for example, topics for discussion included the science of government, delinquent girls, the science of the home, immigration, the effects of philanthropy on government, and industrial Detroit. The women also invited Mrs. W. T. Vernon to give a lecture on her experiences in South Africa and carried on their work with city charities.[63] They frequently discussed female African American authors, such as Harlem Renaissance novelist Jessie Fauset, and they read African American poetry at nearly every meeting.

The Detroit Study Club was one of the first clubs to join the Detroit Association of Colored Women's Clubs, founded in 1921.[64] The association shaped the direction of the study clubs by encouraging them to adopt programs in recreation, civic reform, and public health. Black women also founded women's clubs devoted exclusively to political discussions in the 1920s. The Current Topic Study Club, for example, was organized in 1926 by Mary Belle Rhodes to explore the "knowledge that lies hidden in the brains of its members."[65] About twenty women met every two weeks to discuss current literary and political topics; they also organized charity drives every Thanksgiving. "Seeking to think in broader terms along all lines," these women were part of a new generation of politicized clubwomen engaged in a project of self-education.

Another group of women organized a club with the primary purpose of taking on the "responsibility of citizenship." The New Era Study Club was founded in 1926 by a group of well-educated African American women "of like minds and similar tastes."[66] These women saw themselves as "home-makers" and helpmates to their professional husbands, who had been friends in college. At least two early members, however, were themselves profes-sionals: Gracy Murphy, a lawyer, and Mrs. Norcum, the executive secretary of the Lucy Thurman branch of the YWCA, which replaced the St. Aubin branch. Like members of other clubs, the New Era Study Club members read books and plays, had debates and panel discussions, and held dances, dinner parties, and other social events. The club's exclusive membership was limited to thirty, and it held meetings in the YWCA rather than in private homes. The last two stanzas of the New Era Study Club's song "The Dawn of a Glorious New Era" reflect sentiments common to 1920s study clubs:

> We believe in the glory of woman
> > Her influence, her motherhood blest;
> In facing the great task before us,
> > 'Tis for strength that we ask, not rest
> Strength to serve, through loving and giving
> > And thus make our lives worth living

> Oh hail to our Club and its founders
> > Our weapon for good in our world
> May its influence go ever before us
> > Like a banner of good-will unfurled
> Like a beacon to guide us aright
> > To our heritage—Justice and Might.[67]

Looking back on the work of previous decades, clubwomen had a strong feeling of accomplishment by the late 1920s. The lyrics of their song reflected an image of the clubwoman as a female warrior whose glory, strength, and weapons of goodwill aided in the uplift of the race. By the 1920s, the "in-fluence" of African American women, the "glory of woman," was uncon-tested, and the heritage that early clubwomen left behind certainly inspired a new generation of middle-class African Americans. Many club meetings discussed topics such as "What has the Negro accomplished?" and other re-flections on the past.[68] By the early 1930s, the work of middle-class club-women was becoming secondary to the political and labor organizing of a new decade, and discussions of the "glory of woman" reflected a nostalgia about the clubwomen of previous decades.

Members of black women's clubs in the 1920s expressed a growing interest in the artistic side of the "New Negro." Some focused primarily on African American art and literature, demonstrating a racial consciousness emblematic of the Harlem Renaissance. Even these clubs, however, engaged in charity work. The Golden Rod Social and Art Club, organized in 1925 by Minnie Pearl, for example, had sixteen members who studied art and engaged in "some welfare work."[69] Black women established the Mary B. Talbert Club in 1926 as an art and literary club with a limited membership that met to discuss African American authors of the Harlem Renaissance. In addition, the Talbert Club carried out charity work in the community. Similarly, the New Idea Social Club, organized in 1924, defined itself as a social and literary club. Recognizing the need for additional "safe spaces" in the black community, this club planned to establish a house where African American clubwomen could meet to discuss a variety of topics. The Young Women's Peerless Art Club was organized in 1925 as a discussion and art club specializing in needlework. Although "socializing" was a stated goal of the club, the women who ran it chose the motto "Deeds, not Words," perhaps referring to their charity work.[70]

The dual mission of the 1920s women's clubs was charity and self-improvement through study. Their charity work demonstrated a commitment to community and the NACW's mission of "lifting as we climb." Yet by devoting a substantial amount of time to the study of art and culture, African American women's clubs defined the identity and status of their members as educated and middle class, separate from the masses of working women living on the "wrong" side of Woodward Avenue. As more African American authors were published during the 1920s during the Harlem Renaissance, clubwomen combined their intellectual work with a sense of racial identity and consciousness. Through reading Jessie Fauset, Zora Neale Hurston, Nella Larsen, and other African American female authors, these women defined themselves simultaneously as "race women" and educated members of the middle class. These late 1920s clubwomen also had secular leanings in the material they chose for study and their community work, forming a separate sphere of influence outside of the patriarchal structure of mainline denominations.

The lack of meeting space in the city shaped the nature of women's clubs in many ways. The clubs discussed above had an average attendance of about fifteen women who met in one another's homes—the Detroit Study Club, for example, met on Friday evenings between five and seven o'clock at the homes of members. Having a meeting in one's home meant having the living space and other amenities to host a gathering.[71] Both the limited membership of these clubs and the social rituals surrounding the meetings—tea and card parties, for example—marked their class status. The need to own appropriate clothing and shoes for such events could also be a barrier for women who wished to join clubs. Most clubs also required membership dues, and many were hosted on Detroit's West Side, another indication of the position of literary and artistic clubwomen in the community.[72] None of these clubs, however, set themselves completely apart from the larger black community. Every club was expected to carry out charity work and did, taking particular interest in the plight of African American girls and mothers.

The most overtly political organization of middle-class African American women was the Woman's City Council, founded in 1921, which addressed the needs of children in the community. When the Detroit Community Union asked John Dancy to evaluate this group, he noted that the twenty female members "seem to be high grade," reflecting his recognition of their class status.[73] Neighborhood improvement associations working with the council lobbied city government, monitored the appearance of local neighborhoods, and sought to protect the community's most vulnerable residents. In the early 1920s, for example, the council patrolled the city's school grounds to protect young African American girls from molestation. Woman's City Council women also met incoming migrants at train stations to offer aid and advice. In 1925, the council opened a camp for mothers and their children because no African American families could use the Bay Court Home, a camp for white working mothers and their children established by the District Nursing Society in the early 1920s. The City Council expanded this program to a second camp in 1928.[74]

Another overtly political Detroit club was the Progressive Women's Civic Association, an organization of fifty women established in 1925 specifically to address civic concerns. This association was credited with persuading Kroger grocery stores located in the West Side African American community to hire black clerks.[75] Pressuring Detroit's businesses to hire black workers would be a major concern of women's organizations in the 1930s. The Civic Association, therefore, was in the vanguard of a cross-class movement supporting the goals of economic nationalism. Its larger membership also suggests that it was more inclusive than some of the smaller literary and art clubs.

A similar organization, the Detroyal Gardens Council, was organized in 1924 by ten women as an auxiliary to the Woman's City Council. This group worked in the Eight Mile Road district, an area of particular concern to

Detroit's middle-class leaders because of its large, isolated working-class population. The NACW reported that by the early 1930s, the council had succeeded in "getting police protection, better motion pictures, better deportment at the dance halls and closed quite a few of the vice dens."[76] In addition, it organized a large, successful Girl Reserves Club and helped build a community center. Indeed, the Detroyal Gardens Council was often credited with the rapid improvement of the Eight Mile Road community. This overtly political women's organization successfully combined two major reform strategies: it used older forms of moral suasion to change "deportment at the dance halls" and close "vice dens," and it registered voters in the district and lobbied city government for improvements.

Two related reform efforts converged in the 1920s with the aid of women's clubs—cleanup campaigns and Health Week. In 1923, two African American doctors, Albertus Cleage and Frank P. Raiford, in conjunction with the Detroit Urban League, helped popularize National Negro Health Week in Detroit. Booker T. Washington launched this movement at Tuskegee Institute in 1915, and by the early 1920s, it became popular nationwide. Doctors and Urban League workers visited local churches to educate African American migrants on sanitary measures, particularly those that prevented the spread of communicable diseases such as tuberculosis and smallpox, which were taking a heavy toll on the community.[77] In 1927, the Urban League combined Health Week with Clean Up–Paint Up Week. "We are all determined that nobody shall point to our places and say that they are not well kept," declared Urban League officials. Historian Susan L. Smith argues that linking cleanliness with improved health was a common strategy of black clubwomen: "Community health activists equated health with cleanliness and cleanliness with respectability."[78] The health of individual African Americans became explicitly linked to the beauty of their surroundings in 1920s Detroit.

The Urban League praised the members of the Entre Nous Club on the West Side and clubwomen in the Eight Mile Road district for their efforts in physically improving their neighborhoods and thus elevating community respectability. Prizes of flowers were given to the twenty most impressive properties by the Urban League and the Twentieth Century Club—a prominent women's club founded before the Great Migration.[79] As in other reform efforts, the cleanup campaigns of the Urban League were preceded by the work of women's clubs to improve the appearance of neighborhoods— the outward-facing signs of respectability. The continuing cooperation between the league and women's clubs on such projects reflected the continuing dominance of female respectability as a reform strategy throughout the

1920s. Even the prizes given were highly gendered in this project. Flowers were presumably given to the *women* who improved their properties rather than their husbands, brothers, or sons.

African American women's clubs in Detroit constituted a public sphere, mediating between the needs of private citizens and the state, as in the work of the Entre Nous Club and the Detroyal Gardens Council; however, clubs also constructed new social identities in the community by defining the parameters of club membership and activity. For example, the Elliottorian Business Women's Club, founded in 1928 by Elizabeth Nelson Elliott, was the first women's club in Michigan to focus solely on the work of African American businesswomen.[80] The secretary in charge of coordinating the activities of working women at the Lucy Thurman branch of the YWCA in the late 1920s, Elliott felt that the small group of female white-collar workers in Detroit had the potential to become "a deeply significant and viable community force."[81] The goals of the club were broad: to "stimulate interest" in Detroit's businesses, build an educational program, study the needs of businesswomen, "develop leadership qualities," "promote better community living," and develop professional women to serve in public and private white-collar occupations.[82] After the week of 12 February was declared National Negro History Week in 1931, the Elliottorian Club sponsored the first Detroit celebration of African American history, a testament to the club's broader goals. Club members also raised money to send young women to professional schools in the area and held a beaux arts ball to raise money for a variety of community social services.[83] This type of social event was common among Detroit's elite and middle-class society. Like much club work, it served both to aid working-class families and set educated "respectable" women apart. In order to be a member of the club, a woman had to do work of "a clerical nature" and be of "good standing in her community."[84] The latter subjective requirement excluded female "clerks" working in numbers banks throughout the city, whose salaries and labor were comparable to the Elliottorian members working in black businesses. Overall, the members of the Elliottorian Club accomplished what they set out to: they established themselves as leaders in the community and publicized the role of the African American businesswoman in Detroit.

Clubs with a more working-class constituency also grew during the 1920s but were often connected to a settlement house or church. In these cases, space was provided at an existing institution, which solved the problem of meeting in overcrowded homes but led to increased supervision of club activities. The Sophie Wright Settlement House, for example, set aside one day a week for African American women and men to meet and form clubs such as the Mothers' Club and a girls' domestic science club.[85] Other settlement houses such as the Franklin Street Settlement, the Highland Park Community House, and the Tau Beta Community House offered services to African Americans, although the majority of their work was geared toward immigrant groups in the city.[86] In addition, social clubs throughout the city met in local cabarets or dance halls and were primarily recreational. A 1927 issue of the *Detroit Independent*, for example, announced the founding of a new social club, the Climax Pleasure Club.[87] Although few details about these clubs are known, they were more likely to be heterosocial in nature and did not have the longevity of middle-class women's clubs.[88] Social clubs, however, may have provided opportunities for young working-class women to engage in recreation without being seen as "suspect" by neighbors or family members, keeping their own respectability intact while enjoying commercial leisure.

The authors of the 1926 *Negro in Detroit* study recognized that Detroit's women's clubs had done "more in a community way than any other group."[89] Older clubs, such as the Willing Workers and the Detroit Study Club, increasingly focused on civic reform in addition to continuing their philanthropic and artistic work. Rather than emphasizing the "pseudo-philanthropic" work of the past, black women's clubs were "inaugurating programs designed to foster practical measures."[90] These measures coincided with the Urban League's strategies and reform efforts during and after the Great Migration. Cleaning up neighborhoods and identifying urban problems continued to be part of presenting a respectable community identity throughout the 1920s.

With the advent of the Great Depression, the reform strategies pioneered and led by women's clubs were replaced by more "professional" state-sponsored reform. Ironically, the increasing attention of clubwomen to professional social work and scientific charity led to their decreasing visibility.[91] Meanwhile, the authors of the 1926 study astutely observed that "the colored club women seem to realize as never before the power of good which they possess."[92] Detroit's clubwomen understood that the "power of good" they wielded could be used to change the community's material, social, and political conditions. Indeed, the public sphere that clubwomen created opened a wider black public sphere in which African American public opinion was articulated to white city officials, state agencies, and employers.

The Second Baptist Church and the Secularization of Religion

The growth and diversification of African American neighborhoods and women's clubs were also reflected in black Detroit's religious life. Historian

Robert Gregg has argued that as urban African American communities became increasingly stratified in the decades after the Great Migration, established black churches lost their "central position in the community."[93] Storefront churches, cults, sects, commercial recreation, traveling evangelicals, and new sources of charity all represented competition for large churches such as the Second Baptist Church.[94] The number of black churches in Detroit grew from six in 1910 to sixty in 1923 and continued to expand throughout the 1920s, creating this greater competition.[95] Racial uplift ideology and the social gospel, the powerful undergirdings of the established black churches during the Great Migration, had less appeal by the late 1920s as new institutions and sources of spiritual aid flourished. Yet the membership and influence of the Second Baptist Church continued to grow throughout the 1920s, reflecting the church's ability to adapt to migrants' needs.

Because membership in the Second Baptist Church did not preclude participation in smaller storefront churches, the two were not always in direct competition. Many congregants of the Second Baptist Church also attended storefront revivals or received tips for numbers from a Spiritualist medium, simultaneously aiding in the growth of new congregations and sustaining older ones. What did begin to change significantly was the church's emphasis on moral prescriptions, which decreased as the church was consciously becoming more secular.[96] Religion and class position were still closely linked in this period as elite respectability required membership in an "upper-class" Episcopalian or Methodist congregation. Nonetheless, by the late 1920s, the Second Baptist Church was less concerned with transforming new migrants into "respectable" urban citizens than with offering a variety of services to an increasingly diverse congregation.

In the mid- to late 1920s, new churches were built throughout the city and larger congregations created welfare departments, hired social workers, and provided a wide range of recreational and educational services to complement their spiritual work. This expansion of religious work reflected the diversification of the community and African American residents' growing needs. Over 50 percent of African Americans belonged to a church by the late 1920s, and in order to obtain a seat at the Second Baptist or Bethel AME Church on Sunday morning, congregants had to arrive an hour or more before services started.[97] Community leaders increased pressure on churches to address "modern" urban problems, delegitimizing smaller congregations that lacked employment offices, day care centers, and gymnasiums.[98] As the African American community expanded, mainline churches became a microcosm of the associational life of the city, sponsoring clubs, recreational programs, day care facilities, employment offices, and educational services.

The phenomenal growth in church membership during the 1920s facilitated sharp distinctions in the perceived quality of ministers' and church founders' leadership. Ministers such as Robert L. Bradby of the Second Baptist Church and Bishop William T. Vernon of the Bethel AME Church were recognized leaders in the local African American community and beyond who socialized and worked with heads of industry and local white politicians. These ministers continued to view storefront churches as institutions that held back the social progress of African Americans. Elites measured social progress by the quality of religious practice and the educational status of ministers. "Mental development will cure these people of their weakness for barbaric forms of worship," declared Vernon in 1928.[99] This contrast was also noted in the white press, as in this filmic description of African American religious life in a *Detroit Saturday Night* article: "The hysteric brotherhood walks into only one reel of the film that portrays the religious life of the Negro in Detroit. There are other reels which bring to view thousands of Negroes attending well ordered services in modern churches, pastored by men trained in theological institutions of high standards."[100] The goal of many ministers was to replace "the hysteric brotherhood" with the "well ordered" thousands. Offering a variety of services other than spiritual ones served as a draw for such a transformation.

The Second Baptist Church continued its dominance in the African American community throughout the 1920s, attracting the largest congregation by far, undertaking ambitious expansion, and supporting numerous charity and social service programs.[101] In a photograph that suggests the church's domination of Detroit's East Side neighborhood, Bradby, church officers, and much of the congregation pose outside the church. They are physically part of the neighborhood they inhabit, setting an example for residents while showing their power in numbers—which was particularly significant because the church was located in a "red-light" district.[102] Large numbers also helped ensure relative financial security, and in 1926, the Second Baptist Church purchased an adjoining lot on which it built an annex the next year.[103]

During this period, Bradby and his associates expanded the number of church-sponsored activities. In addition to the older Big Sister auxiliary, Earnest Workers' Club, and missionary society, the church developed numerous other clubs, social service classes, and recreational activities.[104] Church workers targeted these services primarily at the women and girls who made up the majority of the congregation. Just as secular women's

The Second Baptist Church congregants posing outside their church. From John Marshall Ragland, "The Negro in Detroit," Southern Workman *52 (November 1923): 539.*

clubs provided women with increasing opportunities to organize, the Second Baptist Church offered both physical space and an institutional setting for a wide variety of women to pursue both secular and religious activities. Being an active member of the Second Baptist Church had other advantages for women. For example, female entrepreneurs found a ready customer base among their fellow parishioners by advertising in the church's popular publication, the *Second Baptist Herald*. Some women received the church's endorsement of their products and services. The editors of the paper, for example, recommended Hazel Nichols's new "very modern dressmaking establishment."[105] Most of the female congregants lived in the church's environs on Detroit's East Side, and they sought to transform their neighborhood into a model of community betterment.

Many African American women also volunteered or found part-time work in the church. During the 1920s, Sunday schools experienced phenomenal growth. The Second Baptist Church reported a weekly enrollment of 800 in its Sunday school classes by the mid-1920s, and nearly 1,400 African Americans, the majority of whom were women, served as Sunday school teachers or officers in the black Baptist churches in the city.[106] The YWCA also trained Sunday school teachers, and in 1925 alone, 600 African American women participated in its classes. Because few African American women could hope to teach in Detroit's public schools, teaching Sunday school gave them an opportunity to reach out to the community's children. The Second Baptist Church and other large conventional churches also employed secretaries and social service workers.[107] Working and teaching in the church provided much-needed extra income, as well as prestige, for African American women whose neighbors and friends identified them as model "race women."

Central to the expansion of church activities was the Baptist Christian Center, the settlement house associated with the Second Baptist Church. In the 1920s, the center stepped up its outreach to Detroit's African American women by providing a variety of educational opportunities, including classes in household economics, English, home nursing, teacher training, and Christian culture.[108] Although the topics of many of these classes were secular, religious study ran through them all. A visitor in a cooking class in the 1930s reported, for example, that "cooking is combined with a bible class." She continued: "The girls are learning stories and passages from the book of Mark; when they have committed the required material to memory, they will cook a food beginning with the letter M, — Macaroni this time. And so they will continue through the first four books of the New Testament."[109] In 1928, an estimated 1,600 children and young adults enrolled in these programs, making the church part of their everyday lives.[110]

Training girls and young women and "protecting" them from the dangers of the city were the stated duties of the "mothers" in the Second Baptist Church. In the summer of 1928, the church held a mother-and-daughter conference to impart values and life skills to the next generation. Millie Connelly, a church worker who attended the conference, listed the "ideals, virtues and aspirations a young girl must obtain in order to get the best and highest out of life": "First, be true. Next, girls must be pure. Nothing could be any worse than to see a young girl who has ignorantly made a wreck of that which should be her greatest treasure and that is her own growing womanhood. . . . She must keep herself pure. She must be above yielding to the advice of ignorant servants or foolish schoolmates if she would grow into a woman loved and trusted with the greatest and most desired of blessings—a beautiful home life, a noble husband, affectionate and darling children of her own. Third, girls have self-confidence. . . . Fourth, trust in God."[111] This combination of moral purity, chastity, religiosity, ambition, and self-confidence harks back to earlier decades of racial uplift. Within the boundaries of the Second Baptist Church, a bourgeois discourse of respectability remained central to reform work, especially as it applied to girls and women. No longer, however, was this message addressed to incoming migrants who were labeled as inherently "backward." Rather, the new enemies of the female gatekeepers of respectability were from the city itself.

Classes directed at women became increasingly popular throughout the 1920s. The Second Baptist Church's social service and educational department lined up volunteers to teach these classes throughout the community.[112] In addition, church leaders offered special classes, such as one in 1927 for the "leaders of Social gatherings" that taught clubwomen how to organize social events effectively.[113] This class in particular revealed the role the Christian Center played in transforming and reproducing social identities. In many of these courses, professional women such as nurses, stenographers, and businesswomen shared their knowledge with socially mobile women, shaping and defining new occupations. In addition, long-valued skills such as volunteer work and civic activism were taught, as well as African American history and culture. National African American female figures also spoke at the Second Baptist Church about their experiences in racial uplift work.[114] Thus, "race women" who upheld the values of respectability adapted to the changing conditions of urban industrial Detroit in the classroom setting of adult education. The 2,000 women who registered for these courses in early 1927 were proof of the appeal of vocational training, combined with more traditional racial uplift work, among Detroit's women.[115]

Besides providing vocational training for women in dressmaking, domestic service, nursing, and teaching, the center employed several female teachers and social workers.[116] By the late 1920s, both white and African American community leaders lauded the center as one of the most prominent settlement houses in Detroit. The center also solved a perennial problem for working mothers—the need for day care. "Many mothers whose conditions demand that they go out to earn a livelihood during the day have come to the office to see if we could not some way arrange for the proper care of their children during their absence," reported the *Second Baptist Herald*. "Others who would like to have their little children in good hands to know that they were off the streets, not being of school age, while they were called away suddenly have also been desirous of said opportunity."[117] To address this need, the Big Sisters' Home provided a day nursery with "competent nurses and attendants" for a fee of ten cents per child.[118]

In addition to offering educational services and day care, the Second Baptist Church and other churches were major recreation centers for Detroiters. In a survey of 1,000 families, the church was cited as the most popular site of recreation after movies.[119] Church activities included excursions, suppers, plays, recitals, and sports. Many activities were targeted at members of the younger generation, who were most likely to be lured away by commercial recreation.[120] Within the purview of the church, young African American men and women could have picnics, dance, and socialize without fear of criticism from parents or older relatives. This recreational world, however, was not entirely separate from the commercial world of entertainment. Churches sponsored outings to local amusement parks, baseball games, and even movie theaters. "This wider use of the church," wrote the authors of the 1926 study, "is forcing many of the more old fashioned churches to acquire a broader vision of providing facilities for wholesome leisure time activities."[121] These excursions were supervised and the young people were "protected" from exposure to any "undesirable element." Religious recreation, then, was a terrain where respectable leisure activities could be taught and maintained. By redefining "respectable" and "unrespectable" leisure, however, young church members brought secular commercial recreation into the bounds of the church.

Whereas recreational activities provided younger church members with the opportunity to engage in heterosocial leisure without the risk of censure, the large Sunday congregations provided a forum for older Detroiters to display their own status and identities in a communal setting. Women who had gained positions of authority in the church acted out those roles in public before, during, and after services. The dress and deportment of friends and neighbors became central topics of conversation among churchgoers. Older women were equally critical of those who wore "too much finery," which indicated a "sporting life," and those whose clothes were too "southern." Similar judgments were made in the church itself during the service. Although Reverend Bradby was more restrained in his worship style than a storefront preacher, his control over the congregants was minimal during the service. Some women cried out freely; others shouted only at more "appropriate" communal moments. Such public performance marked individuals in subjective ways, just as their clothing and appearance did.

Outside of the churches, distinctions between illegitimate and legitimate religious organizations were part of a larger project of creating a public identity of respectability during the 1920s. The Detroit Community Fund, a secular umbrella group for Detroit's private charities, including the Urban League, mediated the relationship between African American religious charities and the white community. The fund had the ability to undermine the fund-raising efforts of any religious group that social investigators were not familiar with or felt was "suspect." For example, in 1925, an African American preacher, Reverend C. H. Folmar, reportedly visited the Detroit Community Fund's offices to request aid for his United Universal Christian Army, which was operating a much-needed free day nursery for African American children with working mothers. Folmar attempted to use the tools of respectability to gain financial support from fund officials by stating that he was "backed by colored ministers, lawyers and business men representing the better type of Negroes in Detroit."[122] The fund denied aid to Folmar after its investigators found that the day nursery was run in "a dirty, slovenly manner" and that the charity work of the United Universal Christian Army was minimal. The Detroit Urban League was also "emphatic in [its] disapproval" of Folmar's organization and urged white businesses to reject the group's attempts at fund-raising.[123]

Another religious charity organization that came under attack during the 1920s was the Church of God and Saints of Christ. In 1921, this church began to solicit funds from businessmen in Detroit. As in the case of the United Universal Christian Army, these businessmen asked the Detroit Community Fund and the Detroit Urban League to investigate the organization. Dancy reported that it was a "religious sect under the leadership of Elder Wm. H. Merritt" that was soliciting money to operate a home for children in Virginia. Dancy described the membership of the church as "very ignorant" and discouraged businesses from contributing to it.[124] A month later, this opinion became policy as the Detroit Community Fund wrote to Dow Chemical recommending that it not support the group financially because it was "a small Negro mission of the Holy Roller type."[125] Seven years later, this correspondence continued as Dancy reported that the small group had grown to become a "cult believing in a prophet" and that most of the Detroit members were women "who call themselves 'Gleaners'" and solicited contributions.[126] Apparently, the female members of the church had established a women's branch called Sisters of Mercy and Daughters of Jerusalem.[127] These women solicited funds throughout the city to maintain the Virginia orphanage and to earn their own livelihood. Although Dancy and others noted that the Church of God and Saints of Christ seemed to be barely getting by, he felt it was essential to cut off its funding.[128] By directly requesting financial help from the white community in the name of religion and charity, these women circumvented the Community Fund and Urban League's bureaucracy. Rather than presenting a collective identity of "respectable" religion and "scientific" charity, they presented individual identities of needy women and nondenominational religion and were thus censored.

It may be that the United Universal Christian Army and the Church of God and Saints of Christ were fronts for Folmar, Merritt, and their associates to raise money for personal gain. The process by which these institutions were evaluated, however, is telling. Leaders in the Detroit Urban

League and the Community Fund expected religious groups that also provided charity to conform to the same "professional" standards as those of increasingly scientific social work agencies. It was often unrealistic to expect African American charities that had cared for the poor and unemployed without the assistance of public funds or white philanthropy for many decades to meet such standards. Increasingly, African American secular and religious charities were labeled as backward, "slovenly," and unscientific by a growing group of professionals both inside and outside the community. Charity, once a hallmark of respectability, was itself becoming suspect and associated with the informal and "feminine" reform work of the past.

Conclusion

By the time the severe economic deprivation of the Great Depression was being felt in Detroit, the ideology of bourgeois respectability was already in decline. As middle-class African Americans moved out of the East Side neighborhood, their sensitivity to working-class behavior and neighborhood appearance decreased, lessening the elite impulse to police and transform the behavior of incoming migrants. In the 1930s, middle-class African Americans dubbed the East Side neighborhood "Paradise Valley" and described it as a space of commercialized leisure rather than vice. New women's clubs and more secular religious programs incorporated emerging social identities that were not bounded by the old-settler versus newcomer dichotomy. Remarkably, in the face of pervasive racism, African American women effectively developed a female public sphere in which they could articulate their concerns and develop innovative reform strategies.

The Ossian Sweet case demonstrated the power of female respectability in the theater of the courtroom. Nevertheless, the most enduring image of the case was not that of the demure and educated African American female witnesses but that of the African American men who defended their homes against white mob violence. Self-defense and self-determination were strategies that would become more public throughout the 1930s, as working men and women took to Detroit's streets to demand their right to a decent standard of living and protection from racist violence. These strategies were legacies of a working-class notion of respectability that emphasized self-respect. During the next decade, working-class African Americans who fought for their rights in assertive and inventive ways remade respectability.

5 Economic Self-Help and Black Nationalism in the Great Depression

Detroit's a cold cold place: and I ain't got a dime to my name
I would go to the poorhouse: but Lord you know I'm ashamed
I been walking Hastings Street: nobody seems to treat me right
I've got to leave Detroit: if I have to flag Number Ninety-Four
And if I ever get back home: I ain't never coming to Detroit no more.
  Victoria Spivey, "Detroit Moan"

Detroit, with its powerful industrial economy, was devastated by the Great Depression. For its African American residents, unemployment, hunger, homelessness, and fear made Detroit the "cold cold place" that Victoria Spivey sang about in her 1936 blues song "Detroit Moan." In response to the declining conditions, some Detroiters took trains back to the South, where they could grow food more easily and perhaps find employment in service work. Charles Denby, for example, laid off from his job and out of money, soon tired of waiting hours in relief lines to receive a bowl of soup and some crackers. "People ate stale, thrown away food picked out of the garbage," remembered Denby. "I saw families sitting out in the snow with their furniture."[1] When his mother sent him enough money to return to the South, Denby joined his family in Tennessee, where "they had plenty of food but not much money."[2] Most African Americans in Detroit, however, remained in the city and struggled through the depression using a variety of survival tactics. These women and men engaged in social activism, began reform movements, and formed coalitions that challenged existing institutions and ideologies.

In the early years of the Great Depression, many African Americans embraced nationalist strategies. In contrast to the integrationist goals of the Detroit Urban League and the NAACP, these individuals' goal was to build a self-sufficient, independent black community. In particular, activists sought to create new employment opportunities in the black community to offset job losses in the industrial economy. African American women were at the forefront of these efforts in the powerful Detroit Housewives' League and other grassroots campaigns. Nationalist rhetoric tended to stress black women's domestic role while emphasizing the need for working men to protect and defend their wives and children. In part, this shift toward masculine images can be ascribed to the impact of male unemployment on the role of breadwinner. Because men no longer necessarily provided for their families, their ability to protect their families became paramount.

Thus, although bourgeois respectability continued to stress "housekeeping" as the dominant project of racial uplift in the 1930s—emphasizing the importance of presenting a clean and respectable home to neighbors and outsiders—the *defense* of the home and the "nation" was the racial project with the broadest appeal. Nevertheless, the link between these two strategies continued to be female respectability. Nationalist groups stressed a sexual division of labor in which women learned and adhered to standards of cleanliness, housekeeping, hygiene, and education of children. These standards, however, were subsumed in a culture that stressed the masculine project of self-defense and resistance. Depression-era Detroit was a violent place in which union activists, black protesters, and Communist Party members clashed with police officers and white racists. Thus, in the sexual division of labor in social activism, it was masculine calls for self-defense rather than feminine social housekeeping that moved to center stage.

Although the defense of family and community was a largely masculine discourse in 1930s Detroit, women remained as central, if less visible, actors during the Great Depression. Just as the Dress Well Club was a male organization carrying out a feminine style of reform in the early 1920s, the women who fought eviction or joined the Nation of Islam practiced a masculine style of self-defense. In his discussion of abolitionism, James Horton makes a similar point. "For black women no less than black men," he argues, "freedom and dignity were tied to assertiveness, even to the point of violence."[3] The resurgence of a masculine style of reform, however, meant that less attention was paid to African American women's needs, such as child care and vocational training. In addition, African American women no longer served as the central image of racial uplift and urban assimilation. Although some women certainly applauded the decline of the most condescending styles of moral suasion practiced by the Urban League or YWCA workers, there was a price to be paid. Leading institutions and local newspapers were less likely to celebrate African American women as heroines of the race embodying the goals of racial reform.

The decline of bourgeois female respectability and the rise of a masculine discourse of self-defense and self-determination had a number of ramifications for Detroit's black community. First, the visibility of unemployed men overshadowed both the plight of unemployed African American women and the continued struggles that domestic servants faced in an uncertain economy. African American female entrepreneurs, however, continued to be commended for their contributions to the growth of African American businesses, reflecting the increasing prominence of economic nationalism promoted by the Detroit Housewives' League. Meanwhile, prostitutes in the 1930s were no longer primary targets of reformers but instead were viewed as unfortunate by-products of the Great Depression. Second, social activism in the African American community proliferated during the 1930s, effectively undermining the authority of the Detroit Urban League and other established reform organizations. Third, nationalism became a common denominator in the growth of religious organizations during the depression. The Nation of Islam and an increasing number of storefront churches promoted a potent combination of masculine self-determination and female respectability that had wide appeal and undermined established denominations. Finally, the depression greatly blurred the already indistinct lines between the formal and informal economy as numbers bankers and other leisure workers gained respect from community leaders. The East Side neighborhood that had once been referred to as "Black Bottom" was increasingly called "Paradise Valley"—a mecca for numbers runners, cabarets, beauty shops, and other symbols of African American entrepreneurship. Thus, in the arenas of labor, politics, religion, and leisure, the voices of African American racial uplift ideologues were drowned out by the cacophonous choir of African American men and women who were innovating strategies to combat racism and improve their community.

Employment, Unemployment, and Survival

Throughout the 1920s, it was relatively easy for African American men to find wage work in Detroit. Although working conditions were often substandard and wages were relatively low, male employment was not the "problem" that community leaders recognized female employment to be. In the decade following the Great Migration, John Dancy of the Detroit Urban League and other African American leaders, therefore, focused much of their efforts on training and placing African American women in domestic service and attempting to break the color line in female white-collar work. In the Great Depression, this situation was reversed. It became easier to place women in day work than to place men in industrial labor as more factories closed their doors to African American factory workers.[4] No longer was the light-skinned female elevator operator or the well-trained waitress a symbol of the occupational progress of the race. During the depression, male employment became the predominant issue for reformers.

Despite African American leaders' declining concern for female employment, the occupational segregation of African American women in low-paying domestic service jobs was reinforced during the Great Depression by state employment agencies, employer preferences, and widespread discrimination. The number of African American women employed in household service on a national level had increased over 80 percent during the 1920s.[5] In the 1930s, the wages of domestic servants stagnated or dropped to as little as $1 a day. Many of the working-class families in Detroit who had hired household workers once a week or once a month discontinued this practice as the unemployment rate for male industrial workers reached alarming proportions. Some white women, desperate for employment, also returned to domestic service when they found they could no longer obtain white-collar or industrial jobs. Even day work, the mainstay of many African American women and their families, became a scarce commodity during the Great Depression. As jobs in the aboveground economy became more scarce, some women participated in the informal economy, working as prostitutes or numbers runners. These women were not as stigmatized in the African American community as they had been before the depression because their choices were recognized as the product of massive unemployment and poverty rather than immorality or naïveté. Thus, economic uncertainty blurred the lines between "respectable" and "unrespectable" labor in a way that economic prosperity had not.

The hundreds of thousands of Detroit autoworkers who lost their jobs in the early years of the 1930s became national symbols of the ravages of the Great Depression. The unemployment rate for African Americans in Detroit was double that of whites, and they constituted 30 percent of the relief rolls despite making up only 7 percent of the population.[6] Notwithstanding the focus placed on male unemployment, a large number of the estimated 80 percent who were unemployed in the African American community were women.[7] In Detroit, African American female unemployment was devastating, reflected in the high rate of African American families on relief. Ernestine Wright, an African American domestic worker, remembered: "In the

A depression household. Courtesy of Works Progress Administration Collection, National Archives.

early '30s . . . blacks didn't have any decent jobs anyway and lost what they did have, which was domestic work."[8] According to the 1930 census, 25 percent of unemployed women were African American.[9] Many of these women had job histories similar to that of Minnie Parish, who arrived in Detroit from Florida in 1927. Between 1927 and 1930, Parish had nine domestic service jobs. A few lasted for six months or more, but most were relatively brief, and for long periods, she did day work for many different families. During these years, Parish had four periods of protracted unemployment. Prior to the stock market crash, she cited her reason for leaving domestic service jobs as "disagreement with employer," but after 1930, she fell victim to the worsening economy and was unable to find any household labor.[10]

Similarly, Mary Brossard migrated to Detroit from South Carolina in 1922 "to better her living condition." She and her adult son, who was also unemployed, roomed with friends in the city. Like Parish, Brossard had been a day worker throughout the 1920s, suffering periodic but relatively brief periods of unemployment. In 1929, however, neither she nor her son, a laborer, could find steady employment and had to give up their house. They moved in with friends, who, she reported, "give me a piece of bread when they have it and when they don't I don't eat either."[11] Brossard and Parish, along with thousands of other unemployed women, would spend the rest of the Great Depression visiting employment offices throughout the city, hoping to pick up day work and seeking material relief from state charities.

African American women who continued to find jobs knew that their employment was constantly under threat. "I would get a dollar a day, and you couldn't always get a day," recalled Wright, who managed to find day work throughout the Depression. "You'd go to the employment office and sit there for hours all day, and sometimes you wouldn't get a call to come in and do a day's work."[12] By the 1930s, the majority of employed African American women were domestic workers who performed day or part-time work.[13] In 1930, 88 percent of African American female workers were domestics, and 84 percent of domestic and personal service employees in Detroit were African American.[14] The wages earned by these African American women, who often commuted to white homes in the suburbs, became increasingly important as male industrial wages nearly disappeared. "During the dog days of the depression, many black families were held together by the wife," argues historian Norman McRae. "Black women were working in laundries and in the homes of the well-to-do as maids and cooks for two dollars a day plus carfare. Early in the morning, one could see them at transfer points waiting for streetcars and buses."[15] African American families depended on these women, who took drastic pay cuts and traveled long distances to work in private homes.

Throughout the 1930s, African American women continued to be shut out of white-collar and industrial labor, as they had been in the years after the Great Migration. Increasingly, even service work became competitive as white women sought whatever paid labor they could find. Historian Lois Rita Hembold, in her analysis of black and white families during the depression, concludes: "Black women's deprivation was far more severe than that of white women, particularly in regard to jobs."[16] Faced with this deprivation, African American women took on the task of creating new employment opportunities in the formal and informal economies. As in the 1920s, it was the entrepreneurial work of African American women that attracted the community's attention. This labor aided the project of economic nationalism, keeping African American wages in the community, and thus it enjoyed wide support in a period of massive unemployment. By building black businesses, African American women could offer their children some hope of finding future jobs in the community.

Detroit's African American beauty industry, the most significant and widely recognized entrepreneurial endeavor of African American women in the first half of the twentieth century, exemplified this increased focus on local businesses. Although beauty culture had long been lauded as a model of female entrepreneurship, during the Great Depression, African American beauticians and entrepreneurs gained even more prominence as models for the race. Although beauty operators became more competitive during the 1930s because of the Great Depression, in Detroit, African American women continued to establish beauty schools and shops.[17] Their relative success was due, in part, to the popular "Don't Buy Where You Can't Work" campaigns sponsored by the Detroit Housewives' League and the Booker T. Washington Trade Association. Thousands of women who were trained in beauty culture in the 1920s opened shops and schools during the depression or worked as beauty operators in their homes. As more women became successful beauty operators, however, trained operators sought to differentiate themselves from untrained or unlicensed beauticians. Indeed, in this female occupation, successful entrepreneurs sought sharper distinctions between those who worked in the formal economy and those who labored in the ranks of informal workers. As a result, they established professional organizations that lobbied for licensing laws and developed elaborate rituals around education in beauty culture.

Responding to criticism from some African American leaders that the beauty industry was attempting to force black women to emulate white standards, beauty culturalists emphasized the improved image that African Americans could present to the world through the use of their products. According to Kathy Peiss, "beauty culture was a vindication of black womanhood, a way to achieve personal dignity and collective advancement."[18] From the 1900s through the 1920s, the importance of presenting a respectable female image was stressed in advertisements placed by beauticians. Cosmetics and hair and skin products were the tools needed to reach respectability and thus aid in the uplift of the race. In the 1930s, in contrast, many beauty schools and beauticians appealed to the entrepreneurial spirit that had captured Detroit's African American community. "Now is the time to think about your future!," read an ad from Poro of Detroit. "Let Poro's Expert instructors prepare you for your life's work!" Another Poro ad read: "Attention Ambitious Women! Earn Good Profits."[19] Earning profits and establishing a career were foremost in the minds of many Detroiters during the Great Depression.

In October 1937, the owners of the major beauty schools in Detroit met to establish the Michigan School Owners' Organization. Many of these women had attended the seventeenth annual convention of the National Beauty Culturalists' League in New York City the month before and had read about an organization of Chicago beauticians who were attempting to shut down the businesses of unlicensed operators, known as "house shops," and regulate sanitary conditions. The list of schools, all run by Detroit African American women, represented at the meeting at Madam Vivian Nash's Bee Dew Laboratories reflects the phenomenal growth of beauty culture. Although three of the eight schools were branches of national organizations—such as Jessie Morton Williams's Madame C. J. Walker's School of Detroit and Myrtle Cook's Poro Beauty College of Detroit—five were schools founded in Detroit.[20]

Detroit's beauty schools in the 1930s not only competed for students but also rivaled each other in the lavishness of their graduation ceremonies, which were covered by the *Detroit Tribune*, complete with photographs of the attractive young female graduates. In 1938, fifty graduates of Ruby's Beauty University received diplomas at a ceremony held at the Hartford Baptist Church. "Four beautiful silver loving cups will be awarded by the officials of the school for outstanding achievements during the year," reported the *Detroit Tribune*. "One cup will go to the graduating student who has made the highest percentage in theory, and another for the student who has learned to give Marcel waves in the shortest time. There will be a cup for the student rating the highest in decorum and another for the student who has shown the best individual style in coiffeur [*sic*]." The Fleming Beauty School held its graduation ceremony at the Detroit Housewives' League trade exhibit and presented each student with a laurel wreath. Graduates wore academic gowns, and community leaders lauded them as potential future entrepreneurs.[21]

Since African American women lacked other viable job opportunities and access to higher education, receiving a cosmetology degree took on a symbolic importance in the African American community. Graduates earned degrees from institutions registered and approved by the Michigan State Board of Cosmetology and obtained cosmetology licenses that accorded them income and respect.[22] Still, unlicensed operators working out of their homes charged lower prices and represented formidable competition for these new professionals. The success of the cosmetic entrepreneurs drove some operators who functioned in the informal economy out of work, dividing the African American female workforce. Many African American women, however, found that working in beauty parlors was a route to economic independence outside of the unstable and unpopular field of domestic service. Because these jobs were still relatively scarce, other African American women chose to labor in the informal economy.

Unemployment and underemployment of African American women led to an increase in one sector of the informal economy: prostitution. "With the coming of the economic depression prostitution has not prospered but has become a less lucrative and more crowded profession," argued Glen Taylor. "It is my own opinion that the depression has brought no more prostitution but many more prostitutes."[23] In the face of dire economic circumstances and a limited job market, more women chose prostitution as a viable employment option during the 1930s. A decline in male wages, however, led to a corresponding decline in the prosperity of buffet flats and other houses of prostitution and increasing competition among prostitutes. Taylor argued that prostitutes also competed with "the increasingly popular charity girl and with the highly respectable but no longer virginal type of modern girl."[24] These "modern" young women exchanged sexual favors for a night out or viewed sexuality as an expression of freedom and independence.

By the 1930s, working-class migrants had created new social identities that blurred the lines between respectability and licentiousness. Residents did not necessarily vilify women who occasionally turned to prostitution for income. Sociologists St. Clair Drake and Horace Cayton noted that in Chicago "during the Depression years even 'respectable' lower-class families were inclined to be indulgent toward prostitutes. Often their own relatives and acquaintances, or boarders and lodgers, were involved."[25] Indeed, "respectable" individuals and prostitutes were not always easily differentiated in a period of severe economic crisis. Describing the 1930s, researcher Ines Marie Bridges argues: "A lot of the women resorted to prostitution in order to feed their children. . . . Prostitution was more tolerated during those years than it is now."[26] The toleration of prostitutes and sexually active young women marked a period in which female respectability did not carry the weight it had formerly carried.

The presence of prostitutes on Detroit's streets was less troublesome to African American reformers than the large-scale demonstrations and social activism that effectively undermined racial uplift ideologues. Likewise, unemployed women and low-paid domestics were overshadowed by the massive numbers of unemployed industrial workers, whose newfound leisure time and militancy appeared to pose a threat to the city's social order. The women who continued to attract the attention of newspapers and community leaders were female entrepreneurs, primarily beauticians, who represented the ascendancy of businesses owned and run by African Americans. These businesswomen epitomized the hopes pinned on economic nationalism as a strategy of self-sufficiency and self-determination. Rather than representing genteel, respectable race women, beauty shop owners represented the success of a local black economy and the implementation of a policy of economic nationalism.

Class Cooperation and the Housewives' League

The most prominent and successful organization that promoted economic nationalism, the Housewives' League, was developed by Detroit's black women. The founder of the league, Fannie B. Peck, wrote in 1934: "It had been in the minds of our women that they, their husbands and children, were victims of a vicious economic system." [27] By the early years of the Great Depression, the impact of that "vicious economic system" on Detroit's African American community was devastating. Thousands of male industrial workers were unemployed, banks had closed overnight, and Detroit became known as the "city of the dead." [28] It was the sense of emergency engendered by the Great Depression that led working- and middle-class African American women to join forces and exercise their consumer power for the good of the community. The Housewives' League, with its motto "Boosting, Building Business for Bigger and Better Jobs," argued that the labor market for male and female workers could be expanded beyond the purview of white employers by creating and sustaining small businesses owned and run by African Americans. This form of economic nationalism attracted African American women, who took the initiative to create jobs for themselves and their children.

Historians who have discussed the work of the Housewives' League point to the black women's club movement as its direct predecessor. [29] Although women's clubs served as a training ground for many of the league's initial organizers, the large membership of the league, 12,000 women at its height, suggests that it was a more popular and broad-based movement with diverse roots. Working-class women had participated in entrepreneurial projects in the urban North for decades, seeking to expand their extremely limited job opportunities and bring much-needed wages into the family economy.

Female reformers active in the club movement, however, sanctioned only those entrepreneurial projects deemed "respectable" and frowned on African American women who opened storefront churches, participated in the informal economy, or worked in the increasingly popular cabarets and small theaters. Many working-class African American women in Detroit had also been active in nationalist movements before the 1930s, most notably Marcus Garvey's UNIA. Detroit's community leaders criticized these movements in the 1920s because they were thought to reinforce segregation and undermine the formation of a "respectable" community identity.

By the early 1930s, however, clubwomen were less likely to criticize working-class women's public behavior and appearance. Furthermore, unlike the membership of earlier women's clubs, the membership of the Housewives' League was in no way limited—working-class women were actively encouraged to join, to participate in the league's activities, and to develop innovative consumer strategies in their neighborhoods. Finally, the central platform of the Housewives' League was the expansion of the job market for African Americans, a program that acted as a bridge across class interests and ideologies. The Housewives' League encompassed a new generation of female activists who were increasingly politicized and more interested in building coalitions in the African American community than in "uplifting" their working-class sisters. Therefore, only by examining the legacy of the informal economic self-help efforts of working-class women well before the 1930s as well as the ongoing reform efforts of clubwomen can the phenomenal success of this consumer movement be fully understood.

In June 1930, the secretary of the National Negro Business League, Albon L. Holsey, gave a public speech at the Bethel AME Church in downtown Detroit. Holsey addressed the newly formed Booker T. Washington Trade Association, founded by the church's pastor, William Peck, to bolster Detroit's African American businesses on the eve of the Great Depression.[30] Rather than discussing the role of businessmen, Holsey focused on the role of female consumers by describing a recently formed organization of housewives in Harlem. These women had joined together in support of the Negro Business League's Colored Merchants' Association to encourage African Americans to purchase black-made products from black-run stores.[31] Fannie Peck, the wife of Bethel AME Church's minister, was intrigued by Holsey's talk and immediately held a meeting of her own. Recognizing the powerful role that African American women played in business as consumers and inspired by Holsey's description of female activism in New York, Peck issued a call for interested African American women to join her in forming a sister organization to the Trade Association. A few days later, fifty African American women met in the basement of the church and formed the Detroit Housewives' League, whose large and active membership would be credited with helping Detroit's African American community survive the worst years of the Great Depression.[32]

The founders of the league quickly set up a complex but efficient system of disseminating information on the consumer power of housewives. Years of activism and wage work in the city gave league members the experience and knowledge they needed to navigate Detroit's segregated neighborhoods. The officers elected at the first meeting, including Peck as president, formed a central committee that coordinated the efforts of sixteen neighborhood units, which had their own subcommittees and sometimes their own agendas. To be a member of the league, a woman merely had to sign a pledge to support African American businesses and products. This minimal requirement led to the rapid growth of the membership rosters. To further encourage recruitment, the league awarded prizes to the members who secured the most new pledges. Women who had more time to commit served on booster committees of the neighborhood units, forming the backbone of the league's work by canvassing door-to-door, handing out information on African American businesses and products, and recruiting new league members. Boosters also visited businesses in their neighborhoods to encourage them to hire African American youth and stock African American–made products.[33]

Fannie Peck attributed the rapid growth of the league to "the realization on the part of the Negro woman of the fact that she has been traveling through a blind alley, making sacrifices to educate her children with no thought as to their obtaining employment after leaving school. Through the Housewives' League, her vision has been enlarged, and she is now looking beyond the schoolroom to the beckoning light of a 'Better Day.'"[34] This movement "beyond the schoolroom" reflected the understanding of African American women that education alone would not open up employment opportunities for their children. Moving beyond domestic work and factory labor to professional and commercial occupations would require large-scale activism in the African American community. As the Housewives' League's theme song exhorted, "If we our tradesmen patronize / They will our children pay / In their more prosperous day."[35]

In order to facilitate the expansion of job opportunities, a training school for both boys and girls was set up at the YMCA to teach sales and management. A research committee kept track of the state of black establishments and granted certificates of merit to the cleanest, most successful businesses. The women also helped businesses advertise in African American newspapers and circulated information about businesses worthy of African American housewives' patronage. In 1937, for example, the league sponsored a tour of local African American businesses such as the Great Lakes Insurance Company, Old Gov's Coffee Company, and Porter's Cleaning Plant. Reporting on the tour, the *Detroit Tribune* encouraged "all housewives and business women . . . to join this worthwhile organization and help boost Negro business."[36] Other committees visited sick and elderly residents, set up consumer-education programs, and proposed rent-control legislation. As a result, Fannie Peck stated, "many business men of our own group have acknowledged that it was the support of the housewives through the medium of this organization that has made it possible for them to remain in business during the years of the Depression." By 1955, African Americans owned and operated more businesses in Detroit than in any other American city, a direct result of the joint work of the Housewives' League and the Trade Association.[37]

The phenomenal success of the Housewives' League was the result of the convergence of two strands of respectability. For working-class women, for whom entrepreneurship had long been one of the only means of escape from domestic service, the Housewives' League's commitment to supporting small businesses had a strong appeal. Running a beauty shop or lunch counter or working at a black-owned bank or insurance company was the goal of many African American women who were excluded from most industrial and white-collar work. Therefore, supporting the business community not only bolstered male community leaders but also supported an expanding sector of the job market that African American women felt was vital to their own interests. Using the home as an organizing base for such an effort was also a tactic with which working-class African American women were comfortable and familiar. Having a clean, well-kept home had long been a source of pride for all African American women. Courses in household management offered by women's clubs in neighborhood churches, the YWCA, or the Urban League had been second in popularity only to courses in clerical work or other skills that would allow women to leave domestic service. Thus, the blending of economic nationalism and domesticity in a platform of consumer power, without the moralistic prescriptions of bourgeois respectability, was the recipe for a successful "class-bridging" organization.[38]

The extraordinary success of the Detroit Housewives' League, then, represented both the continuity of female activism and a shift in reform discourse from a focus on prescriptive, behavioral norms to a more inclusive ideology of economic nationalism. By the time of Fannie Peck's 1930 meeting, working-class women had already come into contact with the idea of economic nationalism through their participation in the UNIA. In addition, their entrepreneurship in both the formal and informal economies paved the way for their skillful promotion of the Housewives' League's goals. The leaders of the league's central committee relied more on their experience in the club movement, organizing and distributing propaganda efficiently throughout Detroit. It was the cooperation of working- and middle-class women, however, that led to the eventual success of the Housewives' League and the growth of black businesses during the Great Depression.

This cooperation was facilitated by the organizational structure of the Housewives' League, which gave rank-and-file members more autonomy than they had in earlier women's clubs. This autonomy allowed for a careful ideological negotiation of controversial racial issues. Economic boycotts and the reinforcing of racial segregation that might result, for example, were strongly condemned by many middle-class African Americans who had to negotiate with the white community for social services and jobs. Initially, the Housewives' League did not encourage economic boycotts, stating in its joint declaration of principles with the Trade Association that it would not protest against white businesses that had African American patrons but no African American employees. Indeed, in its charter, the league stated that it was not a "protest organization," fending off potential criticisms of militancy. In practice, the league was soon sending committees to white stores to encourage them to hire local African Americans. If the stores refused, they were picketed daily; if they agreed, they were left unmolested, although not promoted by the league. "The Housewives' League was successful in promoting black business," remembered Detroit resident Austin Curtis. "These women would go to the merchants and ask for black products that were produced by African Americans. If they wouldn't carry them, then they would see that people didn't buy there any longer. It was effective"—so effective, in fact, Curtis noted, that "Detroit had the reputation of being the leading city in the nation for black business development and progress."[39] The decision to picket particular stores or use other, more militant tactics was left to individual neighborhood units; thus, the dispersal of decision-making power gave the league's working-class members a louder voice in the community.

One rank-and-file member of the league responded to the charge that boycotts encouraged segregation by noting that "it is not a case of advocating segregation, or of encouraging race prejudice, it is a case of advocating self-respect and thinking as much of ourselves as other races think of themselves."[40] The idea of encouraging "self-respect" was central to many working women's notions of respectability. Self-respect was elevated above the need to present a public face of proper demeanor and nonconfrontation with the white community. Increasingly, middle-class clubwomen also stressed self-respect and self-sufficiency rather than an ideology of racial uplift that seemed increasingly accommodationist by the 1930s. For example, the Advance Guard Club in a middle-class African American neighborhood on the West Side picketed the local Beechwood Theater when it refused to hire a female African American ticket-taker.[41]

Another program carried out by the Housewives' League that appealed strongly to working-class women was a series of classes designed to train and educate children to enter the business world. The enthusiastic response of Detroit youth also added to the energy of the movement and made the league's work a family project. The YMCA school established to train youth in "salesmanship and management of modern stores" ensured both a future generation of skilled entrepreneurs and an available source of labor for immediate employment.[42] If a particular business agreed to employ more African American workers under pressure from the league, it was encouraged to hire a young graduate of the training program whose skills could not be easily challenged. The league also awarded prizes for the best essays written by young adults about Detroit's black businesses. Reporting on the work of the league for the National Association for Colored Women, Elizabeth Davis suggested that this work served a dual purpose by proving that "business is the foundation and backbone of a nation, group or person" and that "there is dignity in labor."[43] For African American mothers concerned about how their children spent their leisure time, the training school offered both future employment and an immediate productive outlet for youthful energy.

The educational work of the league, however, was not limited to children. Designating January as "Thrift Month," league members worked to educate housewives about budgets, savings, and household management. Tips on running economically efficient households were also offered in the Housewives' League's monthly newsletter. Eventually the league designated a theme for every month: February focused on health, March on fire prevention, and so on.[44] Because most African American housewives in Detroit were also paid laborers, tips on budgets, housekeeping shortcuts, children's health, and the like were welcome. The league frequently disseminated its knowledge at public fairs and trade exhibits, which raised money through the sale of canned goods and needlework and spread the program of the league throughout the community.[45] Because the rhetoric in these prescriptive programs was less moralistic than the rhetoric in previous decades, working-class women participated in them with enthusiasm.

By the mid-1930s, league committees began to specialize in particular projects. The sanitary committee encouraged store owners to maintain standards of cleanliness; the membership committee worked to expand the already large membership; the social committee helped merchants design product demonstrations and organized entertainment and exhibits; the speakers' bureau sent representatives of the league's work throughout the city; the program committee organized annual programs for the neighborhood units and the central league; and the education, advisory, music, and drama committees made up the rest of a well-differentiated organization.[46] These diversified activities empowered rank-and-file members. Because the league had so many committees and so many projects, most members could find an area of activity that suited their interests and time commitment. The youth programs also allowed whole families to become involved in the league's work. Indeed, the family was used as a metaphor for the league by organizers. Writing about the league in 1983, Christina Fuqua, one of its founding members, noted: "We always emphasize League, as in family, the joining together of all persons."[47]

Detroit's success with economic nationalist strategies, which were supported by a large cross section of African American women, became a model for African American communities nationwide. The National Housewives' League was formed in direct response to the success of the Detroit league. At a conference in Durham, North Carolina, in 1933, delegates from Detroit presented their work to other female activists from the North and the South. With the support of the National Negro Business League, the National Housewives' League spurred a nationwide "Don't Buy Where You Can't Work" campaign that cast African American women as the central actors in an economic drama of self-help and racial determination. The Detroit Housewives' League, meanwhile, would continue its activities until the late 1960s.

The work of the Housewives' League reflected a set of ideas and strategies that working-class African American women had developed in urban centers over decades. Forced to create employment opportunities where few existed, African American women had become entrepreneurs in small businesses. Some had also risked censure from religious leaders and clubwomen by actively engaging in the informal economy as numbers runners, prostitutes, or performers. As the strategies for reform shifted from a maternalist politics to one focused on racial self-determination, working-class notions of respectability as self-respect became articulated more fully. Thus, it is not surprising that the Housewives' League was founded in the same cultural milieu as former UNIA activist Elijah Poole's Nation of Islam and other nationalist groups. Without the organizational skills and political acumen of female elites such as Fannie Peck, however, the league could not have become so highly articulated and well organized. Ultimately, it was the combination of working- and middle-class members' energy and experience that allowed for the swift and successful development of the Housewives' League.

The Housewives' League was only one example of the diverse street-level activism that marked urban life in Detroit during the 1930s. Because the league was based in the community rather than the industrial workplace, women took the initiative in developing the most effective methods for the promotion of economic nationalism. The cross-class effort that this entailed marked a crucial shift in Detroit's black community. Nevertheless, without the sanction of such "respectable" women as Fannie Peck, the Housewives' League would not have been so widely praised by John Dancy and other male elites. Indeed, the "feminine" nature of the league's work, the emphasis on women's roles as consumers, marked the movement as "respectable" in spite of its militant tactics.

The Diversification of Religion

The advent of the Great Depression marked not only an increase in popular support for economic nationalism but also a proliferation of nationalist sects whose lineage could be traced to Garveyism, storefront churches, the Father Divine movement, and the Moorish Science Temple. Elijah Muhammad, the leader of the Nation of Islam, for example, was a corporal in the UNIA's Detroit division, and Malcolm X's father was the first vice president of that division.[48] Several basic features marked the 1920s and 1930s nationalist/religious groups: strict moral proscriptions, programs of economic self-help, a sexual division of labor and/or worship, a philosophy of racial separatism, a belief in a homeland, and an emphasis on the need for self-defense. In a sense, the UNIA, Moorish Science Temple, Nation of Islam, and other groups combined the devout female religious world of the Sanctified church — including its modest uniforms and moral proscriptions — with a masculine style of discipline and self-defense reminiscent of the rhetoric surrounding the Ossian Sweet trial. The combination of these gendered ideologies with a program of economic self-help and racial nationalism proved to have a potent appeal to working-class African Americans increasingly disenchanted with the Urban League's and NAACP's lack of militancy and policies promoting racial integration.

The growth of nationalism in Detroit, with its valorization of masculine self-defense, can be traced back to the popular Moorish Science Temple in the 1920s. Timothy Drew (who changed his name to Noble Drew Ali) founded the temple in Newark, New Jersey, in 1913. Drew believed that all blacks were in fact "Asiatics" descended from the Moors and urged his followers to abandon the names given to them by white slave owners and take new Asiatic names. In his temples in Pittsburgh, Detroit, Chicago, and elsewhere, Drew taught from the Holy Koran of the Moorish Holy Temple of Science, which combined orthodox Islam with the particulars of Drew's own philosophy. Drew incorporated elements of black Freemasonry in the temple's costumes and rituals, which appealed to working-class African Americans who were introduced to Eastern religions through fraternal societies.

In Chicago and Detroit, the members, who wore red fezzes and refused to be addressed by their Christian names, clashed with police and reformers in welfare offices and on public streets. When sociologist Arthur Huff Fauset interviewed a Detroit policeman about the activities of temple members, the officer became "choleric with anger": "'Those fellows!' he cried out. 'What a terrible gang! Thieves and cutthroats! Wouldn't answer anything. Wouldn't sit down when you told them. Wouldn't stand up when you told them. Pretending they didn't understand you, that they were Moors from Morocco. They never saw Morocco! Those Moors never saw anything before they came to Detroit except Florida and Alabama!'"[49] The defiance of these very visible men and women clearly infuriated white officials and embarrassed the leaders of the Urban League and established black churches, whose image of "respectable" men and women did not include red fezzes.

The Moorish Science Temple also promoted the separation of its members by sex and a set of proscriptions against "immoral" acts that would become part of the Nation of Islam's practices. Drew established a separate female organization, the Sisters National Auxiliary, to promote the political and charity work of black women. Men and women sat apart during mosque services, and members were forbidden to attend movies, dance, use cosmetics, straighten their hair, smoke, and drink. The similarity between these proscriptions and those of the Sanctified church reflected the appeal of such rules to many working-class African American women and men who gained a sense of self-esteem and respect from their involvement in the sect. Although the mosque services did not have the emotionalism of Sanctified services, the Moorish Science Temple did use traditional African American hymns with new lyrics. Thus, "Give me that old-time religion" became "Moslem's that old-time religion."[50] By the late 1920s, some of Drew's associates also began to use the temple as a base for selling a variety of products, including herbs, charms, potions, and literature. This activity was more reminiscent of Spiritualism than Sanctified religion, and the money that was made apparently led to internal strife in the temple. When one of the temple leaders was murdered in 1929, Drew (who opposed the entrepreneurship of his members) was arrested for the murder. After he was released on bond, he too died of "mysterious circumstances," and the Moorish Science Temple disbanded, with the exception of a few small urban mosques.[51] Thus, by 1930, black Detroiters had been exposed to a form of Islam that combined the popular black nationalism of Garveyism with the religious and behavioral discipline of evangelical Christianity.

Into this lacuna stepped Wali Fard Mohammed,[52] who claimed to be Noble Drew Ali reincarnated.[53] It is likely that Fard had been a member of the Moorish Science Temple in Detroit or elsewhere prior to 1930 and wanted to spread the teachings of Noble Drew Ali.[54] His method of doing so proved ingenious and highly successful. Sister Denke Majied, a Detroit follower of Fard, recalled his early work among Detroit's African American women and men:

> He came first to our houses selling raincoats, and then afterwards silks. In this way he could get into the people's houses, for every woman was eager to see the nice things the peddlers had for sale. . . . If we asked him to eat with us, he would eat whatever we had on the table, but after the meal he began to talk: "Now don't eat this food. It is poison for you. The people in your own country do not eat it. Since they eat the right kind of food they have the best health all the time. If you would live just like the people in your home country, you would never be sick any more." So we all wanted him to tell us more about ourselves and about our home country and about how we could be free from rheumatism, aches and pains.[55]

Fard's house-to-house peddling in Detroit allowed him to enter into the informal economic world that was central to the community. His method was similar to that of the highly successful Housewives' League, whose members canvassed neighborhoods to spread information and knowledge that could empower African American women. Fard's peddling also illustrates the intersection between the circulation of money and goods and the circulation of ideas and belief systems in the social terrain of the informal economy. Fard, like Spiritualist mediums who sold dreambooks and incense, linked the economic prosperity of his sect with the religion he preached, joining the secular and the sacred.

Fard began to hold meetings in people's homes, just as a Spiritualist or Sanctified preacher would begin a congregation by holding small informal meetings. As he attracted more attention and followers, he was able to rent halls and convene larger meetings — another parallel to the growth of a storefront church. Four years after he began knocking on Detroit doors, he had a following of between 5,000 and 8,000 members, largely from the Paradise Valley neighborhood.[56] Fard claimed that the teachings of Garvey and Noble Drew Ali foretold "the coming of the new prophet."[57] As in the Moorish Science Temple, new members were given Islamic names. Sister Rosa Karriem said of this process: "I wouldn't give up my righteous name. That name is my life."[58] When welfare workers balked at using the Islamic names, female members of the Nation of Islam fought hard for recognition of their new identities. One client of the Department of Public Welfare who was supplied with food for her family threatened to bring "all of her Mohammedan group to the Community Fund Building" when department officials said they could not read her Islamic name on her grocery orders. To prevent further conflict, the Associated Charities agreed to take her case and accepted her new name.[59] The Department of Public Welfare assigned Muslim clients to black social worker Beulah Whitby when white social workers refused to issue them relief checks in their Muslim names.[60] Such struggles over the names of welfare clients were volatile because they involved control over the very identity of African American women. By changing their names, these women symbolically claimed a new identity that was vocally in opposition to both the dominant white power structure and judgmental neighbors. Having that name accepted by the Department of Public Welfare or other social agencies was an empowering act.[61]

A study of the Nation of Islam conducted by the Department of Public Welfare in the 1930s focused on the increasingly uneasy relationship between female members and public institutions. Comparing clients before and after they joined the Nation of Islam, the investigators found that "the Moslems became more evasive, less cooperative with the case workers, and less interested in securing jobs for themselves. The non-cooperation manifested itself chiefly in resentment toward and interference in their ways of living. They wanted and often demanded aid, but they wished to use it as they chose, and to be let alone. Their evasions appeared to be a defense against interference in their affairs. The servile attitude which has characterized the southern negro for generations was discarded and replaced by one of superiority." The researchers went on to praise the improvement in the "moral tone and self-confidence" of Muslim family members, but they were clearly disturbed by the changed social relationship between these women and public institutions.[62] By taking their children out of public schools and challenging social workers and welfare providers, Muslim women began to change the white image of the "servile" African American migrant. Significantly, it was through an ideology of self-respect rather than bourgeois respectability that this was achieved. Yet some of the tenets of bourgeois respectability were reflected in the teachings and practices of the Nation of Islam.

As in the Moorish Science Temple and Sanctified church, the list of behavioral proscriptions for women in the Nation of Islam was long. "Gluttony, drunkenness, idleness, and extra-marital sex relations . . . were prohibited completely," reported sociologist Erdmann Benyon, who interviewed over 100 Detroit Muslim families. "They bathed at least once a day and kept their houses scrupulously clean, so that they might put away all marks of the slavery from which the restoration of the original name had set them free."[63] The Nation of Islam also reproduced a familiar institution in African American communities: a household-training course for girls and women. Held at the University of Islam, established by Clara Muhammed in 1934, these sex-segregated training classes taught traditional skills of housekeeping and cleanliness, as well as the preparation of food according to the teachings of Islam. The male auxiliary, the Fruit of Islam, was a military organization of young men who were trained to defend their community.[64] Thus, the sex segregation of domestic labor was vigorously promoted by the Nation of Islam, with the more passive role of caregiver assigned to the woman and the more active role of defender and provider assigned to the man.

Despite this rhetoric, in reality, the defense of the Nation of Islam was often carried out by women. For example, the removal of Muslim children from public schools to attend the University of Islam led to the Nation of Islam's most publicized and violent confrontation with Detroit's police department in the 1930s. With the backing of the Board of Education and some African American leaders, the police department stormed the university, sparking a riot among the defiant members of the Nation of Islam.[65] Many of those who placed themselves at risk by barring the police's entry into the school were the young mothers and female teachers who formed the core of the organization. In response to police pressure, the University of Islam moved underground, with members teaching students in private homes.[66] Widely reported in both the white and the black press, the riot marked an increase of interest among Detroiters in the Nation of Islam. Muslim women also supported men in the movement who were arrested and tried in federal court by appearing at trials en masse. In 1935, a courtroom battle between African American women and court officials led to the injury of thirteen police officers and seven court officers.[67] The image of African American women as modest and demure caretakers that was propagated by the Nation of Islam served to elevate them; however, Muslim women also displayed considerable bravery and directly challenged white authority in times of crisis.

Among those who converted to Islam in the early years of Fard's organization was a young autoworker named Elijah Poole. A migrant from Georgia, Poole took the name Elijah Muhammad upon his conversion. In 1932, Fard sent Muhammad to Chicago to set up Temple Number Two, which later became the foundation of the Nation of Islam. Fard was arrested in Detroit that same year and, after his release, moved to Chicago to join Elijah Muhammad. Harassed continually by the police, Fard disappeared in 1934, leaving Elijah Muhammad to assume the mantle of leadership of the most important black nationalist movement of the twentieth century.[68] Poole's, Fard's, and Malcolm X's roots in Michigan are a testament to the mixing of religious, political, and cultural belief systems in Detroit. The popularity of this nationalist movement can be ascribed in part to its potent combination of traditional roles for women and a belief in the need for masculine self-defense. The Nation of Islam, however, was only one of many new religious and ideological groups in Detroit during the 1930s.

One offshoot of the Nation of Islam that caused substantial fervor among Detroit's white community was Development of Our Own, an organization that called for the unity of all people of color against whites. George Grimes founded this organization in 1933; however, its notoriety was largely due to the involvement of Major Satochasi Takahashi, a Japanese immigrant. Takahashi eventually supplanted Grimes as leader and married an African American woman, Pearl Sherrard. Concerned about possible seditious activity because of Takahashi's pro-Japanese sentiments, the Detroit police department assigned two African American police officers to infiltrate Development of Our Own. This investigation led to a raid of the group's headquarters, and Takahashi was promptly deported to Japan in 1934 after the raid. Takahashi's wife carried on the work that he was forced to abandon, and by the late 1930s, Development of Our Own had branches in Mt. Clemens, Roseville, River Rouge, Ecorse, and Eight Mile Road as well as Detroit. Development of Our Own claimed a membership of over 20,000. Although this figure may be exaggerated, Development of Our Own was one of a number of extraordinarily popular nationalist groups during the Great Depression.[69]

In 1943, shortly after a devastating race riot, a white journalist, Phil Adler, wrote an article for the *Detroit News* suggesting that the "Moslem and Shinto cults" of the 1930s were responsible for the assertiveness shown by African Americans in the early 1940s. Beulah Whitby, who worked with Muslim clients in the Department of Public Welfare during the 1930s, concurred. "The Moslem high morale was emulated by non-Moslem Negroes and resulted in a general moral uplift movement," she stated. "What if the Shinto and Moslem paradises promised the gullible ones were distant ephemeral affairs? All paradises are remote and ephemeral. By promising the Negroes a place in the sun alongside of other races, a thing the Negro craves most and which is denied to him, these movements gave him something to look forward to and raised his self respect."[70] Whitby's comments reflected a general agreement by the late 1930s and early 1940s among African American leaders that the growth of Islam was not necessarily detrimental to the community's image. Other religious fringe groups that appeared to be exploiting the poorest African American residents without contributing to moral uplift, such as Spiritualist mediums, continued to cause some consternation among community elites. Many blacks viewed the proliferation of sects during the 1930s, however, as a symptom of the established denominations' failure to address racial problems in cities rather than a sign that African Americans lacked religiosity or respectability.

The proliferation of storefront churches, mosques, and temples during the 1930s was noted by many contemporary religious leaders. Miles Mark Fisher, an African American minister writing in the *Crisis* in 1937, argued for the inclusion of new African American religious movements in the *Census of Religious Bodies*, noting wide-scale denominational decline in urban centers:

> Of course the churches of the last ten years have gone through a depression, but many of them are practically bankrupt not only because of the economic crisis but also because they did not compete successfully with the cults which generally thrived all during the period. Church members have been known to withhold their financial support from the already debt-ridden historical churches and then to give offerings to the cults. Cult literature has been and is sold in abundance to church members. . . . The cults and not the denominations point out directions for organized religion to take.[71]

To Fisher and others, it seemed that the established denominations' search for bourgeois respectability had backfired. "In proportion as the churches are becoming unemotional—fine fashionable and formal," argued Fisher, "their programs become less intelligible to the common man."[72] Fisher noted that women's more prominent role in smaller sects, along with their temperance and teaching of morality, challenged the larger denominations. Sociologists St. Clair Drake and Horace Cayton agreed: "The ban on women pastors in the regular churches has increased the popularity of the Pentecostal, Holiness, and Spiritualist churches where ambitious women may rise to the top." In addition, smaller sects promoted black businesses and carried out charity work, activities previously dominated by large churches.[73] Thus, Fisher viewed the new religious groups as a viable alternative to black Baptist and AME churches, particularly for African American women who sought prominence in religious life.

Female migrants established alternative spaces for their emotional style of worship soon after their arrival in Detroit. By the early 1930s, their storefront churches had become ubiquitous and, as Fisher suggested, challenged the popularity of larger denominations. This process accelerated throughout the Great Depression, and the *Detroit Tribune* and other African American publications contained numerous advertisements placed by new religious organizations hoping to attract congregants. For example, a 1937 ad for the "King David Temple of Truth" publicized a "Monday night school of metaphysics, reading and healing daily." Even middle-class clubs incorporated popular metaphysical and spiritual elements into their activities. For example, the Elliottorian Business Women's Club in 1938 offered "free palm, card, and crystal tea reading . . . [by] Oriental and American readers" at a scholarship benefit party.[74] Despite the popularity of storefront churches, the established denominations never lost significant numbers of congregants. Because most storefront congregations held their services in the evenings, parishioners could easily attend a Sunday service at a large AME or Baptist church as well as attending a Friday night revival in a storefront church or receiving a mid-week reading from a Spiritualist medium. Widespread unemployment also meant that African Americans had more leisure time to go to multiple services and perhaps seek charity from a variety of religious institutions.

In the case of the Second Baptist Church, the early years of the Great Depression marked a growth in the congregation; however, by the mid-1930s, church attendance dropped.[75] This may have been in part an unintended consequence of one aspect of female respectability: dressing up for Sunday services. In Detroit, dressing up for church was an important public ritual for women. Julia Cloteele Page, an African American Detroit resident, remembered: "I wouldn't think of going out without my gloves and my hat. . . . People were very conscientious."[76] As the depression had a cumulative effect on African American families, many women could no longer maintain a wardrobe they considered "suitable" for the public display of a Sunday church service at the Second Baptist Church. "The reason that I joined a small church," reported a woman who left a large Baptist church in Chicago, "was because the people in this church don't pay so much attention to how you are dressed." Another woman complained: "You have to go to one of the large churches early on Sunday morning to get a seat, you have to be dressed in style or you feel out of place, and there is not as much friendship in a large church as in one of these store-fronts." Joining a storefront church could also take the place of joining a women's club, an activity that required money for dues and clothes. "I don't belong to any clubs, but I am a member of the Pentecostal Church," reported a Chicago woman. "It takes money to stay in clubs, and I am not able to make the appearance as far as clothes are concerned."[77]

More than any other factor, the proliferation of small churches, mosques, and temples in the 1930s facilitated the transformation of established churches. In the segregated neighborhoods of the urban Midwest, African American women and men had numerous choices of religious services, ideologies, religious music, and normative teachings. Secular services also challenged the role of larger denominations in the 1930s. Charity work increasingly fell within the domain of public welfare, and recreational activities were sponsored by fraternal organizations, social clubs, and other secular organizations. Recreation could also be found in saloons, apartment rent parties, movie theaters, dance halls, and amusement parks. Historian Robert Gregg has suggested that the 1930s marked a turning point for African American churches, when religion as community — in which the similarities among members of large congregations outweighed the differences — gave way to religion as communion — in which smaller congregations consciously created their association. Thus, argues Gregg, "people were no longer born into a particular church community. Instead they gravitated toward one that met certain economic, social and spiritual needs."[78] In this model, class and culture (as expressed in denominational preferences) became more closely linked during the depression.

Although Gregg's observation that urban dwellers had more denominational choices in the 1930s is accurate, the distinction he makes between the 1930s and an earlier period in which larger congregations made up of different classes had common goals may not be so neat. Detroit's African American community had long divided denominationally along class lines, and even in the relatively inclusive Second Baptist Church, "old-settler" elites looked down on the "newcomer" migrants who joined their church. Reverend Robert Bradby's lack of support for industrial unions also alienated the Second Baptist Church's working-class members during the depression. Even in the 1930s, attendance at small churches was not steady, and many congregants attended more than one church. Thus, "denomination" cannot always be clearly identified. A more accurate picture might present a diverse streetscape of ideologies and religious teachings that paralleled the political ferment of the period. As African Americans became avid creators and consumers of popular and political culture, so too did they create and partake of a diverse religious life. The complexity of this religious culture marked the decline of the established denominations' moral authority in the community, an authority based on a discourse stressing bourgeois norms of respectability and the presentation of a unified community identity. Women in long white Sanctified robes, men wearing fezzes, and strains of gospel music seeping out of storefront windows all undermined a communal image of well-dressed, orderly, Christian citizens.

Storefront churches were remarkably mobile during the depression, moving from place to place as rents became too high or as their congregations moved. This mobility reflected the unstable economic nature of urban Detroit. Blind pigs and buffet flats also had to move frequently, and during the depression, many Detroiters were only one step away from eviction. Ironically, the seeming "decline" of African American religion—or its institutional power in the community—led to a dramatic increase in the number of churches in Detroit. One social scientist has estimated that although African Americans made up less than 8 percent of the population of Detroit in the 1930s, 24 percent of the churches were African American. Nearly half of these churches were housed in storefronts.[79] In his study of African American churches in Detroit, Henry Allen Bullock noted that perhaps the primary difference between "conventional" churches and the storefront churches that gained popularity throughout the 1920s and 1930s was the gender of church leaders. Conventional churches only employed women as secretaries or, in the case of very large churches, social service workers.[80] Storefront churches, in contrast, were often run by women. Thus, a movement away from bourgeois female respectability and self-restraint in worship style was pioneered and promoted by religious women throughout the 1920s and 1930s.

The proliferation of storefront churches that emphasized lay participation in services and attaining status as "saints" or mediums with a unique relationship with God and/or the spirit world marked an alternative inscription of respectability in African American identity. This respectable identity was based not on bourgeois norms but on self-respect and assertiveness. The open expression of identification practiced by members of the Nation of Islam or Sanctified congregations spoke to other members of the African American community about the need to move beyond racial uplift. These women and men expressed powerful resistance to the white power structure and publicly displayed their allegiance to ideologies and beliefs that African American social reformers frowned upon. The fracturing of African American religious identity, then, undermined uplift ideology as a small group of dominant churches could no longer claim to "speak" for the religious masses.

Leisure Work and the Rise of Paradise Valley

In addition to providing alternative worship styles, storefront churches fostered the development of new musical forms and occupations. In the 1930s, the most significant religious cultural development was gospel music; indeed, the depression years were known as the "golden age of gospel."[81] Thomas A. Dorsey was the most prominent gospel composer of this period. Dorsey was a Chicago resident who combined a background of playing piano for blues great Ma Rainey with powerful religious convictions. The new gospel performers, such as Dorsey, not only borrowed musical styles from the blueswomen of the 1920s but also learned from their mobility and commercial know-how. Individual gospel performers and ensembles began to travel throughout the country, performing for different churches and revivals, just as Bessie Smith and her entourage had traveled through cities like Detroit, introducing urban migrants to vaudeville blues. This kind of itinerant performing could enhance personal incomes in the midst of the depression.

When Mahalia Jackson, the most popular gospel performer during this period and perhaps in the twentieth century, sang in churches in Chicago and later throughout the country, she could make as much as $10 a week. "By the time the Depression was over in the late thirties I was earning enough from my singing to keep me away from the maid's work and the washtubs," remembered Jackson.[82] Concerned that her music might not always pay her bills, Jackson used her savings to attend the Scott Institute of Beauty Culture and opened Mahalia's Beauty Salon in 1939, which employed five young women. "I would ride the trains on weekends to sing in churches in St. Louis and Detroit and other cities and then sit up in the day coaches at night to get back to my hairdressing business."[83] Jackson, like many women, did not rely on one means of employment but instead performed music, did occasional domestic work, and opened a beauty salon to ensure her economic survival.

Gospel music in the 1930s provided a viable means of employment and cultural expression that did not have the "immoral" connotations of blues singing; however, the popular success of gospel in the 1930s did not end some ministers' condemnation of the music. Jackson remembered: "They didn't like the hand-clapping and the stomping and they said we were bringing jazz into the church and it wasn't dignified."[84] This criticism of gospel music echoed the wider criticisms of emotionalism in Sanctified religion. Jackson and other gospel singers responded by bringing their music to the storefront churches, where its popularity quickly spread. "In those days the big colored churches didn't want me and they didn't let me in. I had to make it my business to pack the little basement-hall congregations and store-front churches and get their respect that way," remembered Jackson. "When they began to see the crowds I drew, the big churches began to sit up and take notice."[85] Gospel music was a route to respect for Jackson, and by the late 1930s, gospel choirs became a prominent part of services in established urban churches. Through these choirs, according to historian Michael Harris, "women's leadership in Protestant African American churches had found an undisputed sphere of influence and locus of operation."[86] Thus, the innovations of female musicians in storefront churches throughout the 1920s and early 1930s eventually secured for them a position of power in the cultural religious life of established African American denominations. Emotional music with secular roots had finally found a place in the large Baptist and AME churches, completing a process of "cultural southernizing" that began with the Great Migration.[87]

The emergence and popularization of gospel music were related to larger changes in urban African American musical styles that crossed the boundary between secular and sacred. Some music historians have speculated that the use of ragtime piano in gospel music originated in Detroit.[88] In his study of black popular culture, Lawrence Levine argues that many blues and jazz performers first heard piano blues and other urban styles in storefront Sanctified churches.[89] Well-known blues pianists from Detroit, such as Speckled Red and Big Maceo, played in Paradise Valley's bars as well as at private rent parties, but they may have picked up piano styles from Detroit's female gospel musicians or in female-run buffet flats.[90] Despite the influence of female gospel musicians on the popular musicians of the 1930s, however, it was male stars whose names appeared on the handbills advertising secular neighborhood gigs. This marked a shift from the 1920s, when female blues performers dominated the shows at the Koppin Theater and other African American venues. Although blues queens such as Victoria Spivey continued to perform throughout the 1930s, their popularity was on the decline whereas McKinney's Cotton Pickers and other male swing bands were on the rise. Thus, the voices of female blues musicians in the 1920s, the "queens" who were models of mobility and independence to black women, were supplanted by the new swing craze.

Singing and performing were part of a more general expansion of leisure work that occurred in the 1920s and proliferated with the economic crisis of the Great Depression. As with gospel music, much of this labor crossed boundaries between secular and sacred and licentious and respectable. The growth of Spiritualism in depression-era Detroit, for example, was directly related to the phenomenal growth in the popularity of numbers running in the 1930s. During the Great Depression, the ranks of female mediums grew, and the numbers game became the most important segment of Detroit's informal economy after Prohibition ended. As in the Nation of Islam and the political movements of the 1930s, the most visible participants of numbers running were men. Women, however, were direct employees of numbers runners and also gained secondary income through working as mediums, selling dreambooks, or providing numbers in beauty shops and small stores.

As jobs in the formal economy became increasingly scarce, the Great Depression proved to be a considerable boon to the numbers business and therefore Spiritualist churches. One might expect that community leaders who had worked to stymie the growth of the numbers business in the 1920s would be greatly concerned over its rapid growth in the 1930s. In fact, the opposite proved true. Although community leaders focused on the enforcement of norms of respectability in the 1910s and 1920s, by the early 1930s, their primary concern shifted to unemployed male workers and the success of the business community, a community that had begun to include numbers bankers in its ranks. In 1928, the Colored Ministers' Association of Detroit led a "militant crusade" against numbers gambling.[91] Only a few years later, however, the numbers bankers literally bailed out many ministers, saving their churches from repossession and giving generously to community charities. In the early 1930s, one religious leader stated: "'The numbers' is not an evil because the money is spent right in our own community and the bankers are our best charity givers."[92] As charity givers and business leaders, the numbers bankers had established themselves as part of a legitimate economic world in the African American community.

It was this turnaround in the opinion of ministers and secular leaders that Gustav Carlson, in his remarkable 1940 study of Detroit's numbers business, cited as the crucial factor in the legitimation of gambling. In the 1930s, argued Carlson, "number gambling which started out as an illegitimate activity along with other forms of gambling quite suddenly was made a legitimate one in the Detroit negro community by winning to its side the interpreters and guardians of the community's morals, i.e., the ministers, YMCA groups, etc."[93] These "guardians" of the community were swayed in part by the financial assistance they received from the numbers bankers. For example, Reverend William Peck, whose wife was the founder of the Detroit Housewives' League, reported: "The church which I was pastoring needed money to complete a construction contract that had been begun on the church building. Mr. —— did not wait for me to ask help of him but came to me and offered the full amount needed to complete the job."[94] The numbers banker who assisted Peck received gratitude and acceptance into respectable community life. This anecdote also demonstrates the interpenetration of the formal and informal economies as the banker aided not only Peck but also the construction company that received the church's contract.

Numbers bankers were also known for promoting black athletes and baseball teams throughout the country. The famous boxer Joe Louis was backed by John Roxborough, a prominent Detroit numbers banker who was known locally as the "Colored Man's Santa Claus." Louis recalled the general acceptance of the numbers bankers in the African American community in the 1930s: "If you were smart enough to have your own numbers operation and you were kind and giving in the black neighborhoods, you got as much respect as a doctor or lawyer."[95] As the depression worsened, the work of the numbers bankers seemed less like vice and more like big business to community leaders. Thus, men who in the 1920s were considered gangsters and purveyors of vice became symbols of upward mobility, business acumen, and respectable citizenship.

The widespread success of numbers bankers, Spiritualist churches, and purveyors of lucky products during the 1930s was clearly related to the unstable economy of the Great Depression. Ann Fabian has argued that in the nineteenth century the condemnation of gambling allowed an American bourgeoisie to legitimize capitalist speculation.[96] The development of the stock market, which was linked to a national banking system, transformed what had previously been condemned as gambling into legitimate financial practice. Likewise, the bourgeois identity of a "respectable" African American excluded gambling in the 1920s. Urban League officials and prominent ministers encouraged urban migrants to place their earnings in savings banks or invest them in the stock market in the years following the Great Migration. With the dramatic collapse of the stock market and the failure of Detroit's banks, the relationship between a "rational" capitalist economy and a respectable African American identity became strained.

Fabian uses James Weldon Johnson's novel, *The Autobiography of an Ex-Coloured Man*, to describe how a southern African American man could transform his identity by engaging in "economic rationality." The Great Depression, however, marked a very different trajectory for many African Americans.[97] An African American from Pittsburgh, for example, wrote the manager of the New York Stock Exchange in 1931: "After reading in the paper that you were going to hold the daily figures in the exchange to discourage 'Numbers' gambling, the thought came to me that if you would compare the stock gambling with the other you would find that considering it from every angle you would be better off not to make a statement of that kind. My savings of a life time of hard work are all tied up in the stock market at an appalling loss, as you could easily check on the books. . . . Yet I am not a hard loser, but have resorted to the 'Number' game to try and retrieve at least a part of my losses."[98] Having lost a substantial amount of money in the stock market, this individual turned to gambling in the hope of retrieving his life's savings. For this man, as for thousands of others, "legitimate" speculation in a capitalist economy appeared less profitable than gambling in the informal economy.

When they perceived that profits from numbers gambling were being invested in the community rather than lining the pockets of white capitalists, African Americans had an additional motivation to play the numbers. "Number gambling is really not gambling," argued one Detroiter. "You've got a good chance of winning and if you do win you're sure to get your money. That's more than you white folks can say about your gambling."[99] For this African American, numbers gambling provided a direct parallel to the investments whites made in formal economic institutions. Because it was possible to bet as little as a penny a day and the chances of winning were relatively high, many African Americans perceived their form of gambling as more rational than investing in a collapsing formal economy.[100]

In numbers games that were based on stock market reports, which used the final three figures in the Stock Exchange totals as the daily number, the relationship between the formal and informal economy was direct. Letters received by the New York Stock Exchange in the early 1930s indicated that some African Americans assumed the two systems of speculation worked hand in hand. "For many, many weeks I have been trying to 'catch' the New York bond on No. 375," wrote one individual, "and in looking back upon my records for over a year I note this number has never come out on the Bond. . . . Also I note '000' has never dropped—there must be a stock exchange superstition against throwing this particular number. . . . Please let me know if I should continue playing 375 or had I better change."[101] Other letters, many from women, requested either that stock market officials provide early information on stock sales so those numbers could be played or, more directly, that the officials allow a particular number to come up. A typical letter from "a worried mother" reads: "I am writing you this letter for I am a widow with a family of six. . . . I am not trying to get rich quick all I want is this money to save years of hard work which we have spent to get as far as we have. This will carry us over untell [sic] my boy can go to work and pay the rest of the money. So please try and help me by putting out my numbers."[102]

For these African American numbers players, there was little division between the formal and informal economies. One longtime numbers player in Detroit, "Dad" Brooks, explained why he played: "It is a speculation and an investment of money just as the stock market is played[;] it is to gain big money off of a small amount of money . . . so by playing numbers shows [*sic*] you how to invest your little money to help carry the heavy burden."[103] Brooks, like many others, directly equated numbers with the stock market and even suggested that engaging in one form of gambling would be good practice for engaging in the other. Both forms of speculation could potentially be profitable, and increasingly both were considered "respectable." However, most working-class African Americans had access only to speculation in the informal economy, viewing speculation in the stock market as a racially defined practice. Despite this, the stock market and the world of the "formal economy" pervaded the very organization and practice of numbers running. Detroit's numbers bankers formed their own organization and divided the city into districts, as would any business association. Employees of the operations worked in "banks" as "tellers," and according to one contemporary observer, "during the time of the drawing the policy house resembles somewhat the stock exchange during the trading period with men rushing back and forth, numbers being called, and the general loud talking and excitement."[104] In the space of the numbers bank, African Americans became brokers and traders in a local economy of their own making and under their own control.

The relative economic success of the direct and indirect employees of numbers banks, however, should not mask the fact that many of the women and men who bet ten cents a day were in dire economic straits during the 1930s. Mrs. Warren, an African American woman living in Detroit during the Great Depression, when asked why she played the numbers, answered: "I'se jus gotta hit that numbah cause I'se plum outta coal." Another numbers player reported: "If it wasn't for policy I don't know what I'd do. I ain't working and that is the only way I can make some money. . . . An old lady I knows caught fifty dollars last week off policy. She really needs the money because she hasn't any." "I ain't workin' and that is the only way I can make some money," said another.[105] Numbers playing offered these women a slim hope that they could finally pay their bills and have enough food to feed their families. The bankers who controlled the circulation of money in the numbers business were not interested in charity, however; instead, they profited off of many African American Detroiters' despair. They also created jobs and fulfilled some of the promises of economic nationalism. This mixture of exploitation, profit, and job creation also paralleled the contradictions inherent in the formal economy. The informal economic world, as exemplified by the numbers business, was not a premodern "moral economy" but was (and is) an integral part of a larger capitalist economy.[106] Indeed, it is difficult to determine where the informal economy ended and where the formal economy began in interwar African American communities.

By the late 1930s, African American women workers in Detroit could find few job opportunities outside of domestic service. Given these circumstances, the importance of employment in the numbers business, or related entrepreneurial endeavors, was clear to most African American observers. For example, Ulysses W. Boykin, a prominent African American journalist in Detroit, reported that during a rare police raid on numbers banks, 140 African American women were arrested. Writing about this incident, Boykin noted: "The majority of Negro women arrested were clerks and checkers in numbers houses raided by police. Do these figures show that Negro women are more liable to gamble than white women? Or would investigation show that where Negro girls are denied the right to work in banks, and other firms, rather than take the low-paying house-work jobs that are so readily offered, they accept clerical jobs in 'numbers banks' in order to earn a living wage." [107] Boykin's insight reflected a broader understanding on the part of community elites of the function that the informal economy had come to play in the economic life of Detroit. Because African American women continued to be barred from nearly all white-collar work, working in a numbers banks was a necessary and positive alternative to domestic service. Such a job was also preferable to other forms of employment in the informal economy, such as prostitution, a job with declining working conditions and wages in the 1930s.

Entrepreneurs who worked in the informal economy often operated legitimate businesses as well. Ulysses W. Boykin argued that "this illegal source laid the foundation from which several successful ventures grew and subsequently gave legitimate employment to Negro youths trained in business." [108] By the 1930s, numbers baron Bill Mosley had gained controlling interest in the largest African American undertaker business and the largest black cab company in Detroit. He also owned three stores, two poolrooms, and seven houses. The employees of the *Detroit Tribune*, the largest African American newspaper in Detroit during the interwar period, were indirectly supported by investments from the numbers bank that Mosley, the paper's owner, ran.[109] When Mosley died, the *Detroit Tribune* reported that 10,000 mourners went to the funeral, including several of Detroit's most prominent African American ministers, reflecting his stature in the community.[110] Many small businesses, such as grocery stores and barbershops, stayed solvent in part because of their participation in numbers running. Drake and Cayton estimated that 20 percent of the largest African American businesses in Chicago during the 1930s were owned by entrepreneurs in the numbers business. These businesses, they argued, "are those most conscious of the value of public goodwill."[111] By actively giving to local churches and community groups, the numbers bankers fostered an image of themselves as benefactors of the black community. Many African Americans also felt that the successful entrepreneurial activity supported by numbers gambling aided racial uplift, and therefore they viewed the numbers business as a positive force in the community rather than a detriment to the race. During the worst years of the Great Depression, community leaders began to embrace this view of the numbers game as a legitimate form of employment and entrepreneurship.

By the mid-1930s, the numbers bankers had successfully made the transition from the role of gangster to that of businessman through numerous acts of charity and their recognized role as leading employers in the black community. Detroit researcher Ines Marie Bridges, like many others, attributes the success of the numbers game to its legitimacy as a business: "It was very popular in The Bottom because it was inexpensive and convenient; and perhaps because as it grew, it employed many blacks as runners and clerks who could not find more socially acceptable employment elsewhere. . . . Although illegal, the numbers game was not thought of as a vice in The Bottom, because, for some people, it did provide incomes and was a source of funds for legitimate businesses."[112] Even John Dancy, who had banned numbers bankers from league offices in the 1920s, reported by 1940: "Whenever I need financial help for any of my work I can always count on these men."[113] Such largesse was particularly significant in the political climate of depression-era Detroit. By the mid-1930s, there was widespread consensus among black Detroiters that economic nationalism should be promoted through consumer leagues and other programs. Most middle-class African Americans viewed any new businesses as evidence of racial progress, whether or not they were backed by profits gained from the informal economy. Working-class African Americans were hopeful that these businesses would hire black workers, thus freeing them from dependence on white employers. As a result of this cross-class support for African American entrepreneurship, the line between businessmen and criminals was blurred beyond recognition.

At the dawn of World War II, Boykin estimated that the numbers business created a profit of $10 million per year in Detroit, a portion of which went to the female and male clerks, runners, checkers, and players for whom the game was an integral part of everyday life.[114] Although white organized crime was able to take over some of the business by World War II as it sought to replace the gap left by the repeal of Prohibition, the African American numbers business continued to be a large part of the economic life of Detroit in the postwar decades.[115] In their study *Black Metropolis*, Drake and Cayton argue that the success and social acceptance of the "policy kings" (numbers bankers) in Chicago "have given some reality to the hope of erecting an independent economy within Black Metropolis."[116] This same hope had been raised in Detroit by World War II. The interpenetration of the formal and informal sectors in 1930s Detroit was responsible for much of the success of black businesses by mid-century—from local professionals and businessmen giving and receiving numbers to the intimate relationship between the numbers banks and the New York Stock Exchange. Formal and informal labor together could, it seemed, produce a self-sustaining African American economy. Nevertheless, this local economy did not entirely offset the economic devastation of the Great Depression, and deep poverty persisted in black Detroit while numbers running flourished.

Besides being a central economic factor in urban black communities, the numbers game was associated with numerous cultural codes. The language of numbers pervaded African American vernacular during the interwar period. An announcer at a Detroit Stars baseball game would have been likely to say at an opportune moment: "Two strikes, one ball, two down and a gig on base."[117] A "gig" was a form of numbers gambling that involved three numbers, and the word "gig" increasingly was used to replace the number three. Using numbers to replace words and phrases could be particularly useful when one wanted to disguise one's speech from an ignorant observer. A young man who was fouled in front of the YMCA director at a YMCA basketball game was reported as saying: "You 727, try that again and I'll give you a kick in that big 250 of yours."[118] The pervasiveness of the numbers game is also reflected in stories of numbers players who placed successful bets based on dreams or hunches that circulated throughout the African American community and made their way into local papers. Eager players also translated unusual events, such as fires, accidents, or natural disasters, into numbers. When these popular numbers hit, they could temporarily bankrupt local numbers bankers.

Blues singers, the interpreters and creators of African American popular culture, also drew on numbers playing in their songs and performances. In the late 1920s, blues guitarist Blind Blake recorded his song "Policy Blues," with lyrics replete with cultural references to the numbers game:

> Number, numbers, 'bout to drive me mad.
> Number, numbers, 'bout to drive me mad.
> Thinking about the money that I should have had.

I beg my baby, let me in her door.
I beg my baby, let me in her door.
Want to put my twenty-five, fifty-five, seventy-five
In her seven-seventeen twenty-four.[119]

The second stanza is clearly a sexual reference using numbers in place of words. Singing about numbers and other segments of the informal economy such as selling illegal liquor allowed blues singers to connect with their audiences and sell more records. Both performers and listeners delighted in the shared cultural knowledge and language of numbers gambling that outsiders found impenetrable.

All of these cultural practices set African American participants in the numbers game apart from many in the white community and elite African Americans who did not participate knowingly in the informal economy. Intricate knowledge of numbers playing was necessary for entrepreneurs to be successful in the game, such as those who sold tip sheets or ran numbers in their neighborhood. Many of these entrepreneurs were women who continued to benefit from numbers gambling by selling products as part of the "confidence racket." An examination of any African American newspaper published during the interwar period will reveal numerous advertisements for dreambooks and "lucky products" designed to help players pick numbers that were likely to "hit" on a particular day. Dreambooks, which translated symbols that appeared in dreams into numbers, were particularly popular throughout the African American community.[120] Numbers players in Detroit could buy these books at newspaper stands or order them through the mail from advertisements. One Detroit player stated: "I play pretty heavy when I . . . get a good dream. . . . I dream something and then look it up in my dream book. . . . I had a dream last night and I'll play it for three days and it's bound to come out."[121] Through the use of dreams, urban African Americans used personal knowledge for financial gain in a way that directly contradicted the supposed rationality of the formal economy. The interpretation of dreams for profit was also a form of leisure, or play, that many men and women enjoyed spending time discussing and debating.

African American women also sold tip sheets that promised inside information on numbers likely to hit. Some dreambooks and tip sheets were published locally as small pamphlets and sold for an average of ten cents apiece. Popular national publications advertised in newspapers were more likely to have been published in Chicago or Harlem. Thus, numbers players in Detroit supported entrepreneurs in other cities as well as their own, creating a national network of numbers-related businesses. Mediums and beauty operators sold a variety of "lucky products" that, if used properly, would bring good luck to a numbers player. The most popular product in Detroit was incense that, when burned, could bring luck and possibly a vision of the best number to play. Holy oil was popular among African American women, who reportedly added it to their dishwater or washing machine to enhance their luck.[122] Developing and selling lucky products, dreambooks, and tip sheets became a significant subeconomy of the numbers game by the 1930s. None of these activities were strictly illegal, but they would not have existed outside the context of gambling.

During a period of severe economic hardship, Detroit's African American residents had to find alternative means to pay the rent and feed their families. With the repeal of Prohibition and the loss of male wages, the heady days of the buffet flat were waning. The numbers bankers and some of their employees took on the flamboyant identity of the 1920s gangster. When Irene Rosemond moved to Detroit from New York City in the mid-1930s with her middle-class family, she immediately encountered Detroit's codes of class and occupation. "I remember that people were in a state of shock because I had two fur coats," said Rosemond, who had brought her coats from Harlem, where they apparently caused little notice. "Usually the people who wore fur coats were people in the Numbers rackets. Many people said, 'Do you work for the numbers,' I said, 'No.' . . . I don't think they ever believed me." [123] This anecdote indicates both that some female employees of the numbers business could have afforded a fur coat and that to wear such attire in depression-era Detroit was to set yourself apart from others. Rosemond's anecdote also reveals that the influx of large amounts of money into the informal economy complicated the ranking of class identity in Detroit. Should women and men who were recognized as gangsters, numbers runners, or madams be considered members of the elite because of their relative wealth? Or should the "genteel performance" of an older middle-class elite set the standards of class position?[124] Increasingly, the former was true, as numbers bankers were recognized as legitimate businessmen and the older elite lost income and homes to the ravages of the depression. This shift destabilized the link between class identity and respectability. Owning a fur coat, a nice car, or your own home did not necessarily translate into respectability in a period when the surest route to such material wealth was through the informal economy. As a result, creating class distinctions as a project of racial reform became problematic if such distinctions could indicate participation in "suspect" activities.

By the 1930s, numbers gambling was a practice shared by working- and middle-class African Americans. Describing the numbers game in Harlem,

Claude McKay reported: "Numbers is a people's game, a community pastime in which old and young, literate and illiterate, the neediest folk and the well-to-do all participate."[125] Therefore, it was difficult to argue that numbers gambling was a practice of the poor or naive recent migrant. Indeed, in his book *Black Bourgeoisie*, E. Franklin Frazier lamented the pervasiveness of numbers gambling among "Negro society" of the interwar and postwar periods. "It is not unusual," argued Frazier, "for Negro professional men and their wives to play the 'numbers' daily." The popularity of numbers had permeated even the highest levels of the professional class, in Frazier's view. "Even the wives of Negro college professors are sometimes 'writers' or collectors of 'numbers' for the 'numbers racket.'"[126] This cross-class participation in the informal economy was not limited to numbers gambling. One only needs to envision middle-class leisure among whites and blacks drinking in speakeasies during Prohibition to realize that all classes were implicated in the burgeoning of the informal economy. Because local businesses depended on financial backing from such "suspect" sources in the early years of the depression, it is understandable that most professional women and men turned a blind eye to the technically illegal practices occurring in their communities.

Although numbers gambling remained underground, after President Franklin Roosevelt's repeal of Prohibition, former speakeasies became popular cabarets, bars, and restaurants in Paradise Valley. Like the numbers bankers, blind pig proprietors became "legitimate" businessmen and businesswomen in the 1930s. Hastings and St. Antoine Streets, in the heart of the East Side, became known for their nightlife and restaurants. Community leaders celebrated rather than criticized these black businesses. "St. Antoine was quite a mecca," remembered M. Kelly Fritz. "We'd all proceed down St. Antoine to the restaurants. There were all sorts of cafes and what-not there."[127] Southern migrants had become urban entrepreneurs who made use of available resources to expand their opportunities. In doing so, they created a vibrant urban culture that was neither distinctly southern nor emblematic of northern bourgeois respectability. Ironically, the dynamic atmosphere of the East Side had done more to undercut the negative label of "ghetto" than the cleanup campaigns and discipline practiced by the Urban League.

Conclusion

By the mid-1930s, racial uplift ideology in Detroit had been undermined by a variety of factors facilitated by the Great Depression's economic crisis. Male unemployment, the growth of religious sects, and the acceptance of numbers bankers in the ranks of the respectable all eroded a community identity based on self-restraint, decorum, and religiosity. A major symptom of this shift was the emergence of a masculine language of self-defense and self-determination. In a period of social turmoil and violence, defending oneself against police brutality, racist employers, and intrusive state institutions appealed to many black Detroiters. Although this discourse incorporated traditional female notions of caretaking, leaders of these new movements most often invoked the more masculine aspects of the ideology. Nevertheless, African American women were instrumental in the growth of economic nationalism, new religious groups, and social activism. No longer considered the passive victims of migration and urbanization, these women participated in a large-scale effort to explore and develop new, more assertive strategies to obtain civil rights and fight persistent discrimination.

Another significant factor undermined uplift ideologues' authority during the 1930s—the growth of a state apparatus directly providing relief and other services to African Americans. Increasingly, the Urban League, Second Baptist Church, and YWCA no longer acted as intermediaries between the black and white communities, as they had for decades. Industrial unions and new political organizations challenged these established institutions to better represent working-class blacks' interests. New Deal agencies also offered new outlets of charity and employment to the African American community. Often, it was individual African American women who dealt with these organizations, making demands and strategically using available resources in ways that shaped not only the African American community but also the nature of relief and reform.

6 Grassroots Activism, New Deal Policies, and the Transformation of African American Reform in the 1930s

> *Mrs. Roosevelt, I am writing to ask you to please help me to get my job back. I am a widow woman with no means to support myself last year I was laid off the WPA in Dec. and two weeks after I was laid off I lost everything in a fire and I didn't get back on the WPA until February. Please Mrs. Roosevelt help me to get a job I don't care what kind of work it is. I have went every place I know to go and haven't found anything and if I don't find something soon I won't have anyplace to stay. Please help me Mrs. Roosevelt you can send anyone to investigate and they will see my condition. From one of your many friends.*
>
> Annie Perkins to Eleanor Roosevelt, 1 November 1939

In 1939, Annie Perkins, an African American widow, wrote to Eleanor Roosevelt to ask for help getting back her Works Progress Administration (WPA) job. Her letter, and hundreds more like it, signaled a dramatic shift in the lives of Detroit's African Americans. Rather than turning to the Urban League, Second Baptist Church, women's clubs, or other traditional sources of relief and aid, African American women developed a strategic relationship with federal and local agencies to get through the worst years of the Great Depression. This new relationship with the state undermined female uplift ideology and the construction of a respectable community identity. African American leaders and relief clients instead worked to ensure that state agencies reaching out to America's unemployed did not practice overt racial discrimination. Although these efforts were not always successful, the struggles over New Deal policies in the 1930s foreshadowed the civil rights struggles during and after World War II.

By the end of the 1930s, the labor movement had challenged the traditional relationship between Detroit's white elites and African Americans. Early in the decade, organizations such as the Civic Rights Committee (CRC) and the Communist Party persuaded working-class African Americans to look beyond traditional interracial organizations to represent their interests. By the time of the pivotal 1939 strike against Chrysler, the black working class was willing to join the new industrial unions and abandon the conciliatory interracial practices of racial uplift ideologues. This working-class activism reinvigorated the NAACP's Detroit branch and brought a new kind of interracial politics to the city. Rather than focusing on presenting a respectable face to the white community, black labor organizers pushed white employers to recognize their rights as workers. In the process, black activists targeted male workers and emphasized black women's domestic roles.

This focus on masculinity pervaded working-class activism in the 1930s. Robin D. G. Kelley, for example, notes: "The language of masculinity . . . dominated representations of grass-roots organizing" in the Communist Party during a period of relatively high African American involvement. "African American radical writers' and artists' persistent theme of manhood and violent resistance," Kelley states, "struck an enticing chord that probably reverberated louder than allusions to racial pride."[1] In her study of labor organizing in Minneapolis, Elizabeth Faue similarly stresses how masculine narratives of struggle and violence subordinated female activism and agency in the 1930s.[2] Despite this masculine rhetoric, African American women played an active role in working-class mobilization throughout the decade. Their grassroots organizing in the Great Depression's early years laid the groundwork for union activists to build the UAW after the passage of the 1935 Wagner Act. This activism changed the balance of power in black Detroit as industrial unionism supplanted earlier relations between white industrialists and black elites. Likewise, the New Deal undermined black women's relations with traditional African American institutions and gave them new sources of aid and empowerment.

Because of discrimination in both public and private institutions, the history of women and reform differs across racial lines. In the 1910s and 1920s, white female reformers largely excluded African American women from their organizations and ignored them as potential clients, focusing instead on assimilating European immigrants.[3] As a result, black female activists devised a separate network of institutions in their own neighborhoods. These institutions accepted women's simultaneous roles as wage earners and mothers, expanding the definition of maternalism while still emphasizing women's unique roles as nurturers and caregivers.[4] Whereas white reformers generally emphasized the individual cultural assimilation and social mobility of their clients, black reformers devised programs that stressed community strength and racial uplift.

The unique character of black female reform institutions emerged in relative isolation from the state. Without access to the "female dominion" of American policy making in child welfare,[5] black women did not have the opportunity either to lobby or to serve in government agencies. Although many early-twentieth-century black female reformers who called themselves "social workers" were graduates of seminaries, normal schools, or colleges, they did not have equal access to the University of Chicago and other outstanding institutions in the field of professional social work. Thus, until the 1930s, two parallel but distinct reform movements developed. The New Deal, however, brought these movements together for the first time. Traditional African American reform agencies could not handle the growing caseload of the unemployed and poor during the Great Depression. Meanwhile, federal and local state agencies were reaching out to the unemployed to offer unprecedented relief. New ties between African American women and the state accelerated the decline in maternalist rhetoric and female racial uplift ideology in the black community.[6] By the early 1930s, the beginning of a dramatic transition in the relationship of African Americans to federal and local government was under way—a transition in which women played a central role but within male-dominated institutions and with less visibility. Although African American women would continue their charity efforts, the large-scale reform work of the 1930s focused on economic nationalism, unionization, and civil rights. This political work, unlike the assimilation of migrants in Detroit, did not need the backing of female moral suasion for its success.

Because African American organizations had less expertise and resources, as charity became a more interracial project in the 1930s, white-dominated public and private agencies devalued African American reform styles. As social reform shifted from a personalized style to one that was more scientific, "rational," and controlled through large private umbrella agencies and the state, the definition of a "respectable" reformer was based on a changing set of standards. For mediating institutions, such as the Detroit Urban League and the Second Baptist Church, these changes in reform work facilitated a shift away from female respectability. Sex-segregated leisure activities, for example, were stressed less often than the need for young African Americans to have access to commercial recreation in supervised spaces. Decades of African American reform did, however, have an impact on the programs developed by New Deal agencies. Household worker training programs in Detroit run by the WPA and the National Youth Administration (NYA) taught lessons in hygiene and personal appearance as well as domestic science. Nevertheless, these programs were less attuned to the needs of African American women because they insisted that household workers live in their employers' houses. New Deal training programs also had a less holistic approach to education, leaving out the courses on African American history and culture that female uplift ideologues had been careful to include in their programs. Whereas white reformers were concerned primarily with employment and the labor market in the 1930s, middle-class African American women saw employee training as a route to racial uplift.

Despite African American female reformers' decline in prominence during the 1930s, the discourse of female respectability could still be found in a variety of programs. African American women's clubs, for example, continued to meet and expand. The Detroit Association of Colored Women's Clubs had a membership of seventy-three clubs by 1945.[7] Although a focus on bourgeois respectability had retreated to the background, at times, reformers incorporated respectability into public programs such as household worker training projects. Presenting a respectable public self, however, was no longer the best way for working-class African American women to obtain the material goods they needed to survive. Rather, being outspoken advocates of civil rights and demanding these rights from the state were increasingly accepted and effective survival strategies. These new routes to racial empowerment bypassed Detroit's traditional black institutions. Rather than focusing on intracommunity reform, activists in the 1930s were overtly political and directly confronted the white establishment.

Grassroots Activism during the Depression

The lack of job opportunities for African American men and women during the Great Depression galvanized a variety of forms of protest that challenged the Detroit Urban League's preeminence. Some of these groups, such as the Nation of Islam, were overtly nationalist, working to build a self-sufficient and separate black community. Other groups worked in alliance with whites in the well-established tradition of the Urban League and the NAACP and in new organizations with ties to the Communist Party. These groups were central to the success of organized labor by the end of the decade. However, this success was preceded by years of conflict over the role the UAW and the Congress of Industrial Organizations (CIO) would play in black Detroit. After the 1935 passage of the Wagner Act established workers' right to organize and bargain collectively, the national offices of the Urban League and the NAACP actively supported and promoted organized labor. The Detroit branches of these organizations, however, remained tied to a system of corporate paternalism and acted as allies of white industrialists.

The gradual conversion of black Detroit's leading ministers and race leaders to the goals of industrial unionism has been well documented.[8] This conversion, however, was predicated on the establishment of competing organizations and ideologies in the years prior to the successful strikes of the late 1930s and early 1940s. One such organization was the CRC, formed in 1933 by Snow Grigsby, who was dissatisfied with the Detroit Urban League's efforts to place African Americans in prominent positions. Grigsby used the CRC to publicize the abysmal hiring record of the Detroit city government and became a major spokesman in the community for the hiring of African Americans in public jobs.[9] Grigsby himself had hoped to find employment in the public sector after migrating to Detroit from South Carolina in 1923. After a decade of disappointment, an enraged Grigsby compiled a pamphlet detailing the rampant discrimination in hiring by city officials. "We based it on economics," remembered Grigsby, "because we found this: it's not worth anything to be able to go in one of your finest places and sit down to eat, if you don't have the price of a meal. We figure the first thing is to have the job, and other things will automatically follow. Because you will find that the only thing that America respects today is the dollar and the vote."[10]

The significance of Grigsby's pamphlet lies in its explicit challenge to Detroit's African American leaders. In it, Grigsby systematically documented the abominable hiring records of the police department, Board of Education, fire department, and public libraries. Grigsby noted, for example, that none of the nearly 500 clerical workers hired by the Board of Education were African American.[11] Few professionals in the community, argued Grigsby, were members of the NAACP's local branch, which was the logical organization to address the issue of public hiring. "It will be done when our Negro leaders quit being so selfish," declared Grigsby, "and stop using organizations for personal and private business advancement, but use them for the welfare of the masses, and particularly the man who is farthest down. Organizations should be used to open up, rather than cover up."[12] In short, Grigsby was calling for a more militant stand by the middle classes in the face of their failure to convince white city officials to hire trained and educated African Americans. John Dancy's strategy of displaying attractive and well-educated African American women in the past decade had done little to open up hiring; Grigsby's more militant tactic of publicly embarrassing city officials and challenging local elites would prove more effective.

By 1937, some of Grigsby's economic goals for his community had been met. "Negroes operate 358 business establishments in the City of Detroit," noted Grigsby. "This number does not include laundries, barber shops, beauty parlors, dry cleaning, and restaurants. Negroes operate 48 grocery stores and meat markets, 97 restaurants, and 22 drug stores."[13] Despite this short-term economic success, largely due to the initiative of businessmen and women, Grigsby went on to attack community leaders yet again for their shortcomings: "Negro leaders and organizations have been too afraid to go out into the deep where things are rough. They have chosen to stay within a realm of agreement. If the Negroes are going to solve the problem that confronts them in Detroit and America today, we must move out of the realm of agreement into a realm of friction and conflict for the Negro is becoming an economic factor in the scheme of American life. The Negro will never take his place as a respectable citizen until he learns to serve notice on everyone that he is willing to fight for his rightful place in the sun."[14] Respectable citizenship was the common goal toward which both Grigsby and an older African American elite were striving.[15] The difference between them was a matter of tactics. Rather than staying within a "realm of agreement"—characterized by decorum and negotiation with white elites—Grigsby preached action, conflict, and self-defense. These latter attributes were typical of the more masculine styles of racial reform that marked the 1930s.

Holding public forums in neighborhood churches, Grigsby and the CRC raised the consciousness of many in Detroit's African American community. CRC organizers asked, Where are African Americans in the post offices, in our children's classrooms, reading our meters? Rather than telling young African American women that they needed to dress appropriately and behave "like Ladies," the CRC argued that they had the *right* to jobs that were supported by the taxes of the community. Although feminine bourgeois ideals of respectability were largely absent from Grigsby's rhetoric, his campaign improved conditions primarily for educated African American women seeking white-collar work—the same group targeted by the Detroit Urban League in the 1920s.[16]

The efforts of Grigsby's CRC represented only a fraction of African American activism during the early years of the Great Depression, when it was clear that the older organizations and churches could not adequately meet the challenges of massive unemployment and poverty. "Between the unions and the bread lines and the bootlegging and the general bandying-about of civic concerns," remembered Coleman Young of the early 1930s, "the East side was an ideological orgy."[17] This "ideological orgy" undermined the attempt to construct a community identity based on norms of respectability in a dramatic fashion. Rather than presenting a unified and orderly set of demands to the white community, African Americans from all social classes were empowered by the sense of crisis to speak out publicly on a variety of issues. These working-class voices often drowned out the reserved pronouncements of Reverend Robert Bradby and John Dancy.

If one event galvanized Detroit's industrial working class in the early 1930s, it was the Ford Hunger March, the first major battle in the long fight against Ford Motor Company. When the impact of the depression became clear, black and white workers formed unemployed councils to respond to the increasingly frequent evictions of families, demand more relief from state agencies, and provide services such as food and clothing for unemployed people. Communist Party members were instrumental in the organization of these councils, and the ranks of African American members of the party grew dramatically during the depression.[18] In March 1932, the unemployed councils organized a march through Detroit that ended in a rally at the Ford Motor Company's employment office in River Rouge to demand relief for thousands of unemployed Ford workers. Shelton Tappes, who participated in the march, remembered the diverse participants, including "some church groups, some revolutionary party groups. . . . Then there was a group of Baptist. It was a white Sunday School. Then there were several black groups."[19] At the gates of the plant, Dearborn police and private guards hired by Ford attacked marchers with fire hoses and guns. By the end of melee, four men were dead, one an African American, and many more wounded.[20] When organizers discovered that the African American man could not be buried alongside the other murdered marchers, they cremated his body and scattered the ashes over the Rouge plant from a plane.[21] Such dramatic scenes of interracial social protest would mark much of the decade.

In addition to organizing large-scale marches and demonstrations, the unemployed councils protected countless families from eviction. Joseph Billups, an African American activist who led one such council, remembered how this process worked. After council members returned evicted belongings to a house or apartment, "we left the guard there to take care to notify us if the sheriff or deputy sheriff would come back again; but if we put the furniture back they wouldn't bother them unless the landlord paid them again. So very few landlords would pay it again because the same thing would happen over and over." When electricity was cut off by the city, one skilled member of the unemployed councils would reconnect the wiring.[22] The groups who aided evicted families were called flying squadrons and were noted for the speed with which they responded to a call for help.[23] The work of the squadrons was one of self-defense, protecting families from homelessness and violence. Many of the members of the squadrons were African American women who were defending the homes and families they had worked so hard to build.

Besides almost daily clashes with landlords and police, the most distinct memories for many African American residents during the early years of the Great Depression were the numerous meetings and gatherings throughout the city, often in public spaces. "We had meetings on the city hall steps practically every night and the city hall yard would be overflowing—we would have a couple thousand people there every night," remembered Billups.[24] East Grand Circus Park in downtown Detroit became a central gathering site for unemployed women and men, political activists, and curious onlookers after Detroit's new liberal mayor, Frank Murphy, declared it a free-speech zone.[25] "Well you didn't have no trouble in getting a crowd," recalled Billups. "You see at the time there were several different political groups in there. . . . Well we permitted this one to get up and talk and the other one to get up and talk, not two of the same kind. And then the people out there asked questions. We used to have an audience there anytime of night, any time of day in Grand Circus Park."[26] The organizations represented on the Grand Circus Park podium included unemployed councils, the Nat Turner Club organized by African American men and women in response to the Scottsboro case, and many others. It was an interracial group that shared working-class standing in the community. In the early 1930s, this diverse coalition laid the groundwork for the successful organizing of the UAW.

This working-class political activity was anathema to the Detroit Urban League, religious leaders, and even the local NAACP, all of which had linked their fortunes with those of Henry Ford for so many years. "It was not before 1936," argues August Meier and Elliott Rudwick, "that the first significant voices on behalf of the union appeared among the city's Negro elite."[27] Meanwhile, the voices of working-class African Americans were challenging the deafening silence of Dancy and Bradby, who continued to believe that if African American workers could prove themselves worthy of full citizenship, they would eventually obtain it without violence and confrontation. In the face of increased police brutality against African Americans and high rates of unemployment during the 1930s, this passive stance seemed unjust to many.[28] Individuals such as Snow Grigsby represented what Beth Tompkins Bates has called the "new crowd" that challenged the "old guard" of black leaders "who wanted to maintain a somber, reformist stance."[29] By 1935, this "new crowd" began to dismantle the power structure of Detroit's black elite by giving working-class African Americans the opportunity to challenge the limits of reform based on bourgeois respectability.

The NAACP's local chapter was not known for its militancy in depression-era Detroit. Whereas the national NAACP, optimistic about the CIO's professed commitment to interracial solidarity, endorsed industrial unionism in 1936, the Detroit branch refused to participate in organizing drives. Similarly, the Detroit Urban League departed from its national office's policy of supporting industrial unionism. The National Urban League was convinced by 1934 that the federal government would support labor, but Dancy's close alliance with Ford and other industrialists prevented him from endorsing organizing efforts.[30] This leadership vacuum provided an opportunity for new interracial organizations to step into prominence. The National Negro Congress (NNC), for example, was an explicitly prolabor organization with ties to the Communist Party that challenged the local NAACP to support organizing efforts after 1935. Although the success of this group was limited, NNC activists worked with the NAACP, pushing it to change its stance toward labor. "In Detroit," argues Bates, "the interests and needs of black workers increasingly shaped the discourse of the reform agenda in the black community through the combined efforts of the local chapter of the NNC . . . and the new-crowd leaders in the Detroit NAACP chapter, some of whom were members of both the NNC and the NAACP."[31] Grigsby was one such individual who was active in both the NAACP and new organizations like the NNC that challenged Detroit's traditional leadership.

When the local chapter of the NAACP began slowly to shift its allegiance from the white industrialists to the CIO, its membership increased significantly. By the early 1940s, the Detroit local was the largest in the country, demonstrating the benefits of incorporating working-class interests.[32] The relationship between Ford and Detroit's black leaders in the Urban League and large churches, however, had a long and potent history. During and after the Great Migration, black men seeking jobs turned first to the Second Baptist Church or the Urban League. There, Bradby and Dancy had the power to place them in Ford factories. Prominent white industrialists also served on the Urban League board of directors and financed numerous programs in the leading reform institutions during the late 1910s and 1920s. Breaking with the past seemed foolhardy to many in Detroit's black elite. Despite the intransigence of these leaders, the UAW did make major inroads in the black community. The 1939 strike against Chrysler revealed how much progress organizers had made. Nearly 1,700 black workers walked out of the Dodge plant on Detroit's East Side, and despite the company's attempt to recruit black strikebreakers, the UAW managed to maintain enough racial unity to win the strike.[33] The real test of the UAW's ties to the black community occurred two years later, when the union struck against the Ford Motor Company, the largest industrial employer of African Americans in the city, as well as the world. When black workers walked out of the Ford plant, despite the pleas of many black ministers, they signaled their final break with the "old guard."

The abandonment of corporate paternalism and acceptance of unionization by Detroit's black community marked the end of the Detroit Urban League's dominance. The Ford strikers knew they could depend on a new group of black leaders who did not rely on bourgeois respectability to facilitate their relations with the white community. Because women carried the burden of presenting respectability to the public, they became less visible actors in racial reform during the unionization movement of the late 1930s and early 1940s. Nonetheless, union activists appealed to the wives of male workers to persuade their husbands that racial discrimination was no longer prevalent in organized labor. Activist Geraldine Bledsoe remembered that "professional people" in the community "encouraged Negroes to resist the labor movement," but by "working with their wives, especially . . . we finally were able to get the Negro moving into the labor unions."[34] Without female support for unionization, the UAW might have failed to recruit the masses of black industrial workers.

Labor organizers had long emphasized "manhood rights" when making their claims. This rhetoric downplayed the role of women as workers and activists while highlighting their position in the home. For African Americans, argues historian Melinda Chateauvert, manhood rights encompassed political demands for equal rights. "Manhood also signified," she asserts, "the right of black men to protect black women and children from white men, and to preserve the family by restoring mothers to the home. In this sense, manhood rights were not for men only."[35] The secondary rights gained by wives and mothers constituted a claim to respectability, a major goal of the black community during the Great Migration. Chateauvert notes that in the 1930s "female domesticity supported male union activism." Thus, the wives of Ford workers were instrumental in supporting the UAW. Nevertheless, the New Deal promoted the image of the "Black Worker," in which "negroes were men and men were workers."[36] By asserting the rights of black working men in the Great Depression, organizers diminished the public role of women that accompanied racial uplift ideology. Despite this, women as well as men benefited from the campaigns of the UAW and other labor organizations. By the late 1930s, African American women throughout Detroit worked in union auxiliaries and marched in picket lines to demand representation from the industries that had exploited their husbands, sons, and fathers since the Great Migration. Increasingly, these women also demanded equal access to resources from city, state, and federal agencies.

The Great Depression and African American Reform

In the early years of the Great Depression, Detroit was rife with street-level activism by nationalist groups and new interracial organizations that challenged the dominance of racial uplift institutions. After 1935, the drive for unionization had begun in earnest, facilitated by a shift in the political allegiance of Detroit's black community. Like the vast majority of African Americans, Detroit blacks allied themselves with the Republican Party before 1932. In the early 1930s, however, a coalition was developing between organized labor and the "new crowd" of black leadership. Franklin Roosevelt's overwhelming victory in the 1932 election convinced many that the Republican Party's power was quickly diminishing. By the mid-term 1934 elections, the Democratic Party had made major inroads in the black community, winning all of the majority black districts in the city.[37] By Roosevelt's second term, black Detroiters had forged a new relationship with the state. Long ignored by local and national agencies, hungry and homeless families were having at least some of their needs met by relief programs.

The large numbers of the unemployed who crowded Detroit's streets and social agencies transformed the means of dispensing aid to the needy. Detroit, more than any other city in the United States, turned to public relief rather than private charity to deal with its growing social problems even before the New Deal.[38] This transformation impacted the lives of middle-class African Americans who had worked in the city since the early years of the Great Migration in two different ways. On the one hand, these men and women were gratified that Detroit's African American community's needs were finally being at least partially met by public agencies; on the other hand, public relief usurped the role that the Detroit Urban League, established churches, and women's clubs had played for so many years.[39]

In the early years of the Great Depression, the Detroit Urban League was overwhelmed with large numbers of men and women seeking aid. In 1930, Dancy reported that "serried throngs of the unemployed have visited our office in the hope that something might be done to aid them in their struggle for existence."[40] League officials and community groups responded quickly, using fund-raising techniques well-honed through years of organizing. In 1931, one of the worst years of the depression, a group of African American women raised $259 by hosting a Christmas party and promptly spent the money on eighty-nine pairs of shoes and enough clothing for seventy-six indigent children. A black-owned theater on Hastings Street, in the heart of the East Side, raised $102 through benefit performances. The following year, however, the Christmas party raised only $25, and the benefit performances brought in even less.[41] As wages disappeared throughout the community, private charity efforts could not keep up with the unemployed's dire needs. By 1933, African American social workers and reformers were being laid off: two women, for example, who had worked for the Detroit Urban League for more than a decade were fired.[42] Increasingly, the Detroit Urban League and other charity groups turned to Detroit's Department of Public Welfare and the Mayor's Unemployment Committee (MUC) for assistance.

Frank Murphy, Detroit's newly elected mayor, formed the MUC in 1931. Murphy was well known and generally liked in the black community because of his handling of the Ossian Sweet case as a local judge in the mid-1920s. He worked to maintain these ties by appointing John Dancy, the most prominent African American leader in Detroit, as the head of the MUC's Colored Advisory Committee. Dancy was given no funds to disperse directly to needy African Americans; instead, he was responsible for uncovering racial discrimination in the dispersal of public money.[43] This task loomed large because during the first half of the 1930s, African Americans made up as much as 35 percent of the public relief rolls.[44] Other African American reformers worked closely with city officials when the Advisory Relief Council of the Detroit Community Union began to organize the city into districts to better facilitate the relief efforts of private and public charity organizations. The MUC divided the city into the same districts as those used by the Department of Public Welfare, and the Detroit Community Union asked local leaders to form committees to organize relief work.[45] The work done by the district councils was remarkably similar to the work done by the committees that surveyed the African American community in 1920 and 1926 to produce the *Negro in Detroit* studies. In the 1930s, however, the city used the district surveys to ameliorate deteriorating conditions in the African American community and combat discrimination in the dispensing of relief.

When the Advisory Relief Council organized district councils in 1932, it was careful to justify its plan to Detroit's residents and traditional charity givers. "Our cities have grown to be so large and the social machinery has become so complicated that it seems quite impossible for any number of individuals to fit themselves into the scheme of things and to express their feeling of kindliness to their fellowman," the council argued.[46] Rationally organizing the city, it believed, would facilitate the continued expression of "kindliness" by encouraging communication between the residents of a particular neighborhood and the many agencies that sought to serve that neighborhood. In order to carry out this plan, district councils studied the existing resources in each district and the district's needs for recreation, relief, and employment offices. The councils then coordinated the work of private groups with that of the Department of Public Welfare to prevent any duplication of services. Case committees were set up in each district to which local people could refer families for help.[47] Cooperation between a variety of agencies may have prevented the duplication of relief services to individuals and families; however, this seeming "advance" in reform also undercut some African American women's survival strategies. No longer could women easily combine a variety of sources of aid to feed themselves and their families. African American female reformers also lost some of the advantages of the older, less "rational" system of reform. Although many women were active in the district councils, they tended not to hold leadership positions, and the Department of Public Welfare and other white-dominated organizations employed few African Americans.

The Alfred District encompassed the African American East Side neighborhood. This district was considered by many to be the most successful because of local activists' enthusiasm to aid in the study of the community's resources and needs.[48] Since African American church leaders and reformers had asked for greater attention from city officials for so many years, it is no wonder that they welcomed the help of city and state officials. These reformers worked with city officials to prioritize and document the needs of the community. The survey committee compiled district maps that contrasted the amount of commercial recreation (billiard parlors, bowling alleys, and dance halls) with the amount of noncommercial recreation (YMCAs, YWCAs, settlement houses, and recreation centers).[49] This visual mapping of available recreation paralleled the mapping carried out by the Detroit Urban League in the early 1920s. Local community leaders used these findings to demand more workers in noncommercial recreation centers and better regulation and supervision of commercial recreation. By the 1930s, reformers viewed the "victims" of the imbalance of recreation, however, as idle children. This image contrasted with the dominant image during the late 1910s and early 1920s of the African American female migrant who could be lured into a life of vice through commercial recreation.

An increased concern over juvenile delinquency pervaded the reform literature of the 1930s, particularly in discussions of "appropriate" recreational activities. One speaker from the police department's Women's Division alerted a meeting of the district council about a growing problem with girls' gangs, a problem that was particularly pronounced, she argued, on Detroit's East Side. In most cases, suggested the policewoman, young girls who participated in illegal or immoral activity were enticed by an older person who encouraged them to "smoke marijuana cigarettes" or drink alcohol.[50] Reformers also raised concerns in district council meetings about "pri-

Mapping of commercial recreation in the Alfred District, 1934. Courtesy of Archives of Labor and Urban Affairs, Wayne State University.

vate dances, for which music is furnished by mechanical pianos." A representative of the Committee on Youth Legislation explained to the central committee of the council in 1938 that "the leasing of these machines to private parties is a 'racket.' At these house dances often marijuana cigarettes and liquor are sold and rooms are rented to youngsters for immoral purposes. The police are now taking the stand that the nickels put in to produce the music constitute admission."[51] If the hosts of the party charged "admission," the police could argue that the event was commercial recreation rather than a private party and that it therefore could be regulated and supervised. These parties in the majority-black Alfred District were likely rent parties thrown to raise enough money to pay the astronomical rents charged by landlords. Although many of the participants in rent parties were adults, the focus of this discussion was the entertainment's effect on Detroit's youth.

Significantly, although in reform discourse the "victims" of inappropriate recreation shifted from adult women to young women and children, the depiction of these victims as passive was similar to discussions of vulnerable female migrants in the early twentieth century. Other continuities in the district councils' language included the rationale for creating homemakers' clubs. "Realizing that a few unthrifty and slovenly families can give an entire neighborhood a bad reputation," argued the committee that developed homemakers' clubs in the Alfred District, "these clubs have endeavored to get these families interested in the clubs nearest them." [52] Club meetings were held in the houses of members who strove to set an example for others to follow. Unfortunately, when renters made dramatic improvements in the appearance of their homes, landlords often raised their rents.[53] In these examples, bourgeois respectability as a reform strategy operated on a city-wide level, and the programs developed by African American women in the Alfred District were embraced by other white-dominated district councils.

At other times, the district councils dismissed African American reform efforts that came under their scrutiny as unscientific or poorly managed. The director of the Alfred District council, for example, alerted the state unemployment commission about "the growth of certain illegitimate and fraudulent employment agencies operating as labor, religious, and social movements within the Negro community." [54] These allegedly fraudulent agencies might have included Snow Grigsby's CRC, church-based employment agencies, or other legitimate African American reform efforts. To enable the creation of a vast public relief system, however, white leaders argued, the "dependence of Negroes on these agencies of escape and fraud" had to end.[55] The creation of district councils that regulated reform streamlined the creation of a public relief system. At the same time, the district councils began to bridge the gap between private and public, and African American and white, agencies.

The transition from private charity to public relief was not total, and Great Migration–era reform institutions continued to promote programs that emphasized the "respectability" of African Americans throughout the 1930s. In the Eight Mile Road community, the Urban League sponsored "home, garden, and kitchen contests." [56] Some Urban League classes in Detroit also continued to teach bourgeois respectability to young women. For example, in a "bride's class," young women learned "the proper procedure in planning formal and informal teas, bridge parties, dances, buffet suppers . . . proper usage of written social graces," and so on.[57] African American women's clubs such as the Detroit Study Club and the Willing Workers continued their meetings and activities throughout the depression.[58] In 1935, a number of these clubs organized into the Scyades, an acronym for the Sorosis Group, Current Topic Study Club, Youth Council of the NAACP, Atha Study Club, Detroit Study Club, and New Era Study Club. Women from these clubs met annually to celebrate a "Negro woman who has won acclaim in her particular field of endeavor."[59] Mary McLeod Bethune was one of many women honored by Detroit's women's clubs. The Scyades' work in the 1930s was similar in tone and content to clubwomen's work in the 1910s and 1920s; however, community leaders did not hold up these women as exemplars of racial reform.

A typical program launched in the 1930s targeted African American children rather than adults. The Green Pastures Camp, established in 1931 with funding from the Children's Fund of Michigan, was run by the Detroit Urban League. Each of the thirteen cottages in the camp was named after a famous African American, such as Booker T. Washington, Phillis Wheatley, and Paul Laurence Dunbar. The children were expected to learn about the individual for which his or her cottage was named. The camp was staffed by African American college students and was often visited by both African American and white community leaders.[60] The counselors were expected to be role models for the children not only by training them in vocational skills and African American history but, as Forrester Washington noted on a visit to the camp, by serving as examples of proper "deportment, personal cleanliness, and the like."[61] Dancy explicitly used the camp to display the talent and refinement of Detroit's African American youth to an interracial audience. "The visitors at the Camp were usually astounded at the splendid behavior and the excellent manners exhibited by the children," the Urban League reported in 1932. "These lessons taught the children immediately upon their arrival were so indelibly impressed upon their minds, that after three days spent there one would have thought that these children came from the so called best families in Detroit, so excellent was their general deportment."[62] Teaching deportment and good manners and providing recreation and wholesome food were the stated goals of Green Pastures and were strategies reminiscent of the work of the Dress Well Club and other African American organizations primarily interested in constructing a respectable community identity.

The Detroit Urban League also continued its work as an employment agency, a difficult task in the face of massive layoffs. Whereas in the early 1920s African American men were relatively easy to place and African American women were difficult to place in steady jobs, the opposite was true in the early 1930s. In 1930, Dancy reported that "the great majority of placements has been given to women." Of the 1,513 jobs furnished that year, 1,149 went to women and 364 to men. Another 6,986 African Americans who visited the Detroit employment bureau left with no placements at all.[63] Domestic service training classes continued to be held at the Urban League offices as part of the league's effort to make African American women "attractive" employees for white housewives. These classes, however, never regained the popularity they had during the early 1920s, when an Urban League certificate could ensure employment. In 1938, Dancy observed: "It should be remembered that those schools are difficult to operate because the women folk do not take readily to them. They have to be coaxed and coerced into attending."[64] Dancy was correct—African American women reluctantly attended domestic science classes. By the 1930s, many felt such programs were condescending and only marginally related to obtaining employment.

Other social agencies that emerged from the Great Migration managed to survive the economic ravages of the Great Depression and the growth of public charity by accepting New Deal money. The Baptist Christian Center, for example, continued to hold classes and sponsor clubs primarily for African American women and their children.[65] The continuation of the center's work was dependent on a more direct relationship with the state. In 1934, the Department of Education turned to the center when it became interested in setting up a nursery school for undernourished African American children. This plan was carried out in cooperation with the Federal Emergency Relief Association and the city Board of Education, and the staff was made up entirely of WPA workers until the school's closing in 1939.[66] This cooperation was facilitated by the acceptance of the center into the Detroit Community Fund following the visit of a white social reformer, Rosalie K. Butzel, who evaluated the center's programs.

Butzel's evaluation of the center reveals the disjuncture between white and black charity work. "The settlement is not run scientifically according to common standards," reported Butzel; "to some it may appear to put undue stress on the moral rather than the psychological or sociological approach to behavior problems."[67] White reformers commonly criticized African American charity organizations that did not follow the secular and "scientific" approach to reform favored by the increasingly professional class of social workers. Butzel contrasted the "untrained" head of the kindergarten with the professionally trained head of the nursery school: "The difference in their approach was marked. The former gave me a rather confused account of making religious and moral scrapbooks and organizing the Kill Kare Klub, the object of which is to stimulate the members to try to make others happy, while the latter talked of tuberculosis tests, afternoon rest and a balanced diet."[68] For Butzel, the "moral scrapbooks" of the untrained worker could not compare with the familiar scientific language of the nursery school head. The "confused account" given by the African American worker, however, may not have been confused at all to a listener better versed in the traditions of African American female reform. The lack of legitimation given such work by social reformers such as Butzel could be a terrible blow since cooperation with state and federal agencies was essential for charity organizations' survival.

Butzel visited another WPA project, a millinery class in which African American women made new hats from old hats and scraps of material. "The pleasure of hat-making," reported Butzel, "was mixed with the less popular but equally educational hygiene lesson."[69] Lessons on "personal cleanliness" were an indignity these women had to suffer in order to receive the WPA checks they counted on. The reluctance of African American women to sit through personal hygiene lessons paralleled their resistance to the teaching of domestic science at the Detroit Urban League. In both cases, these women had to be "coaxed and coerced" into participating in instruction they found demeaning.

Butzel's complaints about untrained African American reformers were ironic given that many schools of social work excluded African American women. Detroit's Merrill-Palmer School, for example, offered an innovative program in early childhood education but admitted no black women until 1938. That year, school officials enrolled Ethel Childs Baker, the first African American woman to be trained at the school and the last until after 1940. Baker grew up in Detroit and attended Detroit public schools. Because of the lack of educational opportunities in Detroit, she left the city to further her education at Alabama State University, graduating in 1935. After teaching for two years in Alabama, she returned to her native city, hoping to pursue a career as a social worker and teacher; however, the only position available to her was at the Franklin Street Settlement as a volunteer. While working there, she caught the attention of the settlement director, who suggested she continue her studies at the Merrill-Palmer School. While a student at Merrill-Palmer, she could not use the student lavatory or the coat closet. She walked across the street to use the facilities at the public library and ate her lunch alone, ostracized by the white students. Her experiences paralleled those of working-class black women who faced the hate strikes of white women workers in Detroit's factories. Although by the time of her graduation in 1939 she had made a handful of friends among the white students, her enrollment in the school did little to change its emphasis on training and educating middle-class white women.[70] Given the racial prejudice of Merrill-Palmer and other white institutions, Butzel's criticisms of African American women who volunteered their time to help their communities were patently unjust.

Some African American community groups shifted their focus away from moral suasion to focus on juvenile delinquency and cooperation with local and federal government agencies. Reformers founded the West Side Human Relations Council, for example, in 1936, which had a very different set of goals than the Entre Nous Club that had dominated reform in the neighborhood in the 1920s. The council was founded at a meeting of the delinquency prevention committee of the interchurch fellowship. The goals of the council included contacting parents and community leaders about the need to prevent delinquency and studying "the factors tending to cause delinquency," such as "the sale of obscene literature, narcotics, or other injurious matters; the admission of children to places of amusement having doubtful reputations, the loitering of children about places of questionable character," and so on. In addition to focusing on juvenile delinquency, the council was determined to "keep in constant contact with city officials, and cooperate with city agencies . . . to make strenuous efforts to get all the protection and benefits that a community deserves from city, county, and state government."[71] This focus on juvenile delinquency and cooperation with public agencies was typical of the new direction African American reform was taking by the late 1930s.

The participation of African American reformers in interracial public agencies undermined an older generation of reformers who had worked to construct a community identity of bourgeois respectability after the Great Migration. Individual African American social workers and reformers, however, experienced gains during this period. Historian Stephanie Shaw has argued that "black professional women became very important to white public administrators" during the Great Depression.[72] These women acted as mediators between the black community, which was suffering the ravages of the depression, and civic leaders concerned about the possibility of racial unrest. By 1941, 125 African Americans were employed in private and public reform agencies throughout the city. This number represented a substantial increase since the late 1910s and early 1920s, when only a handful of African American women and men worked with the Urban League, YWCA, VNA, or other agencies. By the early 1940s, two African American women, Beulah Whitby and Eliza Grigsby, were supervisors in the Department of Public Welfare, and numerous others worked in the Wayne County Bureau of Social Aid, the CAS, and other agencies.[73] Indeed, employment in public agencies would become an area of growth in African American women's white-collar work in the postwar period.

Cooperation with public relief agencies and district councils gave African American reform groups access to money and political power, both of which aided the community during the Great Depression. That cooperation also led to greater white supervision of African American reformers and social workers, whose work did not always conform to the scientific and "rational" norms of state agencies. Nevertheless, older styles of reform, with an emphasis on public displays of respectability, did not completely disappear. In women's clubs and the Detroit Urban League, middle-class African Americans continued the work they had begun a generation before. The centrality of African American working-class women as the objects of reform, however, gave way to a focus on juvenile delinquency, unemployment, and civil rights. The incursion of New Deal agencies into the lives of African Americans also shaped, and was shaped by, the continuities and disjunctures of Depression-era reform.

New Deal Agencies and Detroit's African American Community

Roosevelt's New Deal policies profoundly transformed the relationship of Detroit's African American community to the federal government. During the early years of the Roosevelt administration, African Americans, from the leadership of the NAACP and National Urban League to the many African Americans who demonstrated against racial discrimination, pressed for racial equality in New Deal programs.[74] When Roosevelt formulated the second New Deal in 1935, the administration made an effort to create more equitable policies for African Americans. The NYA and WPA ran numerous programs in Detroit that employed African American administrative assistants and teachers and welcomed black participants. Although some of these programs reproduced the segmented labor market by training African American women as household workers, they were generally welcomed by Detroit's black residents and engendered a new relationship between African Americans and the federal government. Many African Americans communicated directly with federal agencies or even the president and first lady to demand their rights or critique existing programs rather than relying on the Urban League or other black organizations to act as their intermediaries. These actions reflected reformers' shift from intracommunity work toward electoral politics.

African American women in Detroit received aid from the federal government through WPA projects, NYA training programs, and direct relief.[75] Because local officials had considerable control over how federal public works projects were administered, Mayor Frank Murphy's commitment to equal opportunity and civil rights was essential to ensure that African Americans received their fair share of federal dollars. The oversight of African American leaders such as Dancy and black participants in the district councils helped stem the worst acts of discrimination. In fact, city officials often found themselves in the position of defending the amount of relief Detroit's African Americans received compared to the amount white Detroiters received. In 1939, African Americans constituted 35 percent of both the Detroit public welfare relief rolls and the WPA rolls.[76] Geraldine Bledsoe, an African American placement officer for the Michigan Unemployment Commission, which worked closely with the WPA, recalled the importance of publicizing discrimination in public works and employment services:

> When those offices [employment services] came into existence, it was really a stunning and startling and disheartening thing to see employers asking for workers on the basis of race and color and nationality and religion and complexion within the white group, and complexion within the Negro group, and all these kinds of things that had nothing to do with the person's ability to do the job. And I think this was one of the most significant things that happened during that period, was the growing feeling that a man's religion, and a man's race, man's color, a man's nationality, didn't have anything to do with his capacity to perform.[77]

Empowered by public agencies' recognition that discrimination existed and should be addressed, many African American clients lodged their complaints about the implementation of New Deal policies in Detroit directly with the federal government.

African American women, for example, often wrote letters to Eleanor Roosevelt complaining about unfair treatment on public works projects or asking for direct relief. These letters are a testament to the role Eleanor Roosevelt played as the primary spokesperson for the civil rights community in her husband's administration. The first lady visited Detroit's African American community on more than one occasion, directly communicating with the residents of the city and promising to be their champions.[78] Maxie Craig, a WPA teacher in Detroit, wrote Roosevelt in 1939 praising the speech she had recently delivered to the NAACP's local chapter. "You and your husband have such broad humanitarian views in regard to the minority groups of this nation," wrote Craig, "and are especially considerate of our group, the Negro." Craig, however, was not writing only to praise the Roosevelts' "humanitarian views." She went on to explain that she had been laid off from her WPA job because she roomed with a brother who was employed. "As a teacher of adults I really feel that I am doing something worthwhile," wrote Craig, "helping those of my race who have not had an opportunity to become literate; and to learn something of their own racial background (I also teach Negro History); in order that they might become better citizens of this great free country and at the same time to make an honest living."[79] Craig's eloquent letter elicited an unusually quick positive response: the WPA's division of employment reinstated Craig to her former job.[80]

Eloise Bibb also wrote Eleanor Roosevelt to ask for work after her mother died and she realized she could not make enough money as a seamstress in the midst of the depression. "I am colored," wrote Bibb, "but I know that fact will not make the case less interesting to you."[81] Most likely, Bibb hoped her case would have been of *more* interest to Roosevelt, who was sympathetic to the problems of African American women. Thus, many African American women in Detroit viewed themselves as having a personal relationship with the federal government, from which they could ask, and sometimes receive, aid. This new relationship undercut the ties between these women and the African American reform agencies that had been their sole sources of aid in earlier decades.

Evident in the correspondence to Eleanor Roosevelt from Detroit's women was the emergence of interracial alliances. Gertrude Barrus wrote to Roosevelt on behalf of fifty African American and white women over forty-five who were dismissed from a WPA sewing project. "I think you are the only one will understand," wrote Barrus; "I don't think it is asking too much. To give ous work for what few years we have to stay here on earth to keep our self and loved ones that are helpless."[82] These women requested that a sewing project for older women be established to meet their needs. Drawing on their common experience of age and WPA work, this group of white and black women banded together to request aid from the federal government. Without the interracial programs sponsored by the WPA, such alliances would have been less frequent.

Increased competition for a dwindling number of jobs, however, often exacerbated competition between white and African American women for scarce resources rather than uniting them. Naomi Johnson, an African American seamstress, wrote Eleanor Roosevelt: "I can not get work in shops because they do not hire colored. I could not make enough as a domestic to pay even the rent."[83] Delia Lovelace wrote Roosevelt in 1939 about her difficulties competing with white women for domestic service jobs. Lovelace was a single mother with a six-year-old son. "I lost my job," she wrote. "The lady let me go when I needed my job the most for a white girl." After losing her job, Lovelace managed to get work with the WPA, but she told WPA officials she was married. When the officials found out she was single, they laid her off for obtaining "certification under false pretense." "Mrs. Roosevelt, I need help," wrote Lovelace. "I have always made an honest living. I made a mistake in life, I have outlived it." [84] This letter reflects not only the harsh economic conditions of depression-era Detroit but also the intrusion of the state into the private lives of African American women. Women such as Lovelace felt entitled to support from the federal government in a time of crisis and resented the WPA's demands that they disclose details of their private lives. When she disguised her son's illegitimacy, the WPA took her job away and censured her. Lovelace ended her letter to Roosevelt: "I can't live long like this. I'd rather be dead." Telling her story to the president's wife was a last resort for Lovelace, who felt she had reached the end of her resources.

Lovelace's experience with the state was shared by many other African American women during and after the New Deal. On the local level, Aid to Dependent Children and other state-funded programs sat in judgment of clients' lifestyle, culture, and need. In part, this reflected white reformers' attempt to "assimilate" African American women into the dominant culture using the same kind of reform efforts they had previously used to "assimilate" European immigrants.[85] Because of their focus on assimilation, white reformers did not fully appreciate or incorporate African American women's earlier reform efforts. Yet the practices that New Deal reformers such as Butzel saw as "backward" often challenged racial stereotypes and looked toward uplifting the entire black community through the social mobility of black women. Indeed, if black female reformers' emphasis on day care programs and work training had been part of New Deal programs, welfare today might look very different. Addressing the needs of working mothers had long been a focus of black reform. These needs were never adequately met in national politics during or after the New Deal.

Despite these failures in national policies, African American women felt empowered to write the federal government because of their newly established identities as Democratic Party voters and activists. By the mid-1930s, Detroit activists had forged a new Democratic Party coalition among organized labor, white ethnics, and African Americans. In 1936, this coalition elected Charles C. Diggs as the first African American Democratic representative in the Michigan senate, an election that marked the beginning of black Democratic power in the city of Detroit. In 1939, Ella Spence wrote an appeal to Eleanor Roosevelt on the letterhead of the Negro Division of the Democratic Campaign Committee chaired by Diggs. Spence wrote on

Photograph taken by a social worker of a mother sick in bed with her children attending her. Courtesy of Works Progress Administration Collection, National Archives.

behalf of women who were being laid off from WPA projects because they were married or had dependent children. "You being a woman yourself of sound understanding," she began, "perhaps, you can talk to our President in our behalf. . . . I am working on the WPA and it seems as if all of the women are facing the loss of their job." Although some of these women were put on welfare, Spence protested, "no woman wants that because of their pride." "Can you persuade our President to stop this terrible happening, and that we can retain our work?," asked Spence.[86] By writing from her position as a Democratic Party activist, Spence hoped to gain a greater voice in decision making at the highest level of government, an empowering if not always effective act.

Despite the government's attempts to address racial discrimination in federal policies, the WPA and NYA generally reinforced existing sexual and racial divisions in the workforce. Phyllis Palmer argues that "racial and gender conservatism underlay the moderate reforms of the New Deal."[87] This conservatism was clearly reflected in the government's training programs and work relief. Fearful of creating job competition for white men and women, New Deal agencies went out of their way to ensure that African American women were primarily trained for service work in private homes. Because legislation relating to employment, such as the Social Security Act, did not cover service work performed by African American women, domestic service training programs were among the few federal initiatives that touched the lives of working-class African American women. In Detroit, many women took advantage of these programs and attempted to shape them to suit their own needs, writing letters protesting the cancellation of programs or the laying off of workers. Through WPA-administered household worker training projects, domestic service training, once the domain of the Detroit Urban League and Second Baptist Church, became a federal program.

This program reflected continuities in reform strategies as New Deal workers taught African American women lessons of cleanliness and efficiency; however, it also marked a disjuncture in the administration of reform and the relationship between female workers and reformers. State agencies rather than well-to-do neighbors designed and ran domestic service training, and New Deal workers emphasized bourgeois respectability not for purposes of racial uplift but because they held stereotypes about African American women's lack of skills. Examples of racial stereotyping can be seen in New Deal workers' focus on African American women's "personal hygiene." For example, in a WPA project to help Detroit women become more "employable," the phrases "personal hygiene was stressed" and "personal appearance was stressed" appeared only on black women's records. With the exception of one woman who was a trained beautician, the WPA placed African American women in domestic service while placing white women in a variety of positions, such as saleswoman, secretary, and industrial laborer.[88]

The limited job market for African American women due to racial and gender discrimination was well known to local organizers of federal works projects by the mid-1930s. The respectability of these women, recognized by black social workers in churches or the Urban League, was invisible to white employers despite years of racial uplift work. A 1937 study of African American youth and employment carried out by the NYA resulted in numerous complaints about the lack of job opportunities for even highly trained and educated women. Claire Sanders, a counselor who directed African American youth to employment agencies, stated that "in the majority of cases . . . the employer is not interested in the Negro girl, unless for housework." The director of the Franklin Street Settlement, a settlement house on the East Side, agreed that the "problem of Negro girls is one of securing employment and the conditions are very discouraging." Maude Page, in charge of placing young African American women at the Lucy Thurman YWCA, noted that "qualified" and well-trained women could not be placed in private industry. An investigator for the CAS agreed that the "most serious problem" confronting an African American youth was the fact that "when the youth is trained, he finds so few avenues of employment that he is forced to accept menial and even degrading positions."[89] Despite these findings, both the NYA's and the WPA's work-training programs continued to funnel African American women into service work and did not directly challenge employers' hiring preferences. Although earlier attempts by racial uplift leaders to place well-educated and "refined" black women in visible positions outside of domestic service had a limited impact, state agencies did not attempt to place even token women in white-collar or industrial work.

One of the most disturbing household worker training programs developed by the WPA in Detroit was a "practice house" designed to train young African American men as butlers and cooks. This project epitomized the conservative aspects of training programs that reinforced sex and race discrimination and illustrated some of the negative consequences of federal intervention in African American reform and relief programs. The practice house placed African American men in occupations that they had not held in large numbers since the late nineteenth and early twentieth centuries. To many whites in Detroit, placing African American men in positions that few white men coveted appeared to be a good solution for unemployment. One white doctor telephoned the practice house to say that "he felt it was unfortunate that the colored people had grown so far away from their natural aptitude for household employment and that he was wholeheartedly in sympathy with the program."[90] The *Detroit Free Press* praised the program for "offering an excellent opportunity to Negro boys interested in domestic work."[91] There is some evidence, however, that the young men enrolled in the program were less than enthusiastic about its success. Catherine Murray, director of the WPA's Women's Division in Michigan, reported that "many of them dropped out of the training course before they were certified."[92] It is notable that although the Urban League and the Second Baptist Church had long advocated training African American women for domestic service, they had never designed a program to train young African American men for service work. Male occupational mobility was a primary motivation for southern African Americans to migrate north, and middle-class leaders in the community pointed to the influx of African American men into the industrial workforce as one of the foremost successes of the migration experience. In this case, then, federal programs not only reinforced existing job market segmentation but also brought back a vision of a servile African American male workforce not seen since the Great Migration.

The practice house for boys was part of a larger WPA domestic service training project in Michigan that included the St. Aubin Training Center for young African American women. Like the practice house for young men, this center gave young women, children of families on relief, intensive training for eight weeks and paid no wages but provided room and board. After the young women completed the course, WPA workers placed them as live-in domestic servants in private homes.[93] This practice house was rented from the Second Baptist Church and had formerly been the Big Sisters' Home, where black women had held club meetings, training programs, and charity events since the Great Migration. The practice house, opened in 1935, was initially well received in the African American community because of the sense of continuity between the work of the Big Sisters' Home and the federally funded domestic service training program.[94] WPA administrators agreed to retain some of the original teachers and matrons at the house to ensure greater success. Church leaders also appreciated receiving federal funds in the midst of the depression. When the program was threatened due to the lack of WPA funds in 1937, for example, Bradby wrote the director in Lansing: "I have been the minister here for twenty-six years, and I don't know that I have been able to observe anything that has meant more for the rehabilitation of our girls than the practice house."[95] Bradby's optimistic portrayal of the house, however, disguised the growing tension between the black community's and WPA administrators' perceptions of the program.

The primary source of tension was the placement of young women as live-in domestic servants. New Deal administrators who insisted that young women take live-in jobs found African American household workers intractable. Many African American women refused to accept live-in work, a form of domestic service they believed was demeaning. Sylvia Hartt, the Michigan supervisor of the household workers' training program, reported to the national office of the WPA: "We have had some difficulty placing colored girls due to the fact that they do not want to stay nights in homes where they are employed."[96] The employment services of the Urban League, the Second Baptist Church, and other African American organizations had all offered day work rather than live-in domestic service. The WPA's household worker training service offered no such flexibility. As a result, in 1936, Mamie Bledsoe, the WPA supervisor of the house, reported that "finding the girl to fit the job and job to fit the girl is turning out to be a knotty problem." Several mothers protested that the jobs WPA workers found for their daughters were too hard and underpaid — $6 to $8 a week plus board. "Somehow, something ought to be done in families on WPA," argued Bledsoe, "where the attitude toward the family's becoming independent is so uncooperative."[97] The notion that a $6 per week wage would render a family on relief "independent" was clearly unfounded.

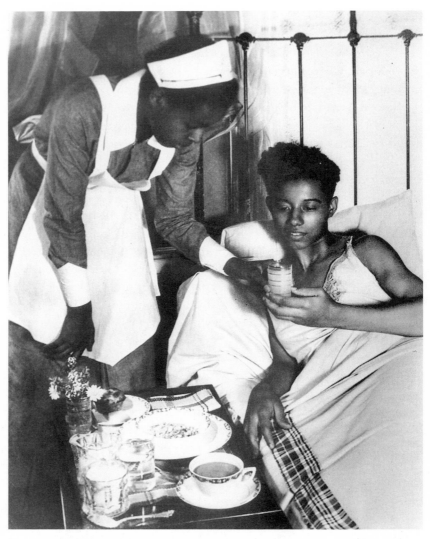

Practicing serving in the WPA household workers' training project. Courtesy of Works Progress Administration Collection, National Archives.

Increasingly, the African American women who attended the practice house used it as a base for activism and social mobility. When house staff members attended an annual YWCA dinner in 1936, they were very surprised to find out that a group of house residents had joined the YWCA's young girls' business and professional program.[98] These residents had no intention of remaining in domestic service but were using the house as a base to gain skills to obtain white-collar jobs. By attending YWCA programs, these young

Learning how to use a washing machine in the WPA household workers' training project. Courtesy of Works Progress Administration Collection, National Archives.

women may have been looking for training that was missing in the curriculum of the practice house but was an integral part of the domestic service training programs run by African American women: training for service to the race, lessons in African American history, and training for greater occupational mobility. The limited goals of the WPA practice house temporarily helped alleviate unemployment problems in some families and employed a few African American teachers but did not fulfill the broader goals of earlier training programs. In addition, because the practice houses were segregated (two white practice houses operated in Detroit during the 1930s), the training program did not reduce the racial stigmatization of household workers.

Although employers continued to view domestic service as a "black" occupation, for the first time in decades, unemployed white women competed against African American women for jobs. By 1932, Mary Anderson, director of the Women's Bureau of the Department of Labor, stated that "particularly in domestic service are Negro women reported to have lost ground."[99] The issue of competition among white and African American domestic workers was raised at the Michigan State Conference on Employment Problems. Lawrence Oxley, the field representative of the U.S. Employment Service, discussing jobs in which African Americans once "had a virtual monopoly," reported: "At one time the Negro domestic seldom had to compete against the white worker. Even in this field today, however, the Negro's job opportunities are perhaps decreasing, for in many states young white girls are being trained for domestic service."[100] The training of white women, reported by Oxley, was carried out in a variety of Detroit WPA and NYA programs. For example, the State Household Demonstration Project, established in 1938, trained white women "of the industrial and unemployed classes to be 'economically independent and get them off the relief rolls.'"[101] The graduates of this course were placed in jobs through the Michigan Unemployment Compensation Commission Employment Service and paid $40 per month while in training. The students' families were all on relief, and the wages brought in by the young women would supplement their families' income.

New Deal workers designed training programs that met the needs of young white women who were willing to live in because their employment was temporary—most expected to marry and practice their domestic skills in their homes after a brief period of wage labor. Betty Chase, state supervisor of the Household Demonstration Project, stated: "The demand for trained household employees exceeds the supply and definite social ends are served, as a trained girl has a greater chance for setting up a good type home of her own in later years." Chase recognized the undesirability of domestic work for white women, to whom other opportunities were available in the past: "The girl trained to consider her service in a good household as a dignified profession need not envy the factory girl."[102] Most unemployed white women, however, did "envy the factory girl," who did not have to face the choice between entering domestic work or suffering economic deprivation. African American women, meanwhile, had even fewer choices, as the willingness of some white women to become household laborers further narrowed their extremely limited job market.

During the 1930s, white and black reformers pushed for the professionalization of domestic work to raise standards of employment and thus the status of employees. Whereas in the 1920s African American women were trained to work in the "modern" technological home, the focus of 1930s domestic labor was on professionalization of both employers and employees. In an address in New York City, Eleanor Roosevelt stated: "We are having less immigration which used to furnish so many household employees, and we have a whole field for employment here if we put it on a professional basis where it will appeal to Americans with professional standards." [103] Thus, training projects of the 1930s were designed to instill professionalism in workers and answer the complaints of employers. The language of professionalization was used by African American and white women to pressure New Deal officials and Congress to include domestic work in the new labor laws that standardized wages and hours. Although this goal was not achieved during the 1930s, the language of professionalization pervaded the programs offered to unemployed workers. This language supplanted the emphasis on domesticity that had dominated the reform discourse of African American training programs for many years and thus undermined one of the major means of transmitting bourgeois respectability to young working-class African American women.

Reformers' emphasis on professionalization, however, did not coincide with the realities of household labor. "The worker who has had no special training whatsoever is at a serious disadvantage in seeking employment in an age that is rapidly becoming more highly specialized," argued Jean Collier Brown of the Women's Bureau. "The present demand for skilled domestic workers, so much greater than the supply, points to an urgent need for better training facilities for such workers." [104] The extent to which domestic work was becoming "specialized" was questionable; if anything, the employment of a day worker who performed a variety of tasks lessened specialization, and the roots of domestic workers' low status went much deeper than the issue of unskilled labor. Therefore, professionalizing domestic work did little to affect wages, hours, and working conditions, particularly without the backing of federal legislation. Geraldine Bledsoe reported on the state of domestic and personal service in 1940 in the "Findings, Report, and Recommendations of the Michigan State Conference on Employment Problems of the Negro." She saw domestic service as holding promise for reform partly because it was "the least standardized, the least modernized, and the most feudal of all work in the Western world" and partly because "it is the only field where the demand for workers continues to exceed by far the supply, without any effective attack on the problem."[105]

Bledsoe described domestic service in Detroit as a "topsy-turvey, crazy quilt situation" in which wages varied from $3 to $15 per week, few workers were "qualified," and conditions came in "every shade."[106] She perceived that "most of the white workers are seeking domestic work temporarily until they, or their men folk, are called back to other jobs. On the other hand, the Negro is seeking household employment as a career and at present has no chance of being absorbed in other fields."[107] This difference reflected white women's willingness to live in and African American women's insistence on day work that allowed them to continue caring for their households.[108] Bledsoe emphasized that although many workers were waiting for job placements, it was impossible to meet the needs of employers. She listed numerous reasons for this dilemma, including the passing down of "deep resentment against household employment" by older African American domestics, the refusal of African American women to stay overnight at employers' houses, white employers' negative perceptions of African American employees, and the lack of standard wages and hours.[109] Discrimination against African American domestic workers by state agencies was prevalent during this period. One study of domestic employment in Detroit noted that the Michigan State Employment Service rarely accepted or referred "a very black Negro woman."[110] Even in the midst of the depression, some African American women openly protested these prejudices and the abysmal working conditions of household labor by refusing to accept domestic service jobs or by encouraging their children to seek other employment.

The problems cited by Bledsoe, coming at the end of two decades of widespread training in domestic science, reveal the inability of training programs to address the complaints of employers and the effects of the lack of regulation on workers' lives. Bledsoe offered several solutions for the problems of domestic workers. The training of older workers and programs in public schools for girls were the main solutions proposed. Requiring potential students to take a "health and personality examination" before entering training programs would diminish the fears of employers. The development of a "professional attitude" on the part of workers, the expansion of Social Security and minimum wage laws, and standard wages and hours would appease workers. Finally, Bledsoe appealed to white employers to "make a really honest effort to abandon the outmoded concepts of the Negro that went out with the minstrel show and to see in this large group of unemployed men and women the solution to a problem that troubled not only Detroit but

500 other cities."[111] Bledsoe believed that these reforms would solve problems inherent in domestic work and aid Detroit's unemployed black women. This strategy, however, did not directly address the problems of the segmented labor market and discrimination practiced by employers. Emphasizing workers' professional status did not sway racist employers any more than emphasizing workers' respectability had in the 1910s and 1920s. In the end, no amount of training or reform of household labor would improve conditions for African American women, who ultimately hoped to obtain jobs in white-collar and industrial work.

Employers' preferences for workers of a particular race or ethnicity had defined the market for domestic workers since the nineteenth century. However, according to Bledsoe, the recognition of this fact by the state bureaucracy sparked an emerging "equal opportunity" movement that eventually opened occupations other than domestic work to African American women. Bledsoe and many other African Americans worked tirelessly in Detroit for the eventual passage of the 1955 Fair Employment Practices Act, which addressed racial and gender discrimination in the labor market.[112] These women and men also fought to get African Americans, particularly African American women, defense jobs during World War II and access to public housing. The experience of working with federal and state agencies during the Great Depression was invaluable to African American activists in the civil rights struggles of the 1940s, the 1950s, and beyond. Meanwhile, the numerous letters written to Eleanor Roosevelt provide eloquent evidence that African American clients of relief agencies raised their voices against employment discrimination and segregation. Together, African American leaders who had gained political clout from their involvement with New Deal agencies and socially conscious African American citizens fought to end overt discrimination in employment and housing in Detroit.

Conclusion

In 1940, Detroit hosted the Seventy-five Years of Negro Progress Exposition to highlight African Americans' many achievements since emancipation. This event signaled the end of an era of racial uplift as the primary ideological base of African American political work. The exhibits at the exposition reflected the accomplishments of the Urban League, the NAACP, and other interracial organizations that had operated in the African American community since the early twentieth century, and they celebrated new alliances and civil rights strategies generated during the Great Depression. Indicative of the new interracial alliances formed in the 1930s was the organizers' effort to gain federal support for the exposition. These organizers submitted a prospectus to the WPA requesting assistance in gathering historical material on African American progress in education, employment, art, science, and other fields. The exposition, assured the writers of the prospectus, "would show very clearly the influences of the various governmental agencies in the development of the total culture of the Negro." By exhibiting the "progress he has made under the American way of life," the exposition would also serve as a "stabilizing influence" in a period of political and economic unrest.[113]

Although the organizers intended the exposition to be national in scope, this plan was scaled down, and the program focused primarily on local accomplishments. The event was divided into nine days, each of which featured a theme such as education, federal employees, business, women, race relations, youth and athletics, and patriotism. These topics reflected both the old—for example, the artistic presentations of clubwomen on women's day—and the new—for example, the honoring of outstanding federal employees on federal employees' day. Thus, the Negro Progress Exposition looked back to a period in which reformers focused on bourgeois respectability and forward to a period when interracial cooperation and state intervention would improve African Americans' lives. Underlying this shift was the pressure placed on Detroit's black leaders by Communist Party members, union activists, and consumer advocates to demand more from white city officials, employers, and the federal government.

Clearly, the positive effects of New Deal policies on Detroit's African Americans were not solely the result of the activism of reformers and community elites. Many ordinary African American women and men demonstrated on Detroit's streets and wrote letters to federal agencies to demand their rights and fight the racism endemic in public works projects. Beulah Whitby remembered: "When I was administrative supervisor at Alfred District there were organizations of clients and they would come to the office and make demands for more adequate budget, more clothing."[114] Welfare clients, along with organized labor, the Communist Party, and the CRC, formed a new organizing base in the African American community. Together, these movements pushed African American women as objects and as visible leaders of reform off center stage.

Conclusion

The truth is that Berry never signed anyone to Motown who needed to be "remade." The uncouth, boisterous, and slovenly couldn't get a foot in the door anyway. Almost everyone who came to Motown wanted to move up in the world. None of us came from homes that didn't teach manners. We were all trying to get ahead, and it's always bothered me that some people have assumed that by accepting what some consider "white" values, we sold out. It's just not true.

Mary Wilson, Dreamgirl: My Life as a Supreme

When Mary Wilson, one of the original members of the Supremes, wrote her autobiography, she took pains to refute what she called the "Motown Myth." The myth was that Berry Gordy, founder of Motown Records, "took a bunch of ghetto kids with no class, no style, and no manners, put them through hours of grueling training in etiquette, choreography, and interview tactics, and then . . . young 'uneducated' blacks suddenly knew how to speak and which fork to use."[1] The young women of Motown, argued Wilson, were hardly uncultured. Members of the Supremes, who grew up in the Brewster projects on Detroit's East Side, were well spoken, well dressed, and ambitious. On the stage, they personified African American female respectability, wearing white gloves and demure clothing. This stage persona, Wilson points out, did not signal an acceptance of "white" values but rather was an extension of the lessons they had learned from their families, churches, and teachers. Like the female migrants of the early twentieth century, Wilson and her fellow artists wanted to "move up in the world" and saw respectability as a route to social mobility. Their respectable identities, however, were rooted in the community from which they came and were not imposed by Motown Records. Likewise, respectable female migrants were not creations of racial uplift ideologues but active agents who shaped Detroit's black community.

There are similarities between Mary Wilson and Mary Etta Glenn, the African American woman whose story began this book. Both sought social mobility and gained it by using Detroit's cultural and economic resources. Glenn and Wilson also employed the lessons of respectability taught to them as children. Rather than being "remade" by social reformers or record producers, these women helped to remake black Detroit. But Glenn's and Wilson's respectability offers only one model of behavior in Detroit's complex African American community. Some city dwellers did reject symbols such as white gloves and embraced an alternative lifestyle in the informal economy. They transgressed elite notions of respectability by "hustling," a term Bettylou Valentine defines as a "wide variety of unconventional, sometimes extralegal or illegal activities."[2] In a period when African American women's job opportunities were extremely limited, hustling became a means of survival and, in some cases, personal expression. During the Great Migration, elites who viewed female migrants as the key to the creation of a respectable identity believed such behavior undermined the entire community. Women, they argued, were the caretakers of homes and neighborhoods and the teachers of children. In their dress and deportment, they embodied the "respectability" of the race as a whole.

Throughout the 1910s and 1920s, some African American women embraced this role by founding women's clubs, working in racial institutions, and pioneering new forms of employment to better the lives of female migrants and their families. Even in this period, however, black Detroiters contested the meaning of respectability. Some working-class women felt their involvement in storefront religion, Garveyism, or numbers running did not necessarily place them outside of the ranks of the respectable. Rather, these activities reflected deep religious beliefs, a commitment to racial advancement, or the economic means to help family and friends. Migrants sometimes resented efforts by the Detroit Urban League, women's clubs, or the Second Baptist Church to change this seemingly "transgressive" behavior. Yet these reform institutions dominated African American community life during the Great Migration. Faced with the virulent racism of white city officials, employers, and white neighbors, black women drew on their experiences in the racial uplift movement to combat segregation and create new opportunities for their daughters and sons.

This strategy was undermined during the Great Depression when the realities of economic survival and a complex urban culture challenged traditional African American leaders. Although bourgeois respectability as a reform strategy never entirely disappeared, economic nationalism and civil rights took precedence during the Great Depression. Masculine rights to a living wage, self-defense, and equality dominated 1930s discourse. In addition, the influx of New Deal agencies into black Detroit weakened the ties between needy Detroiters and traditional black institutions. The origins of this shift to a remade respectability are complex—they include the emergence of black nationalism, a reinvigorated labor movement, and the transfer of black political allegiance to the Democratic Party. Nonetheless, by World War II, the vulnerable female migrant of the 1910s and 1920s stepped off the center stage of reform, and African American leaders no longer condemned black women who transgressed community norms with the same vigor.

Throughout the entire interwar period, African American women challenged racism by actively shaping their own destinies and challenging the status quo. But Detroit's story of migration and resettlement does not end in 1940. Although the Great Migration of the 1910s and early 1920s dramatically increased Detroit's African American population, a second migration brought tens of thousands more African American southerners into Detroit during the 1940s. A story yet to be written is the reaction of the established African American community to this new wave of southern migrants. Were the new migrants given instructions on dress and deportment, as were the earlier arrivals? Were the female migrants targeted as the caretakers of community identity? These questions await further research on Detroit and other cities that were primary destinations of both migrations. It is clear that at the dawn of World War II, the new generation of African American migrants entered a vibrant community relatively united in its efforts to fight job and housing discrimination.

The Detroit of the Second Great Migration was a city in tremendous turmoil. The decade began with a major controversy over African Americans' access to a public housing project in 1942 that was reminiscent of the 1926 Ossian Sweet case. Vocal white opponents protested the inclusion of African American war workers in the Sojourner Truth Housing Project and succeeded in convincing the Federal Housing Administration to restrict the housing project to white families. An interracial coalition formed the Sojourner Truth Citizens' Committee to protest this action, picketed City Hall and the Detroit Housing Commission almost daily, and finally convinced federal housing officials to reverse their decision. The night before the first African American families were scheduled to move into the project, however, a large white mob burned crosses and prevented moving trucks from entering the premises. A riot between blacks and whites erupted, with the police largely taking the side of white residents. Eventually, with the aid of organized labor as well as a liberal interracial coalition, African American tenants successfully occupied the Sojourner Truth Housing Project.[3] The success of Detroit's African Americans in the controversy was due to the experience they had gained organizing and staging militant demonstrations throughout the 1930s. With the strength of interracial coalitions of both social reformers and organized labor behind them, working- and middle-class African Americans banded together to fight a frightening display of white racism in the city.

The Sojourner Truth Housing Project controversy was a harbinger of the disastrous year ahead. Detroit's 1943 race riot was one of the worst of the century and sparked nationwide discussions of how to improve race relations in America. The riot began on 20 June on Belle Isle, a park on an island in the Detroit River. A white mob, formed partly by white sailors from a nearby armory, attacked a group of African Americans. A rumor that the mob had thrown an African American mother and baby into the Detroit River reached the East Side. Marilynn Johnson argues that this rumor reflected a "theme of black male outrage over white violence against women and children."[4] After decades of discrimination, police brutality, and hate strikes, black men were eager to defend attacks on their homes and families and took up the mantle of self-defense. The riot quickly escalated as blacks and whites streamed out into city streets. When the violence ended, the police had murdered 17 African Americans and beaten up dozens of others. In all, 31 Detroiters died and over 200 were injured.[5] After the riot, an interracial Citizens' Committee convened to pressure city officials to respond to the riot. No police officers were censured for their behavior, and few substantial changes were made in discriminatory city policies. Nevertheless, the mayor of Detroit, Edward J. Jeffries Jr., did organize an official interracial committee to improve race relations in the city—a committee that was emulated in cities across the country.

The postwar era in Detroit was marked by more violence, white flight from the inner city, deindustrialization, and a massive loss of jobs in the automobile industry. Despite this bleak picture, African Americans did make some substantial gains. By the late 1940s, African American women, for example, finally broke into industrial and white-collar labor after years of rampant discrimination. African Americans fought racial discrimination in the city on a variety of fronts, including housing discrimination, employment discrimination, and police brutality. Throughout the 1950s and 1960s, African Americans picketed department stores, insurance agencies, and companies that had long refused to hire blacks in jobs that did not require a mop and a broom. Hudson's department store hired its first African American sales-person in 1953 in response to these demonstrations, and other stores eventually followed its example.[6]

Despite these advances in workplace discrimination, by 1967 only 5 percent of Detroit's police department, long known for its brutality against black residents, was African American. In July of that year, Detroit experienced a frightening race riot, with forty-one deaths and scores of injuries.[7] The 1967 riot was sparked by a police department raid on an African American blind pig. After Prohibition was repealed, blind pigs had metamorphosed into after-hours clubs that operated without liquor licenses. These clubs continued to be an important component of Detroit's informal economy. The violent raid on this blind pig escalated into a full-fledged riot after rumors spread that a police officer had brutally attacked an African American woman.[8] As in the 1943 riot, the need to protect black women, and by extension the black community, sparked an angry outcry among African Americans.

Thus, Detroit in the late 1960s resembled Detroit in the interwar period in some ways, as African Americans struggled to maintain their portion of the informal economy and protect African American women from police brutality. The postwar period also saw a resurgence of domestic ideology and a valorization of housewives, which ensured that female respectability would continue to play a role in black Detroit's political culture. In addition, the persistence of racial stereotypes meant that black women often had to prove their respectability before they could demand citizenship and civil rights. It was not until the election of Detroit's first African American mayor, Coleman Young, in 1973 that the city opened jobs for African American women and men in the public sector, including the police department. The city's economy during the 1970s, however, had hit bottom after decades of postwar decline, including the loss of industrial jobs, white out-migration from the central city, and the failure of black-owned businesses. Despite Detroit's dramatic political and economic changes during the second half of the twentieth century, respectability remains a powerful trope, evidenced by contemporary debates over rap music and urban youth culture. Detroit's African American women continue to struggle in a city grappling with segregation, exclusion, and racist stereotyping.

When Motown's young female performers wore their white gloves and took lessons in etiquette, they drew on a legacy of African American female respectability—a legacy that migrants used to construct new lives for themselves and their families. Understanding female respectability's different valences gives us insight into intracommunity debates over social roles, forms of leisure, and political strategies. These dialogues are only heard when African American women's experiences are fully incorporated into the narrative of migration and resettlement. By analyzing those experiences, this book begins the process of uncovering female migrants' myriad stories remembered by poet Robert Hayden and generations of black Detroiters.

Notes

Abbreviations

In addition to the abbreviations listed in the front matter, the following abbreviations are used throughout the notes.

ALUA   Archives of Labor and Urban Affairs, Wayne State University, Detroit, Michigan

BHC   Burton Historical Collection, Detroit Public Library, Detroit, Michigan

DULP   Detroit Urban League Papers, Michigan Historical Collections, Bentley Historical Library, University of Michigan, Ann Arbor, Michigan

HLDP   Housewives' League of Detroit Papers, Burton Historical Collection, Detroit Public Library, Detroit, Michigan

LC   Library of Congress, Manuscripts Division, Washington, D.C.

MHC   Michigan Historical Collections, Bentley Historical Library, University of Michigan, Ann Arbor, Michigan

NA   National Archives, Washington, D.C., and College Park, Maryland; RG 69, Federal Emergency Relief Administration and Works Progress Administration Papers; RG 86, Women's Bureau Papers

SL   Schlesinger Library, Radcliffe College, Cambridge, Massachusetts

UCSP   United Community Services Papers, Archives of Labor and Urban Affairs, Wayne State University, Detroit, Michigan

UCSP-CF   United Community Services Papers, Central Files, Archives of Labor and Urban Affairs, Wayne State University, Detroit, Michigan

Introduction

1. Robert E. Hayden, "From *The Life*: Some Remembrances," in Glaysher, *Collected Prose*, 18–19.

2. See, for example, Meier and Rudwick, *Black Detroit and the Rise of the UAW*; Oestreicher, *Solidarity and Fragmentation*; Zunz, *Changing Face of Inequality*; David Allen Levine, *Internal Combustion*; and Widick, *Detroit*. Although Richard W. Thomas does not limit his analysis to male industrial workers in his important book, *Life for Us*, he downplays conflict in the African American community

and views the industrial working class as the "catalyst for the entire process" of community building (xiii).

3. For a discussion of the distinction between women's history and gender history, see Joan Scott, *Gender and the Politics of History.*

4. Angela Y. Davis, *Blues Legacies and Black Feminism,* xix.

5. For a sampling of this growing literature, see Berkeley, "'Colored Ladies Also Contributed'"; Rouse, *Lugenia Burns Hope*; Hine, "'We Specialize in the Wholly Impossible'"; Salem, *To Better Our World*; Shaw, "Black Club Women"; Lasch-Quinn, *Black Neighbors*; Higginbotham, *Righteous Discontent*; Susan L. Smith, *Sick and Tired*; Knupfer, *Toward a Tenderer Humanity*; and Terborg-Penn, *African American Women in the Struggle for the Vote.*

6. For example, in her pathbreaking book, *Abiding Courage,* Gretchen Lemke-Santangelo notes that her informants "can be characterized as successful migrants" (9).

7. White and White, *Stylin',* 222.

8. See, for example, Kelley, "'We Are Not What We Seem'"; Tera Hunter, *To 'Joy My Freedom,* 145–86; White and White, *Stylin'*; Lawrence W. Levine, *Black Culture*; and Wolcott, "Culture of the Informal Economy."

9. See, for example, Meier and Rudwick, *Black Detroit and the Rise of the UAW*; Korstad and Lichtenstein, "Opportunities Lost and Found"; Stevenson, "Points of Departure"; and Bates, "New Crowd Challenges the Agenda of the Old Guard."

10. My understanding of community incorporates both conflict and consensus, implying, as Earl Lewis has suggested in "Writing African Americans into a History of Overlapping Diasporas," "participation rather than unity of perspective" (780). See also Elsa Barkley Brown, "Negotiating and Transforming the Public Sphere."

11. Working-class respectability has been examined most extensively in British labor history. See, for example, Hobsbawn, "Labour Aristocracy in Nineteenth-Century Britain"; Gareth Stedman Jones, *Outcast London*; and Bailey, "'Will the Real Bill Banks Please Stand Up?'" For discussions of working-class respectability in the United States, see Wilentz, *Chants Democratic*; Rosenzweig, *Eight Hours for What We Will*; and Odem, *Delinquent Daughters,* 43–47.

12. Ross, "'Not the Sort That Would Sit on the Doorstep'" and *Love and Toil.*

13. Ross, "'Not the Sort That Would Sit on the Doorstep,'" 39 (emphasis in original).

14. See Scobey, "Anatomy of the Promenade"; Stansell, *City of Women*; Abelson, *When Ladies Go A-Thieving*; and Kasson, *Rudeness and Civility.*

15. Brian Harrison, "Traditions of Respectability," 183.

16. Higginbotham, *Righteous Discontent,* 14, 15. See also Gatewood, *Aristocrats of Color.* Gatewood states: "Members of the aristocracy of color . . . had great pride in family background, education, and what was called 'respectability,' a term that included good breeding, manners, and proper conduct" (343–44).

17. Knupfer, *Toward a Tenderer Humanity,* 7, 21. Susan L. Smith, in *Sick and Tired,*

also argues that "black club women" imposed "their own standards of appropriate behavior in their efforts for racial advancement" (18). For a similar analysis of black women's clubs, see Hendricks, *Gender, Race, and Politics*. Beverly Guy-Sheftall, in *Daughters of Sorrow*, argues that "a major objective of the black women's club movement was to persuade poor rural black women in the South to embrace the sexual morals of the Victorian middle class" (74). In *Too Heavy a Load*, Deborah Gray White uses the term "middle-class respectability" when discussing the racial uplift work of the NACW. See also Deborah Gray White, "Cost of Club Work."

18. For descriptions of class relations in the African American community that rely on the language of respectability, see Du Bois, *Philadelphia Negro*, 310–11; Drake and Cayton, *Black Metropolis*, 524–25; and Frazier, *Black Bourgeoisie*, 80.

19. See, for example, Carby, "Policing the Black Woman's Body."

20. Lemke-Santangelo, *Abiding Courage*, 11–48; Shaw, *What a Woman Ought to Be and to Do*, 13–103.

21. Shaw, *What a Woman Ought to Be and to Do*, 15.

22. Harley, "When Your Work Is Not Who You Are," 46. In *To 'Joy My Freedom*, Tera Hunter emphasizes the alliances formed by working-class and middle-class women in social reform (130–44). Hunter does, however, acknowledge that middle-class black women criticized working-class women's participation in commercial amusements (154).

23. The notion of circularity is explored by Carlo Ginzburg, a historian of early modern Europe, in *The Cheese and the Worms*, xii, xiv. Similarly, in *In Their Own Interests*, Earl Lewis argues that "segregation led to congregation and a measured autonomy" (90).

24. For example, in *Marching Together*, Melinda Chateauvert argues that "respectability established the political authority of African American women" (xii).

Chapter One

1. Rosetta McKinney to Mary Etta Glenn, 27 August 1922, "Mother" to Mary Etta Glenn, 23 September 1922, and "Aunt Sarah" to Mary Etta Glenn, 29 January 1922, box 16, Glenn Papers, BHC.

2. After Georgia, Tennessee and Alabama were the most common sources of migrants to Detroit because they were due south of Michigan. See Robert W. Adams, "Social Reasons Bring Negroes to Detroit," *Detroiter*, 20 August 1923, 7, 9; Forrester B. Washington, *Negro in Detroit*, vol. 2, chap. 5, p. 100; and Citizens' Research Council, *Negro in Detroit*, sect. 2, p. 14.

3. Citizens' Research Council, *Negro in Detroit*, sect. 2, p. 5.

4. Richard W. Thomas, *Life for Us*, 26–27.

5. A survey of 177 black heads of household was conducted in Detroit in 1920. Of this number, 148 gave social reasons for migration such as unbearable con-

ditions, inferior education, and oppression in the South. Only 29 gave economic reasons for migration north. See Adams, "Social Reasons Bring Negroes to Detroit," 9, and Forrester B. Washington, *Negro in Detroit*, vol. 2, chap. 5, p. 99.

6. Mary Etta Glenn to R. B. Huston, 3 October 1942, box 1, Glenn Papers, BHC.

7. "Mother" to Mary Etta Glenn, 23 September 1922, box 16, Glenn Papers, BHC.

8. "Second Baptist Church," box 9, and "Southeastern Improvement Association," box 15, Glenn Papers, BHC. Glenn became the vice president of the Second Baptist Church's credit union and the chairman of its education department. She was also active in the Detroit chapters of the NAACP and the Urban League.

9. Charles W. Chesnutt, "The Disenfranchisement of the Negro," in Washington et al., *Negro Problem*, 104.

10. Kevin Gaines provides an overview of racial uplift ideology in *Uplifting the Race*. See also his article, "Assimilationist Minstrelsy as Racial Uplift Ideology." Other works on racial uplift ideology include Carlisle, *Roots of Black Nationalism*, 112–20; Moses, *Golden Age of Black Nationalism*; Bardolph, *Negro Vanguard*; Gatewood, *Aristocrats of Color*; Harlan, *Booker T. Washington*; and Higginbotham, *Righteous Discontent*.

11. In *Domination and the Arts of Resistance*, political scientist James C. Scott suggests that communities write "public transcripts," which he defines as a "shorthand way of describing the open interaction between subordinates and those who dominate" (2). For analyses of racial uplift as accommodation, see Gaines, *Uplifting the Race*, and Moses, *Golden Age of Black Nationalism*.

12. See, for example, Harlan, *Booker T. Washington*; David L. Lewis, *W. E. B. Du Bois*; Moses, *Alexander Crummell*; Gabel, *From Slavery to the Sorbonne*; and Deborah Gray White, *Too Heavy a Load*, 87–109.

13. My analysis of uplift ideology follows Evelyn Brooks Higginbotham's view, in *Righteous Discontent*, that the "politics of respectability assumed a fluid and shifting position along a continuum of African American resistance" (187). In her work, the politics of respectability is interchangeable with female racial uplift ideology. For a similar analysis, see Gregg, *Sparks from the Anvil*, 3–6.

14. Cooper, *Voice from the South*, 28 (emphasis in original).

15. See, for example, Margaret Murray Washington, "Advancement of Colored Women," and Hunton, "Negro Womanhood Defended" and "Woman's Part in the Uplift of the Race." Several books celebrating the achievements of African American women were also published in the late nineteenth and early twentieth centuries. See Majors, *Noted Negro Women*; Hallie Q. Brown, *Homespun Heroines*; Hammond, *In the Vanguard of a Race*; Mossell, *Work of the Afro-American Woman*; and Scruggs, *Women of Distinction*.

16. Fannie Barrier Williams, "Social Bonds in the 'Black Belt' of Chicago," 40.

17. Citizens' Research Council, *Negro in Detroit*, sect. 2, p. 16.

18. Forrester B. Washington, *Negro in Detroit*, vol. 2, chap. 5, p. 104. In *Farewell—We're Good and Gone*, Carole Marks counters the image of migrants as rural peasants, stressing the number of southern migrants who lived in cities prior to

the Great Migration (34–35). See also J. Trent Alexander, "Great Migration in Comparative Perspective."

19. Birney W. Smith, interviewed by Jim Keeney and Roberta McBride, 15 June 1969, Oral History Transcript, p. 17, ALUA.

20. See, for example, W. E. B. Du Bois's description of the African American class structure in *Philadelphia Negro*, 310–11.

21. Langhorne, "Domestic Service in the South," 171.

22. Miller, *From Servitude to Service*, 29. This collection of lectures reveals the similarities in the use of racial uplift rhetoric among a wide variety of educational leaders including W. E. B. Du Bois of Atlanta University, Roscoe Conkling Bruce of Tuskegee Institute, and H. B. Frissell of Hampton Institute.

23. Sylvanie Francaz Williams, "Social Status of the Negro Woman." See also A Southern White Woman, "Experiences of the Race Problem."

24. Fannie Barrier Williams, "Awakening of Women," 396. For a discussion of African American women's Progressive Era reform work, see Shirley J. Carlson, "Black Ideals of Womanhood"; Giddings, *When and Where I Enter*; Neverdon-Morton, *Afro-American Women of the South*; Salem, *To Better Our World*; Terborg-Penn, "Discontented Black Feminists"; and Deborah Gray White, *Too Heavy a Load*, 21–86.

25. Barbara Welter first defined the nineteenth-century conception of "true womanhood" in her seminal article, "Cult of True Womanhood." Other important studies of white women's "separate sphere" and cult of true womanhood include Cott, *Bonds of Womanhood*; Smith-Rosenberg, "Female World of Love and Ritual"; and Ginzberg, *Women and the Work of Benevolence*.

26. Anne Firor Scott, *Natural Allies*, 147.

27. See Hobson, *Uneasy Virtue*; Pivar, *Purity Crusade*; and Gilfoyle, *City of Eros*. For a discussion of African American involvement in social purity, see Odem, *Delinquent Daughters*, 26–30, and Simmons, "African Americans and Sexual Victorianism." Tracts promoting social purity aimed at African American women include Eugene Harris, *Appeal for Social Purity*, and Adams, *Negro Girl*.

28. Eugene Harris, *Appeal for Social Purity*, 7–8.

29. Katzman, *Seven Days a Week*, 24. For a discussion of how southern African American women became associated with "dirt," see Tera Hunter, *To 'Joy My Freedom*, 187–218, and Palmer, *Domesticity and Dirt*, 137–52. Both Hunter and Palmer draw on Mary Douglas's pathbreaking work, *Purity and Danger*.

30. Fannie Barrier Williams, "Smaller Economies," 185. In *Upward Path*, Mary Helm, a white woman, also drew a direct connection between the quality of African American homes and the role of women in racial uplift. "The home is the heart of Christian civilization," argued Helm. "From it flows the life-blood of a race or nation. The center of the home is the woman, and its existence for good or bad depends largely upon her as wife and mother. Therefore the right education and training of the Negro woman is of the greatest importance to the future of the race. If she be imbued with the sanctities of life, she will keep herself

and her home pure and clean" (155). For a discussion of the connection between domesticity and respectability, see Shaw, *What a Woman Ought to Be and to Do*, 26–29.

31. Fannie Barrier Williams, "Smaller Economies," 184. For a similar critique of women who saw housekeeping as "drudgery," see Fannie Barrier Williams, "Industrial Education." This article was one of a series of essays on the question of industrial training published from February to July 1904 in the *Colored American Magazine*. Other contributors included Nannie Helen Burroughs, W. E. B. Du Bois, and Kelly Miller.

32. Etiquette manuals specifically written for an African American audience include Armstrong, *On Habits and Manners*; Hackley, *Colored Girl Beautiful*; Northrop, D. D., Gay, and Penn, *College of Life*; Woods, *Negro in Etiquette*; Gibson and Gibson, *Golden Thoughts on Chastity and Procreation*; Floyd, *Floyd's Flowers*; and Charlotte Hawkins Brown, *The Correct Thing to Do, to Say, to Wear*. For a history of etiquette manuals, see Kasson, *Rudeness and Civility*, and Scobey, "Anatomy of the Promenade."

33. Bradford, "Woman," 103–4.

34. Sylvanie Francaz Williams, "Social Status of the Negro Woman," 300. See also Gibbs, "Woman's Part in the Uplift of the Negro Race."

35. Fannie Barrier Williams, "Need of Organized Womanhood," 652. The Atlanta University study by W. E. B. Du Bois and Augustus Granville Dill, *Morals and Manners among Negro Americans*, includes an extensive section on "home life" (67–81).

36. See, for example, Nannie Helen Burroughs, "The Colored Woman and Her Relation to the Domestic Problem," in Penn and Bowen, *United Negro*, 324, 325.

37. Sutherland, *Americans and Their Servants*, 57–58. For discussions of southern white employers' preference for African American servants, see ibid., 40–41; Katzman, *Seven Days a Week*, 24–27; and Salmon, *Domestic Service*, 173–75. For a discussion of domestic service training, see Shaw, *What a Woman Ought to Be and to Do*, 77–78.

38. "The Race Problem—An Autobiography," 587. For other examples of the sexual harassment and rape of African American women, see Denby, *Indignant Heart*, 45–47. Christine and Charles Denby migrated to Detroit in the 1920s. One result of Chief Justice Clarence Thomas's confirmation hearings has been an overdue historical examination of the legacy of the sexual harassment of African American women. See the essays in Morrison, *Race-ing Justice*, and Smitherman, *Race, Gender, and Power*. See also Brown, "'What Has Happened Here.'"

39. Jacqueline Jones, *Labor of Love*, 113.

40. The term "nurse," when applied to southern domestic servants, usually meant an employee whose primary duty was to take care of one or more children. Nurses' work, however, was rarely limited to child care. White employers expected nurses to cook and clean when necessary without complaint.

41. "More Slavery," 197–98. Sexual harassment of African American domestic work-

ers continued well into the twentieth century. For examples, see Tucker, *Telling Memories among Southern Women*, 165, 217.

42. Fannie Barrier Williams, "Northern Negro's Autobiography," 96.
43. Darlene Clark Hine, "Rape and the Inner Lives of Black Women," in DuBois and Ruiz, *Unequal Sisters*, 292, 294.
44. Calderon, *Erma*, 41. When Erma was sexually assaulted by an elderly white man, her mother had him arrested (42–45).
45. Quoted in Alma Blount, "If You Got Time to Lean, You Got Time to Clean," in Hall, *Speaking for Ourselves*, 135.
46. Mahalia Jackson, *Movin' On Up*, 21.
47. Quoted in Guy-Sheftall, *Daughters of Sorrow*, 74.
48. Cooley, *Homes of the Freed*, 87.
49. Historians of Reconstruction have pointed out the salience of household work in the lives of African American women who were freed from field labor. The wrath these women incurred from whites who accused them of having "pretensions" reflected the social status that African American families gained from having a full-time housewife who maintained standards of cleanliness. See Jacqueline Jones, *Labor of Love*, 58–60; Litwack, *Been in the Storm So Long*, 244–45; and Kolchin, *First Freedom*, 62–63.
50. Calderon, *Erma*, 5.
51. Ibid., 11. Erma's mother wiped the stove with a white cloth when she returned home from work to check that her daughter had done the job properly.
52. Mahalia Jackson, *Movin' On Up*, 12. For another example of African American southern housekeeping, see Tucker, *Telling Memories among Southern Women*, 76–77.
53. Quoted in Simonsen, *You May Plow Here*, 41.
54. Quoted in Cooley, *Homes of the Freed*, 64–65.
55. Jacqueline Jones, *Labor of Love*, 86.
56. Du Bois and Dill, *Morals and Manners among Negro Americans*, 50–58. The positive comments on cleanliness far outweighed the negative comments.
57. Higginbotham, *Righteous Discontent*, 214. For a history of the National Training School and its founder, Nannie Helen Burroughs, see Barnett, "Religion, Politics, and Gender" and "Nannie Burroughs and the Education of Black Women"; Harley, "Nannie Helen Burroughs"; Wolcott, "'Bible, Bath, and Broom'"; and Spain, "Black Women as City Builders."
58. Margaret C. Wagner to Nannie Helen Burroughs, 21 February 1932, box 143, Burroughs Papers, LC. Of the dozens of letters requesting information about the school, none expressed an interest in courses in domestic service.
59. Class lists, 1918–31, box 143, Burroughs Papers, LC. The remaining 5 percent of students majored in art, beauty culture, missionary work, social service, or music.
60. Harley, "Black Women in a Southern City."
61. Mildred Holly Farren, student document, n.d., box 153, Burroughs Papers, LC.

62. James D. Anderson, *Education of Blacks*, 61.

63. Melnea A. Cass, interviewed by Tahi Lani Mott, 1 February 1977, transcript, p. 16, Black Women Oral History Project, SL.

64. Ibid., 53–54.

65. Quoted in Hall, *Speaking for Ourselves*, 136.

66. Jacqueline Jones, *Labor of Love*, 128; Dill, "Means to Put My Children Through"; Tera Hunter, *To 'Joy My Freedom*, 56–58, 62–63; Katzman, *Seven Days a Week*, 85–86.

67. Charleszetta Waddles, autobiography, typewritten manuscript, n.d., chap. 3, p. 6, MHC.

68. See Clark-Lewis, "This Work Had an End"; Dill, "'Making the Job Good Yourself'"; Tera Hunter, *To 'Joy My Freedom*, 58–59; and Katzman, *Seven Days a Week*, 90–91.

69. Tera Hunter, *To 'Joy My Freedom*, 60–61, 132–35, 225–27. Although "pan-toting" emerged as a compromise in employer/employee relations after the Civil War, the practice also gave employers ammunition to accuse servants of being dishonest. African American women who attempted to reform domestic service, such as Elizabeth Ross Haynes, recommended that the practice be stopped and domestic servants be paid wages that would allow them to feed their families adequately.

70. The most notable of these was the 1881 Atlanta washerwomen's strike. See Tera Hunter, "Domination and Resistance" and *To 'Joy My Freedom*, 74–97, and Rabinowitz, *Race Relations in the Urban South*, 73–76. For a general history of unionized household workers, see Van Raaphorst, *Union Maids Not Wanted*.

71. For examinations of the employee/employer relationship in domestic service, see Rollins, *Between Women*, and Tucker, *Telling Memories among Southern Women*.

72. Jacqueline Jones, *Labor of Love*, 132–33.

73. "The Race Problem—An Autobiography," 587.

74. Luker, *Social Gospel in Black and White*. For an example of the call for better-educated ministers, see A. W. Pegues, "The Necessity of a Trained Ministry," in Penn and Bowen, *United Negro*, 118–21.

75. I use the term "Sanctified" to describe denominations that sprang from the Holiness revival of the 1870s: the Pentecostal, Holiness, and Primitive Baptist churches and independent denominations. See Hurston, *Sanctified Church*.

76. Quoted in Paris, *Black Pentecostalism*. For a description of the Vineland meeting, see Synan, *Holiness-Pentecostal Movement*, 34–35.

77. For descriptions of northern white missionaries' and teachers' contempt for freedpeoples' religious practices, see Litwack, *Been in the Storm So Long*, 457–62; Montgomery, *Under Their Own Vine and Fig Tree*, 263–67; and Foner, *Reconstruction*, 91.

78. Sernett, *Bound for the Promised Land*, 27–30; Baer and Singer, *African-American Religion*. For an examination of African American ministers' role in the racial uplift movement, see Wheeler, *Uplifting the Race*.

79. Goldsmith, *When I Rise Cryin' Holy*, 57–60; Charles Edwin Jones, *Black Holiness*; Sernett, *Bound for the Promised Land*, 95–96.

80. Ayers, *Promise of the New South*, 401. For an examination of women's role in the Sanctified church, see Gilkes, "'Together and in Harness.'"

81. Adams, *Negro Girl*, 23.

82. Amanda Smith, *Autobiography*, 103.

83. Ibid., 143. For a positive description of ecstatic worship, see White and White, *Stylin'*, 179.

84. Alexander C. Garner, "The True and the False in the Revival Methods of the Race," in Penn and Bowen, *United Negro*, 112. See also S. A. Peeler, "What Improvements Should Be Made in the Religious Worship of the Churches?," in ibid., 146–51.

85. Mahalia Jackson, *Movin' On Up*, 32–33.

86. Maultsby, "Africanisms in African-American Music."

87. Lawrence W. Levine, *Black Culture*, 180.

88. Many female uplift ideologues, however, supported African American women's efforts to open small businesses. See, for example, Alberta Moore Smith, "Chicago Notes."

89. See Barlow, *"Looking Up at Down,"* 41; Tera Hunter, *To 'Joy My Freedom*, 154–61, 168–86; and Carby, "'It Jus Be's Dat Way Sometime.'"

90. For a history of the TOBA, see Daphne Duval Harrison, *Black Pearls*, 4, 23–41; Barlow, *"Looking Up at Down,"* 120–22; and Albertson, *Bessie*, 66.

91. Daphne Duval Harrison, *Black Pearls*, 21.

92. Esther Mae Scott, interviewed by Theresa Danley, 11 August 1976, 3 November 1977, transcript, p. 40, Black Women Oral History Project, SL.

93. Mahalia Jackson, *Movin' On Up*, 36. For an analysis of female blues singers' mobility, see Angela Y. Davis, *Blues Legacies and Black Feminism*, 20, 66–90.

94. Girls' Protective League, "Just Girls," n.d., box 39, folder 10, UCSP-CF. The Girls' Protective League was founded in the 1910s to assist both African American and white female migrants.

95. The literature on women and Progressive Era reform is voluminous. Recent works include Fitzpatrick, *Endless Crusade*; Deutsch, "Learning to Talk More Like a Man"; Trolander, *Professionalism and Social Change*; Hewitt and Lebsock, *Visible Women*; Frankel and Dye, *Gender, Class, Race, and Reform*; and Lasch-Quinn, *Black Neighbors*.

96. For contemporary discussions of reform efforts targeted at African American female migrants, see Matthews, "Some of the Dangers Confronting Southern Girls"; Layten, "Northern Phase of a Southern Problem"; and Kellor, "Southern Colored Girls in the North," *AME Church Review*; "Associations for Protection of Colored Women"; and "Opportunities for Southern Negro Women." In "When Your Work Is Not Who You Are," Sharon Harley suggests that these Progressive Era reform efforts were analogous to the efforts of trade unions because both sought to "prevent working women . . . from being exploited" (50).

97. *Detroit Contender*, 7 May 1921, p. 2.

98. For a history of the Stars, see Bak, *Turkey Stearnes and the Detroit Stars*. See also Miles, "Home at Last," 215–17. Miles notes that "for years the baseball games were the center of a storm of controversy about Negro behavior in public, in which conservative forces continually called upon the masses to restrain their emotions at public functions" (217). See also Citizens' Research Council, *Negro in Detroit*, sect. 7, pp. 14–15. This report estimated that the average African American attendance at Mack Park was 4,500.

99. "Afro-American Rooters Are Best Part of the Shows at Mack Park," *Detroit Saturday Night*, 26 August 1922, p. 2.

100. The separation of classes has a powerful spatial dynamic. Daphne Spain, in *Gendered Spaces*, argues that spatial segregation leads to greater social stratification (15–18). For discussions of how gender inequality becomes part of the built environment, see Hayden, *Grand Domestic Revolution*, and Weisman, *Discrimination by Design*.

101. In "Learning to Talk More Like a Man," Sarah Deutsch describes female urban reformers' efforts to "create space where working women could appear in public without having their virtue questioned by being 'on the streets'" (390). For African American women, whose virtue was always questioned by whites, the imperative to get off "the streets" was even stronger. See also Peiss, *Cheap Amusements*, on the decrease in homosocial space.

102. Quoted in Moon, *Untold Tales*, 33.

103. Quoted in Citizens' Research Council, *Negro in Detroit*, sect. 2, p. 16. For a discussion of the conflict between an older elite and incoming migrants, see Landry, *New Black Middle Class*, 18–66.

104. Katzman, *Before the Ghetto*, 61–62.

105. Because of its proximity to Canada, Detroit was an important last stop on the underground railroad, and many of the ex-slaves who returned to Detroit in the postbellum period had passed through the city in the 1850s.

106. Woodson, *Century of Negro Migration*, 147–66. For descriptions of nineteenth-century migrations to Detroit, see Katzman, *Before the Ghetto*, 61–66, and Deskins, "Residential Mobility of Negro Occupational Groups," 66–78. In "Black Female Workers," Bogart R. Leashore notes that "significant proportions" of Detroit's African American female live-in servants in the late nineteenth century were born in Kentucky and Virginia (118).

107. Katzman, *Before the Ghetto*, 105. See also Oestreicher, *Solidarity and Fragmentation*, 35–36.

108. Katzman, *Before the Ghetto*, 107.

109. Warren, *Michigan Manual of Freedmen's Progress*, 72.

110. Hackley, *Colored Girl Beautiful*, 30–31. See also Davenport, *Azalia*; John B. Reid, "Career to Build"; Gatewood, *Aristocrats of Color*, 138; and Ellistine P. Lewis, "Hackley, Emma Azalia Smith," in Hine, *Black Women in America*, 511.

111. For a description of Detroit's "colored elite," see Gatewood, *Aristocrats of Color*, 124–26.

112. Mrs. Lucien Moore, "First Impressions of a Visiting Nurse," Sixth Annual Report, 1903–4, box 1, Visiting Nurses' Association of Detroit Papers, BHC.

113. The Visiting Nurses' and Visiting Housekeepers' Associations can be considered part of the "female dominion" of American reform efforts. See Muncy, *Creating a Female Dominion*. In "Reconstructing the 'Family,'" Eileen Boris stresses the interactive nature of Progressive Era reform. The intervention of experts in family life, suggests Boris, was "mediated by the gender, class, race, and ethnicity of both family members and interveners" (82). In this case, the racial identity of the client family shaped the white visiting nurse's perspective.

114. Moore, "First Impressions."

115. Minutes of the Board of Trustees, 8 August 1918, box 2, Visiting Nurses' Association of Detroit Papers, BHC. By 1920, three African American nurses were working with the VNA. The pattern of hiring African Americans to work exclusively with the black community can also be seen in the VHA.

116. "Associated Charities of Detroit, Service Reports, Oct. 1912–Oct. 1913," box 5, folder 11, UCSP-CF. A similar disparity existed in Chicago. See Knupfer, *Toward a Tenderer Humanity*, 67.

117. Employment Registers, 1877–82, box 1, Young Women's Home Association Papers, MHC. Approximately one out of forty women were listed as "colored"; notably, several of these specified their desire for "day work" rather than live-in work.

118. For a history of Progressive Era reform in Detroit, see Fragnoli, *Transformation of Reform*. For an examination of African Americans' exclusion from Progressive Era reform efforts, see Lasch-Quinn, *Black Neighbors*.

119. Evans, "Women's History and Political Theory," 129. In *Toward a Tenderer Humanity*, Anne Meis Knupfer argues that "club women's discourse created a 'psychic space,' through which they adapted their language and ideologies to multiple audiences, thereby maintaining their own autonomy and identity" (23). See also Patricia Hill Collins's discussion of "safe spaces" in *Black Feminist Thought*, 95–96, and Griffin, *"Who Set You Flowin'?,"* 9–10.

120. Lillian Johnson, Thirtieth Anniversary Speech, 3 February 1928, p. 1, box 2, Johnson Papers, BHC.

121. Frances Welker, "The History of the Detroit Study Club," 21 February 1956, box 2, Johnson Papers, BHC. See also Warren, *Michigan Manual of Freedmen's Progress*, 142–43; Elizabeth Davis, *Lifting As They Climb*, 331–32; and Gere, *Intimate Practices*, 223.

122. Lillian Johnson, Fortieth Anniversary Speech, 18 March 1938, p. 2, box 2, Johnson Papers, BHC.

123. Yearbook, 1911–12, box 7, Detroit Study Club Papers, BHC.

124. See Elizabeth Davis, *Lifting As They Climb*, 317–21. See also Peebles, "Detroit's

Black Women's Clubs"; Du Bois, *Efforts for Social Betterment*, 45, 76, 102; *Black Women in Michigan*, 6–7; and Hine, *Black Women in the Middle West*.

125. The Phillis Wheatley Association founded homes for young migrant women in cities across the country. See Jane Edna Hunter, *A Nickle and a Prayer*, and Adrienne Lash Jones, *Jane Edna Hunter*. The YWCA named many of its segregated African American facilities after Phillis Wheatley.

126. Elizabeth Davis, *Lifting As They Climb*, 316. See also Miles, "Home at Last," 62–63, and "Eyewitness History," p. 17, reel 2, Second Baptist Church Papers, MHC.

127. Phillis Wheatley Home, document, n.d., box 66, folder 5, UCSP-CF.

128. Mary E. McCoy, Inquiry of the Detroit Association of Charities, 8 March 1910, box 9, DULP. McCoy was also active in the suffrage movement. See Elizabeth Davis, *Lifting As They Climb*, 318.

129. See "National Association for Colored Women" and Hunton, "Detroit Convention."

130. Hunton, "Detroit Convention," 589. Later that year, Hunton herself would be forced to flee Atlanta after that city's bloody race riot. She spent the rest of her life in the North.

131. "National Association for Colored Women," 196–97.

132. Ibid., 197. The same author hints at some discord over the election of officers at the meeting. It was proposed that the election be held in an executive session, with only delegates and alternates attending. The process of removing the women who were not in this group resulted in "quite a commotion" and "much dissatisfaction" (194). The election itself lasted eight hours, suggesting that it generated a good deal of conflict played out through complex parliamentary procedures.

Chapter Two

1. For discussions of female reformers' attempts to sanitize public space, see Deutsch, "Learning to Talk More Like a Man"; Ryan, *Women in Public*, 59–62; Judith R. Walkowitz, *City of Dreadful Delight*, 18–22, 55–57; Stansell, *City of Women*, 63–75; Myerowitz, *Women Adrift*; Elizabeth Wilson, *Sphinx in the City*; and Peiss, *Cheap Amusements*, 163–84.

2. In *"Who Set You Flowin'?,"* Farah Jasmine Griffin analyzes the dominant tropes in a variety of migration narratives. Although some of these narratives—Nella Larsen's novels or Bessie Smith's blues songs, for example—do present complex images of female migrants, most of the Great Migration historiography examines female migrants only as supplementary wage earners. A recent book that integrates gender more fully into Great Migration history is Phillips, *Alabama North*. For a sampling of the vast literature on the Great Migration, see Osofsky, *Harlem*; Spear, *Black Chicago*; Kusmer, *A Ghetto Takes Shape*; Gottlieb, *Making Their Way*; Marks, *Farewell—We're Good and Gone*; Trotter, *Black Milwaukee*; and James R. Grossman, *Land of Hope*.

3. Carole Marks, in *Farewell—We're Good and Gone*, suggests that women are ignored in migration literature because of the "low status" of their paid labor (45). For an overview of African American women and the Great Migration, see Jacqueline Jones, *Labor of Love*, 152–95. For a history of female migrants in California during the second Great Migration, see Lemke-Santangelo, *Abiding Courage*. Darlene Clark Hine, in her insightful article, "Black Migration to the Urban Midwest," suggests that an examination of female migrants would illuminate noneconomic motives for migration. See also Darlene Clark Hine, "Rape and the Inner Lives of Black Women," in DuBois and Ruiz, *Unequal Sisters*, and Hendricks, *Gender, Race, and Politics*, 112–28.

4. See Glen E. Carlson, "Negro in the Industries in Detroit," 59, and Richard W. Thomas, *Life for Us*, 26. Journalists often cited the spectacular increase in Detroit's African American population in articles highlighting the Great Migration's impact. It should be remembered, however, that Detroit's black population in 1910 was only 5,471, which accounts for the dramatically large increase in percentage. For a description of African American migration to Detroit from a white employer's perspective, see Hain, "Our Immigrant, the Negro."

5. Citizens' Research Council, *Negro in Detroit*, sect. 2, pp. 5, 14.

6. The 1920 survey found that labor agents had brought less than 1 percent of migrants, and 91 percent had paid their own way to Detroit, many after living in border cities (Forrester B. Washington, *Negro in Detroit*, vol. 2, chap. 5, p. 104).

7. Ibid.

8. Ibid. In the summer of 1918, however, according to the Travelers' Aid Society, a larger number of women than men arrived. See Olcott, *Work of Colored Women*, 110.

9. Jacqueline Jones, *Labor of Love*, 159.

10. Lasker, "Negro in Detroit," 27; H. O. Weitschat, "Negro 'Coming' on a Hard Road," *Detroit Saturday Night*, 21 January 1928, p. 6. These articles were based on the 1920 and 1926 *Negro in Detroit* studies and interviews with African American reformers such as John C. Dancy, director of the Detroit Urban League.

11. Haynes resigned his post as the National Urban League's executive secretary in 1917 and began working for the Department of Labor as the director of "Negro Economics" in 1918. He apparently conducted his survey of Detroit and wrote this study in the interim. For a longer treatise on the "adaptive" capabilities of migrants, see George Edmund Haynes, *Trend of the Races*.

12. See, for example, Donald, "Negro Migration of 1906–1918," and Emmett J. Scott, *Negro Migration*.

13. See "George Edmund Haynes," in Logan and Winston, *Dictionary of American Negro Biography*, 297–300, and Weiss, *National Urban League*, 30–34.

14. George Edmund Haynes, *Negro Newcomers in Detroit*, 8, 10, 18.

15. See, for example, Thomasson, "Negro Migration."

16. Lett, "Migration Difficulties in Michigan," 232. See also Bethune, "Problems of the City Dweller," and McGuinn, "Commercial Recreation."

17. For descriptions of housing and crowding, see editorial, "Housing Conditions," *Detroit Herald*, 30 October 1916, p. 2, and Len G. Shaw, "Detroit's New Housing Problem," *Detroit Free Press*, 3 June 1917, p. 1.

18. George Edmund Haynes, *Negro Newcomers in Detroit*, 21, 23, 26–27.

19. Quoted in Parris and Brooks, *Blacks in the City*, 93. For a history of the Detroit Urban League, see Richard W. Thomas, *Life for Us*, 49–87; David Allen Levine, *Internal Combustion*, 71–91, 114–24; Miles, "Home at Last"; Boykin, *Handbook of the Detroit Negro*, 24–27; Murage, "Organizational History of the Detroit Urban League"; and Elizabeth Anne Martin, *Detroit and the Great Migration*.

20. Before 1918, the National Urban League was known as the National League on Urban Conditions among Negroes, and the Detroit chapter was known as the Detroit League on Urban Conditions among Negroes; for purposes of simplification, however, I have used "National Urban League" and "Detroit Urban League" throughout.

21. Minutes of the Joint Committee Meeting of the Detroit League on Urban Conditions among Negroes, 16 October 1916, p. 8, box 3, folder 19, UCSP.

22. "The Detroit League on Urban Conditions among Negroes," summary of 1916 survey, p. 1, box 3, folder 18, UCSP. In fact, the Second Baptist Church and several women's clubs had attempted to organize a response to the migration by setting up a boardinghouse for female migrants and stepping up their charity efforts.

23. Ibid. For a more detailed description of the 1916 survey, see Forrester B. Washington, "Report of Secretary to First Meeting of Joint Committee," 17 July 1916, pp. 3–15, box 34, folder 19, UCSP-CF.

24. Forrester B. Washington, "Detroit Newcomers' Greeting," 334.

25. Forrester B. Washington, "Program of Work," 498.

26. Forrester B. Washington, "Detroit Newcomers' Greeting," 334, and "Program of Work," 498; Minutes of the Detroit Urban League, 12 March 1917, pp. 6–7, box 3, folder 21, UCSP.

27. Forrester B. Washington, "Program of Work," 499.

28. Ibid.

29. "Community Dance," in "Report of the Director," 19 January 1917, p. 5, box 3, folder 20, UCSP.

30. Forrester B. Washington, "Detroit Newcomers' Greeting," 335. For a description of the Detroit Urban League's activities during 1916 and 1917, see Report of a Survey by the Detroit League on Urban Conditions among Negroes, 1916, box 3, folder 18, UCSP.

31. "Colored Young Men Form Strong Organization," n.d., box 1, folder 3, DULP. The YNPA was similar to Chicago's Negro Fellowship League, founded by Ida B. Wells-Barnett.

32. "Report of the Director," 12 April 1917, box 3, folder 21, UCSP.

33. "Report of the Director to Monthly Meeting of Joint Committee of Detroit

Urban League on Urban Conditions among Negroes," 12 December 1916, p. 3, box 3, folder 19, UCSP.

34. Quoted in Leonard and Washington, "Welcoming Southern Negroes," 335.

35. Minutes of the Joint Committee Meeting, 16 October 1916, p. 2, box 3, folder 19, UCSP.

36. Ibid. A "mother hubbard" is a long, loose housecoat or dress.

37. Forrester B. Washington, "A Program of Work for the Assimilation of Negro Migrants into Northern Cities," 17 December 1917, p. 17, box 1, folder 8, DULP.

38. Dress Well Club pamphlet, [1918], box 1, folder 8, DULP.

39. Forrester B. Washington, speech to the Dress Well Club, 20 September 1917, box 1, folder 8, DULP.

40. "New Comers' Attention Read Carefully," Dress Well Club card, [1918], box 1, folder 8, DULP. In *Land of Hope*, James R. Grossman has pointed out that "boudoir caps" were considered appropriate attire for southern female domestic workers traveling to work in cities (150–51).

41. Forrester B. Washington, speech to the Dress Well Club, 20 September 1917, box 1, folder 8, DULP.

42. "New Comers' Attention Read Carefully," Dress Well Club card, [1918], box 1, folder 8, DULP.

43. See Weiss, *National Urban League*, 119–20. James R. Grossman, in *Land of Hope*, details similar projects carried out by the Chicago Urban League, YMCA, and *Chicago Defender* (145–60).

44. Detroit Urban League brochure, 1918, box 1, folder 9, DULP. This brochure was originally printed in 1918 and redistributed by John C. Dancy in 1922. See David Allen Levine, *Internal Combustion*, 117. Dancy wrote in his autobiography that 20,000 of these pamphlets were distributed after the second printing. He also remembered that the pamphlet was "very unpopular with some members of the community," indicating that some migrants may have been offended by the condescending tone of the Urban League literature (*Sand against the Wind*, 156).

45. James R. Grossman, *Land of Hope*, 150.

46. Report of the Associated Charities, 1 January–31 December 1919, box 3, folder 9, UCSP. The Urban League board was made up of twenty-six members, thirteen white and thirteen African American, most of whom were active in the Associated Charities. See Dancy, *Sand against the Wind*, 49. The Associated Charities reflected national efforts to rationalize charity during the Progressive period. A 1916 report of the organization argued that "Detroit is now much more efficient than to want to indulge in promiscuous, casual and indiscriminate giving of relief" (Associated Charities bulletin, 26 June 1916, box 3, folder 6, UCSP). The Detroit Community Fund, founded in 1918, disbursed funds to all certified Detroit charities, thus centralizing the city's fund-raising efforts. Therefore, the Community Fund distributed money to the Associated Charities, which then dispersed it to the Urban League. In 1924, the Urban League received permis-

sion to incorporate, which granted the organization independence from the Associated Charities. However, all of the Urban League's fund-raising, as well as that of its affiliated community center and other charity organizations such as the Phillis Wheatley Home, was done through the auspices of the Community Fund, placing it under the direct control of white philanthropists and professional social workers.

47. Minutes of the Joint Committee Meeting, 16 October 1916, p. 4, box 3, folder 19, UCSP.

48. Washington spoke to both the Detroit Study Club and the Willing Workers in 1916 and referred cases to them for investigation. The members of these clubs also assisted the league's fund-raising efforts. See "Report of the Director to Monthly Meeting of Joint Committee of Detroit Urban League on Urban Conditions among Negroes," 12 December 1916, p. 3, box 3, folder 19, UCSP.

49. Minutes of the Joint Committee Meeting, 16 October 1916, p. 3, box 3, folder 19, UCSP. Some delinquent African American girls were sent to the State Industrial School for Girls in Adrian, Michigan.

50. Citizens' Research Council, *Negro in Detroit*, sect. 5, p. 15.

51. Forrester B. Washington, "Report of Secretary to First Meeting of Joint Committee," 17 July 1916, p. 4, box 34, folder 19, UCSP-CF. For descriptions of the housing available to African American migrants, see Jerome Gale Thomas, "City of Detroit," 99–107; Richard W. Thomas, *Life for Us*, 89–102; and Len G. Shaw, "Detroit's New Housing Problem," *Detroit Free Press*, 3 June 1917, p. 1.

52. Stansell, *City of Women*, 74.

53. Forrester B. Washington, *Negro in Detroit*, vol. 5, 123.

54. Forrester B. Washington, "Report of Secretary to First Meeting of Joint Committee," 17 July 1916, p. 12, box 34, folder 19, UCSP-CF.

55. "Negro Housing," 26 April 1924, p. 4, box 1, folder 13, DULP.

56. Forrester B. Washington, "Report of Secretary to First Meeting of Joint Committee," 17 July 1916, p. 14, box 34, folder 19, UCSP-CF.

57. Washington returned to Detroit in 1920 and again in 1926 to direct two large-scale studies of the African American community under the employ of the Associated Charities. In his writings on African Americans, Washington continually referred to the data and experiences he had collected in Detroit. See, for example, Forrester B. Washington, "Recreational Facilities for the Negro."

58. Dancy, *Sand against the Wind*, 56.

59. Ibid., 155.

60. Minutes of the Columbia Community Center, 24 June 1920, box 8, folder 30, DULP.

61. Dancy, *Sand against the Wind*, 51.

62. Minutes of the Columbia Community Center, 31 July 1919, 23 September 1920, box 8, folder 30, DULP.

63. Dancy, *Sand against the Wind*, 145. For a discussion of black women's role in health reform, see Susan L. Smith, *Sick and Tired*.

64. Minutes of the Columbia Community Center, 25 September 1919, p. 4, box 8, folder 30, DULP. The Travelers' Aid Society of Detroit did not work closely with the African American community in the 1910s. The society did, however, occasionally refer migrants to the Urban League, as in this case. By the early 1920s, Dancy was able to convince the Community Chest to hire an African American Travelers' Aid worker who could "divine the needs of the newcomers the minute they got off the train" (Dancy, *Sand against the Wind*, 55).

65. Dancy, *Sand against the Wind*, 156.

66. Minutes of the Columbia Community Center, 24 June 1920, p. 1, box 8, folder 30, DULP. In July and August 1920, the center was visited by "approximately 4,000" people, provided lodging for 16 women, and cared for 392 babies in its clinic. See ibid., 23 September 1920, p. 2.

67. Ibid., 27 January 1921, p. 1.

68. Forrester B. Washington, *Negro in Detroit*, vol. 10. This volume has no page numbers. Washington notes that he is only counting "reputable" churches in this estimate, excluding most storefront churches. For a history of women's role in the black church during the Great Migration, see Sernett, *Bound for the Promised Land*, 115–16, and Overacker, *African American Church Community*, 10–15, 71–110.

69. Forrester B. Washington, *Negro in Detroit*, vol. 10. By 1926, with increased migration, the number of Baptists had risen 66 percent and AME church membership had decreased 15 percent. See Citizens' Research Council, *Negro in Detroit*, sect. 10, p. 3. It should be remembered, however, that some migrants belonged to more than one church.

70. Other African American Baptist churches in Detroit during this period were the Calvary Baptist Church and the Shiloh Baptist Church.

71. Ernestine Wright, quoted in Moon, *Untold Tales*, 94.

72. For a history of the Second Baptist Church, see Shelly, "Bradby's Baptists." See also Miles, "Home at Last," 157–84, and Richard W. Thomas, *Life for Us*, 175–80.

73. "Cavalcade of the Second Baptist Church," 29 March 1937, p. 11, box 9, folder 1, Glenn Papers, BHC.

74. Shelly, "Bradby's Baptists," 7–8; Miles, "Home at Last," 161–62; "History of the Second Baptist Church," 1940, pp. 6–7, and "Eyewitness History," 1976, pp. 19, 45, 46, reel 2, Second Baptist Church Papers, MHC.

75. "Cavalcade of the Second Baptist Church," 14; "History of the Second Baptist Church," 7.

76. Sernett, *Bound for the Promised Land*, 115.

77. "History of the Second Baptist Church," 76, 82, 85, 86.

78. "Cavalcade of the Second Baptist Church," 17; "History of the Second Baptist Church," 81.

79. Forrester B. Washington, *Negro in Detroit*, vol. 10.

80. "Five Glorious Years, Detroit Council of Churches, 1919–1924," p. 6, box 1, folder 1, pt. 2, Metropolitan Detroit Council of Churches Papers, ALUA.

81. "Annual Statement, Detroit Council of Churches," 1920, pp. 10, 14, box 1, folder

1, pt. 2, Metropolitan Detroit Council of Churches Papers, ALUA. The social service department reported that there were 142 dance halls, 756 poolrooms, 152 moving picture shows, and 4 burlesque theaters in Detroit in 1920.

82. "Detroit Protestantism in United Effort," n.d., box 1, folder 1, pt. 2, Metropolitan Detroit Council of Churches Papers, ALUA.

83. "Detroit Churches Illustrate Value of Christian Cooperation," 1922–23, box 1, folder 1, pt. 2, Metropolitan Detroit Council of Churches Papers, ALUA. This document reported that the social service department worked among "the colored people, particularly the new-comers from the South, and has endeavored to strengthen the church and social service agencies which are working among the colored people" (8).

84. Ibid., 11. Both John Dancy and George E. Haynes gave speeches to the council. See "Unity and Strength, 1924–5 Annual Report," p. 12, pt. 2, box 1, folder 2, and "Social Service Department, Minutes," 21 March 1923, box 5, folder 20, pt. 2, Metropolitan Detroit Council of Churches Papers, ALUA. Dancy regularly attended the social service department meetings after May 1923.

85. H. C. Gleiss, General Superintendant of the Baptist Christian Center, to the Detroit Community Union, 11 October 1924, box 75, folder 21, UCSP-CF. The center was run under the auspices of the Advisory Council for Negro Work of the Detroit Baptist Union, an organization of fifty-six Detroit churches, and was located at 1718 Russell Street. It was funded through the Detroit Community Union. See "Baptist Christian Center," n.d., box 6, folder 1, UCSP-CF.

86. "Something Cooking at the Center," Women's American Baptist Home Mission Society flyer, 1946, box 39, folder 18, UCSP-CF.

87. Itemized Report of the Activities of the Christian Center, 28 October–31 December 1921, box 75, folder 21, UCSP-CF.

88. "Christian Center of Detroit Michigan," n.d., p. 3; Joseph Campau, "Baptist Christian Center," November 1939, p. 1; and "Baptist Christian Center," n.d., p. 1, box 6, folder 1, UCSP-CF.

89. Olcott, Work of Colored Women, 5, 6. For discussions of segregated YWCA work, see Lasch-Quinn, Black Neighbors, 131–50; Adrienne Lash Jones, "Struggle among Saints"; and Spratt, "To Be Separate or One."

90. Quoted in Olcott, Work of Colored Women, 110.

91. Quoted in ibid., 112. Although employers relegated most African American women to domestic service after World War I, for a brief period during the war, they worked in tobacco factories, garment factories, and even a few steel mills. After the war, African American women's primary industrial occupation was laundry work. In 1914, the YWCA attempted to establish a "home for colored girls" but claimed there was "not the demand for it that had been supposed." See YWCA Annual Report, 1914, p. 25, box 68, folder 17, UCSP-CF. See also Murtland and Rhinehart, Study of the Educational Aims, 59–60, and Boykin, Handbook of the Detroit Negro, 41–43.

92. Olcott, Work of Colored Women, 112.

93. YWCA Annual Report, 1920, p. 35, box 68, folder 17, UCSP-CF.

94. Murtland and Rhinehart, *Study of the Educational Aims*, 59.

95. The YWCA formed two clubs of service workers in department stores. See ibid.

96. *Blue Triangle*, February 1921, pp. 19–20, box 21, folder 19, UCSP. The *Blue Triangle* was the official publication of the Detroit YWCA. See also ibid., July–August 1921, pp. 20, 22, box 21, folder 20, UCSP.

97. Murtland and Rhinehart, *Study of the Educational Aims*, 59.

98. Ragland, "Negro in Detroit," 537.

99. Murtland and Rhinehart, *Study of the Educational Aims*, 61. Other classes included canning and preserving, basketball, roller-skating, and English. A total of 189 women were enrolled.

100. Ibid.

101. *Blue Triangle*, July–August 1921, p. 20, box 21, folder 20, UCSP.

102. Obituary, *Detroit News*, 17 December 1972, box 1, folder 1, and Dawn Watson, "Michigan's Lady Senator," *Courier*, 6 May 1953, box 2, folder 1, Brown Papers, BHC.

103. "St. Aubin Branch," *Blue Triangle*, February 1921, p. 28, box 21, folder 19, UCSP.

104. Lucile N. to Mary Etta, 12 December 1921, Glenn Papers, box 16, BHC.

105. Forrester B. Washington, "Reconstruction and the Colored Woman," 3.

106. Forrester B. Washington, *Negro in Detroit*, vol. 1, chap. 7, p. 41. Although a small number of black women were schoolteachers in Detroit, Washington estimated that 98 percent of Detroit's African American women workers labored in some form of personal service before 1915. On the employment of African American women in Detroit in the late nineteenth and early twentieth centuries, see Katzman, *Before the Ghetto*, 107–11, and John B. Reid, "Career to Build."

107. See "Distribution of Colored Women in Trade Groups," in Forrester B. Washington, *Negro in Detroit*, vol. 1, chap. 7, p. 43. In this table, the primary occupation for African American women is laundry work, with 295 women employed.

108. Ibid., 42. In "Migration Difficulties in Michigan," Harold A. Lett estimated that African American women made up only 1.8 percent of the female industrial workers in the state of Michigan.

109. "Monthly Report of the Labor Advisor of the Industrial Relations Department of the National Urban League," 1917, box 1, folder 8, DULP.

110. "Facts concerning Negroes in Detroit Industrially, Politically, Educationally, Socially, etc.," 21 November 1925, pp. 3–4, box 1, folder 15, DULP. This document notes that in some cases, white and African American women did work side by side, but it is clear that these instances were relatively rare. For another example of white female clerical workers resisting the hiring of an African American woman, see Dancy, *Sand against the Wind*, 109–10.

111. Forrester B. Washington, *Negro in Detroit*, vol. 1, chap. 7, p. 45. Washington was not the only one who overestimated African American women's entry into white-collar and industrial labor. The Detroit Urban League reported that "colored women have become a leading factor in various commercial and pro-

fessional fields." See "Colored Historical Detroit," n.d., p. 6, box 1, folder 1, DULP.

112. Forrester B. Washington, *Negro in Detroit*, vol. 1, chap. 7, p. 45.

113. Although African American women were generally not included in workplace reform programs, they were at times visited by members of Ford Motor Company's sociological department when their husbands worked in Ford factories. See Meyer, *Five Dollar Day*, and Lindsey, "Fields to Ford."

114. Forrester B. Washington, *Negro in Detroit*, vol. 1, chap. 7, p. 47.

115. Ibid., 48. The higher average wage for white women also reflected their entry into better-paid clerical and sales jobs from which employers barred African American women.

116. Ibid., 49.

117. Detroit Urban League Minutes, 19 January 1917, p. 4, box 3, folder 20, and 8 March 1917, p. 3, box 3, folder 21, UCSP. For a description of "passing" to gain employment during this period, see Drake and Cayton, *Black Metropolis*, 159–71. The authors note that women "passed" for economic reasons in more cases than men, particularly to obtain clerical work (162–63). For detailed discussions of "passing," see Williamson, *New People*, and Gatewood, *Aristocrats of Color*, 175–76, 337–38.

118. Forrester B. Washington, *Negro in Detroit*, vol. 1, chap. 7, p. 51. For a discussion of African American women's awareness of the importance of skin color in employment, see Peiss, *Hope in a Jar*, 230–33.

119. Forrester B. Washington, *Negro in Detroit*, vol. 1, chap. 7, p. 59.

120. Ibid., vol. 1, chap. 8, p. 68.

121. Ibid., vol. 1, chap. 7, p. 56.

122. Ibid., 59.

123. "The Urban League and Its Achievements," speech, n.d., box 1, folder 3, DULP.

124. Dancy, *Sand against the Wind*, 135. Dancy goes on to note that women employees at Hudsons were instructed in clothing and appearance. "The girls always looked so nice in their uniforms," he remembered (136). Soon after placing women at Hudsons, Dancy also obtained some positions for women as elevator operators at Crowleys, another department store. By the late 1920s, African American women were also employed as elevator operators in private apartment buildings. See John Dancy to Glen Carlson, 19 November 1929, box 1, folder 29, DULP.

125. Dancy, *Sand against the Wind*, 136.

126. Mrs. Krolik also served as the chair of the Urban League committee that established the Day Workers' Training School. See "Sketch of the History of the National and Local Urban Leagues," [1933], p. 1, box 34, folder 20, UCSP-CF.

127. "Joint Committee Meeting of Detroit League of Urban Conditions among Negroes," 16 October 1916, p. 6, box 3, folder 19, UCSP.

128. George Edmund Haynes, *Negro Newcomers in Detroit*, 18. For other descriptions of the Krolik experiment, see Forrester B. Washington, "Detroit Newcomers'

Greeting," 334; Elizabeth Anne Martin, *Detroit and the Great Migration*, 19–20; and Richard W. Thomas, *Life for Us*, 32–33.

129. "Report of the Director to Monthly Meeting of Joint Committee of Detroit League on Urban Conditions among Negroes," 12 December 1916, p. 1, box 3, folder 19, UCSP. This report indicated that several African American men were also hired in various capacities.

130. Emmett J. Scott, *Negro Migration*, 131.

131. Minutes of the Detroit Urban League, 8 March 1917, p. 1, and 12 April 1917, p. 2, box 3, folder 21, UCSP. Washington argued that core-making would have "a distinctly uplifting effect on some colored women."

132. Ibid., 8 March 1917, p. 2. Some reformers deemed telephone operators "morally suspect"—Detroit Juvenile Court workers, for example, would not place young women in the telephone exchanges—which may explain why African American women were seriously considered for such positions. See handwritten note attached to ibid., 12 December 1916.

133. Forrester B. Washington, *Negro in Detroit*, vol. 1, chap. 7, p. 57.

134. Ibid. Washington noted that harassment was "an evil which the Y.W.C.A. and other women's organizations have been fighting for some time."

135. Ibid.

136. Ibid., 58.

137. Sutherland, *Americans and Their Servants*, 47; YWCA, "The Employment of Women for Day Work," 1917, box 5, folder 4, UCSP.

138. Wages in the South, however, were significantly less—as little as $1.50 per week for a live-in domestic. See Emmett J. Scott, *Negro Migration*, 16, 130.

139. Quoted in Moon, *Untold Tales*, 115.

140. Ibid.

141. See Frank Marquart, interviewed by Herbert Hill, 24 July 1968, Oral History Transcript, p. 4, ALUA.

142. Quoted in Lerner, *Black Women in White America*, 256. Ross-Haynes also noted that Detroit domestics' wages fell after World War I.

143. Sutherland, *Americans and Their Servants*, 58.

144. Citizens' Research Council, *Negro in Detroit*, sect. 3, p. 26.

145. Ibid., appendix, 27. There were 322 ads listed, 125 requesting "colored" help and the remainder seeking whites.

146. The shift from live-in to day work has been targeted by historians as *the* major change in household labor. However, the sources of this change are in dispute. Social scientists who focus on African American women's agency see their demands for day labor as the primary motivation for the shift. For this perspective, see Clark-Lewis, "This Work Had an End"; Dill, "'Making the Job Good Yourself'"; and Terborg-Penn, "Survival Strategies among African-American Women Workers." Because in the South live-out domestic servants and day work were prevalent, others have seen the regional aspect as paramount. See, for example, Sutherland, *Americans and Their Servants*.

147. The 21 October 1920 issue of the *Detroit Free Press* listed 23 help-wanted advertisements for domestic servants and 4 situations-wanted advertisements placed by black women. The 21 June 1925 issue included 24 help-wanted advertisements and 7 situations-wanted advertisements placed by black women. Of the 11 situations-wanted advertisements placed, 8 women requested day work.

148. John C. Dancy, "Unemployment," 1921, p. 3, box 1, folder 12, DULP.

149. Dancy, *Sand against the Wind*, 52.

150. See Jacqueline Jones, *Labor of Love*, 205–6, and Baker and Cooke, "Bronx Slave Market." Most slave markets in the North emerged during the Great Depression when domestic servants experienced increased competition and severely depressed wages.

151. "Baptist Christian Center," box 8, DULP. Negative descriptions of African American female migrants' skills as domestic servants are ubiquitous. See, for example, George Edmund Haynes, *Negro Newcomers in Detroit*, 18–19. Haynes argued that churches should play a central role in the training of domestic servants, a call that the Baptist Christian Center answered (19–20).

152. Forrester B. Washington, *Negro in Detroit*, vol. 1, chap. 7, p. 52.

153. Dancy, *Sand against the Wind*, 100.

154. The domestic science class offered in the early years of the Columbia Community Center was "intended to be preliminary in character, and to be limited to ten lessons of elementary training in general housework as applied to modern housekeeping—not to include cooking or laundry work." Ten women were trained at a time as day workers, and when certified, they were guaranteed employment and given a reference. See "Columbia Community Center, 1918–1920," box 8, DULP, and "Sketch of the History of the National and Local Urban Leagues," 1.

155. "Sketch of the History of the National and Local Urban Leagues," 1–2.

156. J. E. Leslie, "Colored Women Taught Efficiency," 11 April 1922, newspaper clipping, in Scrapbook, Dancy Papers, BHC. For descriptions of the school, see Dancy, *Sand against the Wind*, 100–101, and Eugene Kinckle Jones, "To the Friends of the National Urban League," 15 June 1918, box 1, folder 9, and press release, [1919], box 1, folder 10, DULP.

157. Dancy, *Sand against the Wind*, 101.

158. Citizens' Research Council, *Negro in Detroit*, sect. 3, p. 26.

159. In 1927, Dancy reported that Goodwill Industries and the Community Fund employed African American female bookkeepers. Three African American women were also employed as nurses for the Board of Health, three as police officers, two in the Girls' Protective League, and two in the VHA. See John Dancy to T. Arnold Hill, National Urban League, 13 September 1927, box 1, folder 21, DULP.

160. Neumann, "Twenty-five Years of Negro Activity in Detroit," 9.

161. Citizens' Research Council, *Negro in Detroit*, sect. 3, p. 26.

162. Miles, "Home at Last," 121. In 1926, only 40 of the 5,856 schoolteachers in Detroit

were African American. See Citizens' Research Council, *Negro in Detroit*, sect. 7, p. 17.

163. According to Miles, "Home at Last," Ester Lowe, an African American school-teacher, taught white pupils in an Italian neighborhood during the 1920s.

164. Ibid., 122–23.

165. Application for employment, June 1928, box 28, folder 15, UCSP. Although historians have noted the power Dancy had in obtaining industrial jobs for African American men, his role in helping women get white-collar jobs has been overlooked. For other examples of Dancy placing African American female white-collar workers, see Dancy, *Sand against the Wind*, 33, 109–10. For discussions of African American social workers in this period, see Daniel J. Walkowitz, *Working with Class*, 51–53, 170–74, and Shaw, *What a Woman Ought to Be and to Do*, 164–210.

166. Minutes of the Detroit Urban League, 8 February 1917, p. 3, box 3, folder 20, UCSP.

167. E. A. Carter to John Dancy, n.d., box 1, folder 18, DULP.

168. "Survey of Education and Training of Social Workers," 1929, box 23, folder 14, UCSP.

169. "Survey," box 23, folders 39, 44, UCSP. Throughout the interwar period, more African American social workers found employment. In 1941, an Urban League report noted that there were 125 trained African American social workers in Detroit. These men and women were employed in the Department of Public Welfare and the Wayne County Bureau of Social Aid as well as the Detroit Urban League and Baptist Christian Center. See Report on Black Social Workers in Detroit, 25 July 1941, box 87, folder 14, UCSP-CF.

170. Notes on genealogy, 21 September 1970, box 1, Glenn Papers, BHC.

171. H. Couldfield to Miss M. E. Graham, 24 August 1922, Correspondence, 1920–47, box 16, Glenn Papers, BHC. For other letters of rejection and a letter that Glenn sent to the Smith-Burden Dry Goods Company seeking employment, see ibid.

172. See Thomas Flaherty, Secretary-Treasurer of the National Federation of Post Office Clerks, to Mary Glenn, 29 September 1925, Correspondence, 1924–54, box 16, Glenn Papers, BHC. See also letters in Correspondence, 1933–45, and Correspondence, 1920–47, box 16, Glenn Papers, BHC.

173. Eugene Kinckle Jones, "Negro in the North"; John Dancy, "The Negro at the Crossroads," 3 March 1927, pp. 3–4, box 1, folder 19, DULP.

174. Neumann, "Twenty-five Years of Negro Activity in Detroit," 14.

175. For a history of millinery and dressmaking establishments run by women, see Gamber, *Female Economy*. Entrepreneurs who worked out of their homes or worked for contractors comprised an important segment of the African American female workforce. See Boris, "Black Women and Paid Labor in the Home" and *Home to Work*, 193–96. For a history of African American women and the beauty industry, see Peiss, *Hope in a Jar*, and White and White, *Stylin'*, 185–91.

176. *Detroit Contender*, 7 May 1921, pp. 3, 6.

177. Citizens' Research Council, *Negro in Detroit*, sect. 4, p. 16. On African American entrepreneurship in Detroit, see Miles, "Home at Last," and Richard W. Thomas, *Life for Us*, 201–14.

178. Peiss, *Hope in a Jar*, 213.

179. *Detroit Contender*, 13 November 1920, p. 11. Poro beauty products and beauticians who were graduates of a Poro school also advertised widely in Detroit. For descriptions of the Walker and Poro companies, see Peiss, *Hope in a Jar*, 67–70.

180. *Detroit Independent*, 10 June 1927, p. 3. By this period, a number of African American beauty schools existed in Detroit, including the Rosilyn School of Beauty Culture. See *Detroit Independent*, 16 September 1927, p. 2.

181. See, for example, Freedman, "Separatism as Strategy"; Fass, *The Damned and the Beautiful*; Hall, "Disorderly Women"; Odem, *Delinquent Daughters*, 188–89; and Douglas, *Terrible Honesty*.

Chapter Three

1. Young, *Hard Stuff*, 20.

2. In *City of Eros*, Timothy Gilfoyle suggests that the "milieu of the underground economy offered a variety of alternative subcultures, some of which countered the dominant, sexually prescriptive mores of the age" (315). The subculture of the informal economy in interwar Detroit similarly undermined the prescriptions of racial uplift ideologues.

3. Luise White, *Comforts of Home*, 1. In "Exploring the Informal Economy," an introductory essay for a special issue of *Social Justice* on the informal economy, Cyril Robinson notes that the informal economy is dependent on the formal economy and vice versa (4–5). For critiques of a false dichotomy of informal and formal economic activities, see Leonard, *Informal Economic Activity*, and Harding and Jenkins, *Myth of the Hidden Economy*.

4. For a sample of the literature on the informal economy, see Ferman, Henry, and Hoyman, "Informal Economy"; Robinson, "Exploring the Informal Economy"; Simon and Witte, *Beating the System*; and Mattera, *Off the Books*. Most of the works on the informal economy have been sociological studies such as those listed above or ethnographic studies of inner-city communities. For examples of the latter, see Stack, *All Our Kin*; Dow, "High Weeds in Detroit"; and Duneier, *Slim's Table*. Discussions of the informal economy in African American history have been largely restricted to the "ghetto school" of urban history, which views criminal activity as evidence of a growing pathological black culture. See, in particular, Spear, *Black Chicago*, and Osofsky, *Harlem*.

5. For a discussion of the importance of Prohibition to the rise of an African American informal economy, see Schatzberg and Kelly, *African American Organized Crime*, 22–25.

6. In sociological and anthropological studies, women's participation in the infor-

mal economy is restricted to mutual aid and self-help activities—nonmonetary exchanges of labor and goods such as housework and child care. Carol B. Stack, in *All Our Kin*, for example, describes these activities as the practice of "swapping" material goods and resources throughout the community.

7. Young, *Hard Stuff*, 17–18.

8. Erenberg, *Steppin' Out*, 234–37. See also Peiss, *Cheap Amusements*; Rosenzweig, *Eight Hours for What We Will*; Cumbler, *Working Class Community in Industrial America*; Couvares, *Remaking of Pittsburgh*; Chevigny, *Gigs*; and Cohen, *Making a New Deal*.

9. See, for example, Charles H. Williams, "Recreation in the Lives of Young People," and Attwell, "Recreation Movement and Colored Americans."

10. Forrester B. Washington, "Recreational Facilities for the Negro," 272.

11. Ibid. "Sitting down" may have referred to a variety of leisure activities, including storytelling, playing music, and singing on front porches, in stores, or at other gathering places.

12. Ibid., 273.

13. Citizens' Research Council, *Negro in Detroit*, sect. 7, p. 10; Ben C. Wilson, "Early Development and Growth of America's Oldest Black Resort."

14. Forrester B. Washington, "Recreational Facilities for the Negro," 278, 281–82.

15. Ibid., 282. For a description of other types of recreation that community elites deemed "respectable" during the 1920s, see Citizens' Research Council, *Negro in Detroit*, sect. 7, pp. 1–9.

16. Quoted in Chauncey, *Gay New York*, 250. For discussions of African American gay and lesbian culture during the interwar period, see Mumford, *Interzones*, 73–92; Chauncey, *Gay New York*, 244–67; and Faderman, *Odd Girls and Twilight Lovers*, 72–79.

17. Chauncey, *Gay New York*, 253.

18. McGuinn, "Commercial Recreation." For another contemporary examination of dance halls and cabarets, see William H. Jones, *Recreation and Amusement among Negroes*, 121–34.

19. McGuinn, "Commercial Recreation," 269–70.

20. Hutzel, *Policewomen's Handbook*, 40–47. Hutzel was the director of the Detroit police department's Women's Division and wrote this handbook based on her experiences in Detroit. For descriptions of such arrests in New York, see Ruth M. Alexander, *"Girl Problem,"* 57–58.

21. Citizens' Research Council, *Negro in Detroit*, sect. 7, p. 16 (emphasis in original).

22. McGuinn, "Commercial Recreation," 272, 279.

23. Ibid., 281.

24. In *The Immoral Landscape*, Richard Symanski argues that prostitution and the spatial configuration of cities are linked. Through processes of segregation and containment, the visibility of prostitutes is limited to low-income neighborhoods.

25. Daphne Duval Harrison, *Black Pearls*, 21. Recent works on the history of African

American female blues performers include Carby, "'It Jus Be's Dat Way Some-time'" and "Policing the Black Woman's Body"; DuCille, "Blues Notes on Black Sexuality"; Peretti, *Creation of Jazz*; Barlow, *"Looking Up at Down,"* 119–81; Ann Douglas, *Terrible Honesty*, 387–433; Deborah Gray White, *Too Heavy a Load*, 126–28; and Angela Y. Davis, *Blues Legacies and Black Feminism*. For descriptions of Detroit's African American music scene during the interwar period, see Björn, "From Hastings Street to the Bluebird"; Barlow, *"Looking Up at Down,"* 283–86; and Hennessey, *From Jazz to Swing*, 109–12.

26. Daphne Duval Harrison, *Black Pearls*, 22.

27. *Detroit Contender*, 7 May 1921, p. 7.

28. Glaysher, *Collected Prose*, 144.

29. Forrester B. Washington, "Recreational Facilities for the Negro," 279.

30. Barbara J. Kukla's *Swing City* describes in detail the variety of clubs, performers, and acts available in urban African American communities during the interwar period.

31. Quoted in Taylor, "Prostitution in Detroit," 32, Harlan Hatcher Graduate Library, University of Michigan, Ann Arbor, Michigan.

32. William J. Robinson, editor of the *Detroit Independent*, quoted in H. O. Weitschat, "Crimes by Negroes Running High," *Detroit Saturday Night*, 24 December 1927.

33. Katzman, *Before the Ghetto*, 171.

34. Citizens' Research Council, *Negro in Detroit*, sect. 2, p. 2.

35. Forrester B. Washington, "Report of Secretary to First Meeting of Joint Committee," 17 July 1916, p. 1, box 34, folder 19, UCSP-CF.

36. George Edmund Haynes, *Negro Newcomers in Detroit*, 8.

37. Dancy, *Sand against the Wind*, 112.

38. The authors of Citizens' Research Council, *Negro in Detroit*, argued: "That this undesireable element was largely responsible for developing future discrimination and race prejudice is the opinion of many of the Negroes who were in Detroit at that time" (sect. 2, p. 2). It is interesting to note that these early participants in the informal economy did not fit easily into the idealistic picture of premigration Detroit drawn by the old settlers.

39. Vice Commission, *Social Evil in Chicago*.

40. Forrester B. Washington, "Report of Secretary to First Meeting of Joint Committee," 17 July 1916, p. 1, box 34, folder 19, UCSP-CF.

41. For a history of Prohibition in Michigan, see Engelmann, "O, Whisky," *Intemperance*, "Separate Peace," and "Booze"; Bak, *Turkey Stearnes and the Detroit Stars*, 128–31; Glazer, *Detroit*, 95; and Miles, "Home at Last," 198–200. In 1918, much of the illegal liquor was smuggled from Toledo, Ohio, where a Prohibition law had not yet been passed. After 1919, Canada was the primary source of illegal liquor.

42. Engelmann, "Separate Peace," 53. Engelmann estimates that the illegal liquor industry was three times larger than the next largest industry, chemical produc-

tion, and was valued at between \$200 million and \$400 million per year. See Engelmann, *Intemperance*, 125.

43. Engelmann, "Separate Peace," 53.

44. Miles, "Home at Last," 198; Young, *Hard Stuff*, 22.

45. Engelmann, "O, Whisky," 503.

46. Murphy, "Bootlegging Mothers," 175.

47. Ibid., 176–77.

48. Mary Johnson, "Barrel House Flat Blues," Paramount #12996, 1930.

49. Bessie Smith, for example, recorded "Moonshine Blues" in 1924 with Irving Johns on piano (Columbia #14018-D, 1924; reissued on *Empty Bed Blues*, Columbia #CG30450, 1972). In this song, Smith sang that she was "drunk all night, baby, / drunk the night before."

50. Engelmann, "O, Whisky," 535.

51. Quoted in Engelmann, *Intemperance*, 128.

52. Ibid., 138–39.

53. Engelmann, "Separate Peace," 54–55, 65. Engelmann argues that of most concern were "school pigs"—blind pigs that operated near high schools to attract adolescent customers. In 1924, Mayor Joseph A. Martin responded to complaints from the Detroit Council of Churches (an organization that included several prominent African American ministers and community leaders) and a Committee of One Hundred by instigating a "decency drive" to "clean up" blind pigs, dance halls, and other "disreputable" businesses.

54. Women as well as men were arrested for running liquor or selling it in blind pigs. See "Criminal Index File," 1926, box 82, Civil Rights Congress Papers, ALUA. This file contains the cases of fifteen women arrested for Prohibition-related offenses and seven women arrested for running or working in houses of prostitution. Unfortunately, there is no indication of race in the file records.

55. Emmett J. Scott, *Negro Migration*, 132.

56. Forrester B. Washington, "Report of Secretary to First Meeting of Joint Committee," 17 July 1916, p. 2, box 34, folder 19, UCSP-CF. Washington counted fifty-four poolrooms by 1928. See Forrester B. Washington, "Recreational Facilities for the Negro," 270.

57. Hendricks, *Gender, Race, and Politics*, 52.

58. Mumford, *Interzones*, 20–28.

59. In *City of Dreadful Delight*, Judith R. Walkowitz argues that prostitutes were "evocative of the chaos and illicit secrets of the labyrinthine city" and represented a "permeable and transgressed border between classes and sexes" (22). Both of these images were of paramount concern to African American reformers attempting to fashion a respectable community identity. Other studies of prostitution during this period include Marilynn Wood Hill, *Their Sisters' Keepers*; Hobson, *Uneasy Virtue*; Mackey, *Red Lights Out*; Pivar, *Purity Crusade*; Rosen, *Lost Sisterhood*; and Mumford, *Interzones*, 93–117. For a discussion of pros-

titution's role in the nineteenth-century informal economy, see Gilfoyle, *City of Eros*.

60. Citizens' Research Council, *Negro in Detroit*, sect. 7, p. 19. Similarly, historian Luise White, in *Comforts of Home*, notes that prostitutes sometimes "made homes" for men who were recent migrants to cities (18).

61. Albertson, *Bessie*, 122. In a memo to the Detroit Board of Commerce, black activist J. H. Porter estimated that there were 1,000 buffet flats in Detroit as well as "questionable rooming houses galore, with many Negro restaurants and eating places" (11 March 1918, box 1, DULP).

62. Bessie Smith, "Soft Pedal Blues," Columbia #14075-D, 1925. For a description of Bessie's experience in the Detroit buffet flat, see Albertson, *Bessie*, 123–24. "Soft pedal" refers to a piano-playing style that was relatively quiet to avoid attracting attention from the police. For example, Thomas Dorsey said he "made good" playing buffet flats in Chicago because he "had the kind of touch, beat and volume the landladies wanted." "I was a soft smooth player and I sang softly with my playing," stated Dorsey, "so I got more work and was better paid than the loud banging type pianist" (quoted in Michael W. Harris, *Rise of Gospel Blues*, 52).

63. Taylor, "Prostitution in Detroit," 13. Taylor suggests that Detroit's white prostitutes were more "individualistic" and African American neighborhoods had substantially more "call flats."

64. Ibid., 105, 111. For a discussion of antiprostitution drives and the increase in the number of pimps, see Hobson, *Uneasy Virtue*, 139–64. Luise White, in *Comforts of Home*, offers a welcome caution that the role of the madam should not be romanticized as oppositional to the role of the pimp (17–18). Madams exploited the labor of prostitutes who worked in their houses. In Detroit, they regularly took 50–60 percent of the money collected by their prostitutes (Taylor, "Prostitution in Detroit," 117). In her autobiography, *His Eye Is on the Sparrow*, Ethel Waters recalls meeting a pimp in Detroit who had "a string of women working on the street with him," indicating that there were some pimps operating in African American neighborhoods (81). See, for example, Slim, *Pimp*.

65. Taylor, "Prostitution in Detroit," 133–34. Taylor conducted interviews with African American prostitutes and published their case histories in her study. For a biography of a white madam who operated in Detroit during the interwar period and employed some African American prostitutes, see McGowan, *Motor City Madam*. McGowan recalled the 1920s and 1930s as the golden days of prostitution in Detroit: "A very popular girl then could earn with tips over two hundred dollars in a twelve hour period. . . . The prostitute now makes far less than her older sister of the roaring twenties" (78).

66. Albertson, *Bessie*, 123.

67. Quoted in Drake and Cayton, *Black Metropolis*, 598 (emphasis in original).

68. George Edmund Haynes, *Negro Newcomers in Detroit*, 21.

69. Because buffet flats were not as visible as street prostitution and were located in

African American neighborhoods, city officials were less concerned about their presence. For example, the Detroit Council of Churches' Public Welfare Committee noted that the "chief evil" of prostitution was "public soliciting on the streets" (Minutes of Public Welfare Committee Meeting, [1922], box 5, folder 18, pt. 2, Metropolitan Detroit Council of Churches Papers, ALUA).

70. "Examples of assistance asked for by various societies and Aid furnished," in Detroit Urban League Minutes, 9 November 1916, pp. 1–2, box 3, UCSP. This document contains several similar investigations of young women at the request of the CAS and the Juvenile Court.

71. Case record, box 12, folder 8, UCSP. I have omitted the last names of all subjects in the case records to protect their identities. For another case in which the Detroit Urban League reported to the CAS that an African American woman ran a buffet flat, see box 14, folder 8, UCSP.

72. Ruth Franklin to John Dancy, 22 January 1925, box 1, folder 14, DULP.

73. Case record, box 12, folder 15, UCSP. Washington reported that upon investigation by the Urban League, Belle was found to be the "lowest type of streetwalker." It is interesting that the investigations by the Juvenile Court and YWCA were not nearly as conclusive. For another case in which a prostitute was given day work, see box 15, folder 8, UCSP. In this case, the Detroit Urban League found that the woman was running a buffet flat. When it was clear that she was being investigated, the woman sent her daughter away to prevent her from being taken by officials.

74. Case record, box 14, folder 8, UCSP; Taylor, "Prostitution in Detroit," 14. In their study of Chicago, Drake and Cayton noted that African American women had a "virtual monopoly" as domestic servants in houses of prostitution before the closing of the "red-light" district (*Black Metropolis*, 248).

75. Taylor, "Prostitution in Detroit," 124.

76. Ibid., 131–32.

77. Quoted in ibid., 132.

78. Quoted in ibid., 29; Citizens' Research Council, *Negro in Detroit*, sect. 7, p. 18. Before 1926, the police department's Women's Division handled prostitution arrests.

79. John Dancy to Rosa M. Mosby, 12 January 1927, box 1, folder 19, DULP.

80. Taylor, "Prostitution in Detroit," 8. Taylor argues that more African American women were arrested because of racial discrimination and that more were imprisoned because they could not pay the $20 fine.

81. Citizens' Research Council, *Negro in Detroit*, sect. 9, p. 17. Although the uneven sex ratio of migrants (more males than females) was often cited as a source of illegal activity in Detroit, it should be noted that in cities such as Washington, D.C., where there were more female than male migrants, the same explanation was used.

82. Taylor, "Prostitution in Detroit," 13–14, 41.

83. Quoted in ibid., 70.

84. Ibid., 73–75, 84. Of eighty-five prostitutes registered at the Social Hygiene Clinic, twenty-seven (32 percent) were African American.

85. Citizens' Research Council, *Negro in Detroit*, sect. 9, p. 30. This version of events was published in the *Detroit Independent*.

86. Unidentified informant, quoted in "Extracts from the Experiences of Various Spiritual Leaders," appendix C-3, in Bullock, "Urbanization of the Negro Church," 50, Harlan Hatcher Graduate Library, University of Michigan, Ann Arbor, Michigan.

87. See Gilkes, "'Together and in Harness'"; Haywood, "Authority and Empowerment of Women"; Baer and Singer, *African-American Religion*, 165; Drake and Cayton, *Black Metropolis*, 632; and Phillips, *Alabama North*, 175–76.

88. See Ira De A. Reid, "Let Us Prey!"; Clark, "Sanctification in Negro Religion"; and Mays and Nicholson, *The Negro's Church*. For a more positive commentary on the growth of storefront churches, see Fisher, "Organized Religion and the Cults." For discussions of storefront churches during the Great Migration, see Sernett, *Bound for the Promised Land*, 188–201, and Phillips, *Alabama North*, 168–80.

89. Citizens' Research Council, *Negro in Detroit*, sect. 10, pp. 17–20. An earlier study came to similar conclusions. See Forrester B. Washington, *Negro in Detroit*, vol. 10. Washington wrote: "It is impossible to find in the Christian religion any justification for such barbaric practices as go on in these so-called churches."

90. This view is reflected in more recent studies of African American religion as well. See, for example, Frazier, *Negro Church in America*, 53.

91. Other storefront churches were Primitive Baptist or Methodist churches that had broken off from larger denominations and so-called cult religions such as the Black Jews.

92. Gilkes, "'Together and in Harness,'" 680. See also Hurston, *Sanctified Church*.

93. Quoted in Drake and Cayton, *Black Metropolis*, 644.

94. Norman Kenneth Miles notes in his dissertation that ironically "few of the mainline churches were able to command the kind of discipline and obedience which characterized some of the smaller sects" ("Home at Last," 184).

95. "One woman who has been in Chicago for 17 years," quoted in Drake and Cayton, *Black Metropolis*, 634. As discussed in Chapter 1, Sanctified churches and emotional worship styles also came under attack in the South. See, for example, S. A. Peeler, "What Improvements Should Be Made in the Religious Worship of the Churches?," in Penn and Bowen, *United Negro*, 146–51.

96. Mays and Nicholson, *The Negro's Church*, 98.

97. Quoted in Fauset, *Black Gods of the Metropolis*, 16. Bishop Robinson founded her church in 1924, and it is still thriving today.

98. Dyson, *Reflecting Black*, 20. In his comparative study of religion, *Ecstatic Religion*, anthropologist I. M. Lewis provocatively argues that female-dominated cults that encourage spirit possession are "thinly disguised protest movements

directed against the dominant sex" because "possession works to help the interests of the weak and downtrodden who have otherwise few effective means to press their claims for attention and respect" (31–32).

99. Forrester B. Washington, *Negro in Detroit*, vol. 10.

100. Clark, "Sanctification in Negro Religion," 547. Clark describes this dancing as individualistic and fitting "into jazz counterpoint" (548).

101. Lawrence W. Levine, *Black Culture*, 179–80; Michael W. Harris, *Rise of Gospel Blues*. For an ethnology of dance and music in Holiness churches, see Boggs, "Some Aspects of Worship in a Holiness Church."

102. The apparent "primitivism" of ecstatic worship attracted writers of the Harlem Renaissance, who both romanticized a rural southern African American past and were enthralled by the music and dances of the Jazz Age. See McKay, *Harlem*, 73–85. In *Black Culture*, Lawrence W. Levine quotes Langston Hughes's memories of a Holiness church in Chicago: "I was entranced by their stepped-up rhythms, tambourines, hand clapping, and uninhibited dynamics, rivaled only by Ma' Rainey singing the blues at the old Monogram Theater" (180).

103. Bullock, "Role of the Negro Church," 29, Harlan Hatcher Graduate Library, University of Michigan, Ann Arbor, Michigan.

104. See Paris, *Black Pentecostalism*; Synan, *Holiness-Pentecostal Movement*; and Chireau, "Conjuring."

105. Baer, *Black Spiritual Movement*, 114.

106. Ibid., 137. See also Bullock, "Urbanization of the Negro Church," 12–14. For an exposition of his beliefs, see "Arrest of Prophet Hurley Desired by So-Called Baptist Leaders," *Detroit Independent*, 14 October 1927, p. 5.

107. Baer, *Black Spiritual Movement*, 83.

108. Gustav G. Carlson, "Number Gambling," 102.

109. Case of Dr. Johnson, quoted in "Extracts from the Experiences of Various Spiritual Leaders," appendix B-1, in Bullock, "Urbanization of the Negro Church," 46.

110. Ibid., 11.

111. Ibid., 2.

112. For discussions of Holstein, who became a major numbers banker and supporter of the Harlem Renaissance's literary prizes, see McKay, *Harlem*, 102–5; David L. Lewis, *When Harlem Was in Vogue*, 129–30; and Watkins-Owens, *Blood Relations*, 143–46. For a history of policy in the African American community, see Fabian, *Card Sharps*, 108–52; Ruck, *Sandlot Seasons*, 140–52; Light, "Numbers Gambling among Blacks"; Haller, "Policy Gambling"; Drake and Cayton, *Black Metropolis*, 478–94; Jervis Anderson, *This Was Harlem*; Watkins-Owens, *Blood Relations*, 136–48; and Schatzberg and Kelly, *African American Organized Crime*.

113. Richard W. Thomas, *Life for Us*, 116. See also Katzman, *Before the Ghetto*, 172–74.

114. See Redding, "Playing the Numbers"; Drake and Cayton, *Black Metropolis*, 478–94; McKay, *Harlem*, 101–16; Richard W. Thomas, *Life for Us*, 116–18; Boykin, *Handbook of the Detroit Negro*, 94–111; Gustav G. Carlson, "Number Gambling,"

127–59; Dancy, *Sand against the Wind*, 114–15; and Allen, "From the Ghetto to the Joint," 237–39.

115. Gustav G. Carlson, "Number Gambling," 54.

116. Charleszetta Waddles, interviewed by Marcia Greenlee, 29 March 1980, transcript, 32, Black Women Oral History Project, SL. See also Charleszetta Waddles, autobiography, typewritten manuscript, chap. 6, p. 6, MHC.

117. Gustav G. Carlson, "Number Gambling," 154. For discussions of the participation of small businesses in numbers gambling, see Schatzberg and Kelly, *African American Organized Crime*, 74–76; Robinson, "Production of Black Violence in Chicago," 308–9; and Haller, "Policy Gambling," 726–30.

118. Bridges, "Paradise Valley," 6, Folklore Archive, Wayne State University, Detroit, Michigan.

119. William Hines, quoted in Moon, *Untold Tales*, 78.

120. One example of a female numbers banker in Harlem was Madame Stephanie St. Clair, who later married the cult founder and labor leader Sufi Abdul Hamid (McKay, *Harlem*, 111).

121. Gustav G. Carlson, "Number Gambling," 107–9.

122. Report of service at St. Ruth's Spiritualist Church, Detroit, Michigan, 18 January 1935, in Gustav G. Carlson, "Number Gambling," appendix C. The italicized words were stressed by the medium.

123. Gustav G. Carlson, "Number Gambling," 111.

124. See, for example, *Detroit Independent*, 30 September, 10 June 1927; *Detroit Tribune*, 27 November 1937; and undated clippings in Bullock, "Urbanization of the Negro Church," appendix D.

125. Unidentified informant, quoted in "Extracts from the Experiences of Various Spiritual Leaders," appendix C-II, in Bullock, "Urbanization of the Negro Church," 49–50.

126. In "'We Are Not What We Seem,'" Robin D. G. Kelley describes the "interior spaces" of public transportation such as streetcars as "moving theaters" (103).

127. Quoted in Gustav G. Carlson, "Number Gambling," 140. Hurley answered the question "Why do you play the numbers?"

128. Miles, "Home at Last," 232. On the history of the UNIA in Detroit, see Richard W. Thomas, *Life for Us*, 194–201; David Allen Levine, *Internal Combustion*, 100–103; Citizens' Research Council, *Negro in Detroit*, sect. 11, p. 6; and Boykin, *Handbook of the Detroit Negro*, 44–45.

129. Deborah Gray White, *Too Heavy a Load*, 124. See also Satter, "Marcus Garvey," 50.

130. For discussions of women in the Garvey movement, see Barbara Blair, "True Women, Real Men"; Tony Martin, "Women in the Garvey Movement"; Seraile, "Henrietta Vinton Davis"; Satter, "Marcus Garvey"; Deborah Gray White, *Too Heavy a Load*, 135–41; and Taylor, "Negro Women Are Great Thinkers."

131. Gary Jerome Hunter, "'Don't Buy from Where You Can't Work,'" 56. Charles C. Diggs Jr., a prominent African American politician, remembered seeing people "in uniforms, parades, and other activity" around the UNIA headquarters on

Russell Street, "as the movement was quite popular" (quoted in Moon, *Untold Tales*, 51).

132. Marcus Garvey speech, New York, 12 March 1922, quoted in Robert A. Hill, *Universal Negro Improvement Papers*, 4:570.

133. Ibid., 6:552. For firsthand accounts of this demonstration, see *Detroit Independent*, 6 May 1927, and *Negro World*, 21 May 1927, pp. 4, 8.

134. Deborah Gray White, *Too Heavy a Load*, 122; Hendricks, *Gender, Race, and Politics*, 127–28.

135. Marcus Garvey, "An Expose of the Caste System among Negroes," 31 August 1923, quoted in Garvey, *Philosophy and Opinions of Marcus Garvey*, 58. Some religious leaders were able to strike back directly at Garvey. African Methodist bishop Charles S. Smith of Michigan, for example, wrote a letter on 25 June 1919 to Attorney General A. Mitchell Palmer recommending Garvey's deportation on the grounds that he was a "Red" and spread "vicious propaganda and fake practices." See Robert A. Hill, *Universal Negro Improvement Papers*, 1:446.

136. Quoted in David Allen Levine, *Internal Combustion*, 103.

137. Dancy, *Sand against the Wind*, 167–68.

138. Robert A. Hill, *Universal Negro Improvement Papers*, 1:413.

139. Smith-Irvin, *Marcus Garvey's Footsoldiers*, 11.

140. Quoted in ibid., 47.

141. Quoted in ibid., 59–60.

142. Deborah Gray White, *Too Heavy a Load*, 137. For a discussion of Amy Jacques Garvey's role in the UNIA, see Taylor, "Negro Women Are Great Thinkers."

143. Josephine Dunkrett, *Negro World*, 10 September 1927, p. 8.

Chapter Four

1. See Drake and Cayton, *Black Metropolis*, 546–50. In *Changing Face of Inequality*, Olivier Zunz states that throughout the 1920s, "blacks became increasingly segregated from whites, drawn into a ghetto solely on the basis of race and without regard to their social status" (354). Although Zunz briefly discusses the middle-class dispersion of African Americans, he discounts its significance because eventually "the ghetto" would incorporate these neighborhoods. See also Jerome Gale Thomas, "City of Detroit."

2. Deskins, "Residential Mobility of Negro Occupational Groups," 79–80; David Allen Levine, *Internal Combustion*, 43. For an examination of the relationship between housing and politics in Detroit in a later period, see Sugrue, *Origins of the Urban Crisis*.

3. For an overview of African American neighborhood development in the early twentieth century, see Taeuber and Taeuber, *Negroes in Cities*, 11–27; Wiese, "Other Suburbanites"; and Sugrue, *Origins of the Urban Crisis*, 37–41.

4. The West Side was also known as the Warren-Tireman District. For descriptions of the West Side, see Richard W. Thomas, *Life for Us*, 101; Dancy, *Sand*

against the Wind, 58–59; Forrester B. Washington, *Negro in Detroit*, vol. 4, p. 119; and Citizens' Research Council, *Negro in Detroit*, sect. 5, p. 11.

5. Dancy, *Sand against the Wind*, 58.

6. Describing the Tireman District, in "Restrictive Covenants," sociologist Harold Black noted: "The dwellings are well-painted and neat in appearance, due to extensive repairing and landscaping by the Negro occupants" (14). See also Sugrue, *Origins of the Urban Crisis*, 38–39.

7. Miles, "Home at Last," 155–56.

8. Gordy, *To Be Loved*, 17.

9. Dancy, *Sand against the Wind*, 59. Girls clubs were also organized in the West Side through a branch of the YWCA known as the West Side Center. See Citizens' Research Council, *Negro in Detroit*, sect. 5, p. 30.

10. Forrester B. Washington, *Negro in Detroit*, vol. 4, p. 119. Amber Cooley Neumann, in "Twenty-five Years of Negro Activity," linked social mobility with residential mobility, noting that in the 1920s, the "more thrifty moved into new sections, bought homes, and attained a decent standard of living" (24).

11. Quoted in Moon, *Untold Tales*, 58–59. Detroit resident Katherine Reid recalled making a similar migration from the East Side to the West Side in the mid-1920s. See ibid., 92.

12. Quoted in ibid., 58. Cureton's emphasis on the importance of homeownership for social mobility is reflected in many other texts during this period. In part, this emphasis is the result of the exorbitant rents charged in the East Side neighborhood by absentee white landlords; however, it may also represent a broader emphasis in the African American community on the need to own land in order to ensure economic stability.

13. H. O. Weitschat, "Detroit's Bulging Black Belt," *Detroit Saturday Night*, 3 December 1927.

14. In "Restrictive Covenants," Harold Black notes that many restrictive covenants during the interwar period specified the exclusion of persons of certain races and prohibited the establishment of blind pigs. One such covenant stated "that at no time shall any part of said land be used or occupied for the manufacture, brewing, distilling, or selling of spirituous or malt liquors . . . nor shall any of said lots be occupied by a colored person" (29–30).

15. For descriptions of the development of the Eight Mile Road community, see Dancy, *Sand against the Wind*, 57; Richard W. Thomas, *Life for Us*, 99–101; David Allen Levine, *Internal Combustion*, 129; Murage, "Organizational History of the Detroit Urban League," 226; and Sugrue, *Origins of the Urban Crisis*, 39–40, 64–72.

16. Quoted in Citizens' Research Council, *Negro in Detroit*, sect. 5, p. 59.

17. Quoted in ibid. For a discussion of southern practices in northern suburbs and criticisms of these practices, see Wiese, "Other Suburbanites," 1516–19.

18. Quoted in Citizens' Research Council, *Negro in Detroit*, sect. 5, p. 31.

19. Ibid., sect. 12, pp. 26–27.

20. Avery, *Walk Quietly*. For information on the West Eight Mile Community Council, which Avery founded in the 1940s, drafts of her novel, and photographs of the early years of the Eight Mile Road development, see Avery Papers, boxes 1 and 2, BHC.

21. Eugene Kinckle Jones, "Social Service Progress."

22. Quoted in Moon, *Untold Tales*, 73.

23. Ibid., 74.

24. Lindsey, "Fields to Ford," 26–27.

25. Joseph Coles, interviewed by Jim Keeney and Roberta McBride, 8 July 1970, Oral History Transcript, p. 4, ALUA.

26. Haldeman-Julius, *Clarence Darrow's Two Great Trials*, 39. For a description of white working-class women's involvement in post–World War II housing riots in Chicago, see Hirsch, *Making the Second Ghetto*, 76–78.

27. Kenneth T. Jackson, *Ku Klux Klan*, 136; Fine, *Frank Murphy*, 154–55.

28. William Pickens to R. L. Bradby, 31 July 1925, in Meier and Bracey, *Papers of the NAACP*, reel 2.

29. I am grateful to Robert Jefferson for sharing his ideas on militarism in African American culture with me. Barbara Blair, in "True Women, Real Men," suggests that gender roles in Garveyism that emphasized separate spheres for men and women countered white stereotypes of "feminine" black men and "masculine" black women.

30. In *Unruly Practices*, Nancy Fraser argues that "citizen" is a male category, particularly in its "soldiering aspect," which she defines as "the conception of the citizen as the defender of the polity and protector of those—women, children, the elderly—who allegedly cannot protect themselves" (126).

31. NAACP press release, 15 October 1925, in Meier and Bracey, *Papers of the NAACP*, reel 2. Similarly, a 24 October 1925 article in the *Baltimore Afro-American* argued: "A man's home is his castle. If he is peaceable and minds his business, neighbors should be peaceable and mind theirs. If they are riotous and vicious in attacking his home, the State should not quarrel if they are killed by the owner of the home protecting his life and his property." See also David E. Lilienthal, "Has the Negro the Right of Self-Defense?," *Nation* 121 (23 December 1925): 724–25.

32. For descriptions of Gladys Sweet, see Haldeman-Julius, *Clarence Darrow's Two Great Trials*, and Weinberg, *A Man's Home*, 7. Observers of the trial often described Sweet as "refined."

33. See Walter White to James P. Johnson, 16 September 1925, in Meier and Bracey, *Papers of the NAACP*, reel 2. According to John Dancy, in *Sand against the Wind*, the Nacirema Club—whose name was "American" spelled backward—was founded by World War I veterans who "wanted a name which suggested patriotism" (123). The club grew quickly and was known for its civic leadership. See also Haldeman-Julius, *Clarence Darrow's Two Great Trials*, 36.

34. Gladys Sweet, handwritten statement, 1925, p. 1, in Meier and Bracey, *Papers of the NAACP*, reel 3.

35. Kenneth G. Weinberg has suggested that Sweet was particularly influenced by the more radical publication, the *Messenger*, in which A. Philip Randolph published this statement in 1919: "We are . . . urging Negroes and other oppressed groups concerned with lynching and mob violence to act upon the recognized and accepted law of self defense" (quoted in Weinberg, *A Man's Home*, 21).

36. Gladys Sweet, handwritten statement, 1925, p. 5, in Meier and Bracey, *Papers of the NAACP*, reel 3; Weinberg, *A Man's Home*, 112. Ossian Sweet was born in Rosewood, Florida, a small all-black town that was decimated by a white mob who murdered residents and burned homes and businesses.

37. Quoted in Arthur Garfield Hays, speech at NAACP annual meeting, 3 January 1926, pp. 5–6, in Meier and Bracey, *Papers of the NAACP*, reel 3.

38. See Vose, *Supreme Court*, and *Washington Daily American*, 19 October 1925, in Meier and Bracey, *Papers of the NAACP*, reel 2.

39. Walter White to R. L. Bradby, telegram, 21 September 1925, in Meier and Bracey, *Papers of the NAACP*, reel 2. See also "Darrow Jeers 'Noble Nordics' before Negroes," *New York Herald Tribune*, 14 December 1925, in Meier and Bracey, *Papers of the NAACP*, reel 2.

40. Walter White to James P. Johnson, 16 September 1925, in Meier and Bracey, *Papers of the NAACP*, reel 2.

41. "Mass Meeting at St. John C.M.E. Church, Interest of Sweet Fund," *Detroit Independent*, 25 September 1925, in Meier and Bracey, *Papers of the NAACP*, reel 2.

42. "The Race's Call," *Detroit Independent*, 23 October 1925, in Meier and Bracey, *Papers of the NAACP*, reel 2.

43. Walter White to James P. Johnson, postscript, n.d., in Meier and Bracey, *Papers of the NAACP*, reel 3.

44. For a description of the case from the prosecution's point of view, see Hilmer Gellein, "The Sweet Trials, 1925–1926," box 1, folder 1, Gellein Papers, MHC.

45. Quoted in Weinberg, *A Man's Home*, 119.

46. "Sweet Jury Disagrees, New Trial in January," press release, 28 November 1925, in Meier and Bracey, *Papers of the NAACP*, reel 3.

47. Ibid.

48. Transcript of second trial, 11 May 1926, in Meier and Bracey, *Papers of the NAACP*, reel 3. For a contrast between the "cultured segment of Negro society" and the "illiterate [white] witnesses," see Cash Asher, "Waiting for a Verdict with Clarence Darrow," *Crisis* 64 (June–July 1957): 326, box 1, Asher Papers, MHC, and Lilienthal, "Has the Negro the Right of Self-Defense?," 725.

49. Transcript of second trial, 11 May 1926, in Meier and Bracey, *Papers of the NAACP*, reel 3.

50. Hays, *Let Freedom Ring*, 229.

51. Transcript of second trial, 11 May 1926, in Meier and Bracey, *Papers of the NAACP*, reel 3. When selecting the jurors, Darrow and the other defense lawyers tried to find whites who employed African Americans in their homes as domestic servants, presumably so this point could be made more effectively.

52. Transcript of closing argument in second trial, 11 May 1926, in Meier and Bracey, *Papers of the NAACP*, p. 16, reel 3.

53. James W. Johnson to Walter White, telegram, [19] May 1926, in Meier and Bracey, *Papers of the NAACP*, reel 3.

54. Miles, "Home at Last," 153. Although it is difficult to trace directly the decline of housing riots to the Sweet case, the wide publicity given the trial in Detroit certainly gave the issue of racial violence more public exposure.

55. See "T. W. McGregor Heads Inter-Racial Board," *Detroit Free Press*, 16 September 1925, in Meier and Bracey, *Papers of the NAACP*, reel 2, and Henrickson, *Detroit Perspectives*, 302.

56. Kenneth T. Jackson, *Ku Klux Klan*, 134–43.

57. Fraser, "Rethinking the Public Sphere," 110. For an overview of new interpretations of Habermas's work, see Craig Calhoun, "Introduction," in Calhoun, *Habermas and the Public Sphere*, 1–48.

58. In her discussion of women's organizations in the 1920s in *Grounding of Modern Feminism*, for example, Nancy Cott notes that clubs tended to have "specialized memberships" that were "instrumentally allied with professional expertise" (95). For discussions of Habermas in African American women's history, see Higginbotham, *Righteous Discontent*, 10–11, and Elsa Barkley Brown, "Negotiating and Transforming the Public Sphere." Higginbotham views the black Baptist church as forming a "counter–public sphere," whereas Brown examines the assumption that the private/public split, on which many feminist critiques of the public sphere are predicated, applies to the African American community.

59. Evans, "Women's History and Political Theory," 130.

60. For a discussion of this transformation in another state, see Stetson, "Black Feminism in Indiana," 296.

61. Lillian E. Johnson, paper presented to the Detroit Study Club, n.d., box 2, Detroit Study Club Papers, BHC. Johnson wrote another paper, "Colored Women in Politics," in 1928.

62. Lillian E. Johnson, "The Newspaper's Part in the Life of Detroit," 13 November 1925, box 2, Detroit Study Club Papers, BHC.

63. Yearbook, 1926–27, box 7, Detroit Study Club Papers, BHC.

64. "Ninetieth Anniversary Celebration, 1898–1988," 1988, box 9, Detroit Study Club Papers, BHC.

65. Elizabeth Davis, *Lifting As They Climb*, 317.

66. Edna Shaw, "Early History of New Era," n.d., p. 1, box 1, New Era Study Club Papers, BHC.

67. "The Dawn of a Glorious New Era," words by Edna Dale Shaw, music by Mary McCree Spaulding, box 1, New Era Study Club Papers, BHC.

68. Yearbook, 1930–31, box 4, New Era Study Club Papers, BHC.

69. Elizabeth Davis, *Lifting As They Climb*, 317.

70. Ibid., 322. In "Cost of Club Work," Deborah Gray White argues that "the purpose of the literary, art, and music clubs . . . was to provide intensive training

and continued practice . . . in dominant high culture" (261). In contrast, I have found abundant evidence in the records of Detroit's women's clubs that African American art and literature were studied and discussed by clubwomen.

71. In her etiquette manual, *The Correct Thing to Do, to Say, to Wear*, Charlotte Hawkins Brown delineates in detail the proper rituals for receiving guests in a "refined" home.

72. In *Black Metropolis*, St. Clair Drake and Horace R. Cayton quote many women who did not join middle-class church congregations or clubs because they felt their dress was not up to the standards of the group or because they could not contribute financially to the church or club. "I'm a lone woman and I have a hard enough time keeping a roof over my head without paying dues here and there," stated one woman (606). Another informant reported: "I plan to join a whist club in the fall. I don't have the clothes or place to entertain" (606).

73. Era Radden Jackson to Mr. Stevenson, n.d., box 1, folder 15, DULP. Jackson was a member of the council, and Stevenson was a member of the Detroit Community Union. Stevenson forwarded the letter to Dancy and asked him about the council's work.

74. Elizabeth Davis, *Lifting As They Climb*, 321–22; Hine, *Black Women in the Middle West*, 15; Era Radden Jackson to Mr. Stevenson, n.d., box 1, folder 15, DULP. For information on the Bay Court Home, see box 1, UCSP. See also *Handbook of Social Work*, 9–10. Bay Court did not admit unmarried mothers or African American families; however, in 1929, five Mexican families were admitted.

75. Elizabeth Davis, *Lifting As They Climb*, 319–20.

76. Ibid., 318–19.

77. Richard W. Thomas, *Life for Us*, 82; Susan L. Smith, *Sick and Tired*, 33–57.

78. Susan L. Smith, *Sick and Tired*, 47.

79. "Health Week Linked with Clean Up–Paint Week," 19 April 1927, box 1, folder 20, DULP.

80. *Black Women in Michigan*, 6. Other professional women's clubs included the Mahoney Professional Nurses' Club, organized in 1924 by Anna Hutchinson Bumbray as a chapter of the Colored Nurses' Association. This group worked to integrate Detroit's hospitals and help educate young African American women in the nursing profession. Mary Eliza Mahoney was the first African American professional nurse to practice in the United States, receiving her degree from the New England Hospital for Women and Children in 1879 (ibid., 6–7). For a comprehensive history of the Colored Nurses' Association, see Hine, *Black Women in White*.

81. Ruth Wills Clemons, "History of the Elliottorian Business Women's Club," n.d., p. 1, box 1, Elliottorian Business Women's Club Papers, BHC.

82. Ibid., 2.

83. "Brief History," n.d., box 1, Elliottorian Business Women's Club Papers, BHC.

84. Bylaws, n.d., box 1, Elliottorian Business Women's Club Papers, BHC.

85. *Handbook of Social Work*, 93; "Comparative Table of Settlement Activities," 23 April 1925, UCSP-CF.

86. Citizens' Research Council, *Negro in Detroit*, sect. 7, p. 7.

87. *Detroit Independent*, 10 June 1927, p. 2.

88. Citizens' Research Council, *Negro in Detroit*, sect. 7, p. 11.

89. Ibid., sect. 11, p. 3.

90. Ibid., 4. Although the authors claim that the clubs abandoned "literary and artistic dilettantism," surviving programs and yearbooks suggest that the study of art and literature continued to have a place in club life.

91. For a discussion of women's decreasing visibility during this period, see Hickey, "Visibility, Politics, and Urban Development."

92. Citizens' Research Council, *Negro in Detroit*, sect. 7, p. 4.

93. Gregg, *Sparks from the Anvil*, 47.

94. Ibid., 48–49.

95. Sernett, *Bound for the Promised Land*, 184.

96. For a discussion of this development, see Frazier, *Negro Church in America*, 51, 84. In *Bound for the Promised Land*, Milton C. Sernett argues that storefront churches did not displace mainline Protestant churches during the Great Migration; however, migrants did transform the culture of mainline churches.

97. Citizens' Research Council, *Negro in Detroit*, sect. 10, pp. 2, 4.

98. The increased professionalization of services in the established African American denominations was facilitated by increased interracial work among Detroit's church leaders. In the mid-1920s, Detroit's Council of Churches established a commission on race relations that coordinated efforts to aid AME and black Baptist churches throughout Detroit and in the new outlying suburbs. This commission organized a conference of church women that included representatives from both the white and African American communities. See "Detroit Council of the Churches of Christ, July–December 1927," p. 13, box 1, folder 2, pt. 2, Metropolitan Detroit Council of Churches Papers, ALUA.

99. Quoted in H. O. Weitschat, "Negroes Pack Churches to Doors," *Detroit Saturday Night*, 1 July 1928, p. 3.

100. Ibid.

101. By 1928, approximately 30,000 African Americans belonged to the twenty-five Baptist churches in the city, of which the Second Baptist Church had the largest congregation. See ibid.

102. Recalling the interwar period, Bradby noted that although "even the Second was in a red light district, I chose to fight it rather than hide my face!" ("Eyewitness History," 1976, p. 21, reel 2, Second Baptist Church Papers, MHC). Not only did Bradby not "hide his face," but he ensured that the entire congregation showed their faces in the community.

103. Shelly, "Bradby's Baptists," 8.

104. See list of meetings in *Second Baptist Herald*, 5 September 1926, reel 9, Second Baptist Church Papers, MHC.

105. Ibid., 18 March 1928. See also the church's endorsement of the Courtesy Chop House run by two women (ibid., 25 March 1928); Shirley Hawkins McCans, "one of the world's greatest spiritual interpreters" (ibid., 26 August 1928); and the "modern" Blue Ribbon Beauty and Barber Shop run by Mrs. Bishop (ibid.).

106. Citizens' Research Council, *Negro in Detroit*, sect. 10, pp. 14, 23; Commission on Missions and Church Extensions, "A Picture of Detroit's Cooperating Churches," 1 January 1928, box 1, folder 2, pt. 2, Metropolitan Detroit Council of Churches Papers, ALUA.

107. Bullock, "Role of the Negro Church," 16, 20, Harlan Hatcher Graduate Library, University of Michigan, Ann Arbor, Michigan.

108. For a typical schedule of classes, see "Schedule, Christian Center," [1925], box 75, folder 2, UCSP-CF. The center offered classes in music, dressmaking, wood carving, and radio and industrial classes for both boys and girls. See also H. C. Gleiss, General Superintendent of the Baptist Christian Center, to Detroit Community Union, 11 October 1924, box 75, folder 21, UCSP-CF. In 1926, 234 adults were enrolled in the center's classes (Citizens' Research Council, *Negro in Detroit*, sect. 7, p. 25). See also *Second Baptist Herald*, 5 September 1926, reel 9, Second Baptist Church Papers, MHC, for an announcement of available classes.

109. Rosalie K. Butzel, "The Baptist Christian Center," n.d., pp. 3–4, box 6, folder 1, UCSP-CF.

110. Commission on Missions and Church Extensions, "A Picture of Detroit's Co-operating Churches," 1 January 1928, box 1, folder 2, pt. 2, Metropolitan Detroit Council of Churches Papers, ALUA.

111. Millie Connelly, "Gleanings from Our Girls Conference," *Second Baptist Herald*, 29 July 1928, reel 9, Second Baptist Church Papers, MHC.

112. Ibid., 26 September 1926.

113. Ibid., 3 January 1927.

114. Madame Tyree, a music instructor at Nannie Helen Burroughs's National Training School for Women and Girls, performed at the Second Baptist Church, Madame Braxton of the Kentucky School for Girls lectured on the training of girls, and Burroughs herself also lectured. See ibid., 3 July, 25 September 1927, 26 February 1928.

115. Ibid., 6 February 1927.

116. "Statement of Organization, Purpose, Methods, Relationships, and Problems," 3 April 1934, box 6, folder 1, UCSP-CF; Dolly Milne, "Report of Dolly Milne, 1925–1926, Juvenile Court Worker," pp. 16–17, box 1, folder 2, pt. 2, Metropolitan Detroit Council of Churches Papers, ALUA.

117. "Day Nursery," *Second Baptist Herald*, 12 September 1926, reel 9, Second Baptist Church Papers, MHC.

118. The Big Sisters' Home was built in 1924 by the Big Sister auxiliary of the Second Baptist Church. It sheltered young African American women as well as providing services such as day care ("History of the Second Baptist Church," 1940, p. 7, reel 2, Second Baptist Church Papers, MHC).

119. Citizens' Research Council, *Negro in Detroit*, sect. 10, p. 9.

120. Ibid., sect. 7, p. 8. See *Second Baptist Herald*, 8 May 1927, reel 9, Second Baptist Church Papers, MHC, for an announcement of a mother-and-daughter banquet. See ibid., 5 June 1927, for an announcement of an excursion to Lake St. Clair.

121. Citizens' Research Council, *Negro in Detroit*, sect. 10, p. 9.

122. Report on the United Universal Christian Army, 3 December 1937, box 92, folder 15, UCSP-CF. See also Daniel C. Walz to Mr. Walborn, 1 February 1926, box 92, folder 15, UCSP-CF. The Detroit Community Fund also passed judgment on Beulah Farms, an African American religious colony based in Ohio. After undertaking an investigation, the secretary of the fund reported that it was "a fanatical religious enterprise" whose leader's "general conduct" in Detroit was extremely suspect (Secretary of the Detroit Community Union to L. B. Kimberly, Briggs Manufacturing Company, 3 September 1921, box 25, folder 5, UCSP).

123. Report on the United Universal Christian Army, 3 December 1937, box 92, folder 15, UCSP-CF.

124. John C. Dancy to William J. Norton, 3 February 1921, box 3, folder 18, UCSP.

125. Secretary of the Detroit Community Union to Guy L. Shipps, 5 March 1921, box 3, folder 18, UCSP. See also Guy L. Shipps to Associated Charities, 2 March 1921, box 3, folder 18, UCSP.

126. John C. Dancy to Victor S. Woodward, 12 September 1928, box 1, folder 24, DULP.

127. Victor S. Woodward to Detroit Community Fund, 19 July 1928, box 1, folder 24, DULP.

128. Interestingly, a welfare worker in Lansing described the members of the Church of God in that city as "average and above the average in appearance, social bearing and deportment." See F. M. McBroom, Community Welfare Fund, to John C. Dancy, n.d., box 1, folder 29, DULP.

Chapter Five

1. Denby, *Indignant Heart*, 37.

2. Ibid., 38.

3. Horton, "Violence, Protest, and Identity," 94. In this essay, Horton contrasts a Garrisonian emphasis on nonviolence and "moral suasion" with calls for more militant action to defeat slavery. For a discussion of masculinity in the black community, see Harper, *Are We Not Men?*

4. See "Conference Minutes, Michigan State Employment Service," 20 November 1937, and Lawrence A. Oxley to Frederick S. Schourman, Acting Director, Michigan State Employment Service, 10 November 1937, in Kirby, *New Deal Agencies*, reel 10; and "Detroit Department of Public Welfare, March Report, 1934," box 8, DULP.

5. Jean Collier Brown, *Negro Woman Worker*, 2. See also Nelson and Farnman, *Women at Work*, 58–64, for an overview of African American women's working conditions during the Great Depression.

6. Fine, *Frank Murphy*, 250.

7. Widick, *Detroit*, 44. Studies of women and employment during the 1930s include Blackwelder, "Women in the Work Force"; Hembold, "Beyond the Family Economy" and "Downward Occupational Mobility; and Scharf, *To Work and to Wed*.

8. Quoted in Moon, *Untold Tales*, 94.

9. "Unemployed" was defined as "out of a job yet able to work and looking for a job." See Kathleen Lowrie, "Unemployed Women in Detroit," 1930, pt. 1, Introduction, p. 2a, box 7, folder 1, NA RG 86.

10. "Women Seeking Employment," 1930, box 7, folder 1, NA RG 86. This survey was filled out by an Urban League representative who interviewed Minnie Parish.

11. Ibid. A page of notes attached to this form includes the quote from Brossard.

12. Quoted in Moon, *Untold Tales*, 114.

13. According to the 1930 census, the majority of the 20,160 employed African American females worked in domestic and personal service. See "Survey, Michigan State Employment Service, Part 2," in Kirby, *New Deal Agencies*, reel 10.

14. "Survey, Michigan State Employment Service," in Kirby, *New Deal Agencies*, reel 10. Nationwide, the number of black women employed in household service had increased by 81 percent from 1920 to 1930. See Jean Collier Brown, *Negro Woman Worker*, 2.

15. Norman McRae, "Detroit in Black and White," in Henrickson, *Detroit Perspectives*, 367.

16. Hembold, "Beyond the Family Economy," 648.

17. For discussions of beauty culture during the Great Depression, see Jacqueline Jones, *Labor of Love*, 214–15; Kathy Peiss, "Beauty Culture," in Hine, *Black Women in America*, 100–104; and Peiss, *Hope in a Jar*, 113–14, 235–37.

18. Peiss, *Hope in a Jar*, 90. For an example of criticisms of beauty culture, see Burroughs, "Not Color but Character."

19. Advertisements, Poro of Detroit, *Detroit Tribune*, 3 July 1937, p. 12, and *Detroit Independent*, 24 October 1931, p. 3. See also advertisement, Ruby's Beauty University, *Detroit Tribune*, 31 July 1937, p. 4.

20. "Beauty Schools in Detroit Organize," *Detroit Tribune*, 30 October 1937, p. 8; "Beauticians to Hold National Confab," *Detroit Tribune*, 11 September 1937, p. 7; "Beauticians Seek to Raise Standards," *Detroit Tribune*, 11 September 1937, p. 2.

21. "Beauty School Grads Compete for Prizes," *Detroit Tribune*, 28 March 1938, p. 3; "Graduates of Beauty Class Given Laurels; Fleming School Holds Tenth Exercises at Trade Exhibit," *Detroit Tribune*, 18 June 1938, p. 2. For descriptions of other graduation ceremonies, see "Poro Graduates Are Addressed by Founder of Poro, Mrs. Malone," *Detroit Tribune*, 11 June 1938, p. 3; "Forty-five Graduates

in Exercises at University," *Detroit Tribune*, 11 June 1938, p. 3; and "Bee Dew Class Get Diplomas; Forty Students Are in Graduation," *Detroit Tribune*, 18 June 1938, p. 10.

22. Poro of Detroit, for example, was approved by the Michigan State Board of Cosmetology in 1935. See "Poro Makes History," in *The Poro of Detroit School of Beauty Culture Yearbook* (1945), in author's possession.

23. Taylor, "Prostitution in Detroit," 33, Harlan Hatcher Graduate Library, University of Michigan, Ann Arbor, Michigan. Social reformers were concerned about the "temptation" of prostitution during a period of high unemployment. See, for example, Bruno Lasker, "How to Meet Hard Times: A Program for the Prevention and Relief of Abnormal Unemployment," *Survey* 45 (5 February 1921), in *Schomburg Clipping File.*

24. Taylor, "Prostitution in Detroit," 33.

25. Drake and Cayton, *Black Metropolis*, 598.

26. Bridges, "Paradise Valley," 5, Folklore Archive, Wayne State University, Detroit, Michigan.

27. "Housewives' Page," in Great Lakes Mutual Insurance Company Report, 1 May 1934, box 1, HLDP.

28. Frank Marquart, interviewed by Herbert Hill, 24 July 1968, Oral History Transcript, p. 2, ALUA.

29. In "Housewives' League of Detroit," Darlene Clark Hine argues that "the organizing activities of the Housewives' League of Detroit were logical outgrowths of the national black women's club movement that flourished throughout the opening decades of the twentieth century" (225).

30. The Booker T. Washington Trade Association is primarily remembered for its weekly luncheon meetings, where businessmen and women discussed entrepreneurial strategies, listened to speakers, and worked to bolster the African American community's economic strength. See Richard W. Thomas, *Life for Us*, 214–21. See also Streator, "Detroit, Columbus, and Cleveland." Streator noted that in 1934, 1,200 small businessmen and women belonged to the association.

31. The Colored Merchants' Association was founded by the National Negro Business League in 1924 and promoted the formation of Housewives' Leagues. See Gary Jerome Hunter, "'Don't Buy from Where You Can't Work,'" 53, and Abram L. Harris, *Negro as Capitalist*, 178–79. The annual convention of the National Negro Business League was held in Detroit a few months after the founding of the Housewives' League, and "organizing the sentiment of women" was one of the major topics of the meeting. See Holsey, "National Negro Business League." For a discussion of the Harlem Housewives' League, see Cheryl Lynn Greenberg, *"Or Does It Explode?,"* 116–17. A similar movement, the Future Outlook League, emerged in Cleveland during this period. See Phillips, *Alabama North*, 190–225. In contrast to the Detroit Housewives' League, the Future Outlook League was widely criticized by Cleveland's elite blacks.

32. For a description of the founding of the Detroit Housewives' League, see Rich-

ard W. Thomas, *Life for Us*, 214–16; Hine, *Black Women in the Middle West*, 20–25, and "Housewives' League of Detroit," 230–34; and Elizabeth Davis, *Lifting As They Climb*, 327–29. Jacqueline Jones, in *Labor of Love*, estimates that 75,000 new jobs nationwide were created by the activism of the Housewives' League (215).

33. Richard W. Thomas, *Life for Us*, 215–16; Elizabeth Davis, *Lifting As They Climb*, 328–29; "Booster Club Has Four for City Canvass, Four Women Boosting Negro Business to Housewives," *Detroit Tribune*, 11 June 1938, p. 2. Similarly, in the 1920s, trade unions experimented with consumer cooperatives that attracted large numbers of working-class white housewives. See Susan Levine, "Workers' Wives," and Frank, *Purchasing Power*.

34. Fannie Peck, "History and Purpose of Housewives' League," 1 May 1934, box 1, HLDP. During this period, many articles appeared in the local black press exhorting African Americans to support local businesses. See, for example, "Jobs for Negroes," *Detroit Independent*, 24 October 1931, p. 3. Snow F. Grigsby, an emerging civil rights leader in the 1930s, also praised the work of the Housewives' League (*X-Ray Picture*, 10, and *White Hypocrisy*, 54).

35. "Housewives' League Rally Song," box 1, HLDP. This song was sung to the tune of "The Battle Hymn of the Republic."

36. "Detroit Housewives' League," *Detroit Tribune*, 7 August 1937, p. 3.

37. Twenty-fifth Anniversary Banquet program, 10 June 1955, box 2, HLDP; "Housewives' League to Observe Birthday," *Detroit Tribune*, 18 September 1937, p. 1.

38. Sarah Deutsch uses this term in "Learning to Talk More Like a Man," 381. She credits Eileen Boris for developing the term to emphasize the continued dominance of middle-class women in most female reform organizations despite large-scale working-class participation.

39. Quoted in Moon, *Untold Tales*, 254. In *Communists in Harlem*, Mark Naison points out that the cross-class cooperation inherent in boycott movements led the Communist Party to oppose them as strategies to offset unemployment (50–51). In Detroit, the Communist Party, active in organized labor and the unemployment councils, also failed to support the work of the Housewives' League and the Booker T. Washington Trade Association.

40. Quoted in Richard W. Thomas, *Life for Us*, 218.

41. "Club Pickets Beechwood Theater," *Detroit Tribune*, 9 October 1937, p. 1.

42. Elizabeth Davis, *Lifting As They Climb*, 327. In order to demonstrate the skills learned by young men and women in these programs, the Housewives' League held public presentations. See "Housewives' Club and Trade Group Hold Joint Meet," *Detroit Tribune*, 26 February 1938, p. 9.

43. Elizabeth Davis, *Lifting As They Climb*, 327.

44. Ibid., 328.

45. "Housewives' League to Sponsor Fair," *Detroit Tribune*, 30 October 1937, p. 2; "Housewives' League to Sponsor Trade Program at Elk Hall," *Detroit Tribune*,

18 December 1937, p. 3; "Thousand Cram into Forest Club to View Eighth Annual Trade Exhibit," *Detroit Tribune*, 11 June 1938, p. 1.

46. Elizabeth Davis, *Lifting As They Climb*, 329. See also "History of Housewives'
League of Detroit," n.d., box 1, Additional Papers, HLDP.

47. Quoted in "The Need for the League Continues," *Michigan Chronicle*, 20 August
1983, box 1, folder 2, Christina Fuqua Papers, BHC.

48. Smith-Irvin, *Marcus Garvey's Footsoldiers*, 15. See also Richard W. Thomas, *Life
for Us*, 199.

49. Quoted in Fauset, *Black Gods*, 43, n. 3. See also Fauset, "Moorish Science Temple,"
and Turner, *Islam in the African-American Experience*, 71–108.

50. Fauset, "Moorish Science Temple," 505–7.

51. Fauset, *Black Gods*, 43–44.

52. Fard was known by many names in Detroit, including Farrad Mohammed,
F. Mohammed Ali, Professor Ford, Walli Farrad, and W. D. Fard. See Lincoln,
Black Muslims in America, 12. I have used the name that appears most often in
accounts of the Nation of Islam's beginnings.

53. Marsh, *From Black Muslims to Muslims*, 51.

54. Some Islamic groups in Detroit prior to 1930 were not part of the Moorish
Science Temple. In her study of the Nation of Islam, Miriam S. Dillon traces
"Mohammedanism" in Detroit back to 1928, and Philip A. Adler, a journalist, re-
ported meeting "Duse Mohammed Ali Effendi," an African American religious
leader who ran a mosque in Paradise Valley, in 1926. See Dillon, "Islam Cult in
Detroit," 11, and Philip A. Adler, "Oriental Influence in Riot Background: Wel-
fare Workers Say Moslem and Shinto Cults Undoubtedly Affected Negroes,"
Detroit News, 26 June 1943, box 70, folder "Phil Adler Series Clippings—1943,"
Civil Rights Congress Papers, ALUA.

55. Quoted in Benyon, "Voodoo Cult," 895.

56. Ibid., 897; Turner, *Islam in the African-American Experience*, 147–73. Officials of the
Nation of Islam estimated the membership at 8,000, whereas detectives of the
Special Investigation Squad of the Detroit police department estimated 5,000.

57. Benyon, "Voodoo Cult," 900. For descriptions of the early years of the Nation
of Islam, see Bontemps and Conroy, *They Seek a City*, 178–83, and Boykin, *Handbook of the Detroit Negro*, 45–46.

58. Quoted in Benyon, "Voodoo Cult," 902.

59. Annual Report to the Board of Directors of the Associated Charities, 6 February
1930, p. 8, box 1, folder 1, UCSP.

60. Shaw, *What a Woman Ought to Be and to Do*, 190.

61. For discussions of the role names have played in African Americans' struggles
for empowerment, see Stuckey, *Slave Culture*, 193–244, and Turner, *Islam in the
African-American Experience*, 156.

62. Dillon, "Islam Cult in Detroit," 13.

63. Benyon, "Voodoo Cult," 902.

64. Predecessors to these sex-segregated organizations were the UNIA's male Universal African Legion and female Black Cross. See Barbara Blair, "True Women, Real Men," and Turner, *Islam in the African-American Experience*, 168–69.

65. Benyon, "Voodoo Cult," 903. Benyon notes that "attacks made on the cult by the Police Department have been instigated usually by the leaders of Negro organizations" (904).

66. Dillon, "Islam Cult in Detroit," 35.

67. Turner, *Islam in the African-American Experience*, 169.

68. Marsh, *From Black Muslims to Muslims*, 54–55.

69. Boykin, *Handbook of the Detroit Negro*, 46–47; Turner, *Islam in the African-American Experience*, 168. Takahashi attempted to return to Detroit via Canada in 1938 but was arrested when he tried to bribe customs officers. Boykin speculated that after his release from Leavenworth in 1943, Takahashi was sent to an internment camp for Japanese Americans.

70. Philip A. Adler, "Oriental Influence in Riot Background: Welfare Workers Say Moslem and Shinto Cults Undoubtedly Affected Negroes," *Detroit News*, 26 June 1943, box 70, folder "Phil Adler Series Clippings — 1943," Civil Rights Congress Papers, ALUA. Development of Our Own appears to be the major "Shinto" cult referred to in the article.

71. Fisher, "Organized Religion," 9. Other African American commentators during this period continued to vilify Sanctified and storefront churches. For example, William A. Clark concluded his long 1937 article "Sanctification in Negro Religion," which decried the emotionalism of Sanctified religion, by stating: "The whole ideology of sanctification, as Negroes accept it, tends to impede progress toward higher cultural levels" (551).

72. Fisher, "Organized Religion," 10.

73. Ibid., 10, 29, 30; Drake and Cayton, *Black Metropolis*, 632.

74. *Detroit Tribune*, 21 August 1937, p. 3; "Elliottorian Business Club Sponsors Scholarship Benefit Party," *Detroit Tribune*, 15 January 1938, p. 5.

75. Shelly, "Bradby's Baptists," 25–31.

76. Quoted in Rosemond, *Reflections*, 69–70.

77. Quoted in Drake and Cayton, *Black Metropolis*, 633, 629.

78. Gregg, *Sparks from the Anvil*, 49. In an earlier study, *Black Religion and Black Radicalism*, Gayraud S. Wilmore argued that the "economic and psychological pressures of the Depression and the brutality of racism drove Negroes deeper within themselves for spiritual resources," alienating them from the large established churches (220).

79. Scheiner, "Negro Church," 99. In *White Hypocrisy*, Snow Grigsby comes up with a similar figure: "The Negroes have 146 churches to a Negro population in Detroit of 136,999, which is 23% of the total number of churches" (40). In *The Negro's Church*, Benjamin E. Mays and Joseph William Nicholson estimated that 45 percent of Detroit's churches were housed in storefronts (219).

80. Bullock, "Role of the Negro Church," 16, Harlan Hatcher Graduate Library, University of Michigan, Ann Arbor, Michigan.

81. For discussions of gospel music during the Great Depression, see Lincoln and Mamiya, *Black Church in the African American Experience*, 361–62; Michael W. Harris, *Rise of Gospel Blues*; Schwerin, *Got to Tell It*; Heilbut, *Gospel Sound*; Phillips, *Alabama North*, 176–80; Sernett, *Bound for the Promised Land*, 208–9; and Lawrence W. Levine, *Black Culture*, 174–89.

82. Mahalia Jackson, *Movin' On Up*, 80.

83. Ibid. Jackson also opened a florist shop in Chicago that she named Mahalia's House of Flowers.

84. Ibid., 63. See also Frazier, *Negro Church in America*, 74.

85. Mahalia Jackson, *Movin' On Up*, 66.

86. Michael W. Harris, *Rise of Gospel*, 269.

87. Sernett, *Bound for the Promised Land*, 208.

88. Boyd, *Jazz Space Detroit*, 8.

89. Lawrence W. Levine, *Black Culture*, 180.

90. Björn, "From Hastings Street to the Bluebird," 257–58. Big Maceo married a woman who ran "a regular blues house party" in Detroit, which increased his popularity. Many of Detroit's piano players migrated from Georgia and began performing in the 1920s; however, it was not until the 1930s that their popularity swelled. For a description of the blues scene in Detroit during the interwar period, see Barlow, *"Looking Up at Down,"* 283–85.

91. Gustav G. Carlson, "Number Gambling," 144. For a general description of numbers gambling in the 1930s, see Redding, "Playing the Numbers," and Drake and Cayton, *Black Metropolis*, 478–94.

92. Gustav G. Carlson, "Number Gambling," 146. The religious leader refused to give his name.

93. Ibid.

94. Quoted in ibid., 148. The name of the numbers banker was withheld. In *Sandlot Seasons*, Rob Ruck describes a similar trend in depression-era Pittsburgh (149–50).

95. Gustav G. Carlson, "Number Gambling," 150; Louis, *My Life Story*, 29–30.

96. Fabian, *Card Sharps*, 5–6. See also Halttunen, *Confidence Men*.

97. Fabian, *Card Sharps*, 108–11.

98. Quoted in Gustav G. Carlson, "Number Gambling," appendix B. In appendix B of his dissertation, Gustav G. Carlson reproduces dozens of letters written to the New York Stock Exchange from the "number playing public." This writer was responding to an attempt by the New York Stock Exchange to prevent the use of daily figures by numbers gamblers by withholding their publication in local newspapers.

99. Quoted in ibid., 145.

100. Gustav G. Carlson reported that in Detroit, one could bet from a penny to a

dollar per day on the numbers. The average bet placed was ten cents, and any wager of more than fifty cents was "uncommon." See ibid., 129.

101. Letter from Tampa, Florida, to New York Stock Exchange, 15 November 1935, in ibid., appendix B.

102. Letter to New York Stock Exchange, 26 January 1935, in ibid.

103. Quoted in ibid., 139.

104. Ibid., 52.

105. Quoted in ibid., 140. Gustav G. Carlson's transcription of Mrs. Warren's dialect reflects his own perceptions of African American speech and not her exact words or inflections.

106. The moral economy of the early modern period placed the good of the community over individual gain and was not an integral part of the emerging capitalist economy. See Thompson, "Moral Economy of the English Crowd." Robin D. G. Kelley applies this concept to the Jim Crow South in *Race Rebels*, 17–34.

107. Boykin, *Handbook of the Detroit Negro*, 97. In *Black Metropolis*, Drake and Cayton quote one informant who said that women who worked for numbers bankers could make $20 a week (494). For a brief discussion of African American women's employment in numbers gambling, see Jacqueline Jones, *Labor of Love*, 213.

108. Boykin, *Handbook of the Detroit Negro*, 94.

109. Gustav G. Carlson, "Number Gambling," 153; Richard W. Thomas, *Life for Us*, 118.

110. Gustav G. Carlson, "Number Gambling," 153–54.

111. Drake and Cayton, *Black Metropolis*, 487. In *African American Organized Crime*, Rufus Schatzberg and Robert J. Kelly also point out that numbers banks gave small loans to local businesses that could not obtain credit from legitimate banks (75).

112. Bridges, "Paradise Valley," 6.

113. Quoted in Gustav G. Carlson, "Number Gambling," 152.

114. Boykin, *Handbook of the Detroit Negro*, 111.

115. Ibid.; "Will White Mobsters Dominate 'Numbers'?," *Detroit Tribune*, 24 September 1938, p. 1. This article expressed concern that African Americans would lose as many as 5,000 jobs if white organized crime successfully took over African American numbers operations.

116. Drake and Cayton, *Black Metropolis*, 487.

117. Quoted in Gustav G. Carlson, "Number Gambling," 132.

118. Quoted in ibid., 133.

119. Blind Blake, "Policy Blues," in Stefan Grossman, *Ragtime Blues*, 89. See also songs quoted in Gustav G. Carlson, "Number Gambling," 136–37.

120. Dreambooks date back to the eighteenth century in America and were sold to both white and black numbers players throughout the nineteenth and twentieth centuries. See Fabian, *Card Sharps*, 142–50.

121. Quoted in Gustav G. Carlson, "Number Gambling," 116.

122. Ibid., 122–25.

123. Rosemond, *Reflections*, 87.

124. This phrase is Willard B. Gatewood's in *Aristocrats of Color*.

125. McKay, *Harlem*, 101.

126. Frazier, *Black Bourgeoisie*, 174.

127. Quoted in Moon, *Untold Tales*, 81.

Chapter Six

1. Kelley, *Race Rebels*, 114. Kelley concludes that masculinity was the "common ground" that united Communists and black nationalists in the 1930s (121).

2. Faue, *Community of Suffering*, esp. 69–99.

3. For discussions of black women's role in the history of welfare, see Gordon, *Pitied but Not Entitled*; Koven and Michel, *Mothers of a New World*; Ladd-Taylor, *Mother-Work*; Lasch-Quinn, *Black Neighbors*; and Mink, *Wages of Motherhood*.

4. In "Power of Motherhood," Eileen Boris argues that black female reformers can be accurately described as maternalist, as that ideology is defined and implemented in the black community. Gwendolyn Mink and Linda Gordon also use the term "maternalist" when describing black female reformers. Molly Ladd-Taylor, however, has called for a narrower definition of maternalism that excludes African American women.

5. Muncy, *Creating a Female Dominion*.

6. For a discussion of the changing roles of black female reformers in the 1930s, see Shaw, *What a Woman Ought to Be and to Do*, 164–210.

7. Hine, *Black Women in the Middle West*, 16. See also Peebles, "Detroit's Black Women's Clubs."

8. See Meier and Rudwick, *Black Detroit and the Rise of the UAW*, 3–33; Richard W. Thomas, *Life for Us*, 271–312; and Korstad and Lichtenstein, "Opportunities Lost and Found."

9. For descriptions of the CRC's work, see Boykin, *Handbook of the Detroit Negro*, 24, 86, and Richard W. Thomas, *Life for Us*, 235–43.

10. Snow Grigsby, interviewed by Roberta McBride, 12 March 1967, Oral History Transcript, p. 4, ALUA. Grigsby continued his activism well into the postwar period. See, for example, his pamphlet, *Taps or Reveille?*, which argued for greater voter participation among Detroit's African Americans.

11. Grigsby, *X-Ray Picture*.

12. Ibid., 8.

13. Grigsby, *White Hypocrisy*, 54.

14. Ibid., 58.

15. Other similarities between Grigsby and leaders such as John Dancy included their opposition to storefront churches. In *White Hypocrisy*, Grigsby argued: "We must stamp out bootleggers in religion. Stop those parasites, who, whenever they can, will get together a sufficient number of poor working women

and open a store front church or a basement church, and peddle a superfluous brand of Christianity at a relative [*sic*] exorbitant price. Some of these men may be sincere, but the majority of them are uninformed lazy louts who would be of greater value to themselves and their race if they were put to work at manual labor" (40).

16. In *Handbook of the Detroit Negro*, Ulysses W. Boykin notes that the CRC "takes credit for being responsible for the selection and appointment of case workers for the Girls' Protective League; Negro representation on the women's division of the Recorders Court; a case worker for the Visiting Housekeeper's Association; a bookkeeper at the Detroit Community Fund; clerks for the Good Will Industries . . . ; nurses for the welfare department" (27). For a description of how Grigsby helped African American men gain employment in the Detroit fire department, see "Marcena W. Taylor," in Moon, *Untold Tales*, 193–94.

17. Young, *Hard Stuff*, 28.

18. The number of active members of the Communist Party in Detroit during the 1930s is unclear, although their influence was certainly significant. See Fine, *Frank Murphy*, 399. In *New Black Middle Class*, Bart Landry argues: "When Communists became active in the black community, black middle-class leaders were soon replaced by more radical leaders or adapted their style to include boycotts, marches, and peaceful demonstrations" (66). For a history of African American involvement in the Communist Party during the 1930s, see Naison, *Communists in Harlem*; Kelley, *Hammer and Hoe*; and Cheryl Lynn Greenberg, *"Or Does It Explode?,"* 97–100.

19. Quoted in Moon, *Untold Tales*, 107.

20. Fine, *Frank Murphy*, 403–5. For a description of the march, see Joseph Billups, interviewed by Roberta McBride, 9 September 1967, Oral History Transcript, p. 1, ALUA; Widick, *Detroit*, 50–53; and Josephine Gomon, interviewed by Jack W. Skeels, 22 December 1959, Oral History Transcript, p. 5, ALUA.

21. Shelton Tappes, quoted in Moon, *Untold Tales*, 107.

22. Billups interview, 4, 9.

23. Gomon interview, 8. Gomon notes that the flying squadrons were probably led by members of the Communist Party.

24. Billups interview, 5.

25. Fine, *Frank Murphy*, 397–98. Despite this designation, Detroit police continued to harass demonstrators who spoke out at Grand Circus Park.

26. Billups interview, 13–14.

27. Meier and Rudwick, *Black Detroit and the Rise of the UAW*, 22.

28. Perhaps the most well known case of police brutality was the murder of a young black boy, James Porter, by two white policemen. Over 5,000 people attended Porter's funeral and a protest meeting that followed, indicating the increased awareness of police brutality. See Widick, *Detroit*, 57. A particularly violent instance of police brutality against an African American woman involved May Smith, who was thrown down a flight of stairs by police officers and died of her

injuries. See case record of May Smith, box 79, "Police Activities—1936 Beatings," Michigan, Civil Rights Congress Papers, ALUA. This collection contains many records of similar cases of police brutality; see boxes 79–80, Michigan, Civil Rights Congress Papers, ALUA.

29. Bates, "New Crowd Challenges the Agenda of the Old Guard," 341.

30. Meier and Rudwick, *Black Detroit and the Rise of the UAW*, 18–29.

31. Bates, "New Crowd Challenges the Agenda of the Old Guard," 369. See also Meier and Rudwick, *Black Detroit and the Rise of the UAW*, 28–29, 80, and Richard W. Thomas, *Life for Us*, 229–35. In 1946, after a decade of organizing, the NNC held its annual convention in Detroit. See "National Negro Congress— 1945–6," box 70, Michigan, Civil Rights Congress Papers, ALUA.

32. Meier and Rudwick, *Black Detroit and the Rise of the UAW*, 78–79. For a discussion of shifting policies in the Chicago chapter of the NAACP, see Reed, *Chicago NAACP*.

33. Richard W. Thomas, *Life for Us*, 298–301; Meier and Rudwick, *Black Detroit and the Rise of the UAW*, 67–71.

34. Geraldine Bledsoe, interviewed by Norman McRae, 1970, Oral History Transcript, pp. 1–2, ALUA.

35. Chateauvert, *Marching Together*, 4.

36. Ibid., 54. See also Deborah Gray White, *Too Heavy a Load*, 165–68.

37. Richard W. Thomas, *Life for Us*, 263–65. See "Summons to Colored Voters," "Organizations, 1921–1969," box 3, Thompson Collection, BHC. This leaflet was distributed by the campaign to elect Charles Digg to the Michigan senate. It urged black voters to "appear at your precinct on November 3, 1936, and cast your vote for your friend, your leader, and your President, Franklin D. Roosevelt, and upon your failure to appear at that time and place herein mentioned you will be liable to four long years of deprivation, starvation, and want for food, clothing and shelter."

38. In *Frank Murphy*, Sidney Fine writes: "Detroit, alone, accounted for more than 25 percent of *all* the public general relief dispensed in the United States in 1930 and more than 13 percent in 1931, and its case load for the fiscal year 1930–1931 constituted about 27 percent of the total case load of the public agencies in seventy principal urban areas" (307).

39. In *Making a New Deal*, Lizabeth Cohen describes a similar pattern in Chicago's African American community (226–27).

40. Annual Report of the Detroit Urban League, 1930, p. 1, box 3, folder 16, UCSP.

41. Ibid., 1932, pp. 2–3.

42. Ibid., 1933.

43. Fine, *Frank Murphy*, 286–87. A letter from Frank Murphy to the editors of the *Crisis* claimed: "The principle of governmental responsibility for its indigent poor has been maintained in this city irrespective of race, creed or color. There has been no discrimination of any kind. . . . We have been criticized at times by the press of the city but we have headed straight toward our plain duty as we saw

it and allowed no prejudice to creep into our program" (*Crisis* 40 [December 1931]: 414).

44. Fine, *Frank Murphy*, 250.

45. Executive Committee of the Advisory Relief Council of the Detroit Community Union, "A Relief Program for Detroit," 17 December 1931, box 139, folder 8, UCSP-CF. For a description of the councils' organization, see Ruth Jennings, "District Councils," *Compass Needle* 1, no. 4 (January 1935): 3, 26–27.

46. Speech, 1 March 1932, p. 1, box 178, folder 18, UCSP-CF.

47. Ibid., pp. 2–3. For a sample of the type of survey carried out by district councils, see "Some of the Facts to Be Discovered through a Recreation Survey," 15 March 1933, box 29, folder 4, UCSP.

48. Initial Survey of Alfred District, 1934, box 180, folder 2, UCSP. The Alfred District also had the largest number of social agencies and charity groups within its boundaries, reflecting decades of social activism by African Americans. See "Detroit District Councils," 5 May 1937, box 177, folder 6, UCSP-CF, and Beulah Whitby, interviewed by Jim Keeney and Roberta McBride, 16 September 1969, Oral History Transcript, p. 6, ALUA.

49. This mapping of commercial recreation includes only spaces that were visible to the survey committee. In fact, numerous speakeasies, private clubs, social halls, and houses of prostitution in this neighborhood were not mapped. Traveling underground recreation, such as rent parties, were also not recognized, although these "problems" were addressed in district council meetings. See, for example, "Meeting of the Central Committee for District Councils," 4 March 1938, box 177, folder 9, UCSP-CF.

50. Minutes of Meeting of Western District Council, 20 April 1937, box 191, folder 4, UCSP-CF.

51. "Meeting of the Central Committee for District Councils," 4 March 1938, p. 3, box 177, folder 9, UCSP-CF.

52. "Homemakers' Clubs, Alfred District Council of Detroit," 28 April 1938, box 180, folder 8, UCSP-CF.

53. Ibid.

54. Birney W. Smith, Chairman, Alfred District Council, to John P. Townsend, Executive Director, Michigan Unemployment Compensation Commission, 17 April 1940, box 180, folder 13, UCSP-CF.

55. Ibid.

56. "Urban League Center," 1937, p. 4, box 34, folder 21, UCSP-CF. For an overview of Detroit Urban League programs, see "Study of Group Work Records, Urban League," 1938, box 35, folder 10, UCSP, and "Urban League Center," 1937, box 34, folder 21, UCSP-CF.

57. "Study of Group Work Records, Urban League," 1938, box 35, folder 10, UCSP.

58. See Detroit Study Club Papers, New Era Study Club Papers, Sorosis Group Papers, and "Golden Anniversary of the Willing Workers, 1887–1937," box 6,

Dade Papers, BHC, and "Elliottorian Business Club Sponsors Scholarship Benefit Party," *Detroit Tribune*, 15 January 1938, p. 5.

59. Scyades Sixth Annual Dinner program, 1941, box 2, New Era Study Club Papers, BHC.

60. Dancy, *Sand against the Wind*, 161–64. In later years, the Urban League extended the work of Green Pastures year-round by creating the Green Pastures Clubs for girls and boys. See Annual Report of the Detroit Urban League, 1944, box 34, folder 16, UCSP-CF. For descriptions of the Green Pastures Camp, see Forrester B. Washington, "Deluxe Summer Camp"; Murage, "Organizational History of the Detroit Urban League," 290–96; and Richard W. Thomas, *Life for Us*, 75–81.

61. Quoted in Richard W. Thomas, *Life for Us*, 78.

62. Annual Report of the Detroit Urban League, 1932, pp. 5–6, box 3, folder 16, UCSP.

63. Ibid., 1930, p. 2. Dancy also noted that "in the so called 'dignified positions,'" the Urban League made some headway, placing three African Americans with the CAS and one with the Associated Charities (4). For similar statistics the following year, see ibid., 1931, pp. 1, 6.

64. John C. Dancy to Kenneth L. Moore, 20 May 1938, quoted in Murage, "Organizational History of the Detroit Urban League," 288.

65. See, for example, Monthly Report of the Baptist Christian Center, October 1939, and "Clubs and Classes, Religious Activities of Baptist Christian Center, 1938–1939," box 6, folder 1, UCSP-CF.

66. Monthly Report of the Baptist Christian Center, November 1939, p. 3, box 6, folder 1, UCSP-CF.

67. Rosalie K. Butzel, "The Baptist Christian Center," 1937, p. 1, box 6, folder 1, UCSP-CF.

68. Ibid., 2.

69. Ibid., 3. See also "Millinery Classes Reopen September 31," *Detroit Tribune*, 18 September 1937, p. 4.

70. Ciani, "Training Young Women."

71. "West Side Human Relations Council," n.d., p. 2, box 5, Dade Papers, BHC. See also *Our Community: Bulletin of the West Side Human Relations Council* 1, no. 2 (1938), Dade Papers, BHC. This newsletter included a statement supporting a "Do Not Buy Where You Cannot Work" program in the West Side, reflecting the wide-scale support for economic nationalism.

72. Shaw, *What a Woman Ought to Be and to Do*, 191.

73. John C. Dancy, report on African American social workers in Detroit, 25 July 1941, box 87, folder 14, UCSP-CF. For a discussion of black social workers during the 1930s, see Daniel J. Walkowitz, *Working with Class*, 170–74. For an account of Whitby's career, see Shaw, *What a Woman Ought to Be and to Do*, 189–92.

74. For a discussion of African American agency in the creation of New Deal policy, see Sitkoff, "New Deal and Race Relations." Other works on African Americans

and the New Deal include Sitkoff, *New Deal for Blacks*; Kirby, *Black Americans in the Roosevelt Era*; Wolters, *Negroes and the Great Depression*; Weiss, *Farewell to the Party of Lincoln*; and Sullivan, *Days of Hope*.

75. For a discussion of African American women and public works projects, see Jacqueline Jones, *Labor of Love*, 216–21.

76. Birney W. Smith, Chairman, Alfred District Council, to John P. Townsend, Executive Director, Michigan Unemployment Compensation Commission, 17 April 1940, box 180, folder 13, UCSP-CF.

77. Bledsoe interview, 2–3.

78. Richard W. Thomas, *Life for Us*, 264.

79. Maxie Craig to Eleanor Roosevelt, 5 July 1939, box 1604, folder 662, A–D, State Series, Michigan, 1935–44, NA RG 69. This letter was written on letterhead from the Edyth R. Thomas Memorial Hospital, where Craig was admitted for high blood pressure. For a history of worker education during the New Deal, see Kornbluh, *New Deal for Workers' Education*.

80. Rosabelle Snohr to Maxie Craig, Information and Adjustment Service, State Division of Employment, 28 July 1939, box 1604, folder 662, A–D, State Series, Michigan, 1935–44, NA RG 69.

81. Eloise Bibb to Eleanor Roosevelt, 28 February 1939, box 1604, folder 662, A–D, State Series, Michigan, 1935–44, NA RG 69. Bibb also suffered from infantile paralysis and walked with a crutch, which would have limited her ability to get a job as a household worker.

82. Gertrude Barrus to Eleanor Roosevelt, 16 August 1939, box 1604, folder 662, A–D, State Series, Michigan, 1935–44, NA RG 69.

83. Naomi Johnson to Eleanor Roosevelt, 16 August 1939, box 1605, folder 662, E–Z, State Series, Michigan, 1935–44, NA RG 69. Johnson was working for the WPA but was laid off after being employed for eighteen continuous months, a common practice. She was writing to ask Roosevelt to get her job back.

84. Delia Lovelace to Eleanor Roosevelt, 23 March 1939, box 1605, folder 662, E–Z, State Series, Michigan, 1935–44, NA RG 69.

85. In *Wages of Motherhood*, Gwendolyn Mink argues that maternalist reformers during the New Deal sought to assimilate poor African American women into the dominant culture (123–50).

86. Ella Spence to Eleanor Roosevelt, 5 January 1939, box 1605, folder 662, E–Z, State Series, Michigan, 1935–44, NA RG 69.

87. Palmer, *Domesticity and Dirt*, 101. Studies of women and New Deal programs include Swain, "ER and Ellen Woodward," and Wladaver-Morgan, "Young Women and the New Deal."

88. Esther Cary, report on WPA project, 23 October 1935, box 1603, folder 661, Women's Projects, Administration, November 1936, WPA Central Files, 1935–44, NA RG 69.

89. Eddie Tolan, "National Youth Administration, Special Report on Negro Youth of Wayne County," 18 June 1937, pp. 5, 7, 9, 10, box 52, folder 4, UCSP-CF.

90. Harriet J. Comstock and Sylvia M. Hart to Ellen S. Woodward, 7 January 1937, box 1604, folder 661, January 1937, WPA Central Files, 1935–44, NA RG 69. See also Cecile Whalen to Catherine Murray, 30 December 1936, box 1605, folder 663, Michigan, 1935–36, WPA Central Files, 1935–44, NA RG 69.

91. "Relief School Trains Boys to Be Butlers and Cooks," *Detroit Free Press*, December 1937, copy, box 1605, folder 663, Michigan, January–October 1937, WPA Central Files, 1935–44, NA RG 69.

92. Catherine Murray to Ellen S. Woodward, Assistant Administrator, WPA, 4 January 1937, box 1605, folder 663, Michigan, January–October 1937, WPA Central Files, 1935–44, NA RG 69.

93. Catherine Murray to Ellen S. Woodward, Director, Women's Work, 27 June 1935, box 1603, folder 661, Women's Projects, June 1935, State Series, Michigan, 1935–44, NA RG 69.

94. For example, Catherine Murray wrote to the administrative assistant in workers' education at the WPA: "I debated a long time about this house, but Detroit advises me it's the best available and because of the interest among the colored women who have been working for this House during the past 31 years, I honestly think it's best to proceed" (31 August 1935, box 1603, folder 661, August 1935, WPA Central Files, 1935–44, NA RG 69).

95. R. L. Bradby to Sylvia Hartt, 31 December 1936, box 1605, folder 663, Michigan, January–October 1937, WPA Central Files, 1935–44, NA RG 69.

96. Sylvia Hartt to Ellen S. Woodward, 11 August 1936, box 1604, folder 661, July 1936, WPA Central Files, 1935–44, NA RG 69.

97. Catherine Murray to Ellen S. Woodward, 21 January 1936, box 1603, folder 661, January–February 1936, WPA Central Files, 1935–44, NA RG 69.

98. Sylvia Hartt to Anna Marie Driscoll, National Supervisor of Household Workers' Training, WPA, 4 February 1936, box 1603, folder 661, January–February 1936, WPA Central Files, 1935–44, NA RG 69.

99. Mary Anderson, "The Negro Woman Worker," *American Federationist*, October 1932, p. 1114, *Schomburg Clipping File*. See also Jean Collier Brown, *Negro Woman Worker*, 2.

100. Lawrence A. Oxley, "Employment Security and the Negro," n.d., p. 57, in Kirby, *New Deal Agencies*, reel 10.

101. Esther Beck McIntyre, *Detroit News*, 27 July 1938.

102. Quoted in ibid.

103. "First Lady at Big Symposium," 1939, *Schomburg Clipping File*.

104. Jean Collier Brown, *Negro Woman Worker*, 14.

105. Geraldine Bledsoe, "Service Occupations," in "Findings, Report, and Recommendations of the Michigan State Conference on Employment Problems of the Negro," 8 October 1940, p. 46, in James R. Grossman, *Black Workers in the Era of the Great Migration*, reel 15.

106. Ibid.

107. Ibid.

108. In the situations-wanted advertisements of the 14 September 1930 issue of the *Detroit Free Press*, eleven of the eighteen black women advertising requested day work. In the 3 February 1935 issue, nine of the thirteen black women advertising requested day work. And in the 31 March 1940 issue, eighteen of the twenty-four black women advertising requested day work. Thus, in this small random sample, 69 percent requested day work.

109. Bledsoe, "Service Occupations," 47.

110. "Study of Domestic Employment," 19 September 1941, box 141, folder 3, UCSP-CF.

111. Bledsoe, "Service Occupations," 48–49. These recommendations parallel ones made by the National Committee on Household Employment, the Women's Bureau, and other reform organizations.

112. Bledsoe interview, 2–3.

113. Prospectus for the Negro Progress Exposition (1938), p. 2, box 1606, folder 663, State Series, Michigan, 1 July 1938–1 November 1938, NA RG 69. The organizers received only $7,500 of federal funds. See "Two Negro Expositions."

114. Whitby interview, 17.

Conclusion

1. Mary Wilson, *Dreamgirl*, 180. For a discussion of the use of bourgeois respectability in Motown, see Suzanne E. Smith, *Dancing in the Street*, 120–21.

2. Valentine, *Hustling and Other Hard Work*, 23.

3. For descriptions of the Sojourner Truth Housing Project controversy, see Richard W. Thomas, *Life for Us*, 143–48; Sugrue, *Origins of the Urban Crisis*, 73–77; and Capeci, *Race Relations in Wartime Detroit*.

4. Johnson, "Gender, Race, and Rumours," 266.

5. For descriptions of the 1943 riot, see Capeci, *Layered Violence*; Richard W. Thomas, *Life for Us*, 166–72; Earl Brown, *Why Race Riots?*; Beatley, *Background Causes of the 1943 Race Riot*; and Lee and Humphrey, *Race Riot*.

6. Darden et al., *Detroit*, 69.

7. Widick, *Detroit*, 166–85; Sugrue, *Origins of the Urban Crisis*, 259–61.

8. Widick, *Detroit*, 168. See also Johnson, "Gender, Race, and Rumours," 271.

Bibliography

Primary Sources

Manuscript Collections

Archives of Labor and Urban Affairs, Wayne State University, Detroit, Michigan
    Civil Rights Congress Papers
    Metropolitan Detroit Council of Churches Papers
    Michigan League for Human Services Papers
    Oral History Transcripts: Joseph Billups, Geraldine Bledsoe, Joseph Coles, Josephine Gomon, Snow Grigsby, Frank Marquart, Birney W. Smith, Beulah Whitby
    United Community Services Papers
Burton Historical Collection, Detroit Public Library, Detroit, Michigan
    Burniece Avery Papers
    Cora M. Brown Papers
    Malcolm G. Dade Papers
    John C. Dancy Papers
    Detroit Study Club Papers
    Elliottorian Business Women's Club Papers
    Christina Fuqua Papers
    Mary E. Glenn Papers
    Rosa L. Gragg Papers
    Lillian Bateman Johnson Papers
    Housewives' League of Detroit Papers
    New Era Study Club Papers
    Carrie B. Riley Papers
    Sorosis Group Papers
    Moses Stewart Thompson Collection
    Visiting Nurses' Association of Detroit Papers
Folklore Archive, Wayne State University, Detroit, Michigan
    Ines Marie Bridges, "Paradise Valley—Detroit's Black Bottom," typewritten manuscript, 1975
Harlan Hatcher Graduate Library, University of Michigan, Ann Arbor, Michigan

Henry Allen Bullock, "The Role of the Negro Church in the Negro
    Community of Detroit," typewritten manuscript, 1935
Henry Allen Bullock, "The Urbanization of the Negro Church in Detroit,"
    report to the Earhart Foundation for Community Leadership, typewritten
    manuscript, 1935
Glen S. Taylor, "Prostitution in Detroit," study for the Earhart Foundation for
    Community Leadership and the Department of Sociology of the University
    of Michigan, typewritten manuscript, 1933
Library of Congress, Manuscripts Division, Washington, D.C.
    Nannie Helen Burroughs Papers
Michigan Historical Collections, Bentley Historical Library, University of
Michigan, Ann Arbor, Michigan
    Cash Asher Papers
    Detroit Urban League Papers
    Hilmer Gellein Papers
    Second Baptist Church Papers, microfilm
    Charleszetta Waddles, autobiography, typewritten manuscript, n.d.
    Young Women's Home Association Papers
National Archives, College Park, Maryland
    RG 86, Women's Bureau Papers
National Archives, Washington, D.C.
    RG 69, Federal Emergency Relief Administration and Works Progress
        Administration Papers
Schlesinger Library, Radcliffe College, Cambridge, Massachusetts
    Black Women Oral History Project

Newspapers

Detroit Contender
Detroiter
Detroit Free Press
Detroit Herald
Detroit Independent
Detroit News
Detroit Saturday Night
Detroit Tribune
Michigan Chronicle
Negro World
Second Baptist Herald

Published Works

Adams, R. A. *The Negro Girl*. Kansas City: Independent Press, 1915.

Armstrong, Mary Frances. *On Habits and Manners*. Hampton, Va.: Normal School Press, 1888.

Attwell, Ernest T. "The Recreation Movement and Colored Americans." *Southern Workman* 52 (February 1923): 78–85.

Baker, Ella, and Marvel Cooke. "The Bronx Slave Market." *Crisis* 42 (November 1935): 330, 340.

Benyon, Erdmann Doane. "The Voodoo Cult among Negro Migrants in Detroit." *American Journal of Sociology* 15 (July 1934–May 1935): 894–907.

Bethune, Mary McLeod. "The Problems of the City Dweller." *Opportunity* 54 (February 1925). Reprinted in *Up South: Stories, Studies, and Letters of This Century's Black Migrations*, edited by Malaika Adero, 109–12. New York: New Press, 1993.

Boykin, Ulysses W. *A Handbook of the Detroit Negro*. Detroit: Minority Study Associates, 1943.

Bradford, B. E. "Woman." *Colored American Magazine* 17, no. 2 (August 1909): 103–4.

Brown, Charlotte Hawkins. *The Correct Thing to Do, to Say, to Wear*. Boston: Christopher, 1941.

Brown, Hallie Q. *Homespun Heroines and Other Women of Distinction*. 1926. Reprint, New York: Oxford University Press, 1988.

Brown, Jean Collier. *The Negro Woman Worker*. Bulletin of the Women's Bureau, no. 165. Washington, D.C.: Government Printing Office, 1938.

Burroughs, Nannie H. "Not Color but Character." *Voice of the Negro* 1 (July 1904): 277–79.

Citizens' Research Council. *The Negro in Detroit: Report of the Mayor's Committee on Race Relations*. Detroit: Detroit Bureau of Government Research, 1926.

Clark, William A. "Sanctification in Negro Religion." *Social Forces* 15 (1937): 544–51.

Cooley, Rossa B. *Homes of the Freed*. New York: New Republic, 1926.

Cooper, Anna Julia. *A Voice from the South*. 1892. Reprint, New York: Oxford University Press, 1988.

Davis, Elizabeth. *Lifting As They Climb: The National Association of Colored Women*. Washington, D.C.: National Association of Colored Women, 1933.

Dillon, Miriam S. "The Islam Cult in Detroit." *Compass Needle* 2 (October 1935): 11–14, 35.

Donald, Henderson H. "Negro Migration of 1906–1918." *Journal of Negro History* 6, no. 4 (October 1921): 383–498.

Du Bois, W. E. B. *The Philadelphia Negro*. 1899. Reprint, Millwood, N.Y.: Kraus-Thompson, 1973.

————, ed. *Efforts for Social Betterment among Negro Americans.* Atlanta: Atlanta University Press, 1909.

Du Bois, W. E. B., and Augustus Granville Dill. *Morals and Manners among Negro Americans.* Atlanta: Atlanta University Press, 1914.

Fisher, Miles Mark. "Organized Religion and the Cults." *Crisis* 44 (January 1937): 8–10, 29, 30.

Floyd, Silas. *Floyd's Flowers, or Duty and Beauty for Colored Children.* Washington, D.C.: Hertel, Jenkins, 1905.

Garvey, Amy Jacques, comp. *Philosophy and Opinions of Marcus Garvey, or Africa for the Africans.* 1925. Reprint, London: Frank Cass, 1967.

Gibbs, Ione E. "Woman's Part in the Uplift of the Negro Race." *Colored American Magazine* 12, no. 4 (April 1907): 264–68.

Gibson, Professor and Mrs. J. W. *Golden Thoughts on Chastity and Procreation.* Atlanta: J. L. Nichols, 1903.

Grigsby, Snow F. *Taps or Reveille?* Detroit: Snow Grigsby, 1956.

————. *White Hypocrisy and Black Lethargy.* Detroit: Snow Grigsby, 1937.

————. *An X-Ray Picture of Detroit.* Detroit: Snow Grigsby, 1933.

Hackley, Emma Azalia. *The Colored Girl Beautiful.* Kansas City: Burton, 1916.

Hain, A. J. "Our Immigrant, the Negro." *Iron Trade Review* 73, no. 11 (13 September 1923): 730–36.

Haldeman-Julius, Marcet. *Clarence Darrow's Two Great Trials: Reports of the Scopes Anti-Evolution Case and the Dr. Sweet Negro Trial.* Girard, Kans.: Haldeman-Julius, 1927.

Hammond, Lily. *In the Vanguard of a Race.* New York: Council of Women from Home Missions and Missionary Education Movement of the United States and Canada, 1922.

A Handbook of Social Work. Detroit: Detroit Community Union, 1926.

Harris, Abram L. *The Negro as Capitalist: A Study of Banking and Business among American Negroes.* Philadelphia: American Academy of Political and Social Science, 1936.

Harris, Ada Newton. "The Influence of Home." *AME Church Review* 3, no. 3 (January 1887): 304–7.

Harris, Eugene. *An Appeal for Social Purity in Negro Homes.* Nashville: Eugene Harris, 1898.

Haynes, Elizabeth Ross. "Negroes in Domestic Service in the United States." *Journal of Negro History* 8, no. 4 (October 1923): 399–413.

Haynes, George Edmund. *Negro New-comers in Detroit, Michigan: A Challenge to Christian Statesmanship—A Preliminary Survey.* New York: Home Missions Council, 1918.

————. *The Trend of the Races.* New York: Council of Women for Home Missions and Missionary Education Movement of the United States and Canada, 1922.

Hays, Arthur Garfield. *Let Freedom Ring.* New York: Horace Liveright, 1928.

Helm, Mary. *The Upward Path: The Evolution of a Race*. New York: Eaton and Mains, 1909.

Holsey, Albon L. "National Negro Business League." *Southern Workman* 59 (October 1930): 464–67.

Hunter, Jane Edna. *A Nickle and a Prayer*. Bloomington: Indiana University Press, 1940.

Hunton, Addie. "The Detroit Convention of the National Association of Colored Women." *Voice of the Negro* 3, no. 8 (August 1906): 589–93.

———. "Negro Womanhood Defended." *Voice of the Negro* 1, no. 7 (July 1904): 280–82.

———. "Woman's Part in the Uplift of the Race." *Colored American Magazine* 11, no. 1 (January 1907): 53–62.

Hutzel, Eleonore L. *The Policewomen's Handbook*. Worcester, Mass.: Columbia University Press, 1933.

Jones, Eugene Kinckle. "The Negro in the North." *Current History* 15, no. 6 (March 1922): 969–74.

———. "Social Service Progress in 1926." *Opportunity* 5 (January 1927): 14–15.

Jones, William H. *Recreation and Amusement among Negroes in Washington, D.C.* Washington, D.C.: Howard University Press, 1927.

Kellor, Frances A. "Associations for Protection of Colored Women." *Colored American Magazine* 9, no. 6 (December 1905): 695–99.

———. "Opportunities for Southern Negro Women in Northern Cities." *Voice of the Negro* 2, no. 7 (July 1905): 470–73.

———. *Out of Work: A Study of Employment Agencies, Their Treatment of the Unemployed, and Their Influence upon Homes and Business*. New York: G. P. Putnam, 1904.

———. "Southern Colored Girls in the North." *AME Church Review* 1, no. 8 (July 1905): 34–39.

———. "Southern Colored Girls in the North." *Charities* 13 (March 1905): 584–85.

Kirby, John B., ed. *New Deal Agencies and Black America*. Ann Arbor: University Publications of America, 1985. Microfilm.

Langhorne, Orra. "Domestic Service in the South." *Journal of Social Science* 39 (November 1901): 169–75.

Lasker, Bruno. "The Negro in Detroit." *Survey* 38 (15 April 1927): 72–73, 123.

Layten, S. W. "A Northern Phase of a Southern Problem." *AME Church Review* 26, no. 4 (March 1910): 315–25.

Leonard, Oscar, and Forrester B. Washington. "Welcoming Southern Negroes: East St. Louis and Detroit—A Contrast." *Survey* 38 (14 July 1917): 335.

Lett, Harold A. "Migration Difficulties in Michigan." *Southern Workman* 56 (May 1927): 231–36.

Lilienthal, David E. "Has the Negro the Right of Self-Defense?" *Nation* 121 (23 December 1925): 724–25.

McGuinn, Henry J. "Commercial Recreation." In *Negro Problems in Cities*, edited by
    T. J. Woofter, 258–81. 1928. Reprint, College Park, Md.: McGrath, 1969.

Majors, Monroe. *Noted Negro Women: Their Triumphs and Activities*. Chicago:
    Donohue and Henneberry, 1893.

Matthews, Mrs. V. E. "Some of the Dangers Confronting Southern Girls in the
    North." *Hampton Negro Conference* 4 (July 1900): 62–69.

Mays, Benjamin E., and Joseph William Nicholson. *The Negro's Church*. New York:
    Russell & Russell, 1933.

Meier, August, and John Bracey, eds. *Papers of the NAACP*. Frederick, Md.:
    University Publications of America, 1986. Microfilm.

Miller, Kelly. *From Servitude to Service: Being the Old South Lectures on the History and
    Work of Southern Institutions for the Education of the Negro*. Boston: American
    Unitarian Association, 1905.

"More Slavery at the South." *Independent* 72 (25 January 1912): 196–200.

Mossell, Gertrude. *The Work of the Afro-American Woman*. Philadelphia: George S.
    Ferguson, 1908.

Murtland, Cleo, and Blanche Rhinehart. *A Study of the Educational Aims and Methods
    of the Young Women's Christian Association of Detroit*. New York: Young Women's
    Christian Association, 1923.

"The National Association for Colored Women." *Colored American Magazine* 11,
    no. 3 (September 1906): 193–97.

Nelson, Eleanor, and Rebecca Farnman. *Women at Work: A Century of Industrial
    Change*. Bulletin of the Women's Bureau, no. 161. Washington, D.C.:
    Government Printing Office, 1939.

Northrop, Henry Davenport, Joseph R. Gay, and I. Garland Penn. *The College of
    Life or Practical Self-Educator: A Manual of Self-Improvement for the Colored Race*.
    Miami: Mnemosyne, 1900.

Olcott, Jane, comp. *The Work of Colored Women*. New York: Colored Work
    Committee War Work Council, National Board Young Women's Christian
    Association, 1919.

Penn, I. Garland, and J. W. E. Bowen, eds. *The United Negro: His Problems and His
    Progress*. Atlanta: D. E. Luther, 1902.

"The Race Problem—An Autobiography." *Independent* 56 (17 March 1904): 586–89.

Ragland, John Marshall. "The Negro in Detroit." *Southern Workman* 52 (November
    1923): 533–40.

Redding, J. Saunders. "Playing the Numbers." *North American Review* 238
    (December 1934): 533–42.

Reid, Ira De A. "Let Us Prey!" *Opportunity* 4 (September 1926): 274–78.

Salmon, Lucy Maynard. *Domestic Service*. 1897. Reprint, New York: Arno Press,
    1972.

Schomburg Clipping File. Alexandria, Va.: Chadwyck-Healey, 1986. Microfiche.

Scott, Emmett J. *Negro Migration during the War*. New York: Oxford University
    Press, 1920.

Scruggs, Lawson A. *Women of Distinction*. Raleigh: L. A. Scruggs, 1893.

Smith, Alberta Moore. "Chicago Notes." *Colored American Magazine* 2, no. 4 (February 1901): 285–91.

Smith, Amanda. *An Autobiography: The Story of the Lord's Dealings with Mrs. Amanda Smith, the Colored Evangelist*. 1893. Reprint, New York: Oxford University Press, 1988.

A Southern White Woman. "Experiences of the Race Problem." *Independent* 56 (17 March 1904): 590–94.

Stevens, S. B. "The Development of Stronger Womanhood." In *Hampton Negro Conference, Number II*, 7. Hampton, Va.: Hampton Institute Press, 1898.

Streator, George. "Detroit, Columbus, and Cleveland: Concerning Mr. Peck and Others." *Crisis* 41 (June 1934): 172–73.

Thomasson, Maurice E. "The Negro Migration." *Southern Workman* 46 (July 1917): 379–82.

"Two Negro Expositions." *Negro History Bulletin* 3, no. 6 (March 1940): 89.

U.S. Department of Labor. *Twentieth Annual Report of the Commissioner of Labor, 1910: Industrial Education*. Washington, D.C.: Government Printing Office, 1911.

Vice Commission of the City of Chicago. *The Social Evil in Chicago: A Study of Existing Conditions*. Chicago, 1911.

Warren, Francis H., comp. *Michigan Manual of Freedmen's Progress*. Detroit: Freedmen's Progress Commission, 1915.

Washington, Booker T., et al., eds. *The Negro Problem*. Miami: Mnemosyne, 1903.

Washington, Forrester B. "Deluxe Summer Camp for Colored Children." *Opportunity* 9 (October 1931): 303–6.

———. "The Detroit Newcomers' Greeting." *Survey* 38 (14 July 1917): 333–35.

———. *The Negro in Detroit: A Survey of the Conditions of a Negro Group in a Northern Industrial Center during the War Prosperity Period*. Detroit: Research Bureau of the Associated Charities of Detroit, 1920.

———. "A Program of Work for the Assimilation of Negro Immigrants in Northern Cities." In *National Conference of Social Work, Proceedings, 1917*, 497–500. Chicago: National Conference of Social Work, 1917.

———. "Reconstruction and the Colored Woman." *Life and Labor* 9 (January 1919): 3–7.

———. "Recreational Facilities for the Negro." *Annals of the American Academy of Political and Social Science* 140 (November 1928): 272–82.

Washington, Margaret Murray. "The Advancement of Colored Women." *Colored American Magazine* 8, no. 4 (April 1905): 183–88.

———. "Club Work as a Factor in the Advance of Colored Women." *Colored American Magazine* 11, no. 2 (August 1906): 83–90.

Wilcox, Ella Wheeler. "On the Making of Homes." *Colored American Magazine* 9, no. 1 (July 1905): 387–88.

Williams, Charles H. "Recreation in the Lives of Young People." *Southern Workman* 46 (February 1917): 95–100.

Williams, Fannie Barrier. "The Awakening of Women." *AME Church Review* 13, no. 4 (April 1897): 392–98.

———. "Industrial Education—Will It Solve the Negro Problem?" *Colored American Magazine* 7, no. 7 (July 1904): 492.

———. "The Need of Organized Womanhood." *Colored American Magazine* 15, no. 1 (January 1909): 652–53.

———. "A Northern Negro's Autobiography." *Independent* 57 (14 July 1904): 96.

———. "The Smaller Economies." *Voice of the Negro* 1, no. 5 (May 1904): 184–85.

———. "Social Bonds in the 'Black Belt' of Chicago." *Charities* 15 (October 1905– March 1906): 40–44.

Williams, Sylvanie Francaz. "The Social Status of the Negro Woman." *Voice of the Negro* 1, no. 7 (July 1904): 299–300.

Woods, Elias M. *The Negro in Etiquette: A Novelty*. St. Louis: Buxton & Skinner, 1899.

Woodson, Carter G. *A Century of Negro Migration*. 1918. Reprint, New York: AMS Press, 1970.

Woofter, T. J., ed. *Negro Problems in Cities*. 1928. Reprint, College Park, Md.: McGrath, 1969.

Secondary Sources

Books and Articles

Abelson, Elaine. *When Ladies Go A-Thieving: Middle-Class Shoplifters in the Victorian Department Store*. New York: Oxford University Press, 1989.

Albertson, Chris. *Bessie*. New York: Stein and Day, 1972.

Alexander, J. Trent. "The Great Migration in Comparative Perspective: Interpreting the Urban Origins of Southern Black Migrants to Depression-Era Pittsburgh." *Social Science History* 22, no. 3 (Fall 1998): 349–76.

Alexander, Ruth M. *The "Girl Problem": Female Sexual Delinquency in New York, 1900–1930*. Ithaca, N.Y.: Cornell University Press, 1995.

Anderson, James D. *The Education of Blacks in the South, 1860–1935*. Chapel Hill: University of North Carolina Press, 1988.

Anderson, Jervis. *This Was Harlem: A Cultural Portrait*. New York: Farrar Straus Giroux, 1981.

Avery, Burniece. *Walk Quietly through the Night and Cry Softly*. Detroit: Balamp, 1977.

Ayers, Edward L. *The Promise of the New South: Life after Reconstruction*. New York: Oxford University Press, 1992.

Baer, Hans A. *The Black Spiritual Movement: A Religious Response to Racism*. Knoxville: University of Tennessee Press, 1984.

Baer, Hans A., and Merrill Singer. *African-American Religion in the Twentieth Century:*

Varieties of Protest and Accommodation. Knoxville: University of Tennessee Press, 1992.

Bailey, Peter. "'Will the Real Bill Banks Please Stand Up?': Towards a Role Analysis of Mid-Victorian Working-Class Respectability." *Journal of Social History* 7 (Spring 1979): 336–53.

Bak, Richard. *Turkey Stearnes and the Detroit Stars: The Negro Leagues in Detroit, 1919–1933*. Detroit: Wayne State University Press, 1994.

Bardolph, Richard. *The Negro Vanguard*. New York: Vintage Books, 1959.

Barlow, William. *"Looking Up at Down": The Emergence of a Blues Culture*. Philadelphia: Temple University Press, 1989.

Barnett, Evelyn Brooks. "Nannie Burroughs and the Education of Black Women." In *The Afro-American Women: Struggles and Images*, edited by Sharon Harley and Rosalyn Terborg-Penn, 97–108. Port Washington, N.Y.: Kennikat Press, 1978.

———. "Religion, Politics, and Gender: The Leadership of Nannie Helen Burroughs." *Journal of Religious Thought* 44 (Winter/Spring 1988): 7–22.

Bates, Beth Tompkins. "A New Crowd Challenges the Agenda of the Old Guard in the NAACP, 1933–1941." *American Historical Review* 102, no. 2 (April 1997): 340–77.

Beatley, George W. *Background Causes of the 1943 Race Riot*. Princeton: Princeton University Press, 1954.

Berkeley, Kathleen C. "'Colored Ladies Also Contributed': Black Women's Activism from Benevolence to Social Welfare, 1866–1896." In *The Web of Southern Social Relations: Women, Family, and Education*, edited by Walter J. Fraser Jr., R. Frank Saunders Jr., and Jon L. Wakelyn, 181–203. Athens: University of Georgia Press, 1985.

Björn, Lars. "From Hastings Street to the Bluebird: The Blues and Jazz Traditions in Detroit." *Michigan Quarterly Review* 25 (Spring 1986): 257–68.

Blackwelder, Julia Kirk. "Women in the Work Force: Atlanta, New Orleans, and San Antonio, 1930 to 1940." *Journal of Urban History* 4 (May 1978): 331–58.

Black Women in Michigan, 1785–1985: A Resource Study Guide. Detroit: Detroit Historical Museum, 1985.

Blair, Barbara. "True Women, Real Men: Gender, Ideology, and Social Roles in the Garvey Movement." In *Gendered Domains: Beyond the Private/Public Dichotomy in Women's History: Essays from the Seventh Berkshire Conference on the History of Women*, edited by Susan Reverby and Dorothy O. Helly, 154–66. Ithaca, N.Y.: Cornell University Press, 1992.

Blair, Karen J. *The Clubwomen as Feminist: True Womanhood Redefined, 1868–1914*. New York: Holmes & Meier, 1980.

Boggs, Beverly. "Some Aspects of Worship in a Holiness Church." *New York Folklore* 3 (1977): 29–44.

Bontemps, Arna, and Jack Conroy. *They Seek a City*. Garden City, N.Y.: Doubleday, 1945.

Boris, Eileen. "Black Women and Paid Labor in the Home: Industrial Homework in Chicago in the 1920s." In *Homework: Historical and Contemporary Perspectives on Paid Labor at Home*, edited by Eileen Boris and Cynthia R. Daniels, 33–52. Chicago: University of Illinois Press, 1989.

———. *Home to Work: Motherhood and the Politics of Industrial Homework in the United States*. Cambridge: Cambridge University Press, 1994.

———. "The Power of Motherhood: Black and White Activist Women Redefine the 'Political.'" In *Mothers of a New World: Maternalist Politics and the Origins of Welfare States*, edited by Seth Koven and Sonya Michel, 213–45. New York: Routledge, 1993.

———. "Reconstructing the 'Family': Women, Progressive Reform, and the Problem of Social Control." In *Gender, Class, Race, and Reform in the Progressive Era*, edited by Noralee Frankel and Nancy S. Dye, 73–86. Lexington: University Press of Kentucky, 1991.

Boyd, Herb. *Jazz Space Detroit*. Detroit: Jazz Research Institute, 1980.

Brown, Earl. *Why Race Riots?* New York: Public Affairs Committee, 1944.

Brown, Elsa Barkley. "Negotiating and Transforming the Public Sphere: African American Political Life in the Transition from Slavery to Freedom." *Public Culture* 7, no. 1 (Fall 1994): 107–46.

———. "'What Has Happened Here': The Politics of Difference in Women's History and Feminist Politics." In *"We Specialize in the Wholly Impossible": A Reader in Black Women's History*, edited by Darlene Clark Hine, Wilma King, and Linda Reed, 39–56. Brooklyn: Carlson, 1995.

Calderon, Erma, with Leonard Ray Teel. *Erma*. New York: Random House, 1981.

Calhoun, Craig, ed. *Habermas and the Public Sphere*. Cambridge: MIT Press, 1992.

Capeci, Dominic J., Jr. *Layered Violence: The Detroit Rioters of 1943*. Jackson: University of Mississippi Press, 1991.

———. *Race Relations in Wartime Detroit: The Sojourner Truth Housing Controversy of 1942*. Philadelphia: Temple University Press, 1984.

Carby, Hazel. "'It Jus Be's Dat Way Sometime': The Sexual Politics of Women's Blues." *Radical America* 20, no. 4 (June–July 1986): 9–24.

———. "Policing the Black Woman's Body in an Urban Context." *Critical Inquiry* 18 (Summer 1992): 738–55.

Carlisle, Rodney. *The Roots of Black Nationalism*. Port Washington, N.Y.: Kennikat Press, 1975.

Carlson, Shirley J. "Black Ideals of Womanhood in the Late Victorian Era." *Journal of Negro History* 128, no. 2 (Spring 1992): 61–73.

Chateauvert, Melinda. *Marching Together: Women of the Brotherhood of Sleeping Car Porters*. Bloomington: University of Illinois Press, 1998.

Chauncey, George. *Gay New York: Gender, Urban Culture, and the Making of the Gay Male World, 1890–1940*. New York: Basic Books, 1994.

Chevigny, Paul. *Gigs: Jazz and the Cabaret Laws in New York City*. New York: Routledge, 1993.

Ciani, Kyle E. "Training Young Women in the 'Service' of Motherhood: Early

Childhood Education at Detroit's Merrill-Palmer School, 1920–1940." *Michigan Historical Review* 24, no. 1 (Spring 1998): 103–32.

Clark-Lewis, Elizabeth. "This Work Had an End: African-American Domestic Workers in Washington, D.C., 1910–1940." In *To Toil the Livelong Day: America's Women at Work, 1780–1980*, edited by Carol Groneman and Mary Beth Norton, 196–213. Ithaca, N.Y.: Cornell University Press, 1987.

Cohen, Lizabeth. *Making a New Deal: Industrial Workers in Chicago, 1919–1939*. New York: Cambridge University Press, 1990.

Collins, Patricia Hill. *Black Feminist Thought: Knowledge, Consciousness, and the Politics of Empowerment*. New York: Routledge, 1991.

Cott, Nancy. *The Bonds of Womanhood: "Woman's Sphere" in New England, 1780–1835*. New Haven: Yale University Press, 1977.

———. *The Grounding of Modern Feminism*. New Haven: Yale University Press, 1987.

Couvares, Francis G. *The Remaking of Pittsburgh: Class and Culture in an Industrial City, 1877–1919*. Albany: State University of New York Press, 1984.

Cumbler, John T. *Working Class Community in Industrial America: Work, Leisure, and Struggle in Two Industrial Cities, 1880–1930*. Westport, Conn.: Greenwood Press, 1979.

Dancy, John C. *Sand against the Wind: The Memoirs of John C. Dancy*. Detroit: Wayne State University Press, 1966.

Darden, Joe T., et al. *Detroit: Race and Uneven Development*. Philadelphia: Temple University Press, 1987.

Davenport, M. Marguerite. *Azalia: The Life of Madame E. Azalia Hackley*. Boston: Chapman and Grimes, 1947.

Davis, Angela Y. *Blues Legacies and Black Feminism: Gertrude "Ma" Rainey, Bessie Smith, and Billie Holiday*. New York: Vintage, 1998.

Denby, Charles. *Indignant Heart: A Black Worker's Journal*. Detroit: Wayne State University Press, 1989.

Deutsch, Sarah. "Learning to Talk More Like a Man: Boston Women's Class-Bridging Organizations, 1870–1940." *American Historical Review* 97, no. 2 (April 1992): 379–404.

———. "Reconceiving the City: Women, Space, and Power in Boston, 1870–1910." *Gender and History* 6, no. 2 (August 1994): 202–23.

Dill, Bonnie Thorton. "'Making the Job Good Yourself': Domestic Service and the Construction of Personal Dignity." In *Women and the Politics of Empowerment*, edited by Ann Bookman and Sandra Morgan, 33–53. Philadelphia: Temple University Press, 1988.

———. "The Means to Put My Children Through: Child-Rearing Goals and Strategies among Black Female Domestic Servants." In *The Black Woman*, edited by La Frances Rodgers-Rose, 107–23. Beverly Hills: Sage Publications, 1980.

Douglas, Ann. *Terrible Honesty: Mongrel Manhattan in the 1920s*. New York: Noonday Press, 1995.

Douglas, Mary. *Purity and Danger: An Analysis of Concepts of Pollution and Taboo.* London: Routledge, 1966.

Dow, Leslie M. "High Weeds in Detroit." *Urban Anthropology* 6 (1987): 111–28.

Drake, St. Clair, and Horace R. Cayton. *Black Metropolis: A Study of Negro Life in a Northern City.* Chicago: University of Chicago Press, 1945.

DuBois, Ellen Carol, and Vicki L. Ruiz, eds. *Unequal Sisters.* New York: Routledge, 1990.

DuCille, Ann. "Blues Notes on Black Sexuality: Sex and the Texts of Jessie Fauset and Nella Larsen." *Journal of the History of Sexuality* 3, no. 31 (1993): 418–44.

Duneier, Mitchell. *Slim's Table: Race, Respectability, and Masculinity.* Chicago: University of Chicago Press, 1992.

Duster, Alfreda M., ed. *Crusade for Justice: The Autobiography of Ida B. Wells.* Chicago: University of Chicago Press, 1970.

Dyson, Michael Eric. *Reflecting Black: African-American Cultural Criticism.* Minneapolis: University of Minnesota Press, 1993.

Engelmann, Larry. "Booze: The Ohio Connection, 1918–1919." *Detroit in Perspective* 2, no. 2 (Winter 1975): 111–29.

———. *Intemperance: The Lost War against Liquor.* New York: Macmillan, 1979.

———. "A Separate Peace: The Politics of Prohibition Enforcement in Detroit, 1920–1930." *Detroit in Perspective* 1, no. 1 (Autumn 1972): 51–71.

Erenberg, Lewis A. *Steppin' Out: New York Nightlife and the Transformation of American Culture, 1890–1930.* Westport, Conn.: Greenwood Press, 1981.

Evans, Sara. "Women's History and Political Theory: Toward a Feminist Approach to Public Life." In *Visible Women: New Essays on American Activism,* edited by Nancy A. Hewitt and Suzanne Lebsock, 119–40. Chicago: University of Illinois Press, 1993.

Fabian, Ann. *Card Sharps, Dream Books, and Bucket Shops: Gambling in Nineteenth-Century America.* Ithaca, N.Y.: Cornell University Press, 1990.

Faderman, Lillian. *Odd Girls and Twilight Lovers: A History of Lesbian Life in Twentieth-Century America.* New York: Columbia University Press, 1991.

Fass, Paula. *The Damned and the Beautiful: American Youth in the 1920s.* New York: Oxford University Press, 1977.

Faue, Elizabeth. *Community of Suffering and Struggle: Women, Men, and the Labor Movement in Minneapolis, 1915–1945.* Chapel Hill: University of North Carolina Press, 1991.

Fauset, Arthur Huff. *Black Gods of the Metropolis: Negro Religious Cults in the Urban North.* Philadelphia: University of Pennsylvania Press, 1944.

———. "Moorish Science Temple of America." In *Religion, Society, and the Individual,* edited by J. Milton Yinger, 498–507. New York: Macmillan, 1957.

Ferman, Louis A., Stuart Henry, and Michele Hoyman, eds. "The Informal Economy." *Annals of the American Academy of Political and Social Science* 493 (September 1987).

Fine, Sidney. *Frank Murphy: The Detroit Years*. Ann Arbor: University of Michigan Press, 1975.

Fitzpatrick, Ellen F. *Endless Crusade: Women Social Scientists and Progressive Reform*. New York: Oxford University Press, 1990.

Foner, Eric. *Reconstruction: The Unfinished Revolution, 1863–1877*. New York: Harper & Row, 1988.

Fragnoli, Raymond R. *The Transformation of Reform: Progressivism in Detroit—And After, 1912–1933*. New York: Garland, 1982.

Frank, Dana. *Purchasing Power: Consumer Organizing, Gender, and the Seattle Labor Movement, 1919–1929*. New York: Cambridge University Press, 1994.

Frankel, Noralee, and Nancy S. Dye, eds. *Gender, Class, Race, and Reform in the Progressive Era*. Lexington: University Press of Kentucky, 1991.

Fraser, Nancy. "Rethinking the Public Sphere: A Contribution to the Critique of Actually Existing Democracy." In *Habermas and the Public Sphere*, edited by Craig Calhoun, 56–80. Cambridge: MIT Press, 1992.

———. *Unruly Practices: Power, Discourse, and Gender in Contemporary Social Theory*. Minneapolis: University of Minnesota Press, 1989.

Frazier, E. Franklin. *The Black Bourgeoisie*. Glencoe, Ill.: Free Press, 1957.

———. *The Negro Church in America*. New York: Schocken Books, 1963.

Freedman, Estelle. "Separatism as Strategy: Female Institution-Building and American Feminism, 1870–1930." *Feminist Studies* 5 (Fall 1979): 512–29.

Gabel, Leona C. *From Slavery to the Sorbonne and Beyond: The Life and Writings of Anna J. Cooper*. Northampton, Mass.: Smith College, 1982.

Gaines, Kevin. "Assimilationist Minstrelsy as Racial Uplift Ideology: James D. Corrother's Literary Quest for Black Leadership." *American Quarterly* 45, no. 3 (September 1993): 341–69.

———. *Uplifting the Race: Black Leadership, Politics, and Culture in the Twentieth Century*. Chapel Hill: University of North Carolina Press, 1996.

Gamber, Wendy E. *The Female Economy: The Millinery and Dressmaking Trades, 1860–1930*. Urbana: University of Illinois Press, 1997.

Gatewood, Willard B. *Aristocrats of Color: The Black Elite, 1880–1920*. Bloomington: Indiana University Press, 1990.

Gere, Ann Ruggles. *Intimate Practices: Literacy and Cultural Work in United States Women's Clubs, 1880–1920*. Urbana: University of Illinois Press, 1997.

Giddings, Paula. *When and Where I Enter: The Impact of Black Women on Race and Sex in America*. New York: Bantam Books, 1984.

Gilfoyle, Timothy. *City of Eros: New York City, Prostitution, and the Commercialization of Sex, 1790–1920*. New York: W. W. Norton, 1992.

Gilkes, Cheryl Townsend. "'Together and in Harness': Women's Traditions in the Sanctified Church." *Signs* 10 (Summer 1985): 678–99.

Ginzberg, Lori D. *Women and the Work of Benevolence: Morality, Politics, and Class in the Nineteenth-Century United States*. New Haven: Yale University Press, 1990.

Ginzburg, Carlo. *The Cheese and the Worms: The Cosmos of a Sixteenth-Century Miller*. London: Routledge, 1976.

Glaysher, Frederick, ed. *Collected Prose: Robert E. Hayden*. Ann Arbor: University of Michigan Press, 1984.

Glazer, Sidney. *Detroit: A Study in Urban Development*. New York: Bookman Associates, 1965.

Goldsmith, Peter D. *When I Rise Cryin' Holy: African-American Denominationalism on the Georgia Coast*. New York: AMS Press, 1989.

Gordon, Linda. "Black and White Visions of Welfare: Women's Welfare Activism, 1890–1945." *Journal of American History* 78 (September 1991): 559–90.

———. *Pitied but Not Entitled: Single Mothers and the History of Welfare*. Cambridge: Harvard University Press, 1994.

Gordy, Berry. *To Be Loved: The Music, the Magic, the Memories of Motown*. New York: Warner Books, 1994.

Gottlieb, Peter. *Making Their Way: Southern Blacks' Migration to Pittsburgh, 1916–1930*. Urbana: University of Illinois Press, 1987.

Greenberg, Cheryl Lynn. *"Or Does It Explode?": Black Harlem in the Great Depression*. New York: Oxford University Press, 1991.

Greenberg, David F., ed. *Crime and Capitalism: Readings in Marxist Criminology*. Philadelphia: Temple University Press, 1992.

Gregg, Robert. *Sparks from the Anvil of Oppression: Philadelphia's African Methodists and Southern Migrants, 1890–1940*. Philadelphia: Temple University Press, 1993.

Griffin, Farah Jasmine. *"Who Set You Flowin'?": The African-American Migration Narrative*. New York: Oxford University Press, 1995.

Grossman, James R. *Land of Hope: Chicago, Black Southerners, and the Great Migration*. Chicago: University of Chicago Press, 1989.

———, ed. *Black Workers in the Era of the Great Migration*. Bethesda, Md.: University Publications of America, 1985. Microfilm.

Grossman, Stefan. *Ragtime Blues*. New York: Oak Publications, 1970.

Guy-Sheftall, Beverly. *Daughters of Sorrow: Attitudes toward Black Women, 1880–1920*. Brooklyn: Carlson, 1990.

Hall, Jacquelyn Dowd. "Disorderly Women: Gender and Labor Militancy in the Appalachian South." In *Unequal Sisters: A Multicultural Reader in U.S. Women's History*, edited by Ellen Carol DuBois and Vicki L. Ruiz, 298–321. New York: Routledge, 1990.

———, ed. *Speaking for Ourselves: Women of the South*. New York: Pantheon Books, 1984.

Haller, Mark H. "Policy Gambling, Entertainment, and the Emergence of Black Politics: Chicago from 1900 to 1940." *Journal of Social History* 24 (Summer 1991): 719–39.

Halttunen, Karen. *Confidence Men and Painted Women: A Study of Middle Class Culture in America, 1830–1870*. New Haven: Yale University Press, 1982.

Harding, P., and R. Jenkins. *The Myth of the Hidden Economy: Towards a New*

Understanding of Informal Economic Activity. Philadelphia: Open University Press, 1989.

Harlan, Louis. *Booker T. Washington: The Wizard of Tuskegee, 1901–1915.* New York: Oxford University Press, 1983.

Harley, Sharon. "Black Women in a Southern City: Washington, D.C., 1890–1920." In *Sex, Race, and the Role of Women in the South*, edited by Joanne V. Hawks and Sheila L. Skemp, 59–74. Jackson: University of Mississippi Press, 1983.

———. "Nannie Helen Burroughs: 'The Black Goddess of Liberty.'" *Journal of Negro History* 81, no. 1 (Spring 1996): 62–71.

———. "When Your Work Is Not Who You Are: The Development of a Working-Class Consciousness among Afro-American Women." In *Gender, Class, Race, and Reform in the Progressive Era*, edited by Noralee Frankel and Nancy S. Dye, 42–55. Lexington: University Press of Kentucky, 1991.

Harper, Phillip Brian. *Are We Not Men?: Masculine Anxiety and the Problem of African-American Identity.* New York: Oxford University Press, 1996.

Harris, Michael W. *The Rise of Gospel Blues: The Music of Thomas Andrew Dorsey in the Urban Church.* New York: Oxford University Press, 1992.

Harrison, Brian. "Traditions of Respectability in British Labour History." In *Peaceable Kingdom: Stability and Change in Modern Britain*, 157–216. Oxford: Clarendon Press, 1982.

Harrison, Daphne Duval. *Black Pearls: Blues Queens of the 1920s.* New Brunswick, N.J.: Rutgers University Press, 1990.

Hayden, Dolores. *The Grand Domestic Revolution: A History of Feminist Designs for American Homes, Neighborhoods, and Cities.* Cambridge: MIT Press, 1981.

Haywood, Carol Lois. "The Authority and Empowerment of Women among Spiritualist Groups." *Journal for the Scientific Study of Religion* 22 (1983): 157–66.

Hazzard-Gordon, Katrina. *Jookin': The Rise of Social Dance Formations in African-American Culture.* Philadelphia: Temple University Press, 1990.

Heilbut, Anthony. *The Gospel Sound: Good News and Bad Times.* New York: Simon and Schuster, 1971.

Hembold, Lois Rita. "Beyond the Family Economy: Black and White Working-Class Women during the Great Depression." *Feminist Studies* 13 (Fall 1987): 629–56.

———. "Downward Occupational Mobility during the Great Depression: Urban Black and White Working Class Women." *Labor History* 29 (Spring 1988): 135–72.

Hendricks, Wanda A. *Gender, Race, and Politics in the Midwest: Black Club Women in Illinois.* Bloomington: Indiana University Press, 1998.

Hennessey, Thomas J. *From Jazz to Swing: African-American Jazz Musicians and Their Music, 1890–1935.* Detroit: Wayne State University Press, 1994.

Henrickson, Wilma Wood, ed. *Detroit Perspectives: Crossroads and Turning Points.* Detroit: Wayne State University Press, 1991.

Hewitt, Nancy A., and Suzanne Lebsock, eds. *Visible Women: New Essays on American Activism.* Chicago: University of Illinois Press, 1993.

Higginbotham, Evelyn Brooks. *Righteous Discontent: The Women's Movement in the Black Baptist Church, 1880–1920.* Cambridge: Harvard University Press, 1993.

Hill, Marilynn Wood. *Their Sisters' Keepers: Prostitution in New York City, 1830–1870.* Berkeley: University of California Press, 1993.

Hill, Robert A., ed. *The Marcus Garvey and Universal Negro Improvement Papers.* 2 vols. Berkeley: University of California Press, 1983.

Hine, Darlene Clark. "Black Migration to the Urban Midwest: The Gender Dimension, 1915–1945." In *The Great Migration in Historical Perspective: New Dimensions of Race, Class, and Gender,* edited by Joe William Trotter Jr., 127–46. Bloomington: University of Indiana Press, 1991.

———. *Black Women in the Middle West: The Michigan Experience.* Detroit: Historical Society of Michigan, 1990.

———. *Black Women in White: Racial Conflict and Cooperation in the Nursing Profession, 1890–1950.* Bloomington: Indiana University Press, 1989.

———. "The Housewives' League of Detroit: Black Women and Economic Nationalism." In *Visible Women: New Essays on American Activism,* edited by Nancy A. Hewitt and Suzanne Lebsock, 223–41. Chicago: University of Illinois Press, 1993.

———. "'We Specialize in the Wholly Impossible': The Philanthropic Work of Black Women." In *Lady Bountiful Revisited: Women, Philanthropy, and Power,* edited by Kathleen D. McCarthy, 70–93. New Brunswick, N.J.: Rutgers University Press, 1990.

———, ed. *Black Women in America: An Historical Encyclopedia.* Brooklyn: Carlson, 1993.

Hirsch, Arnold. *Making the Second Ghetto: Race and Housing in Chicago, 1940–1960.* New York: Cambridge University Press, 1983.

Hobsbawn, E. J. "Labour Aristocracy in Nineteenth-Century Britain." In *Labouring Men: Studies in the History of Labour.* London: Weidenfeld and Nicolson, 1964.

Hobson, Barbara Meil. *Uneasy Virtue: The Politics of Prostitution and the American Reform Tradition.* New York: Basic Books, 1987.

Horton, James Oliver. "Violence, Protest, and Identity: Black Manhood in Antebellum America." In *Free People of Color: Inside the African American Community.* Washington, D.C.: Smithsonian Institution Press, 1993.

Hunter, Tera. "Domination and Resistance: The Politics of Wage Household Labor in Atlanta." *Labor History* 34 (Spring–Summer 1993): 205–20.

———. *To 'Joy My Freedom: Southern Black Women's Lives and Labors after the Civil War.* Cambridge: Harvard University Press, 1997.

Hurston, Zora Neale. *Sanctified Church.* Berkeley: Turtle Island, 1983.

Jackson, Kenneth T. *The Ku Klux Klan in the City, 1915–1930.* New York: Oxford University Press, 1967.

Jackson, Mahalia, with Evan McLeod Wylie. *Movin' On Up.* New York: Hawthorn Books, 1966.

Johnson, Marilynn S. "Gender, Race, and Rumours: Re-Examining the 1943 Race Riots." *Gender and History* 10, no. 2 (August 1998): 252–77.

Jones, Adrienne Lash. *Jane Edna Hunter: A Case Study of Black Leadership, 1910–1950*. Brooklyn: Carlson, 1990.

————. "Struggle among Saints: African American Women and the YWCA, 1870–1921." In *Men and Women Adrift: The YMCA and the YWCA in the City*, edited by Nina Mjagkij and Margaret Spratt, 160–87. New York: New York University Press, 1997.

Jones, Charles Edwin. *Black Holiness: A Guide to the Study of Black Participation in Wesleyan Perfectionist and Glossolalic Pentecostal Movements*. Metuchen, N.J.: Scarecrow Press, 1987.

Jones, Gareth Stedman. *Outcast London: A Study in the Relationship between Classes in Victorian Society*. Oxford: Clarendon Press, 1971.

Jones, Jacqueline. *Labor of Love, Labor of Sorrow: Black Women, Work, and the Family from Slavery to the Present*. New York: Basic Books, 1985.

Kasson, John F. *Rudeness and Civility: Manners in Nineteenth-Century Urban America*. New York: Hill & Wang, 1990.

Katzman, David M. *Before the Ghetto: Black Detroit in the Nineteenth Century*. Chicago: University of Illinois Press, 1973.

————. *Seven Days a Week: Women and Domestic Service in Industrializing America*. New York: Oxford University Press, 1978.

Kelley, Robin D. G. *Hammer and Hoe: Alabama Communists during the Great Depression*. Chapel Hill: University of North Carolina Press, 1990.

————. *Race Rebels: Culture, Politics, and the Black Working Class*. New York: Free Press, 1994.

————. "'We Are Not What We Seem': Rethinking Black Working-Class Opposition in the Jim Crow South." *Journal of American History* 80 (June 1993): 75–112.

Kirby, John B. *Black Americans in the Roosevelt Era: Liberalism and Race*. Knoxville: University of Tennessee Press, 1980.

Knupfer, Anne Meis. *Toward a Tenderer Humanity and a Nobler Womanhood: African-American Women's Clubs in Turn-of-the-Century Chicago*. New York: New York University Press, 1996.

Kolchin, Peter. *First Freedom: The Responses of Alabama's Blacks to Emancipation and Reconstruction*. Westport, Conn.: Greenwood Press, 1972.

Kornbluh, Joyce L. *A New Deal for Workers' Education: The Workers' Service Program, 1933–1942*. Chicago: University of Illinois Press, 1987.

Korstad, Robert, and Nelson Lichtenstein. "Opportunities Lost and Found: Labor, Radicals, and the Early Civil Rights Movement." *Journal of American History* 75 (December 1988): 786–811.

Koven, Seth, and Sonya Michel, eds. *Mothers of a New World: Maternalist Politics and the Origins of Welfare States*. New York: Routledge, 1993.

Kukla, Barbara J. *Swing City: Newark Nightlife, 1925–1950.* Philadelphia: Temple University Press, 1991.

Kusmer, Kenneth. *A Ghetto Takes Shape: Black Cleveland, 1870–1930.* Urbana: University of Illinois Press, 1976.

Ladd-Taylor, Molly. *Mother-Work: Women, Child Welfare, and the State, 1890–1930.* Chicago: University of Illinois Press, 1994.

Landry, Bart. *The New Black Middle Class.* Berkeley: University of California Press, 1987.

Lasch-Quinn, Elisabeth. *Black Neighbors: Race and the Limits of Reform in the American Settlement House Movement, 1890–1945.* Chapel Hill: University of North Carolina Press, 1993.

Leashore, Bogart R. "Black Female Workers: Live-in Domestics in Detroit, Michigan, 1860–1880." *Phylon* 45 (June 1984): 111–20.

Lee, Alfred McClung, and Norman Daymond Humphrey. *Race Riot.* New York: Dryden Press, 1943.

Lemke-Santangelo, Gretchen. *Abiding Courage: African American Migrant Women and the East Bay Community.* Chapel Hill: University of North Carolina Press, 1996.

Leonard, Madeleine. *Informal Economic Activity in Belfast.* Brookfield, Vt.: Avebary, 1994.

Lerner, Gerda, ed. *Black Women in White America: A Documentary History.* New York: Vintage Press, 1973.

Levine, David Allen. *Internal Combustion: The Races in Detroit, 1915–1926.* Westport, Conn.: Greenwood Press, 1976.

Levine, Lawrence W. *Black Culture and Black Consciousness: Afro-American Folk Thought from Slavery to Freedom.* New York: Oxford University Press, 1977.

Levine, Susan. "Workers' Wives: Gender, Class, and Consumerism in the 1920s United States." *Gender and History* 3, no. 1 (Spring 1991): 45–64.

Lewis, David L. *W. E. B. Du Bois: Biography of a Race, 1868–1919.* New York: H. Holt, 1993.

———. *When Harlem Was in Vogue.* New York: Vintage Press, 1982.

Lewis, Earl. *In Their Own Interests: Race, Class, and Power in Twentieth-Century Norfolk, Virginia.* Berkeley: University of California Press, 1991.

———. "Writing African Americans into a History of Overlapping Diasporas." *American Historical Review* 100, no. 3 (June 1995): 765–87.

Lewis, I. M. *Ecstatic Religion: An Anthropological Study of Spirit Possession and Shamanism.* New York: Penguin Books, 1971.

Light, Ivan. "Numbers Gambling among Blacks: A Financial Institution." *American Sociological Review* 42 (December 1977): 892–904.

Lincoln, C. Eric. *The Black Muslims in America.* 3d ed. Trenton, N.J.: Africa World Press, 1994.

Lincoln, C. Eric, and Lawrence H. Mamiya. *The Black Church in the African American Experience.* Durham: Duke University Press, 1990.

Litwack, Leon F. *Been in the Storm So Long: The Aftermath of Slavery*. New York: Vintage Books, 1979.

Logan, Rayford W. *The Negro in American Life and Thought: The Nadir, 1877–1901*. New York: Dial Press, 1954.

Logan, Rayford W., and Michael Winston, eds. *Dictionary of American Negro Biography*. New York: W. W. Norton, 1982.

Louis, Joe. *My Life Story*. New York: Duell, Sloan and Pearce, 1947.

Luker, Ralph E. *The Social Gospel in Black and White: American Racial Reform, 1885–1912*. Chapel Hill: University of North Carolina Press, 1991.

McGowan, Helen [Rocking Chair, pseud.]. *Motor City Madam*. New York: Pageant Press, 1964.

McKay, Claude. *Harlem: Negro Metropolis*. New York: E. P. Dutton, 1940.

Mackey, Thomas C. *Red Lights Out: A Legal History of Prostitution, Disorderly Houses, and Vice Districts, 1870–1917*. New York: Garland, 1987.

Marks, Carole. *Farewell—We're Good and Gone: The Great Black Migration*. Bloomington: Indiana University Press, 1989.

Marsh, Clifton E. *From Black Muslims to Muslims: The Transition from Separatism to Islam, 1930–1980*. Metuchen, N.J.: Scarecrow Press, 1984.

Martin, Elizabeth Anne. *Detroit and the Great Migration, 1916–1929*. Ann Arbor: Bentley Historical Library, 1993.

Martin, Tony. "Women in the Garvey Movement." In *Garvey: His Work and Impact*, edited by Rupert Lewis and Patrick Bryan, 67–72. Mona, Jamaica: Institute of Social and Economic Research, University of the West Indies, 1988.

Mattera, Philip. *Off the Books: The Rise of the Underground Economy*. London: Pluto Press, 1985.

Maultsby, Portia K. "Africanisms in African-American Music." In *Africanisms in American Culture*, edited by Joseph E. Holloway, 185–210. Bloomington: Indiana University Press, 1994.

Meier, August. *Negro Thought in America, 1880–1915: Racial Ideologies in the Age of Booker T. Washington*. Ann Arbor: University of Michigan Press, 1963.

Meier, August, and Elliott Rudwick. *Black Detroit and the Rise of the UAW*. New York: Oxford University Press, 1979.

Meyer, Stephen, III. *The Five Dollar Day: Labor Management and Social Control in the Ford Motor Company, 1908–1921*. Albany: State University Press of New York, 1981.

Mink, Gwendolyn. *The Wages of Motherhood: Inequality in the Welfare State, 1917–1942*. Ithaca, N.Y.: Cornell University Press, 1995.

Mjagkij, Nina, and Margaret Spratt, eds. *Men and Women Adrift: The YMCA and the YWCA in the City*. New York: New York University Press, 1997.

Montgomery, William E. *Under Their Own Vine and Fig Tree: The African-American Church in the South, 1865–1900*. Baton Rouge: Louisiana State University Press, 1993.

Moon, Elaine Latzman, ed. *Untold Tales, Unsung Heroes: An Oral History of Detroit's African American Community, 1918–1967.* Detroit: Wayne State University Press, 1994.

Morrison, Toni, ed. *Race-ing Justice, En-gendering Power: Essays on Anita Hill, Clarence Thomas, and the Construction of Social Reality.* New York: Pantheon Books, 1992.

Moses, Wilson J. *Alexander Crummell: A Study of Civilization and Discontent.* New York: Oxford University Press, 1989.

———. *The Golden Age of Black Nationalism, 1850–1925.* Hamden, Conn.: Archon Books, 1978.

Mumford, Kevin J. *Interzones: Black/White Sex Districts in Chicago and New York in the Early Twentieth Century.* New York: Columbia University Press, 1997.

Muncy, Robyn. *Creating a Female Dominion in American Reform, 1890–1935.* New York: Oxford University Press, 1991.

Murphy, Mary. "Bootlegging Mothers and Drinking Daughters: Gender and Prohibition in Butte, Montana." *American Quarterly* 46, no. 2 (June 1994): 174–94.

Myerowitz, Joanne. *Women Adrift: Independent Wage Earners in Chicago, 1880–1930.* Chicago: University of Chicago Press, 1988.

Naison, Mark. *Communists in Harlem during the Depression.* New York: Grove Press, 1983.

Neverdon-Morton, Cynthia. *Afro-American Women of the South and the Advancement of the Race, 1895–1925.* Knoxville: University of Tennessee Press, 1989.

Odem, Mary E. *Delinquent Daughters: Protecting and Policing Adolescent Female Sexuality in the United States, 1885–1920.* Chapel Hill: University of North Carolina Press, 1994.

Oestreicher, Richard Jules. *Solidarity and Fragmentation: Working People and Class Consciousness in Detroit, 1875–1900.* Chicago: University of Illinois Press, 1986.

Osofsky, Gilbert. *Harlem: The Making of a Ghetto: Negro New York, 1890–1930.* New York: Harper & Row, 1965.

Overacker, Ingrid. *The African American Church Community in Rochester, New York, 1900–1940.* Rochester: University of Rochester Press, 1998.

Palmer, Phyllis. *Domesticity and Dirt: Housewives and Domestic Servants in the United States from 1900 to 1920.* Philadelphia: Temple University Press, 1989.

Paris, Arthur E. *Black Pentecostalism: Southern Religion in an Urban World.* Amherst: University of Massachusetts Press, 1982.

Parris, Guichard, and Lester Brooks. *Blacks in the City: A History of the National Urban League.* Boston: Little, Brown, 1971.

Peebles, Robin S. "Detroit's Black Women's Clubs." *Michigan History* 70, no. 1 (January/February 1986): 48.

Peiss, Kathy. *Cheap Amusements: Working Women and Leisure in Turn-of-the-Century New York.* Philadelphia: Temple University Press, 1986.

———. *Hope in a Jar: The Making of America's Beauty Culture.* New York: Henry Holt, 1998.

Peretti, Burton W. *The Creation of Jazz: Music, Race, and Culture in Urban America.* Chicago: University of Illinois Press, 1992.

Phillips, Kimberley L. *Alabama North: African-American Migrants, Community, and Working-Class Activism in Cleveland, 1915–1945.* Chicago: University of Illinois Press, 1999.

Pivar, David J. *Purity Crusade: Sexual Morality and Social Control, 1868–1900.* Westport, Conn.: Greenwood Press, 1973.

Rabinowitz, Howard N. *Race Relations in the Urban South, 1865–1890.* New York: Oxford University Press, 1978.

Reed, Christopher Robert. *The Chicago NAACP and the Rise of Black Professional Leadership, 1910–1966.* Bloomington: Indiana University Press, 1997.

Reid, John B. "A Career to Build, a People to Serve, a Purpose to Accomplish: Race, Class, Gender, and Detroit's First Black Women Schoolteachers, 1865–1916." *Michigan Historical Review* 18, no. 1 (Spring 1992): 1–28.

Robinson, Cyril. "Exploring the Informal Economy." *Social Justice* 15, nos. 3–4 (1988): 3–16.

———. "The Production of Black Violence in Chicago." In *Crime and Capitalism: Readings in Marxist Criminology*, edited by David F. Greenberg, 301–33. Philadelphia: Temple University Press, 1992.

Rollins, Judith. *Between Women: Domestics and Their Employers.* Philadelphia: Temple University Press, 1985.

Rosemond, Irene, comp. *Reflections: An Oral History of Detroit.* Detroit: Broadside Press, 1992.

Rosen, Ruth. *The Lost Sisterhood: Prostitution in America, 1900–1918.* Baltimore: Johns Hopkins University Press, 1982.

Rosenzweig, Roy. *Eight Hours for What We Will: Workers and Leisure in an Industrial City, 1870–1920.* New York: Cambridge University Press, 1983.

Ross, Ellen. *Love and Toil: Motherhood in Outcast London, 1870–1918.* New York: Oxford University Press, 1993.

———. " 'Not the Sort That Would Sit on the Doorstep': Respectability in pre–World War I London Neighborhoods." *International Labor and Working Class History* 27 (Spring 1985): 39–59.

Rouse, Jacqueline Anne. *Lugenia Burns Hope: Black Southern Reformer.* Athens: University of Georgia Press, 1989.

Ruck, Rob. *Sandlot Seasons: Sport in Black Pittsburgh.* Chicago: University of Illinois Press, 1987.

Ryan, Mary. *Women in Public: Between Banners and Ballots, 1825–1880.* Baltimore: Johns Hopkins University Press, 1990.

Salem, Dorothy. *To Better Our World: Black Women in Organized Reform, 1890–1920.* Brooklyn: Carlson, 1990.

Satter, Beryl. "Marcus Garvey, Father Divine, and the Gender Politics of Race Difference and Race Neutrality." *American Quarterly* 48, no. 1 (March 1996): 43–76.

Scharf, Lois. *To Work and to Wed: Female Employment, Feminism, and the Great Depression*. Westport, Conn.: Greenwood Press, 1980.

Schatzberg, Rufus, and Robert J. Kelly. *African American Organized Crime: A Social History*. New Brunswick, N.J.: Rutgers University Press, 1996.

Scheiner, Seth M. "The Negro Church and the Northern City, 1890–1930." In *Seven on Black: Reflections on the Negro Experience in America*, edited by William G. Shade and Roy C. Hevrenkohl, 92–116. New York: J. B. Lippincott, 1969.

Schwerin, Jules. *Got to Tell It: Mahalia Jackson, Queen of Gospel*. Cambridge: Oxford University Press, 1992.

Scobey, David. "Anatomy of the Promenade: The Politics of Bourgeois Sociability in Nineteenth-Century New York." *Social History* 17, no. 2 (May 1992): 203–27.

Scott, Anne Firor. *Natural Allies: Women's Associations in American Histories*. Chicago: University of Illinois Press, 1991.

Scott, James C. *Domination and the Arts of Resistance: Hidden Transcripts*. New Haven: Yale University Press, 1990.

Scott, Joan. *Gender and the Politics of History*. New York: Columbia University Press, 1988.

Seraile, William. "Henrietta Vinton Davis and the Garvey Movement." In *Black Women and United States History*, vol. 4, edited by Darlene Clark Hine, 1073–90. Brooklyn: Carlson, 1990.

Sernett, Milton C. *Bound for the Promised Land: African American Religion and the Great Migration*. Durham: Duke University Press, 1997.

Shaw, Stephanie J. "Black Club Women and the Creation of the National Association of Colored Women." *Journal of Women's History* 3 (Winter 1991): 10–25.

———. *What a Woman Ought to Be and to Do: Black Professional Women Workers during the Jim Crow Era*. Chicago: University of Chicago Press, 1996.

Shelly, Cara L. "Bradby's Baptists: Second Baptist Church of Detroit, 1910–1946." *Michigan Historical Review* 17, no. 1 (Spring 1991): 1–33.

Simmons, Christina. "African Americans and Sexual Victorianism in the Social Hygiene Movement, 1910–1940." *Journal of the History of Sexuality* 4, no. 1 (1993): 51–75.

Simon, Carl P., and Ann D. Witte. *Beating the System: The Underground Economy*. New York: Auburn, 1982.

Simonsen, Thordis, ed. *You May Plow Here: The Narrative of Sara Brooks*. New York: W. W. Norton, 1986.

Sitkoff, Harvard. "The New Deal and Race Relations." In *Fifty Years Later: The New Deal Evaluated*, edited by Harvard Sitkoff, 93–112. New York: Knopf, 1985.

———. *A New Deal for Blacks: The Emergence of Civil Rights as a National Issue—The Depression Decade*. New York: Oxford University Press, 1978.

Slim, Iceberg. *Pimp: The Story of My Life*. Los Angeles: Holloway House, 1969.

Smith, Susan L. *Sick and Tired of Being Sick and Tired: Black Women's Health Activism in America, 1890–1950*. Philadelphia: University of Pennsylvania Press, 1995.

Smith, Suzanne E. *Dancing in the Street: Motown and the Cultural Politics of Detroit.* Cambridge: Harvard University Press, 1999.

Smitherman, Geneva, ed. *Race, Gender, and Power in the United States: Reflections on Anita Hill.* Detroit: Wayne State University Press, 1995.

Smith-Irvin, Jeannette. *Marcus Garvey's Footsoldiers of the Universal Negro Improvement Association.* Trenton, N.J.: Africa World Press, 1989.

Smith-Rosenberg, Carroll. "The Female World of Love and Ritual: Relations between Women in Nineteenth-Century America." *Signs* 1 (Autumn 1975): 1–29.

Spain, Daphne. "Black Women as City Builders: Redemptive Places and the Legacy of Nannie Helen Burroughs." In *Gendering the City: Women, Boundaries, and Visions of Urban Life*, edited by Kristine B. Miranne and Alma H. Young, 105–18. New York: Rowan & Littlefield, 2000.

———. *Gendered Spaces.* Chapel Hill: University of North Carolina Press, 1992.

Spear, Allen. *Black Chicago: The Making of a Negro Ghetto, 1890–1920.* Chicago: University of Chicago Press, 1967.

Spratt, Margaret. "To Be Separate or One: The Issue of Race in the History of the Pittsburgh and Cleveland YWCAs, 1920–1946." In *Men and Women Adrift: The YMCA and the YWCA in the City*, edited by Nina Mjagkij and Margaret Spratt, 188–205. New York: New York University Press, 1997.

Stack, Carol B. *All Our Kin: Strategies for Survival in a Black Community.* New York: Harper & Row, 1974.

Stansell, Christine. *City of Women: Sex and Class in New York, 1789–1860.* Chicago: University of Illinois Press, 1987.

Stetson, Erlene. "Black Feminism in Indiana, 1893–1933." *Phylon* 44, no. 4 (1983): 292–98.

Stuckey, Sterling. *Slave Culture: Nationalist Theory and the Foundations of Black America.* New York: Oxford University Press, 1987.

Sugrue, Thomas. *The Origins of the Urban Crisis: Race and Inequality in Postwar Detroit.* Princeton: Princeton University Press, 1996.

Sullivan, Patricia. *Days of Hope: Race and Democracy in the New Deal Era.* Chapel Hill: University of North Carolina Press, 1996.

Sutherland, Daniel E. *Americans and Their Servants: Domestic Service in the United States from 1800 to 1920.* Baton Rouge: Louisiana State University Press, 1981.

Swain, Martha H. "ER and Ellen Woodward: A Partnership for Women's Work Relief and Security." In *Without Precedent: The Life and Career of Eleanor Roosevelt*, edited by Joan Hoff-Wilson and Marjorie Lightman. Bloomington: Indiana University Press, 1984.

Symanski, Richard. *The Immoral Landscape: Female Prostitution in Western Societies.* Toronto: Butterworth, 1981.

Synan, Vinson. *The Holiness-Pentecostal Movement in the United States.* Grand Rapids, Mich.: W. B. Eerdmans, 1971.

Taeuber, Karl E., and Alma F. Taeuber. *Negroes in Cities: Residential Segregation and Neighborhood Change.* Chicago: Aldine, 1965.

Tate, Claudia. *Domestic Allegories of Political Desire: The Black Heroine's Text at the Turn of the Century.* New York: Oxford University Press, 1992.

Taylor, Ula Y. "'Negro Women Are Great Thinkers as well as Doers': Amy Jacques-Garvey and Community Feminism in the United States, 1924–1927." *Journal of Women's History* 12, no. 2 (Summer 2000): 104–26.

Terborg-Penn, Rosalyn. *African American Women in the Struggle for the Vote, 1850–1920.* Bloomington: Indiana University Press, 1998.

———. "Discontented Black Feminists: Prelude and Postscript to the Passage of the Nineteenth Amendment." In *Decades of Discontent: The Women's Movement, 1920–1940*, edited by Lois Scharf and Joan M. Jensen, 261–78. Westport, Conn.: Greenwood Press, 1983.

———. "Survival Strategies among African-American Women Workers: A Continuing Process." In *Women, Work, and Protest*, edited by Ruth Milkman, 139–55. Boston: Routledge and Kegan Paul, 1985.

Thomas, Richard W. *Life for Us Is What We Make It: Building Black Community in Detroit, 1915–1945.* Bloomington: Indiana University Press, 1992.

Thompson, E. P. "The Moral Economy of the English Crowd in the Eighteenth Century." *Past and Present* 50 (February 1971): 76–135.

Trolander, Judith Ann. *Professionalism and Social Change: From the Settlement House Movement to Neighborhood Centers, 1886 to the Present.* New York: Columbia University Press, 1987.

Trotter, Joe William, Jr. *Black Milwaukee: The Making of an Industrial Proletariat, 1915–1945.* Chicago: University of Illinois Press, 1985.

Tucker, Susan, ed. *Telling Memories among Southern Women: Domestic Workers and Their Employers in the Segregated South.* Baton Rouge: Louisiana State University Press, 1988.

Turner, Richard Brent. *Islam in the African-American Experience.* Bloomington: Indiana University Press, 1997.

Valentine, Bettylou. *Hustling and Other Hard Work: Life Styles in the Ghetto.* New York: Free Press, 1978.

Van Raaphorst, Donna L. *Union Maids Not Wanted: Organizing Domestic Workers, 1870–1940.* New York: Praeger, 1988.

Vose, Clement E. *The Supreme Court, the NAACP, and the Restrictive Covenant Cases.* Berkeley: University of California Press, 1959.

Walkowitz, Daniel J. *Working with Class: Social Workers and the Politics of Middle-Class Identity.* Chapel Hill: University of North Carolina Press, 1999.

Walkowitz, Judith R. *City of Dreadful Delight: Narratives of Sexual Danger in Late-Victorian London.* Chicago: University of Chicago Press, 1992.

Waters, Ethel. *His Eye Is on the Sparrow.* Golden City, N.Y.: Doubleday, 1950.

Watkins-Owens, Irma. *Blood Relations: Caribbean Immigrants and the Harlem Community, 1900–1930.* Bloomington: Indiana University Press, 1996.

Weinberg, Kenneth G. *A Man's Home, a Man's Castle*. New York: McCall, 1971.

Weisman, Lelie Kanes. *Discrimination by Design: A Feminist Critique of the Man-Made Environment*. Urbana: University of Illinois Press, 1992.

Weiss, Nancy J. *Farewell to the Party of Lincoln: Black Politics in the Age of FDR*. Princeton: Princeton University Press, 1983.

———. *The National Urban League, 1910–1940*. New York: Oxford University Press, 1974.

Welter, Barbara. "The Cult of True Womanhood, 1820–1860." *American Quarterly* 18, no. 2 (Summer 1966): 151–74.

Wheeler, Edward L. *Uplifting the Race: The Black Minister in the New South, 1865–1902*. New York: University Press of America, 1986.

White, Deborah Gray. "The Cost of Club Work, the Price of Black Feminism." In *Visible Women: New Essays on American Activism*, edited by Nancy A. Hewitt and Suzanne Lebsock, 247–69. Chicago: University of Illinois Press, 1993.

———. *Too Heavy a Load: Black Women in Defense of Themselves, 1894–1994*. New York: W. W. Norton, 1999.

White, Luise. *The Comforts of Home: Prostitution in Colonial Nairobi*. Chicago: University of Chicago Press, 1990.

White, Shane, and Graham White. *Stylin': African American Expressive Culture from Its Beginnings to the Zoot Suit*. Ithaca, N.Y.: Cornell University Press, 1998.

Widick, B. J. *Detroit: City of Race and Class Violence*. Chicago: Quadrangle Books, 1972.

Wiese, Andrew. "The Other Suburbanites: African American Suburbanization in the North before 1950." *Journal of American History* 85 (March 1998): 1495–1524.

Wilentz, Sean. *Chants Democratic: New York City and the Rise of the American Working Class, 1788–1850*. New York: Oxford University Press, 1984.

Williamson, Joel. *New People: Miscegenation and Mulattoes in the United States*. New York: Free Press, 1980.

Wilmore, Gayraud S. *Black Religion and Black Radicalism*. New York: Doubleday, 1972.

Wilson, Ben C. "The Early Development and Growth of America's Oldest Black Resort: Idlewild, Michigan, 1912–1930." In *Perspectives of Black Popular Culture*, edited by Henry B. Shaw, 101–8. Bowling Green: Bowling Green State University Press, 1990.

Wilson, Elizabeth. *The Sphinx in the City: Urban Life, the Control of Disorder, and Women*. London: Virago Press, 1991.

Wilson, Mary. *Dreamgirl: My Life as a Supreme*. New York: St. Martin's Press, 1986.

Wolcott, Victoria W. "'Bible, Bath, and Broom': Nannie Helen Burroughs's National Training School and African-American Racial Uplift." *Journal of Women's History* 9 (Spring 1997): 89–110.

———. "The Culture of the Informal Economy: Numbers Runners in Inter-War Black Detroit." *Radical History Review* 69 (Fall 1997): 46–75.

———. "Mediums, Messages, and Lucky Numbers: African-American Female

Spiritualists and Numbers Runners in Inter-War Detroit." In *The Geography of Identity*, edited by Patricia Yeager, 273–306. Ann Arbor: University of Michigan Press, 1996.

Wolters, Raymond. *Negroes and the Great Depression: The Problem of Economic Recovery*. Westport, Conn.: Greenwood Press, 1970.

Woodward, C. Vann. *Origins of the New South, 1877–1913*. Baton Rouge: Louisiana State University Press, 1951.

Young, Coleman. *Hard Stuff: The Autobiography of Coleman Young*. New York: Viking, 1994.

Zunz, Olivier. *The Changing Face of Inequality: Urbanization, Industrial Development, and Immigrants in Detroit, 1880–1920*. Chicago: University of Chicago Press, 1982.

Dissertations and Theses

Allen, Derek Bower. "From the Ghetto to the Joint: A Study of Black Urban Survival Crime in Detroit." Ph.D. diss., Michigan State University, 1989.

Black, Harold. "Restrictive Covenants in Relation to Segregated Negro Housing in Detroit." M.A. thesis, Wayne State University, 1947.

Carlson, Glen E. "The Negro in the Industries in Detroit." Ph.D. diss., University of Michigan, 1929.

Carlson, Gustav G. "Number Gambling: A Study of a Culture Complex." Ph.D. diss., University of Michigan, 1940.

Chireau, Yvonne Patricia. "Conjuring: An Analysis of African American Folk Beliefs and Practices." Ph.D. diss., Princeton University, 1994.

Deskins, Donald Richard, Jr. "Residential Mobility of Negro Occupational Groups in Detroit, 1837–1965." Ph.D. diss., University of Michigan, 1971.

Engelmann, Larry. "O, Whisky: The History of Prohibition in Michigan." Ph.D. diss., University of Michigan, 1971.

Hickey, Georgina. "Visibility, Politics, and Urban Development: Working-Class Women in Early Twentieth Century Atlanta." Ph.D. diss., University of Michigan, 1995.

Hunter, Gary Jerome. "'Don't Buy from Where You Can't Work': Black Urban Boycott Movements during the Depression, 1929–1941." Ph.D. diss., University of Michigan, 1977.

Hunter, Tera. "Household Workers in the Making: Afro-American Women in Atlanta and the New South, 1861 to 1920." Ph.D. diss., Yale University, 1990.

Lindsey, Howard O'Dell. "Fields to Ford, Feds to Franchise: African American Empowerment in Inkster, Michigan." Ph.D. diss., University of Michigan, 1993.

Miles, Norman Kenneth. "Home at Last: Urbanization of Black Migrants in Detroit, 1916–1929." Ph.D. diss., University of Michigan, 1978.

Murage, Njeru Wa. "Organizational History of the Detroit Urban League, 1916–1960." Ph.D. diss., Michigan State University, 1993.

Neumann, Amber Cooley. "Twenty-five Years of Negro Activity in Detroit, 1910–1935." M.A. thesis, University of Detroit, 1935.

Newman, Louise M. "Laying Claim to Difference: Ideologies of Race and Gender in the U.S. Woman's Movement." Ph.D. diss., Brown University, 1992.

Stevenson, Marshall Field, Jr. "Points of Departure, Acts of Resolve: Black-Jewish Relations in Detroit, 1937–1962." Ph.D. diss., University of Michigan, 1988.

Thomas, Jerome Gale. "The City of Detroit: A Study in Urban Geography." Ph.D. diss., University of Michigan, 1928.

Wladaver-Morgan, Susan. "Young Women and the New Deal: Camps and Resident Centers, 1933–1943." Ph.D. diss., Indiana University, 1982.

Index

(n. 46); during Great Migration, 53–
64; and women's employment, 76,
82–83; and domestic service training,
84–85; and leisure, 105–6, 108–10; and
resistance to unions, 214–16; in 1930s,
217–18, 221–23. *See also* Columbia
Community Center; Dancy, John C.
Detroyal Gardens Council, 154–55, 156
Development of Our Own, 188
Dickson, Annie Mae, 24, 29–30
Domesticity, 91; training for, 18–22;
working-class values of, 25–26; and
racial uplift, 26–27; in Sweet case,
142
Domestic service training: in the
South, 18–19, 21–22, 27–29; in 1920s,
83–85; in 1930s, 223, 231–39, 268 (n.
154). *See also* Domestic work
Domestic work, 18, 29–31, 254 (n. 69),
267 (n. 146); and sexual harassment,
18, 22–23, 80; in 1920s, 80–85; in
1930s, 231–39, 302 (n. 108). *See also*
Domestic service training; Employment
Dress Well Club, 57–58, 71, 128, 168,
222

Economic nationalism: in Garveyism,
128–29, 168; in 1930s, 176, 179–80; in
numbers gambling, 198–200. *See also*
Housewives' League
Ecstatic worship, 31–35, 113, 116–17. *See
also* Sanctified church; Spiritualist
church; Storefront churches
Elliottorian Business Women's Club,
156
Employment: during Great Migration,
50, 72–91; and World War I, 72–74,
264 (n. 91); and color discrimination, 77–79; in white-collar work,
85–89; in social work, 86–88, 269
(n. 169); and entrepreneurship, 89–
91; in informal economy, 93–96,

101–26, 198–200, 202–4; in 1930s,
169–76. *See also* Domestic work; Informal economy; Leisure workers;
Prostitution
Entre Nous Club, 70, 134–35, 137, 142,
150, 155–56, 225. *See also* Women's
clubs
Etiquette manuals, 19, 252 (n. 32)

Folmar, Rev. C. H., 163–64
Franklin Street Settlement, 157, 224, 231

Garvey, Marcus, 95, 126–27, 186
Glenn, Mary Etta: and migration, 11–
13, 15, 24, 37, 242, 250 (n. 8); and
employment, 72, 88, 90
Gordy, Berry, 134, 241
Gospel music, 193–94
Grigsby, Snow, 211–12, 214, 221, 295–96
(n. 15). *See also* Civic Rights Committee

Hackley, Emma Azalia Smith, 41–42
Harlem Renaissance, 127, 151, 153, 277
(n. 102)
Hate strikes, 74–75
Hayden, Robert, 1, 246
Haynes, George Edmund, 52–53, 59,
102, 108, 259 (n. 11)
Homosexuality, 98–99
Housewives' League, 168, 169, 173, 176–
83, 185. *See also* Economic national-
ism
Housing, 53–54, 68–69, 280 (n. 12);
crowding in, 14, 59–61; and riots,
131–32, 136, 140–41, 243–45; and sub-
urbanization, 132–40; on the West
Side, 134–36, 150, 154; in Eight Mile
Road development, 136–39, 154–
55, 221; in Inkster, 139; in Highland
Park, 139–40
Hurley, George, 119–20, 126
Hutzel, Eleanore, 111

ciation (UNIA), 95, 126–29, 142, 145, 177, 183

Vernon, William T., 148, 159
Visiting Housekeepers' Association (VHA), 85, 88, 257 (n. 113)
Visiting Nurses' Association (VNA), 42–43, 257 (n. 113)

Waddles, Charleszetta, 30, 122
Washington, Forrester B.: and First Great Migration, 51, 53, 59–60, 68, 262 (n. 57); and women's employment, 73–74, 76–77; and study of leisure, 97–98
Welker, Frances, 44
West Side Human Relations Council, 225
Whitby, Beulah, 188–89, 225, 240
Williams, Fannie Barrier, 6, 14, 17, 21, 23
Wilson, Mary, 241–42
Women's City Council, 154
Women's clubs, 49, 133, 249 (n. 17); in premigration Detroit, 42–48; at Sec-

ond Baptist Church, 64–66, 159–60; at YWCA, 70–71; in 1920s, 149–57, 284 (n. 80); in 1930s, 210. *See also* Detroit Association of Colored Women's Clubs; Detroit Study Club; Entre Nous Club; New Era Study Club; Reform
Workers. *See* Employment
Works Progress Administration (WPA), 207, 210, 223–24, 226–30, 233–36, 240. *See also* New Deal
Wright, Ernestine, 81, 170–71

Young, Coleman, 93, 96, 212, 245
Young Negroes' Progressive Association (YNPA), 55–56
Young Women's Christian Association (YWCA), 18, 31, 38, 46, 88; during First Great Migration, 68–72; in 1920s, 152, 160–61; in 1930s, 231, 234–35
Young Women's Home Associates, 43

Zampty, Charles, 128

Gender and American Culture

Remaking Respectability: African American Women in Interwar Detroit, by Victoria W. Wolcott (2001)

Ida B. Wells-Barnett and American Reform, 1880–1930, by Patricia A. Schechter (2001)

Painting Professionals: Women Artists and the Development of Modern American Art, 1870–1930, by Kirsten Swinth (2001)

Taking Haiti: Military Occupation and the Culture of U.S. Imperialism, 1915–1940, by Mary A. Renda (2001)

Before Jim Crow: The Politics of Race in Postemancipation Virginia, by Jane Dailey (2000)

Captain Ahab Had a Wife: New England Women and the Whalefishery, 1720–1870, by Lisa Norling (2000)

Civilizing Capitalism: The National Consumers' League, Women's Activism, and Labor Standards in the New Deal Era, by Landon R. Y. Storrs (2000)

Rank Ladies: Gender and Cultural Hierarchy in American Vaudeville, by M. Alison Kibler (1999)

Strangers and Pilgrims: Female Preaching in America, 1740–1845, by Catherine A. Brekus (1998)

Sex and Citizenship in Antebellum America, by Nancy Isenberg (1998)

Yours in Sisterhood: Ms. Magazine and the Promise of Popular Feminism, by Amy Erdman Farrell (1998)

We Mean to Be Counted: White Women and Politics in Antebellum Virginia, by Elizabeth R. Varon (1998)

Women Against the Good War: Conscientious Objection and Gender on the American Home Front, 1941–1947, by Rachel Waltner Goossen (1997)

Toward an Intellectual History of Women: Essays by Linda K. Kerber (1997)

Gender and Jim Crow: Women and the Politics of White Supremacy in North Carolina, 1896–1920, by Glenda Elizabeth Gilmore (1996)

Delinquent Daughters: Protecting and Policing Adolescent Female Sexuality in the United States, 1885–1920, by Mary E. Odem (1995)

U.S. History as Women's History: New Feminist Essays, edited by Linda K. Kerber, Alice Kessler-Harris, and Kathryn Kish Sklar (1995)

Common Sense and a Little Fire: Women and Working-Class Politics in the United States, 1900–1965, by Annelise Orleck (1995)

How Am I to Be Heard?: Letters of Lillian Smith, edited by Margaret Rose Gladney (1993)

Entitled to Power: Farm Women and Technology, 1913–1963, by Katherine Jellison (1993)

Revising Life: Sylvia Plath's Ariel Poems, by Susan R. Van Dyne (1993)

Made From This Earth: American Women and Nature, by Vera Norwood (1993)